D0906397

HOUSING AND THE URBAN ENVIRONMENT

A guide to housing design, renewal and urban planning

Barry Goodchild

BA (Hons), MPhil, MRTPI
Reader in Housing and Urban Planning
Sheffield Hallam University

b

Blackwell
Science

© 1997 by
Blackwell Science Ltd
Editorial Offices:
Osney Mead, Oxford OX2 0EL
25 John Street, London WC1N 2BL
23 Ainslie Place, Edinburgh EH3 6AJ
350 Main Street, Malden
    MA 02148 5018, USA
54 University Street, Carlton
    Victoria 3053, Australia

Other Editorial Offices:

Blackwell Wissenschafts-Verlag GmbH
Kurfürstendamm 57
10707 Berlin, Germany

Blackwell Science KK
MG Kodenmacho Building
7–10 Kodenmacho Nihombashi
Chuo-ku, Tokyo 104, Japan

First edition published 1997

Set in 10.5/13 Sabon
by DP Photosetting, Aylesbury, Bucks
Printed and bound in Great Britain by
Hartnolls Ltd, Bodmin, Cornwall

The Blackwell Science logo is a
trade mark of Blackwell Science Ltd,
registered at the United Kingdom
Trade Marks Registry

DISTRIBUTORS
    Marston Book Services Ltd
    PO Box 269
    Abingdon
    Oxon OX14 4YN
    (*Orders:* Tel: 01235 465500
            Fax: 01235 465555)

USA
    Blackwell Science, Inc.
    Commerce Place
    350 Main Street
    Malden, MA 02148 5018
    (*Orders:* Tel: 800 759 6102
            617 388 8250
            Fax: 617 388 8255)

Canada
    Copp Clark Professional
    200 Adelaide Street West, 3rd Floor
    Toronto, Ontario M5H 1W7
    (*Orders:* Tel: 416 597 1616
            800 815 9417
            Fax: 416 597 1617)

Australia
    Blackwell Science Pty Ltd
    54 University Street
    Carlton, Victoria 3053
    (*Orders:* Tel: 03 9347 0300
            Fax: 03 9347 5001)

A catalogue record for this title
is available from the British Library

ISBN 0-632-04101-3

Library of Congress
Cataloging-in-Publication Data

Goodchild, Barry.
    Housing and the urban environment: a guide to
housing design, renewal, and urban planning/Barry
Goodchild.
        p. cm.
    Includes bibliographical references and index.
    ISBN 0-632-04101-3
    1. City planning – Great Britain. 2. Urban
renewal – Great Britain. 3. Urban sociology –
Great Britain. 4. Housing policy – Great Britain.
5. Housing development – Great Britain. 6. Urban
policy – Great Britain. 7. Cities and towns – Great
Britain – Growth.
    I. Title.
    HT169.8.G7G66 1997
    363.5′8′0941 – dc21   97-7651
                                            CIP

Contents

Preface

What types of dwelling are most likely to meet the changing needs and demands of the next decades? What public policy instruments are available to plan the built environment in housing? What measures are available to maintain and improve the quality of the existing stock? What measures are available to promote and control quality in new house building? What is the role of the public authorities that co-ordinate development and the mixture of public and private agencies that undertake development?

These and other related questions define the scope of the present study. They deal with housing considered as environment, as 'habitat', meaning the place in which people live and adapt to their use.

Housing and the Urban Environment brings together research findings and theory from a wide range of professional disciplines. The book is meant for students of town planning and urban design, of residential development and agency, and last, but not least, of housing management and housing policy. It will also be of interest to researchers, policy makers and practitioners within these fields.

The topics covered include:

❏ concepts of housing quality and their application to the built environment
❏ methods of assessing user needs and preferences, including the role of user participation
❏ minimum standards of fitness and design, including the role of the town planning system in controlling design
❏ design standards for social and private housing
❏ area-based and other policies for the renewal of privately-owned sector housing, including the role of slum clearance
❏ the renewal of local authority estates, including the improvement of security and the role of intensive housing management
❏ the management of urban growth, the relation between house building and urban form, the relation between urban planning and the provision of affordable housing
❏ scenarios for the future of British towns and cities.

Acknowledgements

A large number of people have contributed to this book. The author must thank, in particular, Alan Murie, Dory Reeves and Ian Cole, all of whom made extensive comments on an earlier draft.

Chapter 1
Introduction

This book provides a new analysis of housing in Britain. The aim is to provide an analysis of the quality of design, the quality of the building stock and the relation between housing and town planning. Put slightly differently, the aim is to examine those policies and social trends that are relevant to housing considered as 'habitat', meaning the place in which people live and which they adapt to their use.

RELATION TO THE EXISTING LITERATURE

Habitat is of obvious importance. It is important to the quality of life in urban and rural areas. It is central to the comfort, convenience and, in some cases, the health of residents, as well as their consumption of energy and their interaction with other people. As a result, the design and planning of 'habitat' offers a means of encouraging either the integration or exclusion of deprived and minority social groups.

Until recently, however, habitat has not been a central theme in publications on housing. For many years, research priorities have mostly been concerned with issues of access (who gets what type of accommodation), finance (who pays what) and tenure (the varied advantages of owner-occupation, local authority renting and private renting). Official statements of national housing policy have lacked clear objectives or strategy about housing standards or quality. At most, they have merely mentioned, in vague terms, the desirability of ensuring access to a 'decent' home for all. Indeed, most recent policy innovations have sought to reduce the costs of housing. The emphasis has been on quantity rather than quality. The low cost home ownership initiatives of the early 1980s and the housing association initiatives of the 1990s provide examples.

At the same time, the critics of government policy have generally focused on social issues such as affordability, homelessness and the declining output of rented accommodation. Again a tension has existed between these priorities and measures to raise standards.

Moreover, this tension is likely to persist given the financial constraints that will confront any government, whether Conservative, Labour or Liberal, in the immediate future. As a result, neither side of the political divide has wanted to

1

highlight questions concerned with design or the built environment. The difficulty of defining housing quality has also deterred research. Some analysts of housing policy may have even ignored the built environment because they do not know how to provide a critical evaluation.

The renewal of older housing is a partial exception. The existence of long-standing policies to eliminate slums and to reduce the number of unfit dwellings has, since 1966, led the government to undertake regular, five yearly surveys of the English housing stock. These are published in the successive reports of the English House Condition Survey. In 1991, the English survey was supplemented by surveys for Scotland and Wales. Moreover, the pursuit of these policies for housing clearance and renewal has led to the publication of a series of specialist books and monographs, for example *An Introduction to Urban Renewal* by Gibson and Langstaff (1982), *Housing and Urban Renewal* by Thomas (1986), and *Home Improvement under the New Regime* by Mackintosh and Leather (1992).

However, the existing literature on housing renewal has limitations. Gibson and Langstaff (1982) and Thomas (1986) are mostly out-of-date and, in any case, fail to discuss local authority stock or the role of housing building. Their emphasis is overwhelmingly on the renewal and redevelopment of private housing, together with related programmes pursued under the government's inner city policy. Mackintosh and Leather (1992) provide a good up-to-date account of existing practice in the renewal of the private housing stock. However, the scope is also narrow, with little attempt for example, to discuss local authority housing or the development of vacant urban land.

There are other recent exceptions. The growth of housing association house building in the 1990s has led to a wide ranging debate about the design, standards and quality of social housing schemes. Page (1993) has reviewed the external layout and social mix of new housing association estates in an effort to explain why some estates have caused management problems. Likewise, Karn and Sheridan (1994) have analysed floorspace and amenity standards of housing association and privately built dwellings and, especially in housing association schemes, have shown a marked divergence between recommended standards and practice.

A similar interest in housing quality is also apparent in Scotland. *The Physical Quality of Housing*, prepared by Scottish Homes (1996a, p. 3) suggests that, in Britain, policies to maintain and improve the quality of housing 'have moved from the regulation of standards to the encouragement of greater consumer choice'. This shift requires the formulation of a variety of policies that actively seek to promote quality in the existing stock and in new house building.

In addition, broader environmental concerns, for instance about the quality of city life and pollution, have started to influence housing policy. In June 1995, the Conservative government then in power published a White Paper *Our Future Homes*. Most of the policy proposals sought to promote choice and competition. However, the White Paper also contains a chapter entitled 'Housing and the Environment'. This chapter expresses the government's support for sustainable development, defined as 'getting the right kind of housing ... so that the environment is protected and enhanced.' It then lists a series of policy initiatives in favour of the following:

❏ building on urban sites (rather than greenfield sites)
❏ promoting the quality of design and the conservation of the existing stock
❏ improving energy efficiency in housing
❏ introducing environmental audits into housing policies and programmes.

The concept of sustainable development goes beyond the conventional party politics of Left and Right. It also commands significant public support. Few people want to promote pollution or to destroy the natural environment. In many ways, however, the Housing and the Environment chapter was and remains deeply flawed. The definition of sustainability is relatively narrow. It makes little or no reference to building for low maintenance or to the creation of a healthy environment. In addition, concerns with the environment and sustainable development are not fully integrated into housing policy. The chapter discusses quality in design and the conservation of buildings without relating these to the standards and design of social housing or the availability of resources to improve and renew the housing stock. Likewise, the chapter emphasises the importance of building on urban sites without relating this to the expected level of new house building.

The subject matter and the potential literature is large, rich and varied. Much of the task of analysing housing as habitat is to draw together existing knowledge rather than to develop new theories and new knowledge. The literature is very fragmented. It deserves consolidation and systematic assessment.

METHODS OF ANALYSIS

The consolidation of fragmented information implies the existence of some overall framework. What type of framework is the most appropriate?

The role and limitations of history

For most texts in housing studies and town planning, the analytic framework comprises an historical narrative. Malpass and Murie (1982, p. 22) provide a clear rationale for this.

> Housing is a subject in which history is particularly important, most obviously because houses have a long life... Dwellings are the enduring artefacts from earlier periods of social and economic organisation
>
> Second, contemporary housing policy is inevitably heavily influenced by the past, in the sense that dwellings inherited from earlier periods represent both a resource to be utilised and a problem to be dealt with.... Third, ... is the fact that it is not just dwellings but also policy mechanisms and institutional traditions that have been inherited from the past. Housing policy ... is the outcome of a process of accretion over a long period...'

History is too important to be ignored. It is certainly right to argue that dwellings have a long life and that the existing stock is an accretion of past phases of housing development. However, the study of history has pitfalls:

❑ The origins of a phenomenon are not always a good guide to subsequent policy issues. For instance, the reasons for the development of high-rise flats in the 1950s and 1960s are not relevant to policies that aim to ensure their continued popularity in the 1990s.
❑ In addition, history is conservative. History assumes that future trends will continue in much the same way as they have in the past.

The question may be redefined. A distinction may be drawn between the 'grand narrative' and the 'little narrative' of history. The former is based around a single linear theme, invariably linked to concepts of modernity, post-modernity and progress. The latter comprises a series of specific historical examples.

Modernity, post-modernism and the grand narrative

The grand narrative starts with the origins of public intervention in the late nineteenth century and continues to the present day. What might be called 'modern' accounts, those written from the 1940s to the 1970s, generally equate the expansion of public power with social progress. Later accounts are more 'post-modern'. They deal with the eclipse of public intervention during the 1980s and typically suggest the need for new, more democratic methods of public organisation. They provide a more qualified view of progress.

Berry's *Housing: The Great British Failure* (1974) provides an example of a grand narrative of progress, despite the title. 'From the time of the Greeks', Berry argues, 'it has been usual for political thinking to polarise into two schools of thought, those who wish by and large to keep the world as it is and those who wish to change it'. Berry suggests that housing policy in Britain failed owing to the failure of governments and local authorities to commit themselves to radical change. The way forward, Berry argues, is to take responsibility for housing provision away from local authorities and away from private enterprise and to put it into the hands of a national public organisation.

The grand narrative of progress is now obsolete. It leads to total centralisation and an uncritical acceptance of standardisation for its own sake. It also makes demands on public finance to an extent that is unrealistic.

Sim's *British Housing Design* (1993) provides an example of a later grand narrative that recognises the weaknesses of previous forms of practice. *British Housing Design* starts with a review of the evolution of housing design in Britain from before the First World War to the era of high-rise flats in the 1960s. Thereafter, the main emphasis is on how to promote good design. This is to be achieved through the involvement of local people in social housing schemes and, more generally, through a recognition of the varied preferences of different user groups.

Rowe's *Modernity and Housing* (1993) has provided a similar analysis, but with more emphasis on architectural theory. Good practice in housing design, Rowe suggests, involves a balance between two pairs of necessary but contradictory principles (pp. 339–348). These pairs comprise: first, the choice between individualism and the collective, and second, the choice between rational and sensible ways of knowing the world. This latter choice requires a brief explanation. On the rational side of the balance are tendencies towards generalisation, universality and abstraction. On the sensible side are tendencies towards the local and the specific, and towards feeling. Modernism in design failed in the post-war years because it stressed the collective and the rational to the exclusion of everything else. However, modernity and housing need not be out of harmony with one another. A more balanced approach is possible.

To demonstrate the possibility of a more balanced approach, Rowe cites as an example the redevelopment of Byker in Newcastle-upon-Tyne in the early 1970s. The Byker redevelopment is characterised by a combination of high-rise and modern looking low-rise dwellings set in a varied external layout that mostly involves footpath (rather than street) access (Fig. 1.1). Though it is not apparent from the photograph, the scheme is also characterised by vivid colours (red and yellow brick, blue steel roofs and green timber work). Much of the detail of the design was worked out in consultation with local residents.

The post-modern reaction, Rowe suggests, is more a reaction against the worn-out modernism of the 1950s and 1960s. The modernism of the 1920s was a liberating and innovative force. Rowe's account of early modernism focuses on housing design in the Netherlands and Germany. In Britain, it is possible to identify the early garden city movement as a similar force for liberation from the constraints of the nineteenth century city. The architects of the garden city movement, notably Raymond Unwin, sought innovation in housing design, even though their work was not self-consciously and explicitly 'modern'. Moreover, to provide low cost houses, the garden city architects became increasingly concerned about such 'modern' themes as the simplification of form and the standardisation of products (Fig. 1.2).

The qualified grand narrative enables the identification of a series of distinctive themes that have characterised urban policy in the 1980s and 1990s (Goodchild, 1990; 1991). These themes include an increase emphasis in:

❑ housing policy, on choice rather than regulation, much as stated in the Scottish Homes document *The Physical Quality of Housing* (1996)
❑ urban planning, on the promotion of social diversity, rather than 'mass' solutions
❑ urban renewal, on the maintenance and conservation of the existing stock, rather than large-scale redevelopment
❑ design, on the specific characteristic of a place, including the home, rather than standardisation and the repetition of standard building types.

The task now is to contribute to a new interpretation of progress, one that is more sensitive to current conditions. To an extent, this means passing from

Fig. 1.1   Redevelopment at Byker, Newcastle.

Fig. 1.2   An early garden suburb.

concepts of the post-modern to new modern or 'hyper-modern' (*surmoderne* in French), as Ascher (1995) has suggested. Post-modern is a backward-looking concept. Whatever word is preferred, however, possible lines of progress cannot be ascertained through a sweeping historical analysis. The analysis has to focus on the present. It must, in addition, use the results of economic and social research in the formulation of proposals.

The little narrative

A rejection of the grand narrative is not a rejection of all history. Another alternative approach, the 'little narrative', is episodic rather than chronological. It makes no pretence of offering a universal account. Instead, it uses episodes and images to clarify aspects of popular culture.

An example is *Making Space*, prepared by a feminist collective called 'Matrix' and published in 1984. It attempts to work out the connection between gender relations, especially the role of women and the design of the built environment. It uses historical examples to show either how the design of housing has reflected the role of women in the home, or how women might seek to change housing design if they were to acquire greater power and influence. The authors show, for example, how the semi-detached suburban house of the 1930s sought to provide a 'modest retreat for the "little man" ... a nest-like security (or prison) for his wife' (p. 72). In addition, they explore various ways in which cities might be made more supportive to women and to mothers, notably through breaking down the division between home and the workplace.

The strength of the little narrative is to provide a contemporary history rather than a history of the past. The little narrative is more post-modern than even the most revisionist grand narrative. It is more post-modern because it abandons even the suggestion of a single historical framework. Yet, the little narrative does not involve a complete break with the past. Instead, it involves a search for specific historical comparisons and analogies. For a book on housing and the urban environment, this means a recurrent search for specific historic analogies and lessons.

The role of theory

The same distinction between grand and little approaches arises in social theory. Again, the usual approach is to search for big solutions, and big themes. Malpass and Murie (1982) provide an example. The interpretation of history, the authors suggest, should proceed through a double analysis that links local case studies 'with the contemporary theoretical debate about the state in modern capitalist society'. For housing design, this means linking building and floorspace standards of a dwelling to the policy assumptions of the state at the time that the dwelling was constructed.

The analysis of public policy is not the only basis for theory. Rapoport (1982) has argued in favour of cultural theories as a means of explaining housing design and related aspects of the urban environment. In the English-speaking world, Rapoport suggests, an attractive residential environment conveys an image of suburbia.

Theory can provide insights. To provide an example, the former National Community Development Project (Benwell CDP, 1978) has undertaken a case study of post-war local authority housing in Newcastle-upon-Tyne and, in doing this, has related design to the policy assumptions of different political parties. It shows how the flats and maisonettes built at Noble Street between 1956 and 1960 were literally 'slums on the drawing board'. The blocks were built to the lowest design standards at the highest possible density and the cheapest possible cost. The blocks reflected a political belief that the residents of slums deserved no better than the bare minimum and that, in any case, the local authority and central government could afford no better.

Likewise, it is possible to use the suburban ideal as a means of explaining the varied popularity and diverse status of different estates and dwelling types. For example, King (1984) links the popularity of the bungalow in the English-speaking world to the spread of suburbia. Like suburbia, the bungalow offered a way out of the dirty industrial cities of the nineteenth and early twentieth centuries. It offered a way, first for the middle classes and later for other less affluent households, to become owner-occupiers and to pursue a healthy life style in spacious surroundings.

The problem is that theories presuppose a hierarchical pattern of causes. They assume that one fundamental factor explains the workings of social and economic life. For this reason, different theories are difficult to reconcile with one another and are generally incapable of coping with the diversity of practice.

In the case of the human habitat, there is a further problem. The built environment resists theory. The built environment is a real object, part of the world of the senses. How can one possibly understand the social world, and housing is surely part of the social world, from the point of view of an object?

Lefèbvre (1972, French original 1969 and 1985) offers another way forward. He suggests that the built environment may be conceived at different levels of social reality. The first is

'The *level of theory* at which theory merges with ideology, or, if one so prefers, theory is insufficiently distinguished from ideology. This is the level at which architects and planners operate.'

This is the level of strategic, rational planning which involves the forecast of land use patterns over the next five or ten years. It is also the level where the development process is influenced by marketing strategies in the case of private building, and by political assumptions in the case of publicly funded schemes. Because theory and ideology are so intertwined, as Lefèbvre notes, this is also the level of critical analysis, of testing the logic of action and searching out the interests of those involved.

Otherwise, there are two further levels for analysis. These are:

'The *level of application and implementation*, where other factors exist alongside or over and above ideological concerns. At this level, the thoughts and wishes of the architect take practical realities and requirements into account. Some of these are clearly understood, some are not.'

'The *level of urban practice*, defined in terms of a certain way of life, of a certain style (or an absence of style). Here the social activities of a group or an individual are revealed for what they are. At this level, there exists a typology, a feeling, a concrete rationality, which is more impressive and more complex than abstract rationality.' (*Emphasis in the original; translation by the author.*)

The notion of levels of reality may be applied to most forms of housing development. This includes those in which the role of the architect or planner is indistinct or in which the architect or planner is replaced by other actors, for example, by property developers or by other practitioners within local and central government. The point of analysis is to bring the different levels together in an interactive process, whilst simultaneously treating the level of concrete rationality as the main test of success. Again, for a book on housing and the urban environment, this means the constant use of social survey material, where it is available.

FROM THE CONCRETE TO THE ABSTRACT

To discuss housing as habitat implies a distinctive method of enquiry. It means proceeding from the concrete to the abstract. It also means grounding an analysis of public policy in the physical conditions of the housing stock.

The role of the survey

There is nothing new in going from the concrete to the abstract. Early town planning and early housing reformers, in the period between about 1900 and 1920, frequently resorted to the survey as a necessary preliminary to calls for action. Geddes (1915 and 1968) repeatedly argued that public intervention had to be proceeded by a comprehensive survey, a 'concrete study of cities as we find them or rather as we see them grow'. Likewise, the Report of a Scottish Royal Commission (1917, p. 40) used the device of an imaginary tour of a typical Scottish city to introduce the reader to working class housing conditions.

> 'In dealing with the problem of urban housing, it will be best to proceed from the concrete to the more general and abstract questions. If we begin with the actual physical conditions, external and internal, of the houses of a typical Scottish town, and the questions of structure and arrangement dependent on them, we shall be better able to deal with the economic and social factors of domestic life in a modern city, including such problems as those of rent and wages and the demand for a higher standard of comfort and space.'

No single city, even in a small country like Scotland, is completely typical. Nevertheless, as the Scottish Royal Commission showed, it was possible to synthesise the characteristics of different towns and cities into an idealised place.

In the 1990s, the city has a different status in relation to public policy. The post-modern city is more diverse, more fragmented and less clearly defined in relation either to the countryside or, in more heavily populated regions, from other nearby cities. Nevertheless, it remains sensible to proceed from the concrete to the abstract. Moreover, though British cities possess much diversity, it remains valid to assume that they possess shared characteristics. Otherwise, it would not be possible to pursue, or even conceive, national policies in housing and town planning.

A portrait of the British city

Imagine this. Imagine that you, the reader, are visiting a British city that comprises a representative cross-section of the variety of conditions found in all the larger English, Welsh and Scottish cities. This city is an imaginary place, but is also typical of urban conditions in Britain. This is a city that includes the commercial dynamism of London and the extensive areas of older, higher density housing such as are found in the main regional centres, for example Bristol, Birmingham, Manchester and Glasgow. Equally, this is a city that contains dispersed and scattered residential areas of the type that has grown from the 1960s onwards.

Imagine a city that possesses a single dominant centre, largely devoted to business, retailing and public uses, and containing most of the oldest and most prestigious buildings. Housing has largely disappeared from the centre, though the local authority now wishes to convert to residential use some empty property, especially empty floorspace above shops.

Imagine, in addition, a city that possesses a marked contrast between a poor inner area and an affluent ring of suburbs. The inner city comprises a combination of modern, but unpopular local authority flats that were built as part of the slum clearance drives of the 1930s, 1960s and 1970s, and older, privately-owned property. In the North of England and the Midlands, much of the older privately-owned inner city housing comprises rows of small owner-occupied terraces. In inner London and in the largest Scottish cities, blocks of tenements and flats of at least four storeys are more common. Furthermore, in the inner city, there are some streets of larger houses that were once home to the Victorian and Edwardian middle classes, but have long been subdivided into flats for owner-occupiers or multi-occupation for rent.

A proportion of the inner city housing stock requires remedial treatment. The worst local authority estates require a combination of modernisation, design modification and intensive housing management. For the privately owned stock, the problem is mostly of inadequate repair. In contrast, the suburbs mostly comprise detached and semi-detached family dwellings, all well maintained and set in well-stocked private gardens.

The inner city/suburban distinction is the most impressive feature of the British city. The distinction represents the concrete result of the desire of those with sufficient resources, the middle classes and the secure working classes, to move out of the older areas that were built before 1918. The inner city/suburban distinction is not generally found to the same extent in cities in other European countries. Elsewhere in Europe, post-war reconstruction, as in Germany, or relatively late processes of urbanisation, as in France and much of southern Europe, have meant that a higher proportion of the urban area dates from the twentieth century.

In Britain, the inner city/suburban distinction has stimulated a continuous line of urban policy since the 1960s. The fact that the distinction also demarcates a racial divided between a black and brown inner city and the white suburbs has, moreover, heightened its significance. Inner city policy started after the notorious 'Rivers of Blood' speech by Enoch Powell in 1968. The programme expanded again in the early 1980s after riots in multi-ethnic areas in South London, Bristol, Liverpool and elsewhere. Programmes of housing investment have, for the most part, been organised separately from urban programme investments. However, public housing investment has also been targeted on inner city areas. The renewal of the older housing is a constant battle against processes of decay.

Imagine, again, a city that contains areas of wealth and poverty that do not correspond to the inner city/suburban distinction. This city possesses, near the central area, a few wealthy residential areas, either as flats, as in central London, or as tenements as in Glasgow and Edinburgh, or as houses with gardens, as in the prestigious inner suburbs of some provincial cities. Many of these areas are of architectural merit and are classified as conservation areas by the local authority. Some of the most highly valued date from the eighteenth century and comprise rows of large Georgian terraces.

Equally, this city possesses unpopular and isolated peripheral estates. In Scotland, especially in Glasgow, the peripheral estates mostly comprise three and four storey tenements that were built hurriedly in the 1950s to a basic standard. The tenements of these outer estates are often no longer acceptable to households that have a choice in where they live. In the peripheral estates in England, the dwellings were also build hurriedly and to a basic standard. However, they are more likely to take the form of houses with gardens and are, for this reason, more adaptable and more easily upgraded.

The residential areas in this city have a varied reputation. Most are respectable and considered, in varying degrees, desirable. On the other hand, a few areas are considered undesirable, even dangerous and a threat to social order.

Finally, imagine a city that possesses a mixture of change and continuity. Increased affluence, increased car ownership, a growth in single person households and changes in manufacturing and the service industries lead to new demands on the building stock. The city is under constant pressure to expand as individuals, firms and other types of institution seek more space and greater ease of movement.

Yet the physical fabric resists change. This is a city of continuity. It is a place where the street pattern of the city centre dates back many hundreds of years. It is a place where new house building has added less than 1% to the housing stock in recent years; where the scale of investment in buildings and in the infrastructure (for example, sewers and roads) is too great to permit widespread redevelopment; and finally where local pressure groups oppose any proposal that jeopardises their amenity or involves further expansion onto greenfield sites.

What range of public policy instruments is available to promote the quality of housing in such a typical British city? What measures are available to maintain and improve the quality of the existing stock? What measures are available to ensure that developers achieve minimum standards in new housing? What is the relation between standards and quality? What role is played by the public authorities that plan and co-ordinate development and the mixture of public and private agencies that undertake development? What are the themes and trends for the future?

These and other, related questions define the scope of this book.

A summary

Chapters 1 and 2 repeat the method of going from the concrete to the abstract. Chapter 2 starts with a classification of the British housing stock. It then distinguishes between different aspects of housing quality and examines the application of these aspects to the existing stock and to design. The application of concepts of quality in turn presuppose a user-oriented philosophy of design. It is not possible to identify universal priorities for design, only particular priorities that vary according to local circumstances. Participation is one method of assessing the perceptions and requirements of users. It is particularly appropriate for social housing where the occupants lack market choice. Other methods of user research include the analysis of social surveys, the analysis of market choices and the analysis of behaviour.

Chapter 3 starts with an analysis of the official criteria, notably that of unfitness, sub-tolerable housing and overcrowding, that local authorities use to determine whether the condition and use of the existing stock is satisfactory. The chapter than examines the regulation of improved and new housing schemes. It explains how social housing is subject to additional regulation compared to new housing built by private developers. It concludes with an analysis of design controls in town planning, including an analysis of how the assumptions of design control are linked to different concepts of urban design.

Chapters 4 and 5 examine the policy issues that arise in the improvement of the existing stock. Private owners are responsible for the improvement and maintenance of their property. Much of the discussion in Chapter 4 is about how private owners might best be encouraged to invest. Other issues concern the choice between clearance and improvement, and the role of area-based programmes of housing improvement.

Chapter 5 covers local authority and housing association estates, though until recently problems have been concentrated in the local authority sector. The renewal of social housing estates raises issues concerned with crime prevention, housing management, the reduction of child densities and the promotion of social balance. The renewal of so-called 'problem' estates is distinctive partly because social housing agencies have extensive responsibility for allocating homes to tenants, for maintaining the fabric and for keeping good order in their estates. In addition, the renewal of social housing is distinctive because of the concentration of low income households who live there, and because the local authority stock contains a legacy of high density building forms and industrialised dwellings that require environmental improvement.

Chapter 6 covers housing renewal to urban renewal. The main theme is the scope for house building in urban areas. The chapter examines the extent of private house building in urban areas and discusses how public agencies might encourage more urban house building, including more mixed land use development and housing in town and city centres. Much recent discussion is about how and where to accommodate an expected large increase in household numbers. This chapter warns against the use of national target setting, for example, that 50% or 60% of house building should take place on 'brownfield' sites. It also warns against the indiscriminate lifting of existing policies for urban containment. To cope with uncertainties, development plans should include proposals for phased development.

The final chapter, Chapter 7, discusses the most abstract issues. The assessment of future trends is, by definition, an abstract exercise. However, the chapter again repeats the theme of going from the concrete to the abstract. It starts with an analysis of specific possibilities that might affect the development and consumption of housing. It concludes with an analysis of scenarios, including the role of planning and public policy in a changing society.

The examination of possible futures brings the discussion full circle. Futures research is the mirror of post-modernism – the former starts in an analysis of contemporary trends, whereas the latter starts in the philosophy of history and art. Futures research is forward looking, whereas post-modernism is rooted in history. Yet they have similarities. Both are interested in places. Both are concerned with identifying breaks in history. The post-modern break with the past may be understood as a preliminary to attempts to work out a future that is free from the weight of history. Finally, both assume that there is no single logic of change and no guarantee of progress.

Chapter 2
Aspects of housing quality

Quality is an elusive concept. Quality in design may be defined as those aspects of the built environment that are important to people in a historical or cultural context. However, this is a general definition and is not easily applied to housing, without a prior understanding of how people live. Unravelling the concept of quality in housing begs a series of questions. What are the main differences between types of housing and types of layout? What are the advantages and disadvantages of these types? What are the different aspects of quality? How can a designer or developer identify and measure perceptions of quality in different contexts?

A CLASSIFICATION OF HOUSE TYPES

The report of the English House Condition Survey 1991 provides a possible starting point (DoE, 1993). It identifies eight different house types:

'High-rise purpose-built flat: flat in a block of six or more storeys.
Low-rise purpose-built flat: flat in a block of less than six storeys.
Converted flat: flat in a building converted from a house or some other use.
Dwellings associated with a non-residential use.
Bungalow: single storey detached, semi-detached or terraced house (excluding chalet and dormer bungalows).
Detached house: detached house of two or more storeys.
Semi-detached: semi-detached house of two or more storeys.
Medium/large terrace: terraced house of two or more storeys with a usable floor area of 70 square metres or more.
Small terrace: terraced house of two or more storeys with a usable floor area of less than 70 square metres.'

The report of the Scottish House Condition Survey 1991 uses a slightly different classification (Scottish Homes, 1993) (italic text added as explanations):

'Detached houses.
Other houses.
Tenements (*flats arranged around a central stairwell*).

Four in a block flats (*a pair of semi-detached, two storey flats, also known as a cottage flat in England and as a duplex in the United States*).
Conversions.
Tower/deck access blocks.'

Both the Scottish and English classifications include conversions as a separate category. Both include a distinction between flats and houses and are largely consistent with one another. Scottish tenements and four in a block flats may, for example, be treated as subdivisions within the broad category of low-rise flats. The main difference is that the Scottish classification makes no direct reference to the height of a block of flats. Tower blocks are high-rise. However, deck access blocks may be either high- or low-rise.

Both classifications are, of course, a necessary simplification. Flats over shops and flats linked to non-residential property do not fit easily into any classification. Moreover, even a single category such as a semi-detached house may include an enormous variation, for example in its size, construction and room layout.

In addition to house type, it is usual to classify buildings by their age of construction. Whatever classification is used, the results are to an extent arbitrary. In the twentieth century, the First and Second World Wars provide obvious breakpoints, as both caused an almost complete cessation of house building. The year 1975 provides an approximate date for the end of the post-war era of mass slum clearance and mass local authority house building.

Historical classifications refer to the initial date of construction. Few buildings remain unchanged. Successive owners replace window frames and doors, build extensions, update kitchen and bathroom facilities and, in the case of larger properties, make subdivisions to cater for a different, younger type of household. The enlargement of the back extension to incorporate a modern kitchen and bathroom has been a particular feature of the older, pre-1919 housing stock in England and Wales. Of course, not all dwellings are capable of improvement and modernisation. As dwellings age and decay, some are abandoned and then demolished. As a result, the existing distribution of dwelling types is not a reliable guide to the type that existed in the past.

Figs 2.1 to 2.6 provide an illustrated classification of the British housing stock, classified by a combination of its type and age of construction. The advantages and disadvantages of each type is as follows.

High-rise flats (Fig. 2.1) allow more light and air to penetrate to the ground floor in high density schemes. They also allow a higher absolute density than other house types and so save on land costs in areas with high land values. They are relatively expensive to build, however, owing to the incorporation of a lift and the use of unusual and more demanding construction techniques.

High-rise flats are invariably unpopular with households with children owing to the lack of a garden, the difficulty of supervising children playing outside and the risk of accidental falls. They also have other, more general disadvantages. Their scale may seem daunting when viewed from ground level. The widespread use of concrete can create a harsh, drab appearance. Wind problems may arise at

(a)

(b)

(c)

Fig. 2.1   Purpose built high-rise flats (comprising a block of six storeys or more).

Notes: Very few high-rise flats were built before about 1880. The best known surviving examples are in the old town of Edinburgh [Fig. 2.1(a)]. The widespread development depended on the invention of electrical lifts and the use of steel and concrete in building construction. High-rise flats were built in London from the 1890s onwards, mostly for the 'luxury end' of the privately rented and leasehold sector [Figs 2.1(b), Victoria, London and 2.1(c), near to Swiss Cottage, London]. However, most were developed by local authorities from about 1950 to 1970 [Fig. 2.1(d), near to Sheffield city centre]. Cooney (1974) identifies a series of stages in their adoption by local authorities: (1) their advocacy by the architectural profession in the 1920s and 1930s; (2) their experimental use, mostly in London in the 1950s; (3) the publication of national design guides that encouraged their use as a means of reducing the land requirements of slum clearance; (4) their support by large building companies.

(Contd.)

(d)   (e)

Fig. 2.1 *Contd.*
  By the late 1960s, official and public concern about their high costs and social implications led
to a revision of policy. Recently completed high-rise flats are few in number. They are mostly in
the private sector and mostly in London. In the London Docklands private developers have used
the striking image of high-rise flats as a marketing device [Fig. 2.1(e)].

ground level. The best types of high-rise are those that promote the image of
'towers in a park' and relatively low schemes (say of six or seven storeys) that
retain a conventional street layout.

Low-rise flats (Fig. 2.2) are a diverse category. Most flats have some form of
communal access, provided either from a central stairwell, as in a tenement and
in most subdivided houses, or from a balcony or deck. In addition, there are
other types, including those associated with commercial premises (flats over
shops), and flats with separate, independent access to the ground floor (Fig. 2.3).

The varied types of low-rise flats are relatively inexpensive to develop, can be
built to a higher density than houses with gardens and allow the possibility of a
varied external space. Flats over shops have the additional advantage that they
can be built in town and city centres in close proximity to urban facilities and
public transport. The main disadvantage of low-rise flats is the existence of
access stairs and the requirement for communal areas (car parks, open-space,
entrance lobbies, lifts and corridors) that are potentially expensive and difficult
to maintain and that, in some cases, pose security risks.

Of the various types, the deck access and balcony access flats seem to generate
the most complaints from residents. The balcony or deck is exposed to the

(a)

(b)

(c)

Fig. 2.2 Low-rise flats (of five storeys or less) with communal access.

Notes: The different types of low-rise flat are of varied origin. The tenement is organised around a central staircase. In Scotland, the tenement is a traditional house type whose history dates back at least to the eighteenth century. Early examples survive in Edinburgh [Fig. 2.2(a)]. In Scotland, the tenement became the dominant means of working class housing in the nineteenth century, and remains the most common house type in older urban areas [Fig. 2.2(b), Gorgie, Edinburgh]. In London, a similar form of tenement, albeit built of brick rather than stone, evolved in the nineteenth century in response to high land prices and continued to be built throughout the inter-war years [Fig. 2.2(c), Rayners Lane, London]. The word 'tenement' is now seldom used in England. Nevertheless, tenements, defined as flats with a central staircase, continue to be built throughout Britain and have become widely used in private urban renewal schemes, as in Leeds city centre [Fig. 2.2(e)]. This is probably the most common type of low-rise flat.

(Contd.)

(d)   (e)

Fig. 2.2 *Contd.*
The balcony access/deck access flat is essentially an innovation of local authority house building. Most date from the period between about 1919 and 1970. Some of the best known and most distinctive local authority schemes, like the Park Hill flats in Sheffield [Fig. 2.2(d)], are of this type. Recently completed deck access flats are now confined to specialist uses, such as accommodation for elderly people.

weather and is cold in the winter. In addition, it invariably causes over-shadowing to the flat below and transmits noise, especially if the flats are arranged around an enclosed courtyard. Balcony and deck access flats usually have a larger number of units off a common entrance point than other types. This also makes them more difficult to manage.

Bungalows (Fig. 2.4) and other single storey dwellings have significant advantages compared to two or three storey houses. The internal layout is more flexible, as there is no necessity to balance the area occupied by the bedrooms, WC, and bathroom on the upper floor against that occupied by the kitchen and living areas downstairs. In addition, the absence of stairs is easier for people with a disability. Bungalows are not a cheap form of accommodation, however. They occupy a larger area on the ground than a two storey dwelling of the same size. As a result, they require more extensive foundations, a larger roof and more land.

The advantages of *detached* and *semi-detached* houses (Fig. 2.5) have been listed by Lynch (1989).

'(The detached house) receives adequate light and air from its four exposures and provides room for gardening, play, parking and other outdoor uses. It enjoys direct

(a)

(b)

(c)

Fig. 2.3   Other types of low-rise flats, including housing over shops, converted flats and cottage flats.

Notes: It is also possible to identify other types of low-rise flat.

Flats over shops provided the usual living arrangement for trades-people before 1919 [Fig. 2.3(a), Deal, Kent]. Living over a shop is also a frequent feature of tenement housing, though in this case there is no direct internal connection between the flat and the commercial premises. In the 1990s, a growing demand from single people has led to a revival of interest in living in town and city centres. Housing associations have reoccupied empty floorspace above shops and built new schemes [Fig. 2.3(e), Sheffield city centre].

Converted flats include some housing over shops. Otherwise they are mostly formed from large family dwellings. Most conversions are invisible from the outside, except for the existence of multiple names and door bells at the front door [Fig. 2.3(b), off the Finchley Road, London].

(Contd.)

(d)　　　　　　　　　　　　　　　　(e)

Fig. 2.3 *Contd.*

Four in a block and **cottage flats** are distinguished by the existence of independent access to the ground. In Tyneside, the cottage flats were a traditional dwelling type of working class housing in the nineteenth century. The four in a block is essentially an invention of the local authority house building programmes in the inter-war and post-war years [Figs. 2.3(c), Edinburgh and 2.3(d), Sandal, Wakefield].

In 1991, at the time of the last English House Condition Survey, the purpose-built low-rise flat (excluding flats over shops and converted flats) was the most common type of housing association and local authority housing. The converted flat was the most common type of privately rented property.

access to the street and its own private grounds, which can be shielded from noise and view. It can be built, maintained, remodelled, bought and sold independently. It can be constructed at reasonable cost, although it is not the least expensive type of housing. In many parts of the world, it is popularly considered to be the ideal house. It symbolises the individual family.' (p. 272)

'The "semi" has almost all the virtues of a detached house. With three exposed sides instead of four, it can provide private entrances and outdoor areas and relatively few sound separation problems if properly designed.' (p. 276)

The main disadvantages of detached and, to some extent, semi-detached houses are that they are land hungry and sensitive to inflation in land prices. They are also expensive in relation to the provision of infrastructure, for example, roads, water and sewage disposal. Heating costs in a detached house may also be higher owing to the four exposed walls. However, detached houses are well suited to passive and active systems of solar gain.

(a)

(b)

(c)

Fig. 2.4   Bungalows and other types of single storey dwelling.

Notes: Before 1850 much of the rural labouring population lived in single storey cottages of one or two rooms. Much of this is now demolished. Miners' housing in Scotland and the North of England [Fig. 2.4(a), Wibsey, Bradford] and almshouses for elderly people [Fig. 2.4(b), Sandal, Wakefield] took a similar form. However, the word 'bungalow' is a relatively new addition to the English language. It was imported into England in the 1880s and 1890s from India where it had come to denote the type of dwelling commonly used by army officers. Before 1914, bungalows were chiefly used as holiday retreats during the summer. Between the wars, bungalows became fashionable as a simple, easy to run and apparently healthy type of accommodation [Fig. 2.4(c), New Farnley, on the western outskirts of Leeds]. Indeed, bungalows became so popular that they came, in the view of architectural critics, to represent all that was wrong with unplanned, suburban development.

(Contd.)

(d)   (e)

Fig. 2.4 *Contd.*
A demand for bungalows continues as either specialist accommodation for elderly people
[Fig. 2.4(d), Hall Green, Wakefield] or as flexible, general purpose family accommodation
[Fig. 2.4(e), Wakefield]. Bungalows generally command a higher price than a similar two storey
house. However, higher land costs mean that they are now less commonly built than before.

Finally, the *terrace* (Fig. 2.6) combines economy in construction and the use of
land, the provision of a back-yard, or back-garden on one side and access to a
street on the other. It is generally the most cost-effective method of providing a
house with a garden. In a cold, damp climate, the terrace also has advantages of
reduced heating costs compared to semi-detached and detached dwellings. The
main disadvantage is a loss of privacy in the back-garden and, in some cases, a
lack of off-street car-parking.

The distinction between the various house types is a distinction of social
meaning as well as physical form. The report of the English House Condition
Survey 1991 states that 'across all tenures, the lowest income households are
more likely to live in flats' (DoE, 1993, p. 1070). The low status of the flat is not
universal, however. High quality, up-market flats have long existed in London
and in the larger Scottish cities. Moreover, inner city regeneration is currently
leading to the creation of more upmarket schemes elsewhere.

The flat is distinctive in another way. It is poorly adapted to individual home
ownership. The ownership of a flat requires the creation of separate management arrangements (and payments) for the maintenance of the collective parts of
the property, such as the gardens, entrances, stairs and the basic structure. On

(a)

(b)

(c)

Fig. 2.5 Detached and semi-detached houses of two or more storeys.

Notes: Detached and semi-detached houses have a long history as accommodation for farmers and country land owners [Fig. 2.5(a), Hall Green, Wakefield]. In the early nineteenth century, detached houses were seldom used as urban housing. They were out of fashion for the middle classes and too expensive for the workers. Burnett (1991, p. 105) suggests that a middle class preference for detached houses started in the 1820s and arose from an increasing formality of social life. Social interaction was no longer to be left to chance. The house was to be separated from neighbours.

Later, the growth of commuting, based first on local railways, enabled people to live in the suburbs where land costs are usually lower. Here the detached house and to an extent, the semi-detached house could retain the appearance of a country cottage and so provide an escape from the place of work. The garden city and garden suburb, in particular, drew heavily on the imagery of the cottage [Fig. 2.5(b), Hampstead Garden

(Contd.)

(d)   (e)

Fig. 2.5 *Contd.*
Suburb]. The design of the inter-war and post-war semi's is more mundane. Those built by local authorities often have a sparse, utilitarian appearance, especially if built from non-traditional materials such as concrete or steel [Fig. 2.5(d), The Isle of Dogs, London]. Otherwise, most detached and semi-detached houses are designed to express an image of prosperity, individuality and comfort [Fig. 2.5(c), off Rayners Lane, London; Fig. 2.5(e), The Isle of Dogs, London].

Semi-detached and detached houses are the most common types of housing in the owner-occupied sector. Together, they accounted for over half the owner-occupied stock in England at the time of the 1991 House Condition Survey.

the other hand, a block of flats is well suited to communal housing, such as student halls of residences or other housing that contain shared facilities for cooking, eating or recreation.

THE GEOMETRY OF HOUSING DEVELOPMENT

It is also possible to classify the internal layout of house types. The basis of classification is less obvious than in the classification of house types. However, Hillier and Hansen (1984) provide a possible method in what they call a 'space syntax'. This is intended as a compromise between natural or 'ordinary' language and a mathematical language. It uses a 'morphic' language that takes significant elements of natural language, but seeks to work out the arrangements between each in a rigorous, logical, even mathematical manner. In other words,

(a)

(b)

(c)

Fig. 2.6 Terraces and other types of houses with two or more storeys.

Notes: Terraced housing in Britain has two separate origins and is of two overlapping types.

First, larger terraces and medium sized terraces, say those with an overall floorspace of more than 90 m^2, stemmed, as Muthesius (1982, p. 11) has argued, from 'the better kind of narrow house with its front facing the better streets, traditional in London as in the rest of northern Europe'. In the eighteenth century these traditional row houses were incorporated into up-market speculative schemes designed by leading architects to classical principles [Fig. 2.6(a), Edinburgh new town].

Second, smaller terraces evolved from the application of the early building bylaws, in particular their requirement for through ventilation, to older, back-to-back and back court housing in England and Wales (Errazurez, 1946) [Fig. 2.6(b), Wakefield city centre]. The application of the bylaws was not uniform, however. In West Yorkshire in particular, the bylaws did not require through

(Contd.)

(d)   (e)

Fig. 2.6 *Contd.*
ventilation and so permitted the continued use of back-to-back houses until further approvals
were precluded under the Housing, Town Planning, etc. Act 1909.
   The distinction between large and small terraces has persisted throughout the twentieth
century. Larger terraces have provided the basis for architect-designed, up-market schemes,
especially in London [Fig. 2.6(c), Hampstead Garden Suburb]. Small terraces have provided the
usual method of low cost housing for local authorities [Fig. 2.6(d), Deal, Kent] and for private
developers [Fig. 2.6(e), Deal, Kent].

the space syntax allows a geometrical representation of housing design and
housing development.

The starting point of the syntax is a social-spatial element, the 'cell'. As
Ledewitz (1991, p. 261) has explained

> 'In spatial terms, the cell consists of an interior space, an exterior space, a boundary,
> an opening in the boundary (entrance) and an entrance space. The corresponding
> social components are the domain of the inhabitant (interior), the domain of the
> stranger (exterior), the separation or control over interaction (boundary) and the
> opportunity for encounter (entrance), at which point a stranger becomes a visitor.'

From this simple formulation, the space syntax enables a classification of the
internal layout in relation to the degree of depth (the number of doors or access
points between a room and the front entrance); linearity (whether a room opens
off another or from a central hall) and circularity (multiple relationships
between rooms). Figure 2.7 gives examples of dwellings where the rooms are

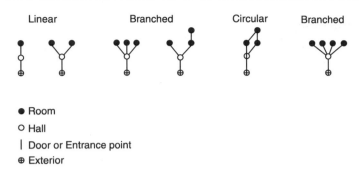

● Room
○ Hall
| Door or Entrance point
⊕ Exterior

Fig. 2.7   The elements of space syntax.

arranged one off each other from the front door entrance (a linear arrangement); where the rooms are arranged around a hallway (a branched arrangement) and where a room has a double point of entry from adjoining rooms (a circular arrangement).

There is no survey that attempts to apply the space syntax to the entire housing stock in Britain. However, Brown and Steadman (1991 a,b) have applied the syntax in a survey of the housing stock in Cambridge. Figure 2.8 provides an extract from the survey report. The report suggests that the frontage of the dwelling (the width of the dwelling facing the street) and the number of rooms on the ground floor are the main determinants of internal layout.

In addition, the results of the Cambridge survey suggest the following.

❏ Narrow fronted dwellings (with a frontage of less then 5 metres) and medium fronted dwellings (with a frontage of between about 5 and 7.5 metres) predominate. The use of a medium or narrow frontage increases the number of dwellings along a road and, in doing this, reduces land and infrastructure costs. In terraced housing, the use of narrow frontages also reduces the amount of external wall in relation to party walls and so reduces building, maintenance and heating costs. Dwellings built by local authorities in the inter-war period are the only common example of wide-fronted terraces and semi's. Model floorplans, for example those published in the Tudor Walters Report (1918), excluded the back extension to reduce overshadowing and favoured medium fronted or even wide fronted dwellings.

❏ Rooms generally offer only one way of reaching the front, either through a hall or through another room. Circularity (multiple links between rooms) is generally absent. The predominance of narrow fronted and medium fronted plan types restricts the possibility of multiple entry points into the same room. Multiple entry points also have the disadvantage that they restrict the use of a room.

❏ The requirements for daylighting in narrow fronted houses ensure a simple distinction between a back room, sometimes supplemented by a back extension and a front room. The back extension is a particular feature of nineteenth century terraces. Another, mostly theoretical possibility, would be to place a courtyard or patio within the building envelope of a narrow fronted terrace house (see Chermayeff and Alexander (1963, pp. 239–245);

2 Room Plans

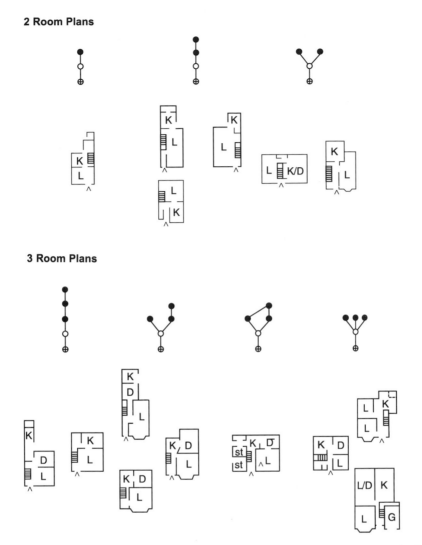

3 Room Plans

Fig. 2.8 Typical downstairs layouts of semi-detached and terraced two-storey dwellings (Brown and Steadman, 1991a).

Colquhoun and Fauset (1991, pp. 50–51). Such narrow fronted patio dwellings allow high levels of privacy and the separation of different household activities. However, they are more difficult to heat and generally require the use of flat roofs which are more liable to water penetration. They are uncommon and do not even figure in the Cambridge survey.

❑ Finally, the distinction between front and back facilitates a distinction between a front 'show' room open to visitors and a rear zone of relative privacy, usually comprising the kitchen. Nearly all small dwellings built before 1939 incorporated such a distinction. Post-war floorplans, especially in local authority housing, show more variety. Local authorities sometimes placed the kitchen at the front, for instance so that the living room might catch the sun. However, a survey undertaken by Birmingham City Council suggests that residents are less likely to complain about the position of rooms if the kitchen is placed at the back, as in the traditional layout (Anon (1988, p. 13).

The geometry of housing design is linked to the geometry of street layout. Martin and March (1972, pp. 35–36) suggest that there are only three basic types of plan form: the pavilion or tower, the street and the court.

'The pavilion is finite in its plan form. The street extends, potentially, infinitely along one axis. The court extends infinitely along two.'

The pavilion includes the detached house, an unusual type of dwelling called the 'quad' house (a block of four dwellings, with each dwelling at a corner) and the tower block. The street layout implies the use of narrow fronted terraces, semi's and most types of flats, except tower blocks. The court allows the possibility of either terraces or flats, but organised in a continuous built form around an external open space (Fig. 2.9).

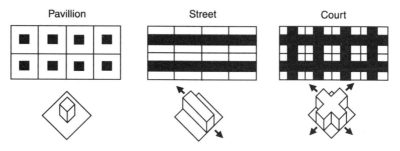

Fig. 2.9   Basic built forms (Martin and March, 1972).

If the distance between blocks is determined purely by conventional spacing standards, for example daylight and sunlight standards or a common privacy standard, the pavilion has the least potential for high density at any given number of storeys. Tower blocks only achieve high densities through their great height. The court has the greatest potential and the street has an intermediate potential (Fig. 2.10).

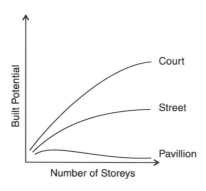

Fig. 2.10   The density potential of different built forms (Martin and March, 1972).

Though Martin and March do not say, courtyard external layouts cannot be applied to most types of housing as a continuous matrix. Such layouts contain no mechanism for road or pedestrian access to the centre. Except in communal housing, for example a university hall of residence or sheltered housing, the court has to be loosened, for instance through the use of a hollow square or the repeated use of 'L'-shaped houses (Fig. 2.11) or some combination of the two.

The repeated use of
'L' shaped (patio) houses

Tenements in the form
of a hollow square

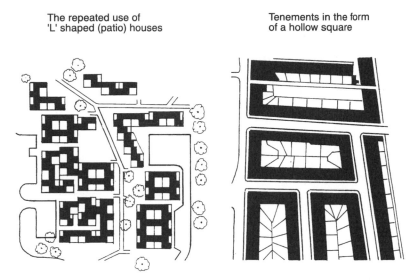

Fig. 2.11 Loosening the matrix of courtyard housing.

The hollow square provides the basic layout of the tenements developed in the nineteenth century in Glasgow, Edinburgh and other Scottish cities (see Fig. 2.11). Dible and Webster (1981) commend a similar pattern of development in urban renewal schemes in Scottish cities. However, current renewal schemes can seldom match exactly nineteenth century layouts. In higher density tenement schemes, such as illustrated, the hollow square layout lacks car-parking and suffers from poor daylighting at the ground floor. The hollow square is not easy to apply to terraces without usually resulting in awkwardly shaped private garden space or no private garden space at all.

The repeated use of 'L' shaped houses, whether repeated as detached or ter-raced units or linked together (Fig. 2.11), leads to a more intricate pattern on the ground than is usually the case for large tenement blocks. The pattern generally involves footpath access and small, patio-like back gardens. Indeed, this type of development is often called patio housing. Crawford (1975, pp. 14–15) suggests that patio houses were an important innovation of local authority housing in the period between 1963 and 1973. However, they have been seldom used there-after. The reasons are not discussed in the literature, but are almost certainly linked to the desire of local authorities and housing associations to provide conventional-looking dwellings and estates, with road access to each property. The limitations of patio houses, like other forms of courtyard development, mean that, in most conditions, the conventional street layout and, therefore, the repeated use of narrow fronted housing forms, provides the highest densities and the most economic type of development of low-rise housing.

CRITERIA OF QUALITY

Discussion of quality implies a search for criteria that may be used to distinguish between good and bad. Clearly, different criteria are likely to be important to different individuals, different social groups and different household types. However, it is also possible to define shared criteria that are more or less common to all residents.

Classifications of criteria

The first step is to distinguish between 'habitability' and what might be called the 'socio-cultural aspects' of quality. Habitability means the extent to which an environment supports human life and health. This is most easily defined in the negative as the absence, within and outside the home, of infectious and harmful living organisms (such as bacteria, moulds, dust mites and their waste products); of harmful inorganic materials, such as asbestos; of polluted air; of noise, glare, dust and contaminated water. Habitability also involves the design of a house that reduces the risk of accidents, for example falls from a window. Habitability is subject to social evaluations, notably about the degree of acceptable risks. Environmentalists, especially those who support the principles of building biology, place more emphasis on health in the home than others (see Kanuka-Fuchs (1993) and Raw and Prior (1993) for examples). However, habitability is essentially about the impact of the environment on the human body. In contrast, socio-cultural aspects of quality are about the relationship between the environment and the user's way of life, social status and daily routines.

Most discussions of quality in housing design focus on its socio-cultural aspects. They focus on how people experience the environment around them; how they interact with that environment; and on how they judge its suitability in relation to their daily routines and their expectations for the future. The question is how to classify these less definable, often more variable qualities into different aspects. Two previous classifications are relevant. First, Lynch (1989, pp.72–77) suggests four main criteria of environmental quality, apart from habitability. These comprise the following:

- ❑ 'sense', concerned with the feel, appearance and identity of a place;
- ❑ 'fit', concerned with matching an environment to user actions;
- ❑ 'access' , meaning the ease with which users can reach other persons, services and resources;
- ❑ 'control', meaning the extent to which the user is free of outside interference.

Rapoport (1977; 1982, pp. 177–183) also distinguishes between four elements of design. These are:

❑ 'space', the organisation of the built environment in a way that links and separates activities, objects and people;

❑ 'time', the daily, weekly and annual pattern of use;

❑ 'meaning', sensory cues, mainly visual cues, that define social status and identity and are often associated with perceptions of beauty;

❑ 'communication', the interaction of different people, including privacy and the control of interaction.

The criteria, both those of Lynch and Rapoport, refer to the urban environment in general. However, they can be readily adapted and applied to housing design, both the interior and the exterior. They can also be roughly related to one another. For example 'sense' relates to 'meaning'; 'fit' to 'space'; 'access' to 'time' and 'control' to 'communication' (Table 2.1).

Lynch's criteria are more easily applied; they relate more readily to desirable qualities. Rapoport's classification is more concerned with different aspects of design; it is more general and more flexible, especially in terms of its treatment of interaction between different people. Neither Lynch's nor Rapoport's classification places much emphasis on security and crime prevention. These may be treated as an aspect of 'control' or communication'. However, security and crime prevention are now so important in the view of residents and so widely discussed in the design literature that they deserve detailed consideration.

Though neither Lynch nor Rapoport say so, it is also possible to collapse the various aspects of housing quality into a simple distinction between the house as a building, located at a specific point in urban space, and the house as a home (adapted from Carlestam, 1989). The house considered as a building and as a location is an object. This comprises what might be called the 'system world' of fit, function and efficiency, making the best use of time and space. Considerations of quality in relation to the systems world of housing apply to virtually any form of accommodation that provides a roof over the head of its occupants. Considerations of quality in relation to the house as home apply most to those places that offer, or have the potential to offer, stability and security to the occupants. The home comprises the 'life world' of the self and others, it covers such issues as privacy and the control of interaction, security and appearance (Table 2.1).

The house as a system

Taken to an extreme, systems analysis leads to a definition of the house as a 'machine for living' or, perhaps more accurately, 'a machine to live in'. The term itself, 'machine for living' is closely associated, for good and for ill, with Le Corbusier and the modern movement in architecture (see Guiton, 1982, pp. 81–82). Le Corbusier's particular concept is not as narrow as it might seem. It does not simply emphasise machine-like efficiency of production and layout. The initial definition, made in 1921, includes a reference to the many necessities of daily life such as 'baths, sun, hot water, cold water, controlled temperature,

Table 2.1 Classifications of housing quality.

	Broad criteria of quality (Lynch, 1989)	Elements of design (Rapoport, 1977–82)	Aspects of quality in housing
The house as a system	Fit Access	Space Time	Flexibility in use Economy in use Access

The house as a home	Sense
	Control
		Meaning,
		Communication
			Privacy
			Security and crime
			  prevention
			Appearance and
			  image

looking after the dishes and plates, health, beauty of proportions'. The reference to 'the beauty of proportions' implies a concern with aesthetics and the appearance of a home. Later discussions of Le Corbusier also make reference to the exclusion of strangers from the home and therefore to privacy.

The interpretation of Le Corbusier is not of great importance, however. A concept of the house as a machine is a legitimate exercise, so long as the qualitative and social aspects of the home are also recognised. More important is to define the type of machine. The house cannot be compared to most types of machine such as a car, washing machine or even a computer. All these serve a limited range of specific functions. In contrast, a house supports a multiplicity of different human activities and actions connected to the daily routines of the occupants, their culture and life-style. The house, if it is to be considered as a machine, has to be considered as a special case. Whereas the typical machine performs certain functions for people, the house enables people to function (Habraken, 1971, pp. 17–18).

Flexibility in use

To say that the house supports a multiplicity of different activities suggests, in turn, that flexibility in use is a prime criterion of quality. To be more specific, flexibility in use implies a flexible internal layout. Whereas the standards of equipment, fittings and finishes can be renewed, improved or added to from time to time, the size of a dwelling is limited by its structural shell and can only be altered at considerable expense. Indeed, in flats, it is usually impossible to increase internal space. The amount and organisation of internal floorspace space is an indicator of long-term economic value and is intimately related to the idea of a house as a place of shelter and comfort.

Movable, time adaptive and 'lifetime' housing

Flexible housing takes various forms. One possibility is to arrange the building structure so that the outside walls carry all the structural loads and the interior is free for adaptation by the occupants as they see fit. Such an approach has long been used in the design of office accommodation and has been a recurrent theme in the history of modern housing design. (See, for example, Dominguez, 1990.) It is also a feature of an innovative housing scheme, 'Midsummer Cottages', completed by the Milton Keynes Housing Association in 1994, that Rudlin and Falk (1995) discuss in a report for the Joseph Rowntree Foundation.

The technology of movable housing has seldom generated public enthusiasm, however. The assembly and reassembly of 'flexible' partition walls involves consideration disruption to household routines, for instance concerning the position of furniture. Moreover, the incorporation of movable partition walls limits the location of electrical sockets and heating appliances. In addition, ease of movement requires the use of lightweight materials that have poorer noise insulation properties than those with conventional building materials.

In any case, flexibility can be promoted through the adoption of simple design guidelines for conventional housing. Examples include:

❑ Rooms and corridors that are larger than the functional minimum permit multiple uses. The bedroom is the best example. If this is of a generous size, it can be used as a study or TV room, according to resident preferences (Bujörklund, 1994). In practice, however, many smaller bedrooms are too cramped even to accommodate a minimum list of furniture requirements, for example a full size bed, a wardrobe, chest of drawers, a dressing table and bedside cabinets.

❑ Square room configurations facilitate variations in furniture arrangements to a greater extent than narrow rectangular rooms (Dominguez, 1990).

❑ The position of doors, 'room openings', may be located to permit different furniture arrangements (Dominguez, 1990).

❑ If the living room and the kitchen can be reached independently and closed off, then the two rooms can be used simultaneously for different purposes. In particular, if the living room is not a passageway to other rooms (as is a frequent design solution in smaller dwellings), it can be used as a spare bedroom by guests (Björklund, 1994).

❑ Even in smaller dwellings, with only two bedrooms, an extra toilet with washbasin is an advantage. The same applies to having an extra sink for washing clothes (Björklund, 1994).

❑ Finally, the floorplan may be modified and expanded in a way that permits a wheelchair user to negotiate the hallways and use the WC (Goldsmith, 1975; JFR Trotter, *Innovations in Social Housing*, No. 3, April 1992).

The implications for wheelchair use deserve more explanation. The conventional design assumptions of the past involve relatively low levels of circulation space. In contrast, if the house is designed for wheelchair users, design must consider the need for a wheelchair to manoeuvre around each room and to go from one room to another. In doing this, the design must assume a turning circle of at least 1.3 m, as used in some European countries, or 1.5 m as is usual in Britain.

The implications may be illustrated with reference to a combined WC/bathroom (see Fig. 2.12). The conventional combined WC/bathroom has a functional minimum of about 2.1 by 1.7 m. An equivalent for a disabled person can take various forms. A full standard room allows a complete turning circle for the wheelchair and also provides easy transfer to the WC. The door opens inward as is the convention in 'ordinary' housing. It is possible to economise on space through the use of a sliding door or an outward opening door. This may also have safety advantages if the disabled person collapses or is otherwise incapacitated in the bathroom. Further economies may be realised through accepting that the wheelchair can negotiate the room, whilst turning round in the hall. Yet even with these compromises, the result is a significantly larger room. (For more detail, see Christopherson, 1995, pp. 29–30; Goldsmith, 1984, p. 150; Scottish Homes, 1996b, p. 4; Voutsadakis, 1989, p. 11.) Designing for disabled people also requires the installation of safety handrails and other equipment, though this has less impact on the room layout and size.

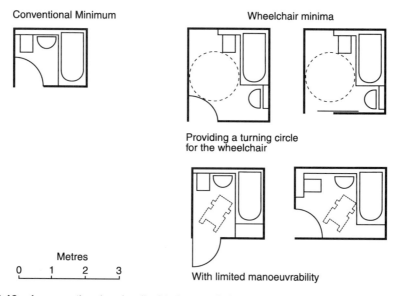

Fig. 2.12   A conventional and a disabled person's bathroom/WC.

The extendible house
Attempts to promote owner-occupation have sometimes led to proposals for another type of adaptable housing. This is the low cost 'extendible' house that the occupier can enlarge once in occupation. Ordinary houses have to be paid for in one lump sum, usually by means of a mortgage or bank loan. The extendible house, at least in principle, offers the possibility of phased development and phased payments.

It is, of course, possible in most low-rise housing to build a single storey flat roof extension at the back or the side. It is more difficult to design a house that is easily extended, without additional expense at the initial stage of construction. 'Contractible' houses, that is, those that can be scaled down when children leave home, are practically non-existent and rarely discussed.

The extendible house is one with a garden, rather than a flat. Additional accommodation is provided either in the roof space, in the private garden or over a garage. Extension into the garden requires either a significant reduction in the size of the garden after alteration or the provision of more land at the stage of initial development. In this latter case, the initial sales price is likely to offer poor value for money, except in areas with low land values. Back extensions may also affect daylight and sunlight, depending on the width of the property. Examples of extendible houses are given in Fig. 2.13.

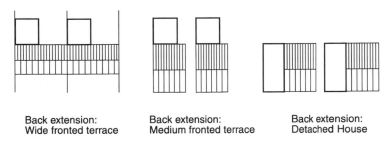

Back extension: Back extension: Back extension:
Wide fronted terrace   Medium fronted terrace   Detached House

Fig. 2.13   Examples of extendible houses in plan form (County Council of Essex, 1973).

In addition, in two or three storey narrow-fronted houses, full height back extensions are often hindered by the use of straight staircases and the lack of a sufficient large internal hall on the upper floor (Fig. 2.14).

Expansion into the roof space is, in some ways, easier. However, it still requires certain features that increase initial building costs. It requires a larger and higher than average loft, without the use of roof trusses as a construction method. It also requires the allocation within the hall of adequate space for the future stairs (see Fig. 2.14).

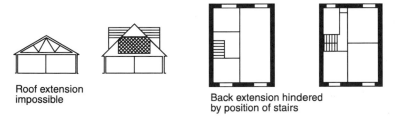

Roof extension
impossible   Back extension hindered
by position of stairs

Fig. 2.14   Some internal constraints on extensions (County Council of Essex, 1973).

There is another objection to the use of extendible housing. The owners of such dwellings may feel trapped, unable to afford to employ contractors to undertake the work and unable to undertake the work themselves owing to a lack of time and relevant skills. Moreover, the financial advantages are generally limited in comparison to the purchase of a finished house of an equivalent size and are sometimes non-existent, even if the alteration work is undertaken on a do-it-yourself basis (HDD, 1980, p. 14). The reason is that piecemeal completion loses the advantages of scale and the relative simplicity of building work that is characteristic of new housing. For all these reasons, developers, both in the private and social housing sectors assume that flexibility is best achieved by giving people the opportunity to move.

Economy in use

Flexibility and convenience in design are always constrained by cost limitations. Cost constraints generally favour the functional minimum or even lower standards and also influence the choice of fittings and services. Clearly it is the task of designers and developers to provide houses that people can afford to buy or rent. However, it is equally important to design and develop houses that people can afford to live in after completion. Economy in use refers to the running costs of a property, both the day-to-day routine costs and more substantial repair costs.

Construction and materials

Economy in use implies, in part, the absence of major repairs. In new housing, the minimisation of repairs means the use of building components with a guaranteed long life and the use of a well-reputed contractor with adequate indemnities and insurance cover. Durability and quality in building construction is mostly a product of workmanship rather than the use of any particular method of construction; for example, traditional brick and block or timber frame. Otherwise, repairs costs are related to age. The report of the English House Condition Survey 1991 suggests that the condition of the building fabric deteriorates steadily until the dwelling is about 70 years old, after which it slows (DoE, 1993, pp. 48–49). The main exception is local authority stock built in the period 1945–1964 whose condition has deteriorated particularly quickly.

Energy conservation

Economy in use is also crucially influenced by the potential for energy conservation. Flexibility in use is likewise influenced. For example, the use of a bedroom as a study in the winter months requires that the occupants can afford an adequate level of heating.

The simplest form of energy conservation is through insulation. The report of the English House Condition Survey 1991 (DoE, 1993, p. 43) suggests that amongst existing houses (excluding flats):

❑ over 90% have loft insulation, though only 8% have insulation at a depth of more than 150 mm;
❑ about 57% have at least some double-glazing;
❑ about 38% have draught excluders;
❑ about 26% have some form of wall insulation.

Loft insulation and draught exclusion can be incorporated into older houses with little difficulty and without major expense. Double-glazing is expensive, but relatively simple to install. It is best incorporated on the occasion that existing window frames are replaced at the end of their usual life expectancy, say after about 30 years.

The incorporation of additional wall insulation is more complex. Most dwellings built since 1980 and virtually all dwellings built since the introduction of higher insulation standards in 1990 were built with wall insulation. Most low-rise dwellings built after about 1920 have wall cavities that may be injected with insulating material. Dwellings built before the First World War, together with buildings using non-traditional concrete systems, have solid walls that can only be insulated through external cladding or internal dry-lining. External cladding changes the appearance of a dwelling and generally requires planning permission. Dry-lining involves a loss of floorspace within a room and may also require the relocation of central heating radiators. The *Energy Report* of the English House Condition Survey provides the most detailed account of the efficiency of the existing stock. The report (DoE, 1996, p. 2) suggests that 'around a quarter of cavity walls are insulated, compared with less than a tenth of solid walls'.

Loft insulation, wall insulation and draught exclusion may be regarded as Stage 1 in the achievement of low energy housing (Fig. 2.15). They comprise the only measures that can be applied as piecemeal improvements within the building envelope of existing dwellings. In new build and in major improvement schemes, the scope for energy conservation is greater. Stage 2 in the achievement of low energy housing is the use of 'passive solar' techniques that involve direct solar heating of the air within a home (see Energy Efficiency Office, 1992; Makkar, 1979).

The typical requirements of passive solar are as follows:

❏ Living areas are located on the south side of houses; circulation, kitchens and bathrooms on the north.
❏ Total glazing is increased beyond that usually possible under the building regulations, with at least 75% of glazing on the south side.
❏ A draught lobby is positioned at the front and back doors.
❏ In the most ambitious schemes, a south facing conservatory is attached to the living room.

In Fig. 2.15, this latter type of conservatory-style house is shown as Stage 3a. Passive solar is not without limitations, however.

❏ In Britain, most useful heat gains are confined to the spring and autumn. In the winter, solar gain is negligible, even in southern England. The sun is low in the sky and cloud cover is persistent. In the summer, solar gain can be excessive and space heating is seldom used anyway. Conservatories are especially liable to extremes of cold in the winter and heat in the summer. They also add to building costs.
❏ It is not possible to guarantee a southern aspect at higher residential densities or in existing built-up areas. Developers argue that the search for a southern aspect reduces the number of dwellings built on a site and upsets their cal-

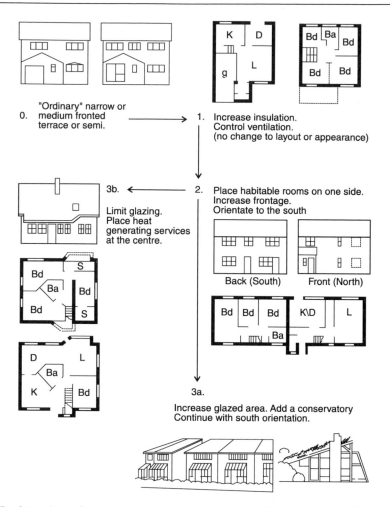

Fig. 2.15 A typology of passive solar house types (adapted from Everett, 1980).

culation of financial viability (Institute of Advanced Architectural Studies, York University, 1993). Moreover, even where a southern aspect is possible, the existence of a pleasant or unpleasant view may suggest a different arrangement.

Solar gain, though desirable, is almost certainly not necessary for low energy housing. In Norway, the State Housing Bank has commended the use of a prototype low energy house where the rooms are arranged around a central core containing the ventilation system, the heating system and the various bathroom and kitchen fittings (Christophersen, 1995, p. 23). This is shown as Stage 3b in Fig. 2.15.

Brenda and Robert Vale (1995) write of their experience in developing a pair of low energy dwellings in Sheffield that:

'with adequate insulation and detailing such measures (as special orientation or passive solar) have little or no additional benefit on a house's thermal performance.'

The Sheffield houses are built with 150 mm of insulation in the walls and under the floor, with 400 mm insulation in the roof, with triple-glazed, draught-proofed windows and with draught-proof, high insulation external doors. The houses are also built to be airtight and use a controlled ventilation system that responds to the moisture content of the air. The elimination of draughts is important in removing perceptions and feelings of cold in a house. However, draught-proofing should not go so far as to avoid any ventilation whatsoever. Otherwise, there is a risk of condensation problems and of poor internal air quality.

Once houses are built to a very high standard of insulation and with controlled ventilation, space heating is usually no longer the main component of domestic energy use. Water heating, cooking and the use of electricity for household appliances is more important.

Further savings can be made through the use of low-energy light bulbs, low-energy refrigerators, specially designed washing machines that use cold water and through the avoidance of remote-controlled audio and video equipment that is left permanently switched on. Otherwise, savings will only occur through the use of 'active solar' devices that provide domestic energy, independently of centrally provided services.

Two types of active solar technology are relevant, namely:

❑ hot water panels
❑ photovoltaic cells that convert sunlight directly to electricity

Both technologies have the advantage that they can be fitted to the older stock. Photovoltaic cells are particularly easy to fit. Experimental low energy houses already use a combination of hot water panels and photovoltaic cells. However, in the absence of technical innovation, growth in their use will, most likely, be slow in a cloudy climate such as that in Britain. Hot water panels and photovoltaic cells both suffer the disadvantage of poor performance in the winter months. Hot water panels are expensive to maintain. Photovoltaic cells, at least in their present form, consume large areas of the roof or the garden if they are to have significant impact on domestic use. Large areas of such cells, in turn, have negative visual effects as they cause glare. Photovoltaic cells are also expensive to manufacture, though costs have declined rapidly over the past two decades.

The search for low-energy consumption has been the main force for technical innovation in housing design during the past two decades. The search for innovation in turn begs the question of identifying criteria to guide design. Makkar (1979) suggests the following. (Italic text is added to clarify the original.)

'a)   No architectural compromises are made in order to save energy.
       For example, the dwelling should be satisfactory on all the other criteria that define housing quality.
 b)   Comfort levels are not reduced.'
       For example residents should not have to reduce the temperature in the living room or hall to save heating costs.

'c) The life styles of the people living in the houses are not affected.'
*For example, residents should not have to undertake complex procedures to
manage heating and ventilation systems in the dwelling. They should be able to
take baths and run electrical equipment at any time they wish.*

'd) The procedures for building the houses are common knowledge and do not
depend heavily on exceptional skills and materials.'
*To promote the widespread use of low energy measures, innovation should use
known technology and should avoid equipment that requires specialised exper-
tise to install and maintain.*

'e) The various measures taken are "economic" i.e.: they are affordable at least in
principle.'
*The crucial economic consideration is the payback period, meaning the time
necessary for the savings of reduced energy consumption to counter a combination of the capital cost of the investment, the likely cost of any additional
repairs and maintenance work and, in the most complete accounts, the likely cost
of raising the finance.*

The economic criteria are, in some ways, the most significant. In new housing,
the payback period constrains the type of energy-saving measure. The overwhelming impression is that the benefits of conservatory-style extensions and
active solar devices are, at present, too uncertain to justify their general use in a
British climate. They are only likely to prove economic if the investor takes a
very long-term view, say over 30 or even 60 years. Enhanced insulation and
controlled ventilation, with solar gain as an occasional optional extra, provide
the most cost-effective ways forward.

In the improvement of the existing stock, the payback period is a potential
influence on whether an investor is prepared to install *any* energy saving measure. The *Energy Report* of the English House Condition Survey (DoE, 1996, p.
243) suggests that,

' except for households in the least energy efficient dwellings there is likely to be little
financial motivation to undertake energy improvements per se. Energy measures on
dwellings with SAP (*Standard Assessment Procedure*) ratings greater than 20
(*excluding the most inefficient 15% of the stock*) generally have "simple payback
periods" ... of 10 years or more.' (*Italics added to clarify the text.*)

In fact, the *Energy Report* almost certainly exaggerates the financial advantages of energy saving. The so-called 'simple payback period' excludes the costs
of borrowing money to finance the work.

The motivation for improvement must therefore come from other sources. In
owner-occupied property the installation of double glazing is usually the most
valuable type of energy-related investment. It is driven by the need to replace
existing defective timber window frames and to reduce maintenance cost. A
desire to increase heating efficiency may be a consideration, but is clearly not the
only consideration (DoE, 1996, pp. 199–200). Likewise, in social housing
schemes, most energy conservation measures take place in the context of broader
measures of modernisation and repair (p. 243).

Otherwise, the main motive is a desire for a warmer, more comfortable home. The *Energy Report* (DoE, 1996, pp. 243–244) states that:

'On improvement, households with previously below average expenditure tend to increase their spending with new opportunities for whole house heating and the fear of excessively high fuel bills removed. Such households, including many who have traditionally been content to live with inefficient heating facilities and low thermal standards, appear more than willing to maintain, or even to raise their level of spending to achieve the comfortable conditions now within their grasp.'

Savings are mostly realised at the extremes. Savings are possible where those low income households, for whom heating is a major proportion of the budget, are able to avoid living in very inefficient property. Savings are also made amongst those households who are able to live in the highest quality, most efficient property. Otherwise, energy expenditure remains much as before.

Access

If a house is indeed a 'machine for living', as Le Corbusier suggested, the criterion of access is the most important aspect of its external layout and location. Access means the degree to which users of the proposed scheme can reach other persons, relevant services, resources or information and work. Access covers approaches by foot, private car, public transport and occasionally by lorries and other larger vehicles. In practice, however, the most significant issues have risen from the steady and apparently unstoppable growth of motor traffic.

Access by car is an obvious prerequisite for an adequate housing scheme. However, the traffic generated by easy access is also a problem, especially where the speed or volume of traffic is high. Moving vehicles, particularly heavy goods vehicles and buses, cause a series of obvious problems. They disrupt the safety of residents. They deter parents from letting children play outside. They cause problems of noise, polluted air and dust. They sever pedestrian movement, say from the house to local shops or local parks. They consume valuable urban space. Vehicles and their associated infrastructures, such as road signs and markings, are also visually intrusive.

Until the 1970s, the consensus in the design literature was that, within cost and density constraints, more space should be allocated to cars in residential areas. More space was needed to ensure that cars and lorries could pass one another. In addition, more space was needed to ensure that all cars could park off the road. The provision of more and more space for cars was admitted to increase the risk of car accidents for pedestrians. However, this risk was offset by the use of road and footpath layouts that separate pedestrians and vehicles and exclude through traffic from residential areas.

Car-orientated layouts generally proved expensive to develop in terms of land requirements and road construction. They were also unattractive in their domination by concrete or tarmac surfaces. As a result, in the 1970s and 1980s, designers and developers invented new forms of 'reduced standard' road layouts that use a combination of design measures to reduce the speed of motor traffic. These layouts abandon pedestrian footpaths or pavements and so require pedestrians and cars to use the same surface. The abandonment of the footpath, together with the less generous road standards, permits higher density layouts with no loss of garden size.

The use of shared surfaces might be thought to increase the risk of traffic accidents. However, this risk can be avoided by ensuring that:

❑ as before, through traffic is excluded from residential areas;
❑ the new type of road is only used for small groups of houses, say up to 30 dwellings;
❑ through the careful design of the road, drivers are encouraged and required to moderate their speed.

The risk of serious accidents, those involving personal injury, is practically zero for a small cul-de-sac, irrespective of whether it is provided with a foot-path. For this reason, the case for shared surfaces is endorsed by the government in its Design Bulletin 32, *Residential Roads and Footpaths* so long as the various design conditions are satisfied (DoE and DoT; also see Noble *et al.* 1987).

For all their advantages, reduced standard road layouts are not a panacea. They cause problems of access for large delivery vehicles and for the removal of dustbins. When first introduced, they also generated mixed views amongst residents. In 1979 and 1980, the Buildings Research Team at the former Oxford Polytechnic undertook a large-scale survey of the residents of a sample of estates with reduced standard road layouts. Most residents, all local authority tenants, thought that the estates were safe. However, a substantial number of residents thought safety was a problem, especially where children were involved. Residents saw potential hazards, even though there was no evidence of increased risks of accidents and even though these new road layouts reduced traffic speeds (Jenks, 1983).

The planning of existing built-up areas has followed a similar pattern. In the 1960s and 1970s, the main theme was 'traffic management'. In this, local authorities attempt to channel through traffic into a series of priority roads through measures, such as one way streets, road closures and no entry signs, that stop access to residential areas or make access so circuitous that it is not worthwhile for a driver to search for short cuts. The main limitation of traffic management is the impact on residents living on the main routes. Traffic management diverts traffic to places where residents already suffer most from the effects of traffic. In addition, local authorities have worried that such diversion could overload through routes.

Since the 1980s, public authorities have paid more attention to so-called 'traffic calming' measures that slow down traffic, without preventing access. Traffic calming does not eliminate the need for traffic management. It offers a range of new measures that may be applied separately or in combination.

Examples of traffic calming measures including humps in the road, the narrowing of the carriageway at key points, small roundabouts and, in the most fully worked out examples, the redesign of the street with new pedestrian areas and a variety of new materials, trees and shrubs. The aim is to slow down traffic either through causing physical discomfort to drivers or through the use of visual cues that impress on the driver that this is not a conventional road. In such traffic calming areas, local authorities have the power to introduce a speed limit of 20 mph (Fig. 2.16).

The impact of the first traffic calming measures has been summarised by Llewelyn-Davies (1994b, pp. 53–54). They have had clear benefits in reducing the speed of traffic and in terms of accident prevention, with a 75% reduction claimed for the first 20 mph zones. However, in contrast to the use of similar measures in other European countries, traffic calming in Britain has somewhat ignored its potential to improve the environment of residential areas. Traffic calming in Britain has seldom used extensive landscaping measures or paid much attention to ways of reducing traffic noise. The reasons for the lack of landscaping are seldom discussed. The additional costs are an obvious constraint, and it is likely that local authorities would not be prepared to take the risk of large trees causing damage to nearby buildings.

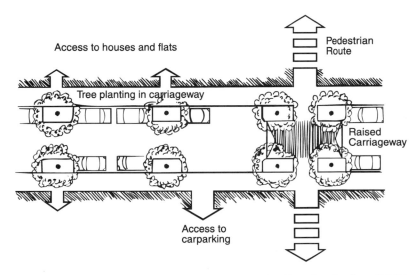

Fig. 2.16   An indicative traffic calming street (Kassel, cited in Llewellyn Davies, 1994b).

Traffic calming measures, even the best designed measures, have various limitations:

❑ They can sometimes cause problems for emergency vehicles.
❑ They raise a potential conflict of interest between car users and pedestrians. The main beneficiaries are children, elderly people and other pedestrians. Though most residents generally welcome traffic calming, a minority complain that they cause inconvenience, damage to vehicles or look unsightly (Windle and Mackie, 1992).

❑ The full range of traffic calming measures cannot always be used in high density areas, characterised by small terraces, flats or multi-occupied dwellings. The reason is that in such high density areas car-parking takes place in the street and consumes space that would otherwise be used for landscaping.

❑ Traffic calming cannot be used in streets with high levels of through traffic, unless the local authority or other public agency accepts the case for broader measures to discourage vehicle use.

The need for access raises different issues in the older, higher density urban areas than in the newer, lower density suburban and edge of city schemes (Hedges and Clemens, 1994, p. 128; Pharoah, 1992). In the older areas, social and shopping facilities are often close at hand. Likewise, these areas are generally well-served by public transport. In most cities, the most frequent public transport routes are those that lead in and out of the town or city centre along the main radial routes. The main issue in these older areas is to divert and slow down private motor traffic, including heavy vehicles. The means to do this are now well established.

In the newer suburban and out-of-town areas, developers have mostly assumed, from the outset, that the car will serve the majority of travel needs. In dwellings built for sale, for example, the usual selling point is their access to the motorway network or their convenience for motorised commuting. The schemes are nearly always provided with a road layout that avoids problems of through traffic. However, these newer areas often lack services and facilities, such as shops, health facilities and a local library. Moreover, the low density of development is often insufficient to justify a frequent bus service. This being so, if people wish to walk to local services from their home or even to use a bus service, they are likely to have to choose a house built in a small urban infill scheme or an older house.

The house as home

Aspects of quality relating to the concept of the house as home differ, in many ways, from concepts relating to the house as a system. Whereas the latter refer to the organisation of activities, the house as home refers to the relationships within a household, to their relation with the environment they inhabit and with other people. The house, considered merely as a system, becomes a home through a process of 'personalisation'. In this process people move in, choose furnishings and decor (and sometimes make structural improvements) to express their identity. Cooper Marcus and Sarkissian (1986, p. 63) explain personalisation as follows,

> 'Most people need, if not to design their dwellings, at least to give them some touch of uniqueness that says: "This is mine: it is a reflection of me/my family; and I/we are worthy and unique beings." '

Personalisation assumes the ability of the occupiers to control a territory, free from unwanted intrusion. It literally means making a house 'personal'.

Privacy and the control of interaction

Personalisation and territory are abstract concepts. A more familiar, more concrete expression of the same phenomenon is the desire for 'privacy'. In principle, privacy is simple to define. It means the ability of individuals and families to lead their own lives without either interfering – or being interfered by – the lives of others. Privacy is not always easy to achieve, however.

Requirements of privacy

Three overlapping types of privacy may be identified, depending on the source of intrusion, for example whether in the house or outside, from neighbours or strangers. Each type has different implications.

First, privacy means avoiding problems with neighbours. People with different life styles may have to live close to one another, especially in high density housing and flats. Though the outcome is dependent on the precise mix of residents, some types of housing and some types of layout are less likely to cause problems than others. For example, shared housing, in which residents share a WC and bathroom, requires the greatest co-operation amongst the occupants. Independent units in a block of flats with shared entrances and shared bin stores generally require more co-operation than houses with a separate ground floor entrance.

For conventional low-rise 'estate' housing, comprising a mixture of terraces, semi's or detached, Karn and Sheridan (undated, 1994 or 1995) list the main features that are likely to reduce neighbour conflict:

❑ marked parking spaces for visitors' cars;
❑ separate driveways and separate front paths;
❑ front doorways that don't look directly into each other;
❑ unobtrusive spaces for rubbish bins;
❑ space out of sight of neighbours to repair a car or keep a boat or caravan.

The existence of clear boundaries between one property and another is also important in minimising disputes.

Second, privacy means a sense of seclusion. It means freedom from over-looking and freedom from intrusive noise. Privacy as seclusion overlaps privacy as freedom from neighbours. Privacy can be achieved either by keeping people at a distance or by a combination of screening and noise insulation. Upper income groups, especially those that live in detached houses in the suburbs, create privacy by purchasing space around their home. Others living at higher densities in terraces and flats can enhance their seclusion through living behind fences, hedges and curtains. Nevertheless, the achievement of seclusion in higher density schemes is usually more limited.

A design handbook prepared by the Building Research Establishment lists the main principles in designing for seclusion, what they call 'acoustic and visual privacy' in higher density areas, where separation of one dwelling from another is not possible (Anon, 1993). (Italic text is adapted from the original or from from Cooper Marcus and Sarkissian, 1986, pp. 94–101.)

❑ 'Adopt the screening methods used for reducing noise...'
  For example:
  ○ *provide good sound insulation materials in walls and floors;*
  ○ *place footpaths away from windows to reduce noise from passers-by;*
  ○ *reduce noise coming from children: ... incorporate a park into the estate or keep family homes away from those associated with single or young couples;*
  ○ *arrange the layout of dwellings so that old people ... are protected from the noise generated by the younger households.*
❑ 'Maintain a careful balance in the levels of screening.'
  Some occupants, particularly the elderly, like views of activity as well as greenery, and parents like to be able to watch over their children.
❑ 'Provide where possible an enclosed garden in which children can play safely and which occupants can use in private.'
  Ensure that the private garden space is screened from public view, for instance from adjacent footpaths and from the view of neighbouring houses, and is clearly delimited from any adjacent communal area or public open space.
❑ 'Position windows where they are unlikely to interfere with privacy.'

Third, privacy means freedom from disturbance from other people, either visitors or members of the same household, within the home. The determining factor for such internal privacy is the number of different rooms in relation to household size, together with the relation amongst the members of the household. The implication for design is to provide extra smaller rooms rather than fewer larger rooms.

It is possible to link the different types of privacy through a hierarchy of needs and expectations, depending on living standard. Willis (1963) suggests that

> 'When housing conditions are bad or there is little space and much overcrowding, privacy from other members of the family is the first and most important priority.'

Once problems of overcrowding are resolved, the relationship to neighbours comes into prominence. Finally, once problems of overcrowding and problems with neighbours are resolved, expectations about privacy increase to include:

❑ personal independence, the ability of different members of a household to be on their own when they wish and to undertake different activities in different rooms;
❑ seclusion from being overlooked.

The ideas of Willis were developed from open-ended interviews with a small representative sample of people living in London in the early 1960s. Willis characterised a concern with the implications of overcrowding and with neighbour problems as a working class view of privacy. A concern with personal independence and with seclusion was a middle class view. Willis also showed that problems with neighbours arose most frequently in shared accommodation and flats and led to a strong desire not just for a separate kitchen and WC but a separate 'street' door.

There are no later studies of the full range of concepts of privacy in and around the home. However, Oseland and Donald (1993) have examined public conceptions of privacy in relation to the use of rooms in owner-occupied housing. The home, the authors suggest, is not a wholly private domain, but is viewed as a mixture of social areas, such as the living room, and personal areas, notably the bedroom.

Ambiguities and limitations of privacy

Ideas of privacy have political implications. Privacy favours the individual and the family rather than the community. It is always subject, for this reason, to potential challenge from those who favour collective action as a basis for urban planning. For instance, Day (1993, p. 160) complains that the exaggerated advocacy of privacy can encourage 'a tendency to take for yourself whenever you can' and can 'in society at large' undermine civilised values.

The key word is 'exaggerated'. The need for private space always has to be tempered by the provision of public open space and by the establishment of links, not just between the private and the public, but also between housing and other land uses. Moreover, urban planning cannot accept separation as the only way in which individuals can achieve privacy. Separation implies low densities, urban dispersal and the consumption of greenfield sites.

On the other hand, it would seem naive to suppose that urban planning either could or should cram people together in flats or high density/low-rise schemes in the hope that they will get to know each other and form a community. Even if they do get together, the result may be an increased level of neighbour dispute. Some balance is necessary.

Security and crime prevention

Privacy is an exercise in social control. Security and crime prevention is another dimension of the same theme. Much of the public concern and much of the unpopularity of local authority estates, especially the high density estates, concerns their apparently high crime rates. Moreover, as crime rates and especially burglary rates have increased in the 1970s and 1980s, more attention has had to be paid to crime prevention in other types of housing, including conventional suburban estates.

There are no particular types of housing or environment that can be described as completely 'secure' or 'crime free'. However, some places and some buildings are clearly more at risk than others. American research suggests that virtually all types of crime are concentrated into 'hot spots' (Sherman, *et al.* 1989). British research is more fragmentary, but in the case of burglaries, it also shows a degree of concentration in specific places and types of property (Mayhew *et al.* 1993, pp. 45–50). A property that is burgled once is, for example, much more likely to be subject to repeat burglaries (see also Farrell, 1992).

The variation in crime rates is partly determined by the social composition of different urban areas, by variations in local subcultures and, in addition, by what Shapland *et al.* (1994, p. 11) call the 'action space' of offenders. For most of the time, most offenders behave like ordinary people and like to operate either in their home area or along the routes that lead from their home to local shops, to entertainment centres or to their work. The occupants of houses and commercial properties in different areas are therefore likely to be at varied risk of crime, irrespective of the details of the design and layout. The impact of design and layout may be small in comparison to these other factors. The significance of the impact is certainly a matter of debate. However, even within small areas with a similar social compositon, crime rates may vary significantly. Micro-environmental or design factors also influence the incidence of crime (Bottoms *et al.* 1987).

Defensible space

Much of the architectural and planning literature on crime prevention focuses on what might be called the larger design elements concerned with the layout of streets and buildings. Jacobs (1961) first suggested that urban design might influence community safety and crime The safest streets, argued Jacobs, were those where the buildings were oriented to allow for natural surveillence by residents and where, in addition, there were sufficient numbers of pedestrians to provide 'eyes on the street'.

Thereafter, the analysis of safety and crime prevention has led to two distinct and, in some ways, conflicting solutions. These are:

❏ the defensible space thesis, worked out in most detail by Newman (1972) in the United States and applied in Britain by Coleman (1985), where the emphasis is on the division of urban space into manageable zones that encourage community control;
❏ measures to integrate estates into the surrounding street network, worked out by Hillier *et al.* (1987).

The defensible space concept is the most widely discussed method of crime prevention in housing layout. It possesses a series of recurrent themes:

❏ the use of houses with gardens rather than flats;
❏ where flats are unavoidable, the use of small blocks with a limited number of households (between say eight and twenty depending on age), using the same entrance;
❏ the provision of clearly defined gardens, fences and gates in low-rise housing; the incorporation of all potential public space into private gardens and the clear separation of private and public space;
❏ the promotion of more effective means of surveillance of space around the

home, including public footpaths and road spaces; the provision of better lighting;

❏ the use of a series of culs-de-sacs, intended to deter entrance from strangers; the removal of escape routes such as overhead walkways and back-footpaths;

❏ the promotion of a sense of neighbourliness that enables residents to identify anyone who does not belong.

A degree of support for the defensible space thesis is given by the results of *The 1992 British Crime Survey* (Mayhew *et al.* 1993, p. 48). This is a large-scale survey of the pattern of crime as revealed by the respondents to a questionnaire survey. The report states that:

'Houses are less at risk of being burgled than other types of accommodation, regardless of the sort of area where they are located and any other factors. Houses differ from other types of dwellings (flats, maisonettes, rooms and bedsits) in that they are, by definition, self-contained, with separate (rather than communal, and possibly open) entrances. Their greater privacy may help keep burglars out.'

Some support is also given by an analysis of police crime statistics in North-ampton and the London Borough of Harrow. This suggests that burglary and theft from outside the house are reduced if the front is subject to surveillance from over the road (Poyner and Webb, 1991).

Otherwise, it is not easy either to prove or disprove the defensible space thesis. The different elements interact with one another, with the attitudes and expectations of residents and offenders and with general trends in crime. The usual method of demonstrating a causal link is through a mapping exercise in which specific design features are related either to the presence or the absence of crime. However, correlations are not equivalent to causes and may have more than one explanation.

Doubts about the validity of the thesis are reinforced by the experience of the Mozart Estate in the London Borough of Westminster. Here, in 1986, the local authority demolished four overhead walkways on the advice of Coleman that this would limit access to and from the estate. A subsequent evaluation con-cluded that the demolition had made no difference to local crime rates and that, in addition, the incidence of burglaries was not related to the size of the block (Osborn, 1993, p. 46).

The defensible space thesis should not, however, be judged purely in terms of its record in reducing the incidence of crime. Even if the impact on crime rates is uncertain, the defensible space thesis makes sense as a device for reducing the fear of crime. The defensible space thesis favours an idealised suburban layout comprising a row of family houses, with a private garden at the front and rear and overlooking a quite street. Thus it uses a familiar environmental image which, irrespective of its value as a crime prevention measure, is perceived as safe, respectable and is particularly well-suited to the rearing of children (Rapoport, 1982, 137–176).

The estate layout is, moreover, easily adapted by private developers. Indeed, in some ways, the defensible space layout is too easily adapted by private developers. Defensible space amounts to little more than an endorsement of the status quo.

An additional strength of defensible space is that its themes of surveillance and defensibility are consistent with another, less well-known theory of environmental preferences, that of 'prospect/refuge'. This assumes that people prefer and feel safer in an environment in which they can simultaneously watch out for strangers and other sources of danger (prospect) and avoid being seen by others (refuge). Prospect/refuge theory is an evolutionary theory that is grounded in the needs of survival of primitive man (Appleton, 1984). It does not deal specifically with crime as a hazard. Moreover, its original formulation places too much emphasis on refuge as a hiding place rather than a place where people can find mutual support. Nevertheless, for people living in a city, the analogy between primitive survival and the need to avoid crime and violence is close enough to make the theory relevant. For example, it is likely that, in areas with a known reputation for crime, people will usually consider as unsafe any streets or open spaces that are unlit at night or that offer hiding places for potential offenders (Loewen *et al.* 1993).

Fear of crime may, of course, be a fully justified and rational response to a rising crime rate and to incidents that have occurred to oneself or to others. However, the fear of crime can sometimes become irrational and exaggerated. The ability of the defensible space thesis to combat the fear of crime provides a means of improving the confidence of individuals in their local community.

Finally, the defensible space thesis has the advantage of defining an environment which is less likely to suffer serious effects from vandalism in comparison with a high density flatted estate. A suburban layout comprising two storey houses is not vulnerable to the failure of the lifts in the same way as a high-rise block. Likewise, unlike a deck-access scheme or some very high density low-rise estates, a typical suburban estate has no noisy footpaths or walkways running very close to the windows of habitable rooms of adjacent dwellings.

Figure. 2.17 shows two residential layouts that Furbey and Goodchild examined in a survey in the winter of 1981/1992. The defensible space layout comprises a series of small culs-de-sac, with semi's. The other layout comprises a significant element of footpath access, with a lack of front gardens and a lack of surveillance over car-parking and over the footpath network. Residents were more likely to complain about vandalism to the estate that lacked defensible space principles (Furbey and Goodchild, 1986a).

The main limitations are as follows. First, the treatment of open space is subject to different interpretations. Coleman (1985, pp. 44–47) argues against any form of open space that cannot be supervised either by an individual dwelling or by a small group of dwellings. In practice, according to Coleman, this means an estate layout that allocates all potential open space to private gardens (1985, p. 172). In contrast, others argue that public open space retains value in urban areas as a place where local people can meet, see one another and

Fig. 2.17 Defensible space: a comparison of two estates (Furbey and Goodchild, 1986b).

where local youth can undertake recreational activities (Perkins *et al.* 1993, pp. 44–45). The incidence of crime and vandalism in public parks and gardens is easily exaggerated.

The distinction between the opponents and supporters of open space is not large, however. Both parties would argue that housing design should eliminate small 'scraps' of open space and landscaping. Both link the value of open space to their use by a community. Unused space may allow the planting of trees and shrubs and may soften the landscape, but is of much less social value.

Second and more important, the exclusion of strangers takes no account of the extent to which acts of crime and vandalism are undertaken by local residents (Mawby, 1977). If most crimes are committed by local residents, say local youth as is often the case, the exclusion of strangers will have no impact on crime levels.

Moreover, even if the exclusion of strangers were to provide an effective means of stopping crime, this is not the only aspect of site layout. The exclusion of strangers, combined with related calls to reduce so-called 'escape' routes implies restrictions on access. This can be taken too far; it can lead to a sense of isolation and stop local residents from walking to local shops, local parks, schools and other facilities. It can also promote social exclusion. Damer (1974), for instance, used the term 'dreadful enclosure' to describe a severely deprived local authority estate in Glasgow.

Integrating streets into an urban network

The opposite of enclosure and exclusion is to integrate an estate into the urban street network. This is the main theme of Hillier's attempt to work out an alternative to defensible space. Hillier *et al.* (1987) show that the 'encounter rate', the number of pedestrians encountered on a street already falls away towards the centre of local authority estates in a manner that is not typical of older residential areas. So, he would argue, why promote even more pedestrian exclusion? Why not open up local authority estates to pedestrian movement and, in doing this, integrate these estates into the urban street network?

A desire to integrate modern estates in the urban street network, including Hillier's proposal, can be understood as a restatement of nineteenth century town planning principles which aimed, through a mixture of clearance and regulation, to break up the impenetrable alleyways of slum areas. The reconstruction of Paris in the 1860s, undertaken by the Baron Haussmann, is the best known example. The result of Hillier's proposal would be to recreate an urban landscape comprising terraces and four storey or higher tenements laid out in a loose geometrical pattern. Many would welcome this as an alternative to both the 'modern' blocks which disregard conventional street layouts and to the low-density suburban estates promoted by Coleman and others.

Such an integrationist approach is not without problems, however. First, Hillier's work has a specific weakness. It ties a potentially attractive aesthetic solution to a contentious assertion that social life is becoming progressively weaker in the modern city.

> 'It is often said that cities are mechanisms for generating social contact. Looking at what has been done to cities in the past quarter century, one may doubt the generality of this principle. The city in its modern transformation seems more a mechanism for keeping people apart in conditions of high density, the under-use, non-use and abuse of space – the 'urban desert effect' – are the distinctive products of the modern transformation of the city.' (Hillier *et al.*, 1987, p. 247)

Social life is diminished, Hillier argues, by the tendency for modern housing estates, notably local authority estates, to possess a street layout that isolates them from their surroundings. Even if this assertion could be substantiated, it seems odd to assume that casual encounters with pedestrians in a street are a significant source of social contact, more significant than, say, encounters at work or in pubs and clubs.

Second, measures to integrate estate roads into the broader road network ignore the conflicting requirements of pedestrians and a motor car. The nineteenth century boulevard or avenue involved relatively slow moving horse-drawn carts and carriages sharing the same surface as pedestrians. Modern motor vehicles do not readily mix with pedestrians, except under the strictly controlled circumstances of a traffic calming scheme. Moreover, the potential for pedestrian face-to-face contact is influenced by the amount of motor traffic in a street. The higher the level of motor traffic and the wider the street, the less is the potential for social interaction and for surveillance from one side to another.

Indeed, measures to protect residential areas from through traffic may actually promote social interaction, even if these same measures form a physical barrier to movement with the rest of the city.

The integrationist approach has been subject to less evaluation than the defensible space thesis. Osborn's review of local crime prevention initiatives mentions only one example, that of the Studley Estate in Lambeth. Here Hillier argued in favour of the creation of integrated routes through the estate to promote pedestrian movement. In fact, before Hillier's proposal was implemented, an independent crime survey showed a concentration of crimes and thefts against the person on the edge of the estate, especially near an underground tube station. High integration of the urban street network and high pedestrian encounter rates coincided with a high crime rate (Osborn, 1993, p. 41).

Though Hillier and Coleman generally present their ideas in opposition to one another, they have much in common. Both rely on statistical correlations rather than the perception of an area by its residents; and both would, if applied on a large scale, lead to a loss of diversity in urban design. The concept of defensible space is, for example, as much a universal, standardised blueprint as the modernist, design solutions condemned by Coleman in *Utopia on Trial* (1985).

The main implication is for a balance between accessibility and isolation. On the one hand, a residential area should be protected from unnecessary and unwanted pedestrian and vehicular traffic. On the other, the residential area should not be isolated. Urban design should seek to avoid what Jacobs (1965, pp. 271–283) has called 'the curse of border vacuums', dead-ends whose isolation encourages a sense of social and physical exclusion.

The smaller elements of design
The defensible space thesis, together with the similar prospect/refuge theory, also has implications for the detailed design of housing. For example, Stollard *et al.* (1991, p. 71) write:

> 'Projections on the façades of the dwelling which impede the line of vision should ... be carefully considered. Window design is an important factor when considering how to provide good lines of natural surveillance at the front of ground floor units. Oriel or bay windows are pleasing design features and also provide good lines of surveillance.... Recessed doors can provide cover for the would-be intruder and should therefore be avoided.'

However, the minor elements of design cannot be analysed purely as a response to theoretical statements in the same way as building layout and street layout. Crime prevention in relation to the minor elements is mostly an exercise in learning from experience and from research. The main lessons may be summarised.

❑   The results of the British Crime Survey suggest that the presence of security devices in a property (the provision of a burglar alarm, of window locks and of double or dead locks lowers, but does not eliminate, the risk of burglaries (Mayhew *et al.*, 1993, p. 48). More sophisticated security devices are of doubtful value as they can easily hinder the daily routines of the occupiers, are potentially dangerous in the case of fires and still fail to deter professional burglars.

❑ The analysis of police statistics, together with the views of police crime prevention officers, suggest that:

○ Burglary is reduced by the avoidance of features that can be used as a ladder to provide access to upper floor entry points. For example, downpipes and gutters have to be carefully detailed to avoid their use as climbing aids (Stollard *et al.*, 1991, p. 73).

○ For blocks of flats with communal access, the bare minimum is the provision of a secure external door that works on an intercom system so that unwanted visitors do not gain access to the internal circulation areas (Goodchild *et al.*, 1997). The provision of a door entry system is now standard practice in the design of local authority and housing association flats.

○ Car crime (both theft of cars and theft from cars) is reduced, though not eliminated, through the provision of a hardstanding or garage within a private garden area. Car crime is more common if the car is parked in the street, in a communal parking area or somewhere distant from the house. Likewise, theft from garages is more common when these are located away from the house they serve (Poyner and Webb, 1991).

○ Theft of personal belongings from outside the home is reduced, though again not eliminated, by the provision of secure external storage, by the blocking off of access to the rear and by the provision of a reasonably sized front garden, say with a depth of at least 3 m (Poyner and Webb, 1991).

❑ Finally, interviews with burglars suggest that the most vulnerable property is that characterised by:

○ the front doors concealed from neighbours, for example, by a hedge;

○ easy access to the rear where it is possible to break through doors or windows unobserved;

○ obvious signs of wealth;
(all reported by Gaskell and Pugh, *The Sunday Telegraph*, 19 February 1995);

○ evidence of current occupation (Brown and Bentley, 1993; Goodchild *et al.*, 1997).

An objection is sometimes raised that the incorporation of crime prevention measures in one scheme merely displaces crime elsewhere. For example, a burglar may merely avoid a house with a burglar alarm in favour of another nearby without. The objection is often theoretical. The scale of displacement has been subject to virtually no research. However, even if displacement exists, this does not reduce the interest of the individual householder or property owner in measures to reduce the risk of crime in their property. From the viewpoint of the individual the extent of displacement may even be regarded as an indication of success. In any case, crime prevention measures may be introduced progressively, first into one place and then into another, until offenders have nowhere else to go.

Markers and signs of order and disorder

Crime prevention through the built environment rests mainly on the offender's or potential offender's perception of a lack of opportunities. In part, the perception of opportunities may be influenced by the permanent arrangement of the built environment, by the layout of streets and the design of buildings. In addition, such perception may be influenced by more transient aspects of the built environment, derived largely from the degree of care that residents exercise over their community.

For instance, one might hypothesise that offenders will be deterred by signs of an orderly watchful community, as represented by neighbourhood watch stickers, evidence of guard dogs, such home 'personalisation' as family names on doors or the maintenance of well stocked front gardens. Conversely, one might hypothesise that offenders will be encouraged by signs of disorder, or 'incivilities' as they are sometimes called in the technical literature. Some of these signs are social. They are related to the type of person present in a street, for example drug addicts, youth gangs or prostitutes. Other signs are essentially physical. They comprise evidence of vandalism, graffiti, litter, dilapidated exteriors and empty property (see also Wilson and Kelling, 1982).

The link between such visual markers and the incidence of crime is the basis of many local crime prevention initiatives, notably the management initiatives inspired by the Priority Estates Project. These generally seek to promote community development and control, whilst simultaneously removing physical incivilities such as dilapidated or empty buildings.

The link is subject to mixed evaluations. The 1988 British Crime Survey suggests that the presence of a Neighbourhood Watch scheme has little impact on the incidence of crime in an area, though it has advantages in bringing residents together (Mayhew *et al.*, 1989). On the other hand, Hope and Hough (1988) have used information from The 1988 British Crime Survey to show a correlation between the evidence of incivilities, measured by the residents' perception of drunks and tramps on the street, of litter and of teenagers hanging around and the overall crime rates in different residential areas. Residents are more likely to perceive incivilities as common in those areas with the greatest risk of crime. Likewise, interviews with burglars have sometimes revealed an awareness of their part that they they have to be more careful in neighbourhood watch areas (Brown and Bentley, 1993).

Appearance and ambience

Issues of privacy and security overlap those of what Lynch calls 'sense', meaning the way in which the environment affects our senses of hearing (the ambience of a place) and sight (the appearance of a place). Privacy is promoted by an absence of noise and the absence of the opportunities for overlooking. Likewise, the way in which visual markers and signs may deter or encourage crime has a broader implication in showing the significance of appearance and image in the environment.

The sensuous characteristics of the home are sometimes dismissed as mere aesthetics. However, aesthetics are important in defining the identity and individual character of the home. In relation to the interior, Björklund (1994, pp. 43–44) provides a good summary of the characteristics of the beautiful home. Though written about the experience of housing in Scandinavia, the summary is of wider relevance.

> 'Views, both outside the within, light and space give character to the home. The home should provide varied experiences not only during the day but throughout the year, providing places with atmosphere and character, be well-lit, exhibit openness and provide seclusion. It is a matter of the orientation of rooms, their inter-relationship, design and lighting, the colour of surfaces and the smell and resonance of materials.'

The main factors are:

> 'Through views and space
> Pleasant proportions
> Beautiful light and sunshine
> Views in different directions
> Genuine and beautiful materials
> Bay windows, glazed sections etc.'

In relation to the siting and external environment of the dwelling, the sense of spaciousness is again a consideration. The sense of spaciousness, as represented in the view from the kitchen or the living room, is, for example, more important as an influence on satisfaction than the provision of a sunny, south-facing aspect (Markus *et al.*, 1972). Indeed, the sense of spaciousness is so important that Rapoport (1982, pp. 162–169) has argued that the perception of a residential area as 'low density' is the crucial factor in determining whether an estate or neighbourhood is attractive.

However, the sense of an attractive environment cannot be reduced to either the sense of spaciousness or the existence of low densities, even perceived low densities. Were this to be so, the only attractive housing in Britain would be located in suburban estates built after 1919. Much depends on the expectations of users. People expect suburban areas to be characterised by a sense of spaciousness and greenery and judge these areas accordingly. However, they judge other areas, for example the city centre, in other ways.

Moreover, there are examples of high density residential areas, for example, the tenements of Glasgow's inner city, that provide an acceptable and attractive environment for their occupants, at least as attractive as suburban low-rise housing (see Dible and Webster, 1981). Residents may forego the advantages of living in a spacious suburb for the possibility of living in a fashionable urban neighbourhood, with good access to cultural facilities and the work place. The preference for urban rather than suburban housing is mostly one of age and life style. Younger, more mobile and childless individuals are almost certainly more likely to prioritise urban living in comparison with families with children. National tradition is also relevant. In Scotland there is a tradition of living in tenements that is largely absent in England and Wales.

Other factors, apart from spaciousness, influence the views of residents. For example, an attractive environment is generally one that its residents perceive as:

❑ enjoying peace and quiet, the absence of mechanical or human noise;
❑ avoiding an institutional appearance such as is more appropriate to an office block or a hospital;
❑ conforming to established notions of what home should look like, with a sloping roof at the front (rather than a flat roof);
❑ safe, without graffiti or evidence of vandalism;
❑ well maintained and clean, without overgrown or unattended front gardens in the immediate vicinity.

The characteristics of a typical poor quality environment are, naturally, a rough mirror image of a good environment. The Report of the English House Condition Survey 1991 suggests that the quality of the local environment can be judged on two overlapping dimensions (DoE, 1993). These are:

❑ its overall impression;
❑ the nature and severity of specific environmental problems, notably those linked to:
  ○ an unkempt area (problems with litter, rubbish and dumping);
  ○ maintenance (poor conditions of roads, paths, pavements or street furniture);
  ○ industry (problems of industrial noise, waste or pollution);
  ○ traffic (including problems of car parking);
  ○ noise (problems with railway or aircraft noise).

Of these various problems, the surveyors employed by the English House Condition Survey reported that problems with traffic 'are by far the most significant', followed by problems with maintenance and the area being unkempt (DoE, 1933, pp. 89–91). Residents generally give a slightly different emphasis. The English *Housing Attitudes Survey* found that crime was the most frequently mentioned problem in an area and that, amongst the various noise nuisances, noise from neighbours was the most frequently mentioned (Hedges and Clemens, 1994, pp. 126–127).

THE ANALYSIS OF USER NEEDS AND PREFERENCES

The analysis of quality separates the different aspects of the house as a system and the house as a home. Some way has to be found of putting the different pieces together. This is essentially the process of design.

Good practice in housing design may be understood as a process of empathy with the users. Empathy means a double process of imagination. It means imagining what the scheme might be like on completion. It also means imagining how this scheme will relate to the experience of the occupants.

Empathy is only the starting point. It may draw on the designer's previous experience. It may also draw on the designer's knowledge of previous schemes and precedents that have proved successful. However, given the variability of meanings of the home, empathy always has to be supplemented by a reliable knowledge of the users requirements and wishes.

In principle, there are three main methods of assessing user preferences and requirements. These are:

❏ those based on the direct involvement of the user in design;
❏ those based on questionnaires and surveys;
❏ those based on an analysis of behaviour.

User consultation and participation

Where users or potential users constitute a relatively small group and where they are easily contacted, they may participate directly in the design process. Participation is a relatively recent innovation in the history of housing design. In planning, the idea of participation became widely recognised in the late 1960s at about the time of the publication of an official report *People and Planning* (MHLG, 1969). In the architectural profession, the idea of participatory design only became widely accepted with the publication in 1987 of *Community Architecture* by Wates and Knevitt. Thereafter, the case for participation has been widely endorsed amongst those involved in social housing, notably by the Institute of Housing and the Royal Institute of British Architects (1988), and by the National Federation of Housing Associations (Duncan and Halsall, 1995).

Rationales for participation

In part, participation has been advocated as a means of giving residents a feeling of self-importance and control. Participation, it is said, promotes democracy, personal development and initiative. It increases the accountability of fossilised professions and public services. This is an essentialist or fundamentalist argument. Participation in housing design is desirable in itself, especially for low income people that possess few other ways of either influencing their environment or influencing the administration of public services.

In addition, it is suggested that participation improves the quality of design. This is an instrumentalist or expert argument. Participation is considered a useful instrument of providing professional experts with relevant information about a site and about the likely wishes of residents. It is a tool of good design and a means of avoiding the mistakes of the past. Indeed, according to its supporters, participation is the most powerful tool that an architect can use to improve the quality of a design.

Turner (1976) and Ward (1976) provide the best known examples of the essentialist case. Both writers are mostly concerned with self-help and self-build in housing. Ward even calls for 'an anarchist approach' to housing in which all organised provision fades away in favour of self-build and squatting. For Turner, participation is a means of stimulating 'industrial and social well-being'.

'When people have no control over, nor responsibility for key decisions in the housing process, on the other hand, dwelling environments may instead become a barrier to personal fulfilment and a burden on the economy.' (p. 6)

Anarchism in housing can be partially applied to self-build and similar types of development where the future occupier either undertakes the design and construction work or commissions the architect and the building contractors. This type of development has grown substantially over the past 15 years and gives users a combination of lower development costs and more choice in design. Self-build is not completely anarchic, however. Self-builders generally have to raise finance from banks and building societies. They have to satisfy the financial institutions that the house will be well built and saleable in the case of a default. This generally limits the scope for innovative designs. Self-builders also operate within the framework of the building regulations and planning controls.

Otherwise, unadulterated anarchism is a nonsense. It would mean the end of conventional housing association and local authority housing provision, even the end of conventional owner-occupied housing. In most conventional housing, people live in dwellings whose design they have not influenced.

Moreover, it is surely wrong to say that this lack of control necessarily becomes a barrier to personal fulfilment. People may wish to express and fulfil themselves in other ways apart from building or designing a house. They may wish to express their talents and abilities through their work, through a hobby or a sport. Even if they wish to express themselves through their home, piecemeal do-it-yourself work, decorating and gardening may be sufficient. There is no evidence that participation is necessary to secure high levels of satisfaction amongst residents. Satisfaction with housing is influenced by many factors. It is even possible for tenants to express dissatisfaction with the process of participation, whilst still expressing satisfaction with the completed scheme (Goodchild, 1987, p. 311).

If anarchism is put to one side, the main application of the fundamentalist or essentialist argument is to rehabilitation schemes, especially to rehabilitation schemes in social housing. In such schemes, the support of tenants is a prerequisite for its success. Support has to be secured from individual tenants in respect of proposals for the remodelling of the interior. Support also has to be secured from the majority of all local residents for proposals affecting the estate as a whole. Otherwise proposals may simply be paralysed in local disputes. (See Sim, 1993, pp. 155–159.)

Moreover, in the rehabilitation of an existing estate, participation has other advantages. It brings people together. It involves them with their neighbours and offers a vehicle for community development, encouraging residents to think about the future in social and economic terms, as well as design.

A report by the National Federation of Housing Associations, prepared by Duncan and Halsall (1995, p. 2) provides an example of the alternative, less radical expert view. The report states that:

> 'At its best design participation involves both tenants and architects in shared creativity. . . . The sharing of imagination and creativity . . . , if carried out in an open and responsive way by all parties, is stimulating and mutually rewarding. . . . It means that the design ideas in both concept and detail have been "tested" and considered at an early stage and that potential mistakes or inappropriate choices or decisions are more likely to have been avoided.'

Again, the case for participation is stronger for rehabilitation schemes than for new housing. In new housing, it is generally not possible to identify the occupant in advance. In new social housing schemes, participation in design requires the pre-allocation of dwellings to particular households before they are built. Except in schemes involving a combination of demolition and redevelopment, this is generally impractical.

Moreover, participation in the design of new housing increases development costs. It increases administrative costs because staff have to attend more meetings. It increases design costs and slows down the design process owing to the need to prepare alternative proposals and revisions. Finally, it leads to increased construction costs as it reduces the scope for standardisation in design and tendering documentation. In rehabilitation, local variations in design, with their likely additional costs, are often unavoidable owing to site constraints. In new housing, they can be avoided.

Even in rehabilitation, however, participation is not a panacea. The views of residents have to be tested against established notions of good practice. Llewelyn-Davies (1994b, p. 91) give an example in the redesign of a local authority estate in London. Here, tenants would choose car-parking provision in preference to play areas and landscape nearly every time, unless the implications and disadvantages were carefully explained.

The most difficult exercise in participation is where the designer faces a different or unfamiliar culture. This is a situation where the designer cannot readily communicate with a user or where the designer cannot readily use his or her experience to understand the needs of the user. In such circumstances, participation is more necessary, but is also more difficult to achieve. Documents have to be translated. A translator has to be present during meetings. Otherwise, the best way is that suggested by Lynch (1989, p. 104).

> 'The designer must move with caution, leaning on local information, previous studies and cultural precedent. He' (*or she – Lynch uses both terms*) 'focuses on basic needs such as vital support, makes flexible plans open to user intervention, and emphasises the training of local professionals.'

Different types of participation

The advocates of participation often talk about a ladder of public involvement that ranges from no public influence at one extreme to full community control at the other. The ladder was first worked out by Arnstein (1969) to clarify citizen participation in the American model cities programme. This was the first national urban policy in the United States. As originally conceived, it implied that all those involved in urban policy, including the provision of social housing, should seek the maximum level of participation. Subsequent adaptations use more neutral language and use the ladder to classify participation exercises (Fig. 2.18).

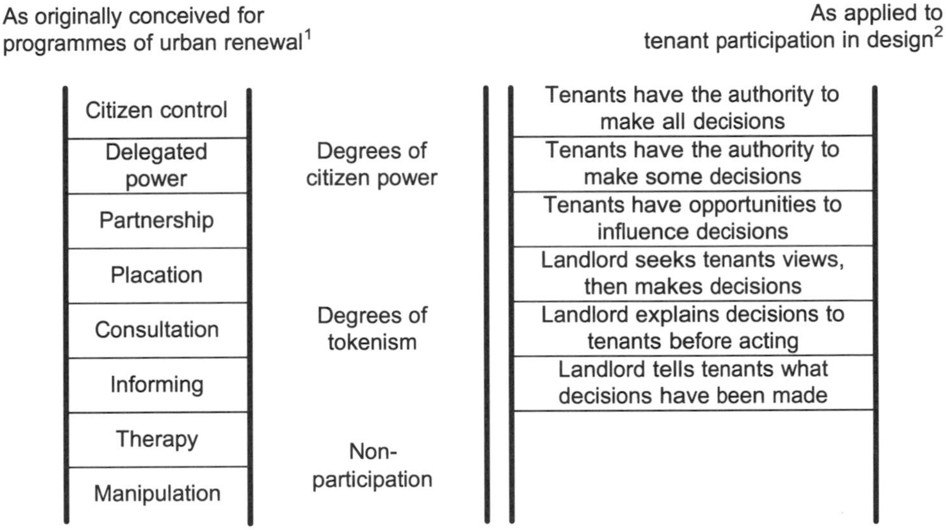

As originally conceived for programmes of urban renewal[1]		As applied to tenant participation in design[2]
Citizen control	Degrees of citizen power	Tenants have the authority to make all decisions
Delegated power	Degrees of citizen power	Tenants have the authority to make some decisions
Partnership		Tenants have opportunities to influence decisions
Placation	Degrees of tokenism	Landlord seeks tenants views, then makes decisions
Consultation	Degrees of tokenism	Landlord explains decisions to tenants before acting
Informing		Landlord tells tenants what decisions have been made
Therapy	Non-participation	
Manipulation	Non-participation	

[1] Arnstein (1969).
[2] The Institute of Housing and the Royal Institute of British Architects (1988).

Fig. 2.18   The ladder of citizien participation.

The essentialist position implies full citizen control in all circumstances. The expert position implies a degree of scepticism about the feasibility of full control. However, the expert position is unlikely to be so cautious or so cynical as to recommend participation as 'therapy' or 'manipulation'.

The levels of therapy and manipulation require clarification. Some participation exercises may be interpreted as therapy because they are intended to ease the fears of a community about the future. Others might be regarded as manipulation because they are mostly intended to persuade a local community to support a proposal. However, neither the advocates of participation nor the practitioners are likely to talk openly about such intentions. Ideas of therapy and manipulation indicate bad faith and are, by definition, excluded from guides to good practice.

In any case, the distinction between levels is not fixed. Different participants may define a participation exercise variously as 'manipulation', 'consultation' or 'partnership' depending on their interests and degree of scepticism. Moreover, participation exercises may change as they proceed. It is possible that an exercise that starts with an element of manipulation may eventually allow residents to influence the outcome. Conversely, the exercise may start with the promise of full participation, only for the social housing or planning agency to reject the residents' preferred solution.

The distinction between types of participation may be restated as a distinction between different types of method. Informing, consulting and placation imply what Bishop *et al.* (1994) call 'one way' techniques of participation. They imply a situation in which the professional designer merely provides information without the possibility of an effective reply. In contrast, citizen control, delegated power and partnership imply a combination of one way and what Bishop *et al.* call 'interactive methods'.

These latter higher levels of participation imply one-way methods to start the process. This is necessary to inform residents about the aims of a project, to outline possible choices and to indicate the constraints on choices. An indication of likely constraints is always desirable to reduce the risk of raising expectations in a way that the sponsoring agency cannot achieve. However, higher levels of participation also imply interactive methods that give people an effective say in the outcome.

One-way methods include drawings and artists impressions, slide shows, talks and visits to other sites. Ash (1985) has reviewed the effectiveness of different methods used in a housing co-operative in Liverpool. Members of the co-op were asked to say which methods were the most helpful.

'In order, these were visits, talks and slides. The architect's traditional means of conveying information, by drawings, was at the bottom of the list and models were next to bottom, much to the surprise of the architects. The use of the projector and question sessions were in the middle.'

These one-way methods are usually packaged together in a combination of public meetings, exhibitions or publicity leaflets. The use of visits presupposes a slightly different context. Such visits provide a realistic way of illustrating the implications of design choices. However, they can only involve a small number of residents and are potentially time-consuming.

The simplest interactive method is to ask residents or possible residents their main priorities. For instance, in a series of meetings, the residents of an improvement area might be asked a simple open-ended question: 'What would make ... a better place to live in?'

Otherwise, interactive methods generally involve some form of intensive process of working out alternative designs in a public arena. Members of the public are given the opportunity to prepare lists of priorities and to make choices about where buildings and other design elements are to be sited. Simply made, moveable models are often a feature of this type of exercise. In an estate layout, for example, the houses may be represented by wooden blocks that the residents can move about as appropriate. In the future, computer-aided design may be able to simplify the making of design choices and provide a more effective simulation of the outcome. However, at present, computer-aided design is too expensive and too complex for widespread use (Bishop *et al.*, 1994, p. 13).

Interactive design has generated its own terminology. This includes 'design days', planning weekends', 'planning for real'. However, these are mostly distinguished by the time span of the participation process and the origins of the ideas. The techniques do not vary greatly.

The provision of independent technical advice is a potential problem in participation. Funds are available for the training of tenant representatives. However, the training is general and more about raising the confidence of tenants, rather than proving technical skills in design or the making of financial estimates. Most housing associations and local authority housing departments use their own professional staff or external professional staff hired to act on their behalf. These professional staff are not independent. They work for the social housing agency. It is conceivable that, in some circumstances, the tenants might wish to consult other expert opinion.

In participation exercises in town planning, the availability of independent advice is more important. Participation exercises in town planning may involve a conflict between residents and the commercial interests of developers and land owners. Moreover, in the case of major schemes, participation exercises in town planning may culminate in a local public enquiry where alternatives proposals and the views of objectors are subject to detailed cross-examination. As a result, access to independent advice may be crucial to the outcome.

Free or reduced price technical advice is available through the planning aid service of the Royal Town Planning Institute, the Association of Community Technical Aid Centres and from individual planners and architects who are interested in the subject. However, free advice is not always available. Many local groups would not even know where to look for such advice.

User surveys

Questionnaire surveys are closely related to, and complement, exercises in providing a broad, representative statement of local views, whereas participation generally allows a small number of residents to discuss points in detail. Moreover, like participation exercises, questionnaire surveys may be classified according to the degree of influence of residents.

Some questionnaires allow residents to express their priorities and their preferences for different types of scheme. These may be understood as consultation surveys. Others provide background information to the designer. They seek to assess the performance of housing in use, as experienced and perceived by the occupants after six months or more of occupation.

Consultation surveys

The assumption of consultation surveys is that residents should be allowed to respond in terms of the trade-offs and conflicts that the process of design has to resolve. In doing this, the aim is to assess the relative priorities of typical residents, to determine whether residents' priorities correspond to those of the professional design and to promote innovation. Consultation surveys are directly linked to participation in design and have grown, from the mid 1970s onwards, alongside the movements for tenant involvement and community architecture.

The simplest consultation survey is similar to the simplest exercises in interactive participation. Residents are asked to list their priorities for their local neighbourhood or for their own home. The analysis of the results then assesses which items are mentioned most frequently.

The mere listing of priorities fails to consider the likely costs. However, it is also possible to identify spending priorities within realistic financial constraints. A good example is the 'Priority Evaluator' technique used by the former Milton Keynes Development Corporation (1975). In this, residents were presented with a matrix that illustrated key aspects of housing quality and standards and that gave residents the ability to choose the type of accommodation that best met their expectations (Fig. 2.19).

Bedrooms	Lounge/dining room	Bathroom/toilet	Built-in storage
1 double + 2 singles −25p	Basic lounge/basic dining area −15p	Combined upstairs or downstairs −15p	No storage −10p
2 double + 1 single 00p	Basic lounge/larger dining area 00p	Separate upstairs (or downstairs) −10p	Limited storage 00p
2 doubles + 2 singles +25p	Larger lounge/basic dining area 00p	Combined upstairs/ toilet downstairs 00p	More storage +10p
3 doubles + 1 single +50p	Larger lounge/large dining area +15p	Separate upstairs toilet/shower downstairs +15p	Much more storage +20p

Notes: The original Priority Evaluator contained twelve different aspects of housing, including aspects relating to the exterior. The items marked in grey indicate the original standard of the property.
Source: Milton Keynes Development Corporation Planning Directorate (1975).

Fig. 2.19   An extract from a Priority Evaluator matrix.

For each aspect of quality, the matrix indicated three or four levels of provision ranging from the barest minimum to the above average. For each level of provision, the matrix indicated a price, measured as the difference in weekly rent level compared to their present level. Residents were therefore able to decide whether they were willing and able to pay for additional features compared to the standard of their existing house. If they were willing and able to pay for a better house, they were able to select priorities amongst these different features.

Finally, if they were to face reduced financial circumstances, they were able to select those aspects of quality that were least worth retention.

The Priority Evaluator is distinctive in the way it allows residents to vary their spending on housing. Another approach is to ask tenants to select priorities amongst a series of options that cost about the same. Duncan and Halsall (1995, p. 8) give the example of an illustrated questionnaire used to assess alternatives in the redevelopment of the Manor Estate in Sheffield. Previous consultations had shown that safety and security were key issues. In response, the architects asked the residents to rank different ways of achieving security under a series of different headings covering, among other things, such items as house security equipment, type of front entrance, front and garden layouts, the location of play areas and play spaces and the design of fencing, hedging and walling. Each heading represented a page in the illustrated questionnaire. Residents were able to rank the alternatives for each heading in order of priority and to add comments were appropriate.

The identification of priorities is essentially about the details of design in concrete cases. The Priority Evaluator used in Milton Keynes requires a series of baseline costs that are related to the existing home of a respondent. Likewise, the illustrated questionnaire used in Sheffield involves a series of modifications to existing house types. Both methods need to be explained in detail to respondents, are potentially time-consuming and are, for this reason, better suited to group discussion rather than large-scale sample questionnaires.

In the private sector, market researchers have independently worked out what might be called 'deeper' methods of exploring priorities. These methods include group discussions; projective techniques using sculpture, collage and cartoons; role playing and 'enabling techniques' that allow the consumer to express or portray what would bring them satisfaction (Birks and Southan, 1992). The aim of such consumer research is to quantify different segments of the market and to sensitise builders and the manufacturers of home furnishings to the preferences of each segment.

Environmental psychologists have used similar methods to define the qualities of the home. In Denmark, for example, the Institute of Future Studies has worked out, through group discussions, a series of visions of the dream home (see *The Futurist*, January/February 1993). The classification comprises four overlapping types:

❏ Those who see the home as a source of security generally prefer a traditional family house with garden.
❏ Those who see the home as a physical expression of family life generally want a spacious house where different rooms can express the complementary aims of family togetherness and individual relaxation.
❏ Those who use their home as a showcase for visitors emphasise stylishness and status.
❏ Finally, those who place most of their life priorities on outside interests want a house of more or less spartan efficiency.

These 'deeper' methods of analysis have exactly the opposite strengths and weaknesses to the detailed assessment of design priorities. They are rich in generalities, but not easy to apply to specific cases. Their main use is at an early stage in design, before detailed consultation or market testing.

Surveys of housing in use

Irrespective of the care undertaken in determining preferences in advance, it is also sensible to assess the quality of housing after completion. Such 'satisfaction surveys', as they are often called, have a longer history than consultation surveys. They date back to the first attempts in the 1930s and 1940s to apply the principles of social science to public policy. In Britain, the first substantial survey is almost certainly *An Enquiry into People's Homes*, prepared by Mass Observation (1943). The aim was to guide planners and architects in the reconstruction programme expected after the end of the Second World War.

Surveys of housing in use continued to be undertaken throughout the 1950s. Hole and Attenburrow (1966) record that, in 1956, researchers at the Building Research Station interviewed 252 people living in small terraced houses to ascertain the acceptability of different arrangements for storage. Later, in the 1960s and 1970s, the Ministry of Housing and Local Government and subsequently the Department of the Environment undertook a series of surveys to evaluate the tenants' views of newly completed local authority estates. These surveys were less specific and less technical than the earlier work of the Building Research Station. They attempted to develop a broad view of the reasons that contribute to the residents' satisfaction with their home (Burbidge, 1975). This particular series of survey research is largely responsible for the subsequent description of surveys of user response as 'satisfaction surveys'. Another term, mainly of American origin, used to describe this type of survey is 'post-occupancy evaluation'.

The direct involvement of the Department of the Environment in satisfaction surveys largely ceased in 1981, when a Conservative government decided to end local authority house building. By this time, the practice of satisfaction surveys was also under attack in the design journals on the grounds that it said little about the priorities of residents for the future (Donnelly, 1980). However, satisfaction surveys have not completely disappeared. The language of housing policy in the 1980s and 1990s, with its emphasis on 'choice', has encouraged housing associations and local authorities to undertake their own surveys of tenant satisfaction, mostly in relation to satisfaction with the management service (see Prescott-Clarke *et al.*, 1993). In addition, general housing surveys, notably the quinquennial English House Condition Survey and the *Housing Attitudes Survey*, have included specific questions about satisfaction and attitudes towards the built environment.

With few exceptions, satisfaction surveys have not been sponsored by private developers. Market research undertaken for private developers may include a question about satisfaction. However, market research surveys generally place more emphasis on product development and are best described as exercises in consultation and the identification of priorities.

Typical patterns of response

The scope and content of a satisfaction survey is best defined by the rules of good practice. If the survey is to achieve reliable and valid results, the questionnaire should cover background material relating to the social and economic characteristics of the resident and his or her household, including their previous housing experience. It should cover all the main aspects of housing quality, at least in outline, including floorspace and internal layout, heating and insulation, location and the external environment. More specialised surveys are possible, for instance enquiries into privacy or security, but should seek to place this particular aspect into context. Finally, most surveys include a question that seeks to provide a global evaluation of the home as a place to live.

The results generally show the varied factors that influence housing quality. A list of likes and dislikes may, for example, generate more than 80 different features relating to either the inside, the outside, to the rents or other costs or to the neighbours. Some satisfaction surveys include more than 50 separate questions on different aspects of housing quality. It is impossible to give an item by item summary.

More important are the attempts to identify the main influences on satisfaction. The usual method is to relate the statistical pattern of responses to the question (or a series of questions) about overall satisfaction to responses about particular aspects of the environment. It is also possible to search for similarities in response to specific aspects of the home, for example space within the home, the dwelling unit as a whole or the area outside the home, without relating these to an overall question about housing satisfaction. Canter (1983; 1985) has advocated this latter approach, calling it 'facet analysis'. However, facet analysis is most suited to evaluating places in relation to the social roles and activities of their occupants. It is less suited to analysis of feelings or preferences, or analysis of the home in relation to personal or social identity (Sixsmith, 1986).

In virtually all types of satisfaction surveys, the usual method of analysis involves a search for the most influential perceived aspect of quality. Assessing the impact of actual variations in housing quality requires additional information. Either the researcher examines the pattern of results in different settings and infers the implications of these differences, or the survey includes a house-by-house assessment of the physical condition and layout, undertaken by a trained independent surveyor. The English House Condition Survey provides an example of the latter.

Most published reports of surveys concern the experience of living in social housing estates. The reports consistently indicate that the appearance of the estate and the buildings is the single most important factor influencing residents' feelings towards the home (see DoE, 1972; Furbey and Goodchild, 1986b; HDD, 1981). Tenants are most satisfied if they state that the estate, especially the approach to their house, is attractive to look at. In contrast, if residents are asked directly what they most dislike or like about their home, the surveys generally indicate a different pattern. The most important aspects of design are those concerned with the equipment standards of the dwelling, such as the heating system, the size of rooms or the parking facilities.

The discrepancy between the statistical determinants of satisfaction and the tenants' own views is open to different explanations. One possibility is that the factors associated with an attractive environment are less easily conceptualised and so more easily ignored in direct discussions. Another possibility is that appearance is a sensitive issue that respondents are unlikely to reveal through direct questioning. Since the meaning of architecture is transmitted mainly through a series of visual cues, a question concerning whether a person likes the appearance of their house comes close (or as close as any question in such surveys) to asking whether that person likes the social meaning of the home as well. The home is a potential representation of the good taste of the self and so a representation of beauty. Equally, the home is a facade that is presented to others (see, for example, Cooper Marcus and Sarkissian, 1986, pp. 45–62; Duncan, 1985; Almendola, 1989).

There are few detailed studies of the determinants of satisfaction in owner-occupied or privately rented housing. The reports of the English House Condition Survey are the main exception. The report of the 1976 survey states that, for a representative national sample of households, it is not easy to relate the statistical pattern of overall satisfaction to a series of questions about particular aspects of the accommodation. Nevertheless, of all aspects included in the questionnaire, the general state of repair of the property, followed by the attractiveness of the surroundings of the dwelling were the most important influence (DoE, 1979, p. 10). Later reports give similar results. The report of the 1991 survey repeats the distinction between the statistical determinants of satisfaction, mostly relating to appearance and the more concrete aspects of quality identified by residents (DoE, 1993, p. 123).

It is also possible to use the results of satisfaction surveys to classify the responses of different household types. Three main types may be distinguished, namely:

❑ households with children;
❑ adult households of one and two persons without children;
❑ retired or pensioner households.

Sometimes, households with children are subdivided into those with young children, aged under 5 years old, and those with children aged between 5 and 16.

Members of households with children make the most intensive demands on their home. They are invariably more critical of all aspects of housing design. In addition, as is well known, households with children also have a particular aversion to living in a flat.

Members of pensioner households generally report more satisfaction with their existing accommodation, though they are more likely to complain about vandalism and the disruptive effect of children's play. In addition, elderly people are often more reluctant to contemplate moving. Finally, adult households without children have a pattern of likes and dislikes that is intermediate between households with children and pensioner households. They are less critical than households with children, but more likely to move than elderly households. (See Burbidge, 1975; Furbey and Goodchild, 1986b.)

The relatively high levels of satisfaction amongst elderly households is surprising, given that elderly people are often more vulnerable to adverse conditions in their dwellings or their neighbourhood. Various explanations are possible. The Report of the English House Condition Survey 1976 links housing satisfaction with the state of repair of a property to the length of residence of the occupier (DoE, 1979, p. 24). As people settle into a home and stay there for many years, they become less aware of its defects, as these latter are determined by an independent surveyor.

In contrast, a Scottish survey shows that, amongst elderly people, there is no relation between length of residence and satisfaction (Aspinall *et al.*, 1995, p. 19). Moreover, the length of residence cannot explain the tendency for elderly households to be more satisfied with newly completed dwellings. Other explanations are that:

❏ old people are less willing to articulate dissatisfaction (Burbidge, 1975, p. 159);
❏ many older people lack viable housing alternatives and are reluctant to admit dissatisfaction with a situation that they cannot change (Christensen and Carp, 1987, p. 46);
❏ over the life cycle, aspirations usually become lower and more realistic, that is, by the age of 60, most people will have found and moved into a house that they find satisfactory and, finally, that the current generation of elderly have experienced a particularly marked improvement in housing conditions through their life (Aspinall *et al.*, p. 4, 9, 43).

The distinctive responses of elderly people implies a separate statistical analysis of the main influences on their satisfaction. A US study of public sector housing suggests that, whereas the main influence on the satisfaction of families is appearance, the main influence on the satisfaction of the elderly is their sense of control, meaning the amount of perceived privacy in the home, the extent to which they could make changes to the interior, as well as their feeling part of the neighbourhood and being safe from accidents outside (Selby *et al.*, 1987, p. 32–33).

The Scottish survey, analysed by Aspinall *et al.*, 1995, suggests that the most important influences are whether the occupants report damp in their home, whether they have central heating and whether they are able to suggest improvements. However, the analysis is based on a survey of housing needs, rather than a full satisfaction survey, and makes no mention of factors such as appearance, privacy or their sense of control. Aspinall *et al.* also undertook in-depth interviews. These indicate a wide range of factors relating to the interior and exterior and suggest that no single factor is dominant.

Other social differences, such as gender, class and ethnic status are less amenable to examination through satisfaction surveys. Gender differences have been widely studied. It is possible to show that women, in their role of mothers and housewives, are likely to stay in and around the home for longer periods than men and are, as a result, more vulnerable to any inconveniences or design errors. It is also possible to show that, in family households, women and men generally use the home in a different way and that, in particular, women spend more of their time in the kitchen and in child-rearing activities (Ahrentzen, 1989). Women are generally more involved in their home and are able to provide a richer, more complex account of the various meanings of the home (Gurney, 1995, p. 316).

However, it is much more difficult to say that women and men define the qualities of the home in a different way or provide a significantly different evaluation of where they live (Smith, 1994). Likewise, it is difficult to find surveys where the satisfaction of women residents is significantly higher or lower than men. For example, the report of the *Housing Attitudes Survey* states that: 'Differences by gender tended to be very small' (Hedges and Clemens, 1994, p. 130). Other factors, such as the age of residents, the type of household and the respondent's previous housing experience, are generally more important.

Issues of reliability and method

Both consultation and satisfaction surveys enable users to express their wishes and needs in the most direct and detailed way. However, they encounter problems of reliability. How does the interviewer know that the articulated responses actually reflect the views of the users?

Surveys invariably involve a difficult choice about sample size and the depth of analysis. Should the interviews concern a large number of people to enhance statistical validity/ If so, the questionnaire is likely to comprise simple closed questions that can be analysed in quantity. In contrast, should the interviews concern a smaller number of respondents and involve an in-depth enquiry? If so, the interview is likely to generate a rich body of information that is not easy to quantify or to compare with other studies.

Moreover, both consultation and satisfaction surveys risk imposing frameworks on users. Actual decision-making situations may involve different and more complex choices than is possible in a consultation survey. Likewise, in satisfaction surveys, residents are asked to consider their home in a way that many might not have done previously. The respondents of user surveys are notoriously reluctant to express dissatisfaction. As a result, the analysis of the determinants of resident satisfaction rests on relatively small differences in overall satisfaction levels, say in the range between 65% and 80% of different samples and subsamples.

The interpretation of satisfaction surveys is also subject to uncertainties. The degree of satisfaction is crucially related to the respondents' expectations. People living in poor quality housing may express satisfaction because they know nothing else. Conversely, those who have experienced an improvement or rehabilitation programme might express dissatisfaction because he or she can see missed opportunities. (See Niner and Forrest, 1982, p. 83.)

Doubts about the reliability of surveys are compounded by the fact that most are undertaken by a housing agency that has some interest in the outcome. The agency may wish to emphasise its good record in providing satisfactory housing. If so, it is likely to emphasise the existence of a high level of satisfaction and fail to examine possibilities for improvement. Conversely, the agency may be searching for financial support to undertake a modernisation or renewal scheme. If so, it is likely to emphasise the scale of dissatisfaction and the need for action.

However, the possibility for bias is not confined to satisfaction surveys. Participation sometimes suffers the same tendency. This is why Arnstein's ladder of participation includes levels of manipulation and therapy. The possibility of bias also arises in other types of housing research, for instance assessment of 'need'. Properly conducted, surveys of housing preferences and surveys of housing satisfaction remain a valid method of research.

The analysis of behaviour

The analysis of behaviour is qualitatively different from participation exercises and the use of questionnaire surveys. The latter involve some form of social communication between the designer and the user. The designer and the user talk to one another, even if, as in many questionnaire surveys, the discussion is through an intermediary, such as an interviewer. In contrast, the analysis of behaviour involves an analysis of what users do – what type of environment they choose to inhabit and their actual use of the environment. The analysis of behaviour involves such questions as: Where have people moved? What type of housing did they move into? Once they had occupied their new home, did they use the public space?

The analysis of choices

The analysis of behaviour starts with the analysis of how people choose a place to live. Such analysis is implicit in the logic of private development. House building is a capital intensive exercise. House builders must therefore always be aware of the type of housing that sells quickly if they are to maintain their profits. The analysis of choices enables the identification of concrete examples of successful designs and layouts. The developer uses his (or sometimes 'her') experience to judge the potential of a site. Sometimes the personal judgement of the developer is tested against the views of a professional consultant. Whatever the details, the method of analysis invariably involves a search for comparables.

For small sites, say under 50 dwellings, the usual questions are: what types of house and what price level is typical of the surrounding area? For larger sites, other questions arise: what type of housing has sold in towns and cities of an equivalent size, with an equivalent socio-economic mix and an equivalent rate of population growth?

The analysis of choices also provides a way in which designers can learn about popular culture and its implications. For example, the American architect Robert Venturi (1972; 1976), one of the leading advocates of popular, post-modern styles in urban design, has suggested that ordinary speculators' housing, together with the advertising material used to sell such housing, provides the best starting point for understanding contemporary meanings of the home. In Britain, Forty and Moss (1980) suggest that the dominant image is a combination of continuity, permanence, comfort and efficiency. Consumers want a home whose interior is comfortable and efficient. However, they also want a home that, on the outside, looks traditional. This preference for tradition in turn leads to a preference for country cottages and houses in small country towns.

Analyses of advertising images offer an idealised interpretation of preferences. The analysis of actual consumer choices, the pattern of demand, is more realistic but has other limitations. The pattern of demand generally provides a weak source of information about the details of design. Most estate agents and builders argue that the most common influence on choice is the location of a house rather than its design. Moreover, the analysis of market demand makes no allowance for the way in which available choices are structured by the practices and expectations of providers or compromised by financial constraints.

A further complication is that people make choices for either positive or negative reasons or for a combination of the positive and negative. People may find a place positively attractive or simply less unattractive than somewhere else. The balance between positive and negative factors is not easy to determine unless research concerns the motives of a house purchaser or tenant. For example, it is commonplace to observe that people leave inner city areas for the suburbs. However, this does not mean that the movement cannot be reversed, given new types of inner city development. The only way of assessing the prospects for inner city development is through an assessment of the motives and perceptions of those who move.

The observation of use

Once people have moved to a place, the direct observation of behaviour can reveal patterns of use. The observation of behaviour is most commonly used to clarify issues in the design and improvement of parks, streets and other public spaces. For the interior of the home, designers seldom undertake direct observation themselves. Instead they use the results of previous observational exercises that have attempted to measure the space requirements of different activities.

Observation of behaviour in public spaces

In relation to the design of the space outside the home, Hester (1975, pp. 148–150) suggests that observational techniques are of little value in generating ideas and aims, or in choosing between different options. However, they can test whether people actually use a place in the way they say they do in their survey responses or participation exercises. Observation can help fix the position of footpaths, paved areas and seats. It can also help clarify the problem when one group of users complains about another group – for example where local residents complain about the behaviour of local youths.

In addition, observation can identify priorities in crime prevention work. Observation can reveal the number and type of people in a street (whether they are alone or in groups, whether they are men or women). In doing this, observation can establish the character of the street and whether it is likely to appear threatening to most people. Observation can also establish the incidence of anti-social behaviour (drunkenness, shouting, youths hanging around). Finally, it can measure the extent of what are sometimes called 'incivilities'. These are environmental problems that arise from misuse and include litter, dog muck, vandalism and graffiti. Observation of the number and type of people in the street is recommended by Shapland *et al.*, 1994, p. 68) as a preliminary for area-based crime prevention exercises. The measurement of incivilities was a crucial element in the correlation studies undertaken by Coleman (1985) in an effort to demonstrate the validity of the defensible space thesis.

Observation of behaviour requires the preparation of a schedule to ensure consistency amongst the surveyors. The observation itself should be undertaken in an unobtrusive way and must be repeated to give valid and reliable results. Observation should be undertaken at different times of the day, different days of the week and, if possible, at different seasons of the year. Observation is not a cheap method.

Observation within the home

The desire of residents to maintain their privacy limits the scope of direct observation within the home. Use of the home is a frequent theme in surveys undertaken in the 1950s and 1960s in Britain. However, most studies merely asked residents to record their use of rooms, for example through completing a daily record of household activities and routines.

The observation of use may still proceed in a laboratory setting, for example through filming or video-taping people in a simulated residential setting. Such techniques are common in the field of ergonomics, which is the study of the working environment in relation to its comfort, ease and safety of use. They have also been applied in housing to establish architectural guidelines for the design of rooms. (See Wilson, 1982.)

The kitchen is especially suited to ergonomic research. A teaching guide *Living with Technology* prepared by the Open University explains why this is so (The Course Team, 1988).

'... There are many aspects of cooking and food preparation that can be thought of as needing rational organisation and functional space planning. For example, preparing a meal can be described in terms of a sequence of actions something like: taking raw food from storage (e.g. from the refrigerator), initial preparation (such as washing, peeling and mixing), putting into cooking container, placing in or near the cooker, final preparation, serving. So the kitchen equipment could be planned in convenient locations for this sequence of activities, such as having a sequence of equipment: refrigerator, worktop, sink, worktop. This sequence allows the cook to move efficiently from one "work station" to the next as the food is sequentially processed from raw to prepared, cooked and served states.'

The usual assumption is that the main 'work stations', comprising the cooker, the sink and the refrigerator, are located closely together in a convenient 'work triangle' (see Fig. 2.20). The Building Research Establishment suggest, for example, that, from the central front of the units, the user should generally have to walk between 3.3 m and 6.6 m (Anon. 1993, p. 250).

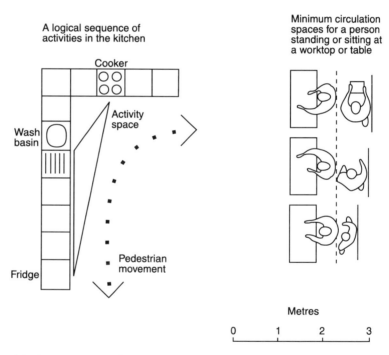

Fig. 2.20   A logical sequence of activities in the kitchen (DoE, 1971: Anon., 1993).

Food preparation is a frequent source of accidents, such as burns and scalds and falls whilst trying to reach out-of-reach storage. The design of a logical, convenient sequence of kitchen workplaces minimises the risk of accidents. In particular, as part of this aim to reduce accidents, good practice requires the following:

❑   As far as possible, through circulation should be separated from food preparation areas. In addition, through circulation should never obstruct a person working at a cooker or cross the route between the cooker and the sink (see Fig. 2.20; also DoE, 1971, p. 6; Anon., 1993, p. 250).

❏ The cooker or hob unit should not be placed under a window because there is a risk that the curtains might catch fire and because it is dangerous to open or close the window while leaning across the unit (Anon., 1993, p. 258).

Ergonomic research also makes sense in relation to designs for the aged and infirm. Many elderly people do not fully admit to experiencing difficulties in moving around a house and in undertaking housework. As a result, the observation of behaviour in an experimental laboratory study, despite its artificial quality, may provide a more reliable source of information than a questionnaire survey (Rennie, 1981).

Ergonomic research is not without ambiguities. Should the aim be to establish floorspace guidelines that allow the maximum freedom and ease of use? Or should more restricted spaces be accepted if this is necessary for economic or other reasons? The ergonomic research of the Department of the Environment led to the publication of *Activities and Spaces* (Noble, 1982). Apart from a few activity spaces that involve safety considerations, for example space in front of a cooker, *Activities and Spaces* gives three measures, with the smaller and larger dimension varying by about 20% from each other. *Activities and Spaces* assumes, in other words, that dimensional data are, to an extent, variable and that people may adapt their behaviour and choice of furniture to the type of dwelling in which they live, whether, for example, the conversion of older property, the design of high quality 'executive dwellings' or the development of small 'starter homes' for first-time purchasers (Fig. 2.21).

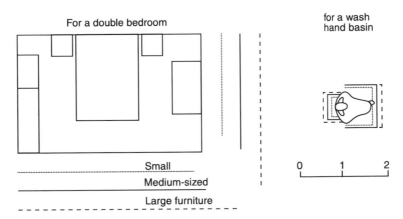

Fig. 2.21 The variable geometry of activity spaces.

In practice, even the minimum guidelines do not always conform to the room dimensions. *Activities and Spaces* gives space in the bedroom for a person to move around and make a bed, as well as space for a bedside table and a wardrobe. The third bedroom in starter homes and low cost social housing schemes is often too small for this.

A further complication is that ergonomic research, together with the design guidelines that they have generated, is mostly concerned with physical space and with quality in relation to the house as a system. Personal and social space must also be considered. Oseland and Raw (1991) have shown that, in the case of small starter homes, the occupants' assessment of adequacy of space is more determined by the number of people in the dwelling than by its physical size. Likewise, the Building Research Establishment noted that 'in most households, the kitchen is far more than a workplace: it is the focal point for much social activity' (Anon., 1993, p. 239).

The observation of use is clearly of limited value. Yet, even a limited method of enquiry has its value. The guidelines generated through the ergonomic research in the late 1970s, including those that led to the preparation of *Activities and Spaces*, still provide a useful discipline in the preparation of floorplans. Similar guidelines exist in most other European countries. They enable the dimensions of the human body and the likely use of the house to be taken into consideration from the outset. Likewise, the observation of behaviour in the street and other open spaces can supplement social surveys and participation exercises.

CONCLUSIONS

Analyses of housing quality lead to limited conclusions. The main points may be summarised.

❑ Housing quality has a series of components, all of which involve an interaction between social, personal and physical factors. Components relating to a house as a system involve an interaction between the physical fabric of the house and the convenience, safety and comfort of the occupants. Components relating to the house as a home – the privacy of the home, its security and its image – assume a relation to other people whose behaviour is capable of influence through design.

❑ Despite the existence of these distinct components, satisfaction with the house and, more generally, the experience of the house is unitary. The components must all be considered in an evaluation of housing quality in a specific place.

❑ Perceptions of housing quality, much like satisfaction with the home, are invariably relative and liable to change. It is not possible to generalise about priorities and only possible to identify priorities for design in particular situations. It is not, for example, possible to say that issues relating to the house as a system are more important than issues relating to the house as a home or vice versa. Residents judge different aspects as more important in different situations. Moreover, different household types – family households, childless adults and pensioner households – generally evaluate the environment in a different way.

The various uncertainties emphasise the importance of testing possible designs against the likely views and needs of users. Each of the available sources of information (direct participation, questionnaire surveyors, the analysis of existing choices and the observation of behaviour) has its own pattern of advantages and disadvantages. None is superior to another in any absolute sense Instead, the main question concerns the choice of method in any particular situation.

User-oriented research raises a question: Which user is the most important? Only in very limited exercises, such as when designing a new house for a single individual or household, is the user easy to ascertain, easy to consult, articulate about his or her needs and wishes and identical with the paying client. Even in the design of a single house, the needs and wishes of different members of the household, including children, may be different. It is easy for those who have less purchasing power or who are less articulate to lose out. However, the existence of different users is not an argument against user-orientated research. The existence of different users is, instead, an argument in favour of attempting to satisfy as many different views as possible.

In large scale schemes and in schemes undertaken in an urban setting, there are other interested parties, for example, the views of neighbours whose privacy may be affected or the views of passers-by or, in mixed use schemes, the views of commercial property users. The greater diversity of interested parties is a distinguishing feature of exercises in urban renewal and urban planning compared to those that only involve the design of housing. The potential conflict between car users and pedestrians, including children, is a particular source of difficulty in larger scale exercises in urban renewal and urban design. Again, the diversity of users is not an argument against user involvement or user research. It is, instead, a reason why the process of urban planning should always be organised in a way that allows each interest group, and not just the powerful, to have a say in the outcome.

Chapter 3
Regulatory frameworks

The interest of governments in the built environment is narrower than the interests of residents, property owners and developers. Direct government intervention is largely confined to an exercise in regulation in which a public agency (or sometimes a private agency that acts on behalf of the public interest) ensures that conditions in the existing stock or in new housing conform either to a series of specific standards or, sometimes in town planning, to a more general policy statement. The standards and policy statements define a condition that is socially or politically unacceptable at a given point in time. They ensure consistency in the treatment of individual cases and provide a starting point for public action.

MINIMUM STANDARDS FOR THE EXISTING STOCK

The identification of standards is similar to the analysis of quality in that both presuppose a series of classifications. Standards vary according to whether the object of regulation is new house building or the existing stock. In addition, in relation to the existing stock, the form of the standard varies according to the type of environmental problem.

In relation to the existing stock, separate types of standard have emerged to cover:

❑ the condition and amenities of a dwelling, as expressed in the concept of unfitness;
❑ its occupancy, as expressed in the concept of overcrowding.

Unfitness, overcrowding and related issues of public health

The concept of unfitness is the oldest and, in many ways, the most important way of defining unsatisfactory housing. The term arose in the Artisans' and Labourers' Dwellings Act 1868 (commonly called the Torrens Act), the first Act that enabled local authorities to demolish unhealthy dwellings and to take enforcement action against their owners (Moore, 1980, p. 20). In Scotland, the term 'unfit' has, since 1969, been replaced by the concept of a house that falls below the 'tolerable standard', though the legal function of the standard remains fundamentally unchanged. In England and Wales the term persists to the present, albeit in a revised and more precise form.

The application and enforcement of the minimum standard is subject to omissions. For example, the courts have ruled that the fitness standard cannot be enforced for temporary accommodation such as bed and breakfast hotels, mobile homes and caravans. In addition, the standard cannot be enforced on dwellings owned by the same local authority as would undertake enforcement. The local authority cannot undertake enforcement on itself (R. v. Cardiff CC *ex parte* Cross, 1982; Burridge and Ormandy, 1993, p. 413). There are other possible remedies, however. A tenant may take action against the local authority under Section 11 of the Landlord and Tenant Act 1985 to ensure that the property is kept in repair. A tenant may also take action under Section 79 of the Environmental Protection Act 1990 (formerly part of the Public Health Act 1936) against premises that are in such a state that they are prejudicial to health or a nuisance, and against any noise which is prejudicial to health or a nuisance.

The 1954 definition of 'unfit'

The first national statutory definition dates from the Housing Repairs and Rent Act 1954. Before this, the definition was made largely by local authorities in the light of local circumstances. The 1954 definition was repeated in the Housing Acts 1957, 1969 and 1985 and remained largely unchanged until the coming into force in 1990 of the Local Government and Housing Act 1989.

The definition was not strictly speaking a standard. It merely listed those factors that should be considered when determining whether a house is unfit, namely repair; stability; freedom from damp; natural lighting; ventilation; water supply; drainage and sanitary conveniences; and facilities for storage, preparation and cooking of food and for the disposal of waste water. The test of unfitness was, as Cullingworth (1966, p. 178) once stated:

> 'Whether a major defect in one of these matters or an accumulation of lesser defects in more than one, renders the house "not reasonably suitable for occupation".'

Yet this term 'not reasonably suited for occupation' was not defined. The standard was subjective and capable of different interpretations, especially between different local authorities.

This question of subjectivity was discussed in the Denington Report (CHAC, 1966). The committee responsible for this report was established 'to consider the practicability of specifying objective criteria' for the minimum standard. It concluded that an element of subjectivity is unavoidable but that the standard may be applied more consistently if supplemented by explanatory notes. The committee prepared its own guidance notes and these were endorsed by the Ministry of Housing and Local Government in Circulars published in 1967 and 1969.

The section dealing with dampness is typical of the level of detail in the guidance notes. It is also typical of the committee's intention to exclude trivial or easily corrected faults from the definition.

> 'Any dampness should not be so extensive or so pervasive as to be a threat to the health of occupants. Such items as a small patch of damp caused by defective pointings around window reveals or door jambs or by a defective rain water pipe are due to disrepair rather than inherent dampness. Care must also be taken not to be misled by temporary condensation.' (Anon, 1981)

Even with a degree of guidance there still remained much scope for the possibility of subjective variation. For example, the proportion of houses suffering some form of dampness is very high. A national sample survey of 1000 dwellings, undertaken by the Building Research Establishment in 1978, found that 46% of those interviewed reported a condensation problem somewhere in their home and that 20% reported a problem with mildew (Hunt and Gidman, 1982, pp. 122–123). Some reduction is necessary if the problem of unfitness is not to become unmanageable. But how is this reduction to be achieved? For example:

❑ Should seasonal mould growth be excluded, even if this lasts all winter?
❑ Is the number of rooms affected by dampness relevant?
❑ Should dampness in the living room or bedroom count as more serious than that in the kitchen or the bathroom?
❑ Should penetrating dampness count as more serious than condensation?
❑ Should, in the case of condensation, the form and extent of heating be considered?
❑ Finally, should the age and vulnerability of the occupants be considered? Should the degree of dampness, prejudicial to health, be defined with reference to the likely effects on a fit young adult or a young baby or a vulnerable old person?

A series of questions are posed for which there is no easy answer.

At a local level, in the context of the slum clearance programmes of the 1960s and early 1970s, the various uncertainties could be resolved in a public inquiry held to determine the validity of a compulsory purchase order. However, in the context of surveys intended to measure house conditions, variations in the interpretation of the fitness standard created numerous difficulties. For example, an attempt to standardise the results of the 1976 and 1981 English House Condition Surveys led the report of the latter survey to increase the estimate of unfitness in the former by about 40% – a very large correction indeed (DoE, 1982).

The tolerable standard

In Scotland, the difficulty of interpreting the fitness standard led to the development of an alternative concept: that of the tolerable standard. The latter dates from the report of a sub-committee of the Scottish housing advisory committee (the Cullingworth Report) (SDD, 1967). Until then, Scottish practice had followed that in England and Wales, though with some detailed variations.

The Cullingworth committee sought a more radical departure than that recommended for England and Wales by the Denington committee. It sought to replace the nineteenth century concepts of 'insanitary' and 'unhealthy' housing with a standard more concerned with 'the expected standards of modern living' (SDD, 1967, p. 27). It also sought a more objective definition that would admit less variation between local authorities and would be expressed in positive terms with reference to a notional 'satisfactory' standard. The use of the phrase 'satisfactory', the committee noted, also had the advantage that it made unnecessary a discussion of whether a house 'is not reasonably suitable for occupation'.

The tolerable standard, as put into effect in the Housing (Scotland) Act 1969, uses specific criteria and specific amenities and services, such as the provision of an internal WC. The approach is similar to that of the Cullingworth committee. However, the original intention of the Cullingworth committee to create a radically different standard of social acceptability has meant little in practice. With the exception of an internal WC, the amenities listed in the tolerable standard are not expensive or difficult to provide compared to the earlier definition. For example, the minimum standard for artificial lighting and heating may be satisfied by an electrical socket in each room. The treatment of dampness is particularly restrictive. The standard refers to rising damp and to penetrating damp, but not to condensation.

The standard of fitness from 1990 onwards

The fitness standard in England and Wales was reviewed in a Green Paper *Home Improvement – A New Approach* (DoE, 1985). The starting point was similar to that of the Denington committee 20 years before. Again the main criticism of the test of unfitness was the way in which it was open to different interpretations. Again, the report accepted that the Department of the Environment should provide more guidance on the interpretation of the standard. Unlike the Denington committee, however, the Green Paper argued that more guidance was insufficient without a revision and clarification of the standard. The best way forward was to remodel the definition of fitness on the Scottish tolerable standard, whilst simultaneously changing the way the standard is used so that it would also define eligibility for mandatory grant aid.

This reference to 'eligibility' requires more detailed explanation. The old definition of unfitness was concerned only with those circumstances that would require clearance or would lead to clearance in the absence of remedial work. The old standard of unfitness was an 'intervention' standard. It defined the obligations of the local authority to intervene and the obligations of the owners if they wished to avoid enforcement action. In contrast, the new definition of unfitness, as proposed in the 1985 Green Paper, was intended to act both as an intervention standard and as an 'eligibility' standard that defines the rights of the owner to receive grant aid for improvement.

Further clarification is necessary. Burridge *et al.* (1993, p. 89) state that the new fitness standard amalgamated a target standard and the intervention standard. However, this is misleading. Neither the 1985 Green Paper nor the 1989 Act had such an implication. Local authorities may still require owners to undertake works in excess of the fitness standard for receipt of a discretionary grant, where such a grant is made available.

The role of the new fitness standard as an eligibility standard meant, in turn, that it incorporated a requirement for the 'standard amenities' of a fixed bath, wash hand basin, a sink, an internal WC and a hot and cold water supply. This latter concept of standard amenities originated in the House Purchase and Housing Act 1959 and provided the definition of those requirements that were subject to mandatory grant aid (Moore, 1987). It retains this function in Scotland, though a general improvement in housing standards means that it is less important than before.

The Local Government and Housing Act 1989 incorporated the new standard in a form that largely followed the recommendations of the 1985 Green Paper. The standard came into force in 1990, at which time the Department of the Environment published extensive guidance notes. The details are shown in Table 3.1, together with the details of the old fitness standard and its Scottish equivalent.

Table 3.1   Minimum standards: a summary of their contents.

The fitness standard 1954–1989	Scottish tolerable standard 1969 to date	New fitness standard 1990 to date	Definition
●	●	●	Adequate repair
●	●	●	Structurally stable
●	●	●	Substantially free from rising or penetrating damp
●	—	●	Substantially free from condensation
○	●	✳	Satisfactory access to external doors
●	●	●	Adequate natural lighting and ventilation
●	●	●	Adequate piped supply of wholesome water
●	●	●	Satisfactory facilities for drainage and sanitation
●	●	●	Satisfactory facilities for cooking and waste disposal
—	●	●	A sink with hot and cold water
—	—	●	Wash basin, fixed bath or shower
—	●	□	Internal WC
—	●	●	Satisfactory artificial lighting
—	●	●	Satisfactory heating
—	—	—	Adequate insulation
●	—	—	Satisfactory in terms of overall condition

○: introduced in 1969.
✳: in the case of multi-occupied properties, adequate means of fire escape are required under a revised section 352 of the Housing Act 1985.
□: the precise definition is of a 'suitably located water closet'.
Notes: The list of criteria is a general indication of the contents. The detailed wording varies. The detailed wording and application also varies for houses, flats and houses in multiple occupation (HMOs). In an HMO, different households may share a WC without the property failing the fitness standard.

Thereafter, the concept of fitness as an eligibility standard came under attack. An eligibility standard presupposes the availability of sufficient funds to ensure that owners can exercise their right to grant aid. In practice, however, local authorities administered the system of grant aid in the context of spending restriction that denied any such right. In response, the Housing and Construction Act 1996 states that improvement grants are available at the discretion of the local authority. This being so, the unfitness standard has again reverted to an intervention standard, a guideline for public action, though the standard itself has remained unchanged.

The 1990 fitness standard is simultaneously more comprehensive and narrower than its predecessors. As well as including the former standard amenities, the new standard is more comprehensive in making a reference to artificial lighting and heating, the latter being a requirement that was omitted in the proposals included in the 1985 Green Paper. At the same time, the standard is narrower in the exclusion of internal layout and in the way, like the Scottish tolerable standard, it comprises a list of specific requirements based on notions of adequacy and sufficiency.

In other respects, for example in the treatment of dampness or repair, the standard remains much the same as before. Local authorities continue to judge fitness on the basis of whether a defect renders the house 'not reasonably suitable for occupation'. Moreover, they continue to make this judgement in the light of advice that, in the words of the relevant Circular, the primary consideration is that of 'safeguarding the health and safety of any occupants'. Discomfort, inconvenience and inefficiency are regarded as 'relevant' but of 'secondary importance only' (DoE, 1990a, p. 34).

The interpretation of the new standard has been examined in a series of case studies of 24 local authorities undertaken by Burridge *et al.* (1993). The study shows that local authorities generally experienced little difficulty in either understanding the new standard on its introduction or in applying the standard on a uniform basis. However, the study also notes, like the Denington committee did many years before in 1965, that complete or total objectivity is impossible. In particular, judgements about unfitness were influenced by the purpose of the assessment, whether it was made for the purpose of grant aid or for taking some form of enforcement action such as the serving of a repairs notice or demolition order. Local government officers generally adopted a more generous and more demanding interpretation of the fitness standard if the assessment was for the provision of grant aid. They were more cautious and restrictive in their interpretation of the fitness standard if they were making an assessment for enforcement action.

Uncertainties in the interpretation of standards is particularly marked in the estimation of costs. The Report of the English House Condition Survey 1991 states that, at November 1991 prices, the average cost of remedying unfitness was about £3301 per dwelling (DoE 1993, p. 63). In the same year, the average local authority mandatory grant aid for unfit dwellings was much higher, about £8500 (1993, p. 63; also see Leather, 1993).

There are a variety of possible reasons why grant aid to rectify unfitness should prove so expensive. Grant aid is given to a specific sector of the population (usually low income owner-occupiers, often living in very poor condition property), whereas the survey data is an average of the remedial costs for all unfit properties. However, uncertainties in the fitness standard is one relevant reason. Local authorities may take a different view of the scale of works required. They may require additional work, above the minimum fitness standard, to ensure that the property remains in a reasonable condition and does not deteriorate quickly. Moreover, as part of this, they are sometimes prepared to fund work for problems that only become apparent once the contractors have started and are, therefore, invisible to a surveyor.

Another question is whether the list of relevant considerations exclude anything that might also render a house unfit for human habitation. For local authority officers, as revealed in the survey undertaken by Burridge (1993), the most frequently cited omissions concern internal layout and insulation. The respondents wanted to reinstate internal layout to prevent a loss of privacy (for example, one bedroom entered through another) and safety (for example, steep or winding staircases). They wanted the inclusion of insulation to prevent excessive heat loss.

The exclusion of insulation is probably the most significant omission. To an extent, insulation is included under the heading of 'adequate heating'. The guidance notes state that (DoE, 1990a, p. 49):

'In deciding whether a dwelling-house is or is not unfit, the authority should consider whether the dwelling-house currently has for heating a main "living" room, provision for fixed heating capable of efficiently maintaining the room generally at a temperature of 18 deg. C or more when the outside temperature is –1 deg. C, and for the other main habitable rooms, provision for heating capable of maintaining an equivalent temperature of 16 deg. C. or more[1]. The authority should also have regard to whether the construction and condition of the dwelling-house prevents excessive heat loss and whether the overall level of provision for heating, when combined with adequate ventilation, is sufficient to prevent both condensation and mould growth prejudicial to health.'

However, the heating standard is severely qualified. The guidance notes only talk of fixed heating 'capable of maintaining' the relevant temperature. They do not specify that the fixed heating is likely to maintain the relevant temperature within a reasonable budget.

In fact, a substantial proportion of homes do not achieve the minimum in cold weather in winter. In England, the most recently published national sur-

---

[1] The recommended minimum temperature levels are largely consistent with international practice, as recommended by authorities in France and the United States, as well as by the World Health Organisation. The only difference is that some authorities suggest that elderly people require a higher minimum standard, say 20–21°C, owing to their more sedentary life style (Collins, 1993, pp. 120–121). The question of maximum temperatures is also discussed in the international health literature, but is of little practical importance in Britain.

vey of house temperatures is that undertaken by the English House Condition Survey in the winter and spring of 1991 and 1992 (DoE, 1996, p. 154). This shows that, during a period of relatively mild weather, about 29% of households failed to meet the minimum heating standard in some way. 19% of households failed to meet one of the two minimum standards (either 18°C in the living room or 16°C in the hall). Another 10% failed to meet both minimum standards. Though the survey report is not completely clear, most of the cold dwellings were fit according to the current definition. Only a small minority of energy inefficient homes, about 1 in 16 of such properties, were unfit (DoE, 1996, p. 3).

The definition of 'fixed heating' is, in any case, very weak. The guidance notes state that a 'suitably located (13 amp minimum)' electric socket, capable of supporting a portable heating appliance, is sufficient to satisfy the standard (DoE, 1990, p. 50). An electrical socket can hardly be regarded as a fixed heating appliance. At the most, an electrical socket allows the use of a portable electrical heater. The use of portable heaters, especially gas and paraffin heaters, increases the risk of accidents in the home.

It is possible to identify other candidates for inclusion in the fitness standard. The Civil Rights (Disabled Persons) Bill, introduced unsuccessfully into Parliament in 1994, proposed that owners should be obliged to make buildings accessible to disabled people. This would have had very similar effects to the inclusion of disabled persons' access in the unfitness standard. Another possible candidate is room size, though this is covered in a slightly different way in the concept of statutory overcrowding.

Notwithstanding the various omissions, the new standard is a more stringent test of unfitness than its predecessor. The Report of the English House Condition Survey 1991 shows that many more dwellings are made unfit as a result of the additional requirements in the new standard than have been made fit as a result of the exclusion of internal layout and overall condition. Moreover, regardless of the effect of the changes in statutory definition, the numbers of unfit dwellings have also increased as a result of a hardening of views about the type of dwelling that is suitable for habitation. The interpretation of the standard has become slightly more demanding. For example, if the new standard is applied to the 1986 survey data, the estimated number of unfit dwellings in that year would increase from 910 000 to 1 662 000, with changes in interpretation accounting for the majority of the increase (DoE, 1993, pp. 68–70).

Trends in stock condition

The overall condition of the English housing stock improved since 1986. In 1986, about 8.7% of the English housing stock was unfit under the new standard. In 1991, the equivalent proportion was 7.4%. Indeed, it is possible to show a sustained improvement since the first English House Condition Survey in 1966. Progress has been substantial, but much still needs to be done.

In Scotland, in 1991, about 4.7% of the occupied stock was below the tolerable standard. The 1991 survey was the first national survey in Scotland. Thus no reliable comparisons can be made with earlier periods.

The type of person living in poor condition housing has been summarised by Mackintosh and Leather (1993, pp. 30–31). The occupants are likely to have a lower than average income. They are likely to comprise a mixture of people at the start and in the later stages of their housing career. Middle aged households tend to be better housed than either young people living independently of the family home or old people. Finally, the occupants of poor quality housing include a disproportionately large number of people who originated from the New Commonwealth countries or from Pakistan.

Properties in the privately rented sector are, on average, in the worst condition. In 1981, surveyors employed by the English House Condition Survey estimated that almost 30% of privately rented dwellings were classified as amongst the worst property (measured in relation to the cost to rectify problems of unfitness and disrepair) (DoE, 1993, p. 76). Privately rented property also contained a disproportionate number of difficult-to-heat homes (DoE, 1996, p. 3). The greater than average age of privately-rented dwellings combined with relatively poor maintenance and low levels of central heating served to exacerbate heating problems in this sector.

The privately rented housing sector is relatively small in comparison to either the social housing or owner-occupied sectors. In 1991, 9% of the occupied housing stock was owned by private landlords (DoE, 1993, p. 5). The large size of the owner-occupied stock meant that this sector contained nearly half (49.2%) of the worst 10% of dwellings (again, measured in relation to the cost to rectify problems of unfitness and disrepair) and nearly half (47.9%) of all the dwellings with poor energy efficiency (i.e. with a Standard Assessment procedure rating of less than 20) (DoE, 1993, p. 78; DoE, 1996, p. 262, Table A6.1). Within the owner-occupied sector, single or two person elderly households account for most of those who live in the worst 10% of the housing stock (DoE, 1993, Table A11.6). Elderly owner-occupiers are also less likely to undertake repairs and improvements (DoE, 1979).

What of the future? The report of the English House Condition Survey 1991 states that the reduction in unfitness in the period from 1986 onwards was probably caused by the high level of activity in the housing market in the late 1980s (DoE, 1993, p. 69). Much improvement is undertaken by individuals in the first few years after buying a property. People undertake improvement at this time mainly because they are less settled and more willing to tolerate the disruption. In addition, they are sometimes required to undertake repairs by a mortgage lender.

The market conditions in the 1990s have been depressed. Moreover, this depression has not been countered by an increase in public expenditure on repairs and improvement. It is possible that, in the 1990s, owner-occupiers have been more willing to undertake improvements without moving. It is possible, therefore, that the depression in the housing market has had little impact on the condition of the housing stock. On the other hand, it would surely be wrong to assume a continuation of previous trends. The progress of the past cannot be taken for granted and may not continue.

In the longer term, the changing social composition of owner-occupation is a cause for concern. The Report of the English House Condition Survey 1991 notes that between 1986 and 1991 owner-occupiers have risen from 38% to 41% of people in the lowest income group (DoE, 1993, p. 103). The change is small but is an extension of a trend that has continued for many years. Owner-occupation has moved downmarket. As these low income owner-occupiers grow older, they are likely to encounter growing difficulties in maintaining and improving their property. The growth of owner-occupation has had some beneficial aspects. Owner-occupiers at least have an interest in maintaining their property. The main question is whether they can afford to do so and have the necessary skills, time and energy either to do the work themselves or to involve a private building contractor.

Overcrowding

Unlike the standard of unfitness, the overcrowding standard has not been revised for many years. The present definition, as stated in the Housing Act 1985 remains the same as that in the Housing Act 1935. There are two related requirements:

❑ A room standard
❑ A space standard.

The room standard is contravened when the number of persons sleeping in a dwelling and the number of habitable rooms (including the living room) is such that:

❑ Two adults of opposite sexes who are not living together as husband and wife sleep in the same room.
❑ Children of more than ten years sleep in the same room.

The space standard is contravened when the total number of persons living in a house is over-occupied in relation to its size. The Act provides a schedule that relates room sizes to the maximum permitted number of people allowed to live there. For example, the minimum size of a room capable of occupation by a single adult is 70 sq. ft. (about 6.5 m^2). The Act also specifies that no account shall be taken of a child aged under one, and that a child aged between one and ten should be regarded as the equivalent of half a person. The minimum size of a bedroom for a child aged between one and ten is 50 sq. ft. (about 4.65 m^2).

The occupants of a dwelling have to be living in overcrowded conditions on a permanent basis for the dwelling to be classified as overcrowded for the purpose of local authority action. Temporary and seasonal forms of occupation do not constitute overcrowding.

The overcrowding standard arose in the late nineteenth and early twentieth centuries from a desire amongst reformers to discourage incest, to promote clean living conditions in the home and to reduce the risk of infectious diseases, notably those diseases such as tuberculosis that are spread on the breath of an infected person. The reduction of overcrowding was a central aim of housing policy before 1935. The overcrowding standard remains relevant as a means of justifying public intervention in extreme cases, but is often considered inadequate.

For example, is it correct to treat the living room as a potential bedroom? If the aim of an overcrowding standard is broadened to include the reduction of mental stress or the protection of personal privacy, as the World Health Organisation (1972) and Ineichen (1993) have suggested, the living room should surely be excluded. Again, why is about 6.5 m^2 considered the minimum size of a room capable of occupation by an adult or by an adult and a child of less than one year? If the aim of the overcrowding standard is to reduce household accidents or to promote healthy child development, a more generous floorspace standard is surely necessary.

The English House Condition Survey and the General Household Survey use a different and more generous measure of overcrowding called the bedroom standard. This excludes the living room as potential sleeping accommodation, but includes any room of whatever size so long as it is actually identified as a bedroom in the course of an interview with a member of the household. Again, the standard requires children of different sexes and aged more than ten years to sleep in separate rooms. In addition, any single person of 21 years or more is deemed to require a separate room.

On the measure of the bedroom standard, just under 3% of all households are living in overcrowded accommodation, according to the Report of the English House Condition Survey 1991 (DoE, 1993, p. 33). Amongst owner-occupiers, families of Asian origin in smaller, pre-1919 terraced housing are more likely than others to live in overcrowded conditions. In the social housing sector, lone parent families, unable to move from a small flat, experience the highest incidence of overcrowding (1993, p. 36).

Overcrowding has consistently declined since the nineteenth century. Much of this has been due to general social and economic change. Family and household sizes have declined. House building rates have outstripped population growth. However, for low income families, public sector intervention has, almost certainly, been crucial This intervention, whether in the form of 'bricks and mortar' subsidies (that aim to increase the supply of low cost housing) or means-tested personal housing allowances, allows low income families to live in larger properties than they would otherwise be unable to afford.

Why are minimum standards so narrowly defined?

The unfitness and overcrowding standards raise a series of interrelated questions. Why is the emphasis on public health, rather than social acceptability? Why, even as a statement of health standards, are the standards of fitness and overcrowding phrased in such a restrictive way?

Financial and other resource constraints provide an obvious, albeit partial answer for caution. Any increase in standards begs the question: who will pay for the improvement? The occupiers of a dwelling classified as unsatisfactory may not be able to afford the higher rents or the higher mortgage repayments of a higher quality dwelling. Governments can subsidise the difference, but they also have other priorities.

The problem of Houses in Multiple Occupation (HMOs) provide an example. Such houses contain a high proportion of unfit properties, properties in disrepair and properties in unsatisfactory management (LRC, 1994, p. 17). They also frequently suffer the additional problem of fire risks. Local authorities have a discretionary power under the Housing Act 1996 to ensure that landlords register HMOs (defined for this purpose as dwellings containing two or more households who share all or some of its facilities – the bathroom, kitchen or WC). They also have the power to enforce standards of management, as well as the conventional fitness standards on their owners.

However, even if the standards of accommodation are poor, HMOs meet a social need. They provide relatively cheap housing for mobile young people, including students and for those in urgent housing need. Rents are invariably lower than for self-contained flats. The London Research Centre has summarised the results of a survey of the occupants of HMOs that 'while HMO tenants might welcome legislation or official action to improve dwelling standards, they would not wish this to lead to increased rents or a further reduction in supply' (LRC, 1994, p. 24). Local authorities must always balance the need for enforcement against the need to maintain a low cost housing stock.

Another resource constraint concerns the availability of technical staff and the staffing costs involved in processing enforcement action, especially if this involves the serving of a statutory notice and subsequent court action. Many local authorities would argue that they possess inadequate staff to enforce even current fitness standards other than on a piecemeal, discretionary basis. The Audit Commission (1991, p. 11) has estimated that, in the financial year 1989/90, 'despite the considerable staff resources devoted', statutory notices were served only on about 5% of those dwellings that were unfit or otherwise required attention under the housing legislation.

A lack of resources is not the only constraint. In relation to owner-occupied housing, local authorities are often reluctant to take any action that might adversely affect the property rights of an individual or might be interpreted as an invasion of personal privacy. Unfitness and overcrowding are more than a desirable minimum. They define a minimum to which the owner or the occupier (in the case of overcrowding) must ensure conformity or risk some legal sanction such as compulsory purchase or the serving of a repairs notice in the case of unfitness or, in the case of persistent overcrowding, a fine.

Enforcement of stricter overcrowding standards would prove especially difficult. Local authorities can exercise discretionary powers to rehouse families from property which is overcrowded on the bedroom standard or overcrowded on a more generous standard. However, they would almost certainly not want any additional compulsory responsibilities of inspecting houses and of serving notices on the occupants of overcrowded dwellings to move to a larger house, with all the disruption and financial implications implied by such a move.

A related problem concerns the tendency for the residents of poor quality housing, and again owner-occupiers are the most prone to this tendency, to perceive the quality of their home in a more favourable light than is typical of a professional surveyor or environmental health officers. For example, a survey of the experience of slum clearance in Birmingham, undertaken between October 1986 and September 1988, found that a majority of those living in clearance areas believed that the condition of their home was acceptable (Heywood and Naz, pp. 157–158).

The impact of social factors on health

In the case of the fitness standard, a further complication is that the pattern of poor health in British cities is no longer always related to the physical characteristics of the building stock. The worst problems are not always found in those residential areas with the oldest housing stock or with the highest proportion of unfit dwellings or, in Scotland, sub-tolerable housing. Instead, health problems are concentrated in local authority estates and in other areas with a concentration of low income households.

For example, Byrne *et al.* (1986) provide an analysis of health conditions in different local authority estates in Gateshead (Tyneside), based on a questionnaire survey of residents. In this survey, residents were asked to rate their record of health, including the health of their children and to report any problems with the condition or design of their home. The report of the survey (p. 124) concludes that:

> 'In all indicators, people living in "difficult to let" housing areas reported more illness and inferior health status than did people living in other housing areas. Consistent differences between housing areas were found which could be explained more by the location of a dwelling than by dwelling type.'

The concentration of health problems in poor local authority estates does not suggest that the standard of fitness is irrelevant. For example, it would be foolish to suggest that dampness in the home has no effect on the health of children. It is possible to show that dampness has an adverse impact on health even after controlling for possible confounding factors such as household income, the extent of cigarette smoking in the house, unemployment and overcrowding (Stewart, 1994, p. 4). Regulation of the built environment, one might reasonably argue, should be based on the precautionary principle. Risks should be considered, even if proof of their consequences cannot be demonstrated (Mant and Muir Gray, 1986, p. 43).

In any case, within the local authority stock, there are sometimes marked health variations that can only be explained by variations in physical conditions. The former, now demolished Divis flats in Belfast provides an example. Blackmon *et al.* (1987) have shown that the health conditions of children and adults here were significantly worse than in the Twinbrook estate, another typical local authority estate in Belfast, even though poverty and unemployment were widespread in both.

The most likely explanation is that problems of poor condition interact with other factors that influence the health of residents. These other factors are easily identified. For example:

❑ Low income residents may be unable to heat their homes to a temperature that avoids condensation in the winter. The Scottish House Condition Survey 1991 notes, for example, that condensation is more common in dwellings occupied by single parent families, by large families and by households with an unemployed head of household (Scottish Homes, 1993, p. iii). Poverty, just as much as poor standards of insulation, prevents people from warming their home.

❑ Some estates may contain a concentration of children living in high-rise flats. Living in a high-rise flat increases the risk that a child will suffer accidental death and injury from a fall. It also places more stress on the mother (Littlewood and Tinker, 1981).

❑ Finally, the sense of deprivation in these poor estates may cause depression and mental illness (Ineichen, 1993, pp. 47–48). In the London Borough of Hackney, for example, Woodin *et al.* (1996) have shown how the rehousing of tenants from particularly poor and depressing living conditions in the Holly Street estate led to an increased sense of well-being and a reduction in the demand for local medical services. The higher morale of tenants, after rehousing, meant that they felt better able to deal with problems. (See Chapter 5: Case study 2: 'The Holly Street estate, Hackney'.) If this is so, it is also likely that declining living conditions will have the reverse effect, leading to a decline in morale and an increased demand for medical services.

The implications of overcrowding are slightly different. The extent of overcrowding, as revealed in the Report of the English House Condition Survey 1991 (and using the definition incorporated therein), is generally higher in local authority owned dwellings than in the owner-occupied or privately rented sectors (DoE, 1993, pp. 32–33). Within the local authority sector, many of the least popular estates are characterised by high levels of dwelling occupancy, by, for example, a concentration of households with children living in two bedroom flats. It is possible, therefore, that the relationship between poor health and overcrowding is closer than that for the relationship between poor health and unfitness.

On the other hand, it is possible that, other than in extreme circumstances, the relationship between overcrowding and health is also relatively weak. Walmsley (1988, p. 138) concludes a review of the international literature with the statement that:

'... the effects of crowding tend to be mild ... many people are remarkably good at adjusting to crowding and thereby vitiating its detrimental consequences... In other words, it may not be crowding per se but only uncontrollable crowding that is responsible for the negative effects . . . Indeed, it is likely to be powerlessness to control a situation which leads to a sense of crowding.'

Likewise, Myers *et al.* (1996) state that US research has never shown a consistent relationship between crowding and poor health. Myers *et al.* also show that, at present, patterns of crowding in the US are essentially linked to the distribution of newly arrived Asian and Hispanic households who 'may not perceive the harmful effects of overcrowding that are assumed by the housing policy standards' (p. 81). The varied experience of different ethnic groups leads Myers *et al.* to reject the relevance of overcrowding to public policy. Any standard of overcrowding is likely to represent a type of ethnic imperialism which imposes the views of the majority on a minority. Though Myers *et al.* do not say so, this is laissez-faire post-modernism, *par excellence*. Increased ethnic and cultural diversity, it is said, has undermined the case for the standards that guided the introduction of modern town planning and modern housing policy in the first half of the twentieth century.

An alternative view is that it is only through the maintenance of minimum standards that different ethnic groups are able to pursue distinct life styles. In Britain, overcrowding is also associated with larger Asian households. However, the overcrowding standard in Britain is so minimal that problems of ethnic imperialism surely do not arise.

Whatever the precise cause, the link between poor health, poverty and living in unpopular local authority estates demonstrates a case for housing improvement even in areas without a concentration of unfit dwellings or of statutory overcrowding. The link reinforces the arguments made in favour of the priority estates project, estates action and other similar policies that seek to improve living conditions in local authority estates. In addition, the link focuses attention on the need for housing measures to be accompanied by other social and economic measures that protect and enhance the incomes and living standards of poor people. Indeed, one might argue that the promotion of good living conditions, through a combination of housing and income redistribution measures, should be the main policy priority, rather than technical alterations to the definitions of unfitness and overcrowding.

Priorities for the future

If the minimum standards are to be improved, there are clear priorities:

❑ The standard of tolerable housing in Scotland could include a reference to condensation.
❑ The fitness standard and the tolerable standard could be expanded to include a reference to dangerous design features and to the level of insulation in a dwelling.
❑ Alongside the existing punitive overcrowding standard, a new standard of 'over-occupancy' could be created to permit people to move to larger or more suitable dwellings if they so wished. This new standard would only

treat bedrooms as suitable sleeping accommodation. It would also make a more realistic assessment of the space required for household safety and for children's play.

The external environment

Standards of the external environment are concerned with physical conditions and with amenities. In this sense, they are analogous to the standard of unfitness and are distinct from overcrowding as the latter is essentially about use. However, standards of the external environment are not easy to incorporate into the housing legislation and, with a few limited exceptions, have not been so incorporated. Standards of the external environment are mostly outside the control of the individual owner or occupier and they generally require larger scale public intervention if conditions are to be improved.

The absence of environmental standards in the housing legislation was criticised in the reviews of the fitness standard undertaken, in the mid 1960s, by the Denington and Cullingworth committees. The Cullingworth report even went so far as to propose a new statutory provision for an Area of Unsatisfactory Environment (SDD, 1967, p. 36). Such an area was defined as one in which

> 'the majority of the houses fall below the Standard for a Satisfactory House, or where the arrangement of the streets is unsatisfactory, or where there are unsatisfactory environmental conditions such as those of noise, smell, dust, dirt, smoke, inadequate open space (including play space for children) or inadequate provision for the garaging and parking of cars.'

Declaration of an Area of Unsatisfactory Environment would enable a local authority to undertake a comprehensive local programme comprising improvement or clearance or a mixture of the two.

Later research sought to develop the recommendations of the Denington and Cullingworth committees so that a systematic survey of environmental quality could be undertaken. For example, in 1968 the Scottish Development Department proposed a 'Housing and Environmental Defects Index' as a means of assessing house conditions, including the condition of the external environment, in a uniform and consistent manner. The environmental schedule of the survey form referred to six factors: parking, noise, the presence of nearby industry, greenery, the quality of view and the existence of litter. Other indexes were prepared by the Ministry of Housing and Local Government for England and Wales, by individual local authorities and by Parry Lewis at the University of Manchester.

The proliferation of quality indices was evidence of confusion. Each approach had its own strengths and weaknesses and gave different results. Each could therefore be said to be arbitrary and subjective.

The difficulties were later summarised in *Housing Requirements: a guide to information and techniques*, published as a guide for local authorities in the preparation of local housing strategies (DoE, 1980b, p. 80). Assessment of environmental quality, it was suggested, raised a series of questions that were unanswered and perhaps unanswerable. (Italics are added to the text for clarification.)

'a) what are the main problems which a survey should cover?' ...
(*Should, for example, vandalism be included?*)
'b) who defines these problems? Professionals may fail to appreciate the attitudes of neighbourhood residents, but they, in turn, may be conditioned to accept a poor environment.
c) can surveyors be trained to provide consistent judgements?
d) how can the effects of problems be aggregated and compared?'

Thereafter, proposals to survey and measure the quality of the urban environment have largely disappeared from the technical literature in housing and environmental health. They persist in town planning, but only in the different context of defining good quality urban and rural landscapes that merit protection.

In the 1980s and 1990s, discussions of environmental standards have mostly focused on pollution. The Association of Metropolitan Authorities (AMA, 1981) has, for example, proposed that a new clause is inserted in the housing legislation to enable clearance in areas badly affected by pollution such as noise, vibration, smell, fumes, smoke, artificial lighting and the discharge of any solid or liquid substances. Likewise, Burridge *et al.* (1993, p. 75) have suggested that a new requirement is added to the definition of unfitness to the effect that the dwelling is 'Free from any threats to health and safety from the immediate locality.'

A degree of caution is necessary. Improvements or even clearance and relocation is an unrealistic way of tackling problems of pollution, if extensive urban areas are affected. For example, house improvement or clearance is unlikely to provide an effective way of tackling the noise and air pollution caused by motor traffic. For extensive forms of pollution, including most caused by motor traffic, the most effective remedy is to tackle the problem at source and to ensure that the polluter pays for preventative measures.

Even if the source of pollution is local, there is a further qualification. Given that the expectations of residents are themselves conditioned by the environment in which they live, the test of environmental quality would have to be stringent and would also have to include procedures for consultation with local residents. The environmental problems would, in other words, have to be so overwhelming and of an inherently permanent nature to make demolition or possibly improvement the most practical solution. Particularly bad cases of traffic pollution provide a possible example.

STANDARDS FOR NEW HOUSING

Standards in new housing are best understood as the mirror image of unfitness. The latter is a negative standard that defines what is undesirable and unsatisfactory. In contrast, the former is more positive. It specifies the type of dwelling that should be developed to provide an asset to the community in the long term.

New house building only adds very small numbers of dwellings to the existing stock. From the mid 1970s onwards, new house building has only added 1% or less to the existing stock. Nevertheless, the development of a house is an expensive undertaking and results in a design and a form of construction that cannot be easily changed after completion. It is sensible, therefore, to ensure that the dwelling is built to a standard that maintains its continued durability and popularity for many years ahead.

Differences between social and private housing

Standards in social housing have two main characteristics:

❑ First, the standards are usually specified in greater detail than in private housing;
❑ Second, the specification of standards raises a policy conflict between quality and quantity, between building a smaller number of good quality dwellings and a larger number of adequate dwellings.

The determinants of design in private and social housing

The role of standards in social housing may be clarified. For those who advocate high standards, the aim is generally to break the link between housing and poverty. This is a long-standing view that dates at least to the origins of Council housing at the end of the First World War. The case for high standards was, for example, put, in 1923, by John Wheatley, at that time Labour front bench spokesman on housing. Faced with a proposal for smaller Council houses, with no parlour (a second living room on the ground floor), Wheatley accused the government of building 'hutches' rather than homes, of,

> 'stereotyping poverty in housing … and giving Parliamentary acceptance to the permanency of class distinctions.'

In contrast, for cost conscious officials and politicians in local and central government, the main task has been to build as many houses as possible within a minimum budget.

The distinctiveness of social housing is related to their dependence on public money. As a result of this, the choice of standards is a public issue, capable of resolution only through an explicit policy decision as to what tax-payers and tenants can and should pay. In contrast, in the private sector, housing design is more likely to be defined as a private matter to be settled by the market, as represented in the relation between the consumer and the developer.

To an extent, the dominance of the market in private sector design has a party political aspect. The Conservative government elected in 1979 and re-elected three times thereafter consistently argued in favour of deregulation. However, the sentiments of the Conservatives amounted to little more than a restatement of a long-standing status quo. The Conservatives did not, for example, deregulate building and planning control in England and Wales. Indeed, in relation to insulation, standards are now more stringent.

Moreover, Labour policy has not been greatly different from that of the Conservatives. The traditional Labour position, as represented for example by John Wheatley, was to raise working class housing standards through the construction of good quality Council houses. The imposition of higher standards on privately-built housing was unnecessary. The Labour government that was in power from 1974 to 1979 took a slightly different position, but was also sceptical of either the feasibility or desirability of higher standards in dwellings built for sale. A circular, *Housing: Needs and Action*, advised local planning authorities not to impose floorspace controls on new housing for fear that this might prevent the development of low cost 'starter homes' (DoE, 1975).

There is another difference between private and social housing. In contrast to most build-for-sale schemes, a local authority or a housing association is likely to possess a continuing responsibility for the property after completion. This continuing responsibility, in turn, encourages a concern with specification standards, those covering the standards of materials, fittings and finishes, so that maintenance costs can be minimised in the long term.

Moreover, as part of this concern with long-term maintenance, some housing associations, probably accounting for about a third of the build for rent programmes in England for rent, take out insurance to cover future building defects with the Housing Association Property Mutual (HAPM). This is a specialist insurance company that was first established in 1990 in response to a loss of public funding for major repairs. The coverage with HAPM is for a longer period than that usually available for private owners (20 or 30 years rather than 10 years) and is based on a more stringent assessment of drawings at the design stage, as well as through inspection on the site during construction.

The withdrawal of the private developer after completion also means there is no agency capable of undertaking long-term maintenance of public open space and landscaped areas. Private developers are more likely than social housing developers to locate all open space within private gardens. They believe that the provision of private gardens is preferred by consumers. Moreover, they use semi-detached and detached forms of houses that facilitate such provision.

Change and continuity in procurement and development

In the 1990s, the distinction between private and social housing has, in some ways, become blurred. Housing associations have replaced local authorities as the providers of new housing. At the same time, housing associations have increasingly used 'design and build' procurement methods that rely more heavily on private sector methods.

The old procurement method involves a series of separate distinct stages:

❑   the specification of a design for each scheme, usually by an architect;
❑   the preparation of bills of quantities, usually by a quantity surveyor;
❑   putting the scheme out to tender, usually to a number of different builders.

Design and build brings these stages together. The housing association puts the scheme out to tender, without a bill of quantities, and requires the contractor to work out the details of design. Design and build has advantages for the housing association in making the contractor liable for the risk of cost overruns and delays. It also has advantages for the private contractor in increasing his/her discretion over the details of design.

In many ways, however, the changes of the 1990s are less than they seem. Housing associations still retain traditional procurement methods, with bills of quantity for a minority of prestige schemes and schemes designed for special needs. In addition and more importantly, even if housing associations use design and build procurement, they still generally restrict the building contractor to a statement of specifications, known as the 'employer's requirements'. Moreover, they generally employ quantity surveyors in the role of 'employer's agent' whose task is to ensure that the contractor conforms to the employer's requirements. Indeed, some large housing associations use design and build contracts whilst retaining control over the design of the basic floorplans.

Design and build is a legal term that defines who bears the burden of risk. Another way of classifying procurement methods is through a distinction between contractor-led and client-led approaches. Contractor-led procurement involves the contractor preparing the design and more or less requires a design and build contract. Client-led procurement gives the main responsibility for design to the housing association and may be pursued through either a design and build contract or the traditional contract, with bills of quantity.

The distinction between client-led and contractor-led procurement is common in the technical literature, though the terminology varies. Contractor-led procurement has also been called 'developer-led procurement' by the Social Housing Unit of the House Builders' Federation (undated, probably 1994) and the housing association as 'dispurser' by the Audit Commission (1996, pp. 41–42). The alternative method of 'client-led procurement' is also called 'employer-led procurement' and 'develop and construct'. For the Audit Commission this alternative approach is the housing association as 'developer'. Another term used in housing association development is the 'package deal'. This may be regarded as contractor-led, with the land (as well as the designs) provided by the contractor.

The continued use, in client-led procurement, of a statement of employer's requirements and of the employer's agent is open to the criticism that it fails to realise the full potential of design and build procurement. The Social Housing Unit of the House Builders' Federation suggests that client-led procurement leads to discontinuity of design and construction, the duplication of effort in design and the inclusion of unnecessary design features. The Federation is a private sector body. So it might be expected to support a contractor-led approach. However, Winch and Campagnac (1995), writing as independent researchers and drawing on the experience of social housing in France, also suggest that the level of detail in a typical employer's requirements inhibits innovation by the contractor.

The advantages of contractor-led procurement are not always apparent. It does not lead, on average, to reduced building costs. There is virtually no cost difference between contractor-led procurement and its client-led alternative (see Goodchild *et al.* 1996; Audit Commission, 1996, p. 42). Moreover, many housing associations consider that it is in their long-term interests to maintain control over design details.

The present system is, nevertheless, top-heavy with controls. Given the desire of the building contractors for increased flexibility, a possible way forward is to simplify the statement of employer's requirements, whilst giving the HAPM the main responsibility for quality control in matters relating to durability. The HAPM guarantee of a 30 year life for all the main construction details is surely sufficient.

Procurement methods may also vary as to whether they involve competitive or negotiated tendering. The Audit Commission (1996) suggests no difference in the costs of the two approaches. Moreover, Winch and Campagnac (1995) argue in favour of negotiation on the grounds that this leads to better co-operation between the client and the contractor and is more likely to encourage innovation.

However, cost data prepared by the Building Cost Information Service (BCIS) and covering the whole construction industry suggests that negotiated contracts are consistently more expensive. For example, in February 1995 the BCIS reported that open competition was the least expensive form of procurement. Negotiated contracts were, on average, 12% more expensive than the mean of all projects. Negotiated contracts are also less open and less accountable than open, competitive tenders. They may be justified for particular reasons, for example if the contractor owns the site or if the contractor is able to participate in the financing of a scheme. If possible, however, they should be avoided.

In addition to competitive and negotiated contracts, social housing agencies may also sign a serial contract with a building contractor. In this, the contractor agrees a fixed price, usually adjusted for the likely effects of inflation, for the superstructure of a series of standardised house types. This stage of the procurement is usually undertaken by means of a competitive tender. However, the housing agencies and the contractor negotiate the site development costs for each scheme and any unusual costs that might arise from difficult ground conditions.

Serial tendering invariably involves contractor-led procurement. The contractor needs to know and control the basic parameters of design to make an accurate estimate of superstructure costs. Serial tendering was the basis for an experimental programme, so-called 'Operation Breakthrough', introduced by the Housing Corporation from 1992 to 1995. The initiative provided a way in which small housing associations could combine into local partnerships. However, it had no advantages in reducing costs compared to conventional scheme-by-scheme competitive tendering (Goodchild *et al.*, 1996). The main reason was that serial tendering includes an element of negotiation when applied to specific sites.

A White Paper, *Our Future Homes*, published in 1995, proposed a more radical change to procurement methods. The proposal was to introduce legislation 'to allow profit-making companies and other bodies to compete alongside associations to provide social housing'. The proposal was later dropped. Though the reasons are not completely clear, the most likely explanation is that the government was unable to find a simple way of making the proposal attractive to private contractors, whilst also realising reduced construction costs.

The extent of recent changes may be qualified in another way. Housing associations and local authorities have undertaken shared ownership and build for sale schemes for many years, since at least the 1970s. Where housing associations have built or improved property for shared ownership or for sale, they have found that buyers hold them responsible for the quality of the property. Housing associations have been seen as a 'caring' institution looking after the interests of their customers rather than a private firm which seeks to maximise profits (Valerie Karn, personal communication). The distinction between private developers and social housing agencies is maintained by public perception, almost independently of detailed changes in the procurement method.

Likewise, the distinction in financial responsibility and social purpose remains much as before. Most housing associations build to meet social needs rather than consumer demand and they rely on a combination of private finance and housing association grant. The size of grant aid relative to privately raised finance has declined since 1988. In England, the proportion is now less than 50% (Saw, 1996). However, the availability of grant aid still remains crucial to the schemes going ahead. Moreover, there is little sign that housing associations will expand into unsubsidised speculative build for sale schemes. The continuing commitment of housing associations to a social or charitable ethic is one reason. In addition, however, only the very largest developing housing associations possess either the technical skills or the land reserves to compete directly with private developers.

The various differences in the methods of raising finance, in the process of housing development and in the expectations of users define the main policy questions. Local authorities and housing associations must meet the building regulations and the requirements of planning authorities in exactly the same way as private builders. However, they must also meet additional standards of good practice. In local authority and housing association housing, the main policy question is to define the type of housing that offers good value for money and meets social needs. In private housing, the main policy question is to define the scope of the building and planning controls and to ask whether voluntary, non statutory control by the NHBC is sufficient.

Standards for social housing

The adequacy of housing standards is determined by historical expectations. Standards are invariably judged in relation to current practice in the recent past and to the possibilities for the future. In the case of development by social housing agencies, the clearest and most comprehensive statement of good design practice remains the report *Homes for the Future* prepared as a response to the introduction in 1981 of new control procedures for local authority housing (Institute of Housing, Royal Institute of British Architects, 1983). *Homes for the Future* starts with a reflection on an earlier report, *Homes for Today and Tomorrow* prepared by the Parker Morris committee (MHLG, 1961). The latter report, it was noted, still stood as a reference point in the design of local authority housing.

Endorsement of the Parker Morris report means, in turn, endorsement of Parker Morris floorspace standards as an essential component of minimum housing standards. These comprise a matrix of minimum floor areas related to the number of people expected to live in a dwelling (see Table 3.2).

Table 3.2 Parker Morris floorspace standards (m^2).

Dwelling	Expected occupancy (no. of persons)					
	6	5	4	3	2	1
Floorspace (excluding storage)						
3 storey house	98.0	94.0				
2 storey centre terrace	92.5	85.0	74.5			
2 storey semi or end terrace or maisonette	92.5	82.0	72.0			
Flat	86.5	79.0	70.0[†]	57.0	44.5	30.0
Single storey house	84.0	75.5	66.0	57.0	44.5	30.0
Storage						
Houses*	4.5	4.5	4.5	4.0	4.0	3.0
Flats and maisonettes (inside)	2.0	2.0	2.0	1.5	1.5	1.0
Flats and maisonettes (outside)	1.5	1.5	1.5	1.5	1.5	1.5

* Some of this may be on the upper floor, but at least 2.5 m^2 should be at ground level.
[†] 67.0 if there is balcony access.
Notes: Two WCs are required in two and three storey houses, in maisonettes of five or more persons, and in flats and one storey houses with six or more persons.

As is conventional in housing design in Britain, the floor area measures the space between the inner leaf of the external walls, and includes the space occupied by the internal partition walls, the hall, entrance area and staircase where the latter exists.

Parker Morris floorspace standards have long been more generous than those prevailing in the smallest privately built dwellings. They were justified, because in the words of *Homes for the Future*, 'Tenants are more likely fully to occupy a dwelling than in the private sector and are less able to move to suitable accommodation when their needs change.'

Despite the endorsement of Parker Morris floorspace standards, the most distinctive aspect of *Homes for the Future* is the breadth and comprehensiveness of its concern. The Parker Morris report had emphasised floorspace as the most important indicator of quality. In contrast, *Homes for the Future* emphasises the importance of other factors, notably:

❑ measures to promote energy conservation, to be achieved through a combination of enhanced insulation, in excess of the building regulations then in operation; improved draught-proofing; as well as more effective methods of controlled ventilation intended to reduce condensation;

❑ an increased emphasis on costs in use; that is an increased emphasis on the maintenance and running costs borne by the tenant and landlord after completion;

❑ measures to safeguard the quality of external spaces, based on the allocation of an adequate budget for landscaping, the clear definition of private and public space and the provision of adequate space for access and car-parking.

Trends in standards after 1981

The publication of *Homes for the Future* may have encouraged local authorities to maintain their standards. However, it had no official status and did not alter the policies of the Conservative government then in power. The report was prepared against a background in which ministers argued against 'profligate' local authorities. Indeed, in 1981, the government abolished Parker Morris standards as obligatory requirements in England and Wales. It is not possible to trace trends in design standards at a national level after 1981. A study of new house building in Greater London undertaken in the period from 1981 to 1984 shows that one in three London boroughs had approved new housing at below Parker Morris standards during this time (GLC, 1986).

In the early 1980s, new housing association housing largely escaped any cutbacks in the design standards. Basic standards were laid down by the Housing Corporation (1983) in its *Design and Contract Criteria*. While the criteria made no explicit reference to Parker Morris floorspace standards, the approach was generally similar in the way that the design of the dwelling was related to the activities undertaken in each room. In the case of the dining and living areas, the criteria advised housing associations to consult *Space in the Home*, a companion document to the Parker Morris report and to provide drawings showing the position of furniture (another recommendation of the Parker Morris report).

In contrast, from the late 1980s onwards, the Housing Corporation emphasised cost effectiveness in a way that, in the view of most observers, has largely eclipsed any commitment to design standards. Housing associations are now subject to competitive bidding procedures that provide financial rewards for cost reductions, but none for the maintenance of standards. As a result, housing associations that seek to maintain standards are always at risk of losing financial allocations to others that are prepared to compromise.

Housing Corporation guidelines, as published in *Scheme Development Standards* (1993), are less prescriptive than before. The guidelines mostly comprise a series of questions, for example:

'Dwelling layout minimises noise transmission?
Convenient relationship between rooms?
Circulation space sensible for the room activities?
Adequate space for sensible furniture arrangements?'

A study undertaken by the National Federation of Housing Associations shows that the average area of newly built housing association homes in the financial year 1989/90 had fallen by about 10% since 1987/88. In the latter financial year 53% of housing association general needs housing was built with a floor area 5% or more below Parker Morris (Walentowicz, 1992). By the time of a later survey, undertaken by Karn and Sheridan (1994) and covering the year 1991/92, the equivalent figure had risen to 68%.

Standards of specification have also fallen since 1988. In a paper prepared for a Joseph Rowntree Inquiry into design standards, Bowron (1992, unpublished) provides a list of typical savings. This includes the provision of chipboard floors that are more vulnerable to damage from water leaks, cheap partition wall with less acoustic insulation, fewer and cheaper kitchen and bathroom fittings, no external lighting, single rather than double-glazed windows, lower quality softwood window frames and reduced fencing and paving. The implication is that housing associations have attempted to minimise initial costs in a way that risks causing increased costs and an increased need for component replacement in the long term. The external environment is another cause for concern. The desire of housing associations to minimise development costs has also led to increased densities and a reliance on unattractive rows of terraces, with on-street or grouped parking and bin stores at the front.

The publication of Karn and Sheridan's survey in 1994, together with dissatisfaction amongst housing associations led, in 1995, the Housing Corporation to revise its statement of scheme development standards. Housing associations must now show how the floorplan accommodates a minimum list of furniture. There has been no repeat study of housing association standards to determine the impact of this new requirement. However, there have been examples where housing associations have had to upgrade design standards to ensure compliance to the new requirement.

Housing association development has not been subject to such intensive competitive pressures in Wales and Scotland. In Wales, floorspace is regulated by a series of model floorplans. In Scotland, floorspace standards have probably not fallen as far as in England, though full statistics are not available. In Northern Ireland, the Housing Executive has managed to persuade the government to retain Parker Morris standards.

Towards a revised framework of standards

The underlying question remains the extent to which housing associations and local authorities should break the link between income levels and housing standards. Should they seek to provide homes of which the occupants can be proud in the long term? Or should they simply attempt to provide houses of a minimum standard at the minimum cost?

Questions about social purpose can only be resolved through political debate. However, it is possible to indicate the standards that housing associations or local authorities should adopt if they wish to provide good quality homes, of which the residents can be proud for many years ahead.

❏ In respect of building quality, the standards imposed by HAPM are almost certainly sufficient. The 35 year guarantee offered by HAPM is exceptionally long in comparison with other building insurance guarantees either in Britain or elsewhere in Europe.

❏ In respect of floorspace standards, Parker Morris standards surely remain the best test of adequacy. They have the merit that they specify a minimum for the whole house, given conventional assumptions about household activities and furniture dimensions. The standards remain more generous than those prevailing in lower priced private housing. However, the average occupancy rates of social housing schemes also remain higher (Karn and Sheridan, 1994, p. 94). Moreover, neither housing associations nor local authorities are able to change their allocations policies in a way that reduces occupancy, unless they abandon their priority in favour of housing those in need.

In many ways, Parker Morris floorspace standards are not generous.

   o Parker Morris standards are not a departure from long-standing notions of good practice in local authority housing. The recommended minimum for a family house is, for example, very similar to the minimum recommended by the Dudley Committee in 1944 and smaller than some of the floor plans shown in the Tudor Walters report in 1918.

   o The standards are not generous compared to the equivalent standards used in many other European countries. A comparative study of housing in France and Italy, undertaken by a firm of consultants, SPAZIDEA (1992, p. 36), states that, in the social housing sector, the minimum reference standard for a dwelling of four habitable rooms is $77\,m^2$ in France and $85\,m^2$ in Italy and that the equivalent standard for a dwelling of five habitable rooms is $93\,m^2$ in France and $95\,m^2$ in Italy. Habitable floorspace, as measured int he SPAZIDEA report, excludes the space of walls and internal partitions, steps and stair-cases, lifts and the surrounds of windows and doors. The definition is tighter than that conventionally used in Britain, including that of the Parker Morris report. In practice, the reference standard in France and Italy is not very different from the Parker Morris minimum.

○ The standards assume a relatively 'tight-fit' between floorspace, household activities and a list of minimum furniture requirements (Rapoport, 1968). Smaller dwellings lead to a series of design compromises. An analysis, undertaken by the former Greater London Council, has indicated the problems of terraced family houses that fail to meet Parker Morris standards (GLC, 1986, insert between pages 24 and 25). The problems include the following:

> '1. Space in the entrance is severely cramped ... There is no place to store a pram or bicycle indoors.
> 2. Passage from the garden to the kitchen is through the living area.
> 5. The limited floorspace on the ground floor makes it impossible to include either a sideboard in the dining area, seating in the cooking area or a washing machine and/or dryer anywhere ...
> 6. Circulation around all the bedrooms is virtually impossible ...'

Figure 3.1 provides an example of a Parker Morris and a reduced standard terraced family house that is characterised by these problems. In addition, the Parker Morris house possesses more storage.

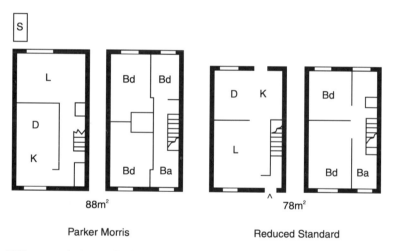

Fig. 3.1 Differences between Parker Morris and smaller dwellings.

To say that Parker Morris standards are not generous begs the question as to whether they should be upgraded. A marginal increase is almost certainly desirable to promote better disabled persons' access. However, floorspace is not the only attribute of housing quality. The demand for floorspace has to be traded against the desire for housing that is inexpensive to heat, is set in attractive surroundings and possesses a degree of privacy. The most recently completed survey of tenants' views of different floorspace standards remains a survey undertaken in 1982 of four estates in Sheffield. This suggests that tenants notice even small reductions in floorspace compared to Parker Morris. On the other hand the results also suggest that, if standards are to be improved beyond Parker Morris, floorspace is not the main priority. The spontaneous comments of respondents indicate that the heating system is potentially both the most liked and the least liked feature of a home, depending on whether or not the heating system is efficient and cost effective. The statistical pattern of responses suggest that the appearance of the estate is the most important influence on overall satisfaction (Furbey and Goodchild, 1986c; Goodchild and Furbey, 1986).

Towards a revised project control system

The achievement of high standards requires a sympathetic administrative framework. There are two possible methods.

❏ First, the relevant supervisory agency (for example, the Housing Corporation for housing associations in England or its equivalents in Wales and Scotland) could introduce a system of quality labelling to encourage the achievement of higher standards. Achievement of the quality label could, for example, justify a higher level of grant aid.
❏ Second, the relevant agency could provide more design guidance, including the provision of design and equipment standards and model floor plans. Conformity to the guidance would be considered a condition of grant aid. This is already in practice in Wales.

The first method, involving the possibility of an additional cost allowance for good quality schemes (1993) is recognised to an extent in the Housing Corporation's *Scheme Development Standards* (1993). However, there is at present no system of quality labelling that would enable the consistent application of a higher grant rate. Established quality labelling systems already exist in France and Switzerland. In France, the quality labelling system (QUALITEL) applies to protection against noise, likely heating costs, the cost of maintenance of the external walls and roof, the quality of the plumbing and sanitary equipment, the quality of electrical sockets and artificial lighting and protection against summer heat. In Switzerland, the quality labelling system places more emphasis on location and the amenities of a neighbourhood.

Whatever the contents, the preparation of a quality labelling system requires some ground rules. Harrison (1996) recommends the following:

'– easy to follow layout, clear and concise,
 – information on how to assess each issue and why it is important,
 – extensive use of diagrams to clarify issues,
 – non-additive indices – danger of a single quality score,
 – weighting used to determine relative importance of issues,
 – weightings arrived at by consensus;
 – use of alternate weightings to reflect special requirements,
 – graphical output should show strengths/weaknesses of a scheme very clearly.'

The weighting of different elements is not easy, however. The experience of surveys of housing in use is that the priority given to different aspects of design is sensitive to the type of question and method of analysis and that, in any case, the weighting is likely to vary for different household types (households with children, adult households and pensioners) and in different situations. Some aspects of housing quality, security and appearance are, in any case, not easy to measure.

A key criterion is simplicity. The French QUALITEL system does not provide a comprehensive measure of housing quality. It merely lists some of the easily measured attributes of the building fabric and its fittings.

The second method of quality control, the introduction of a tighter framework of design standards, may proceed through a statement of requirements or a set of standard house plans or a combination of the two. Tai Cymru, the Welsh equivalent of the Housing Corporation, uses a range of standard house plans to control quality. However, this is very prescriptive and would almost certainly prove too rigid in the diversity of different situations and different housing associations in England. A statement of requirements would surely be sufficient.

In some ways, the introduction of standards is a return to the system of project control used in local authority housing in the 1970s. However, the system used in the 1970s failed to produce good quality housing because the design requirements were limited to the achievement of Parker Morris floorspace standards. Local authorities maintained Parker Morris standards, but sought high densities in an effort to reduce overall building costs. Any reformed system should avoid these failings, through specification of a wide range of design criteria.

The implementation of design standards requires procedures for inspection and enforcement. Inspection may be undertaken either in advance or after completion. The latter is more flexible, though it has the disadvantage that, once schemes are completed, the designs cannot be changed. If the inspection were to find that a social housing agency had failed to conform to the minimum standards, the responsible agency could easily impose an appropriate financial or other sanction.

Universal design standards

Though there is no definitive official statement, the public regulation of house building may be understood as serving three main aims: the promotion of health and safety; the protection of natural resources, including the conservation of energy; and the protection of basic amenities and comfort standards. These are, of course, very broad aims that are open to multiple interpretations. In the control of private housing, there is no single benchmark of design standards such as is provided by the Parker Morris report or *Homes for the Future* for social housing.

Existing forms of regulation

The existing framework of administrative control may be summarised.

❑ First, developers have to secure planning permission and can expect planning authorities to require modifications if a proposal has an adverse effect on its surroundings, either an adverse visual impact, as in a conservation area, or an adverse effect on traffic levels, pedestrian or vehicular safety or on some other aspect of public well-being, including the potential for crime and vandalism. Planning authorities can control design by requiring modifications at the time of approval or by attaching conditions to the granting of planning permission, for example about landscaping or the use of building materials.

The scope of design control is sometimes qualified. The Department of the Environment gives advice to local planning authorities in England in *Planning Policy Guidance: Housing* (DoE, 1992c). This states that planning authorities should only refuse permission for a specific reason and should not interfere in the marketing strategies or commercial judgements of developers. However, planning authorities are in a strong position to exercise design controls over the external environment, if they see fit. They know that most developers want to avoid the delays involved in an appeal and that the limits of planning control are not always precisely defined.

The scope of control over floorspace and internal layout is more restricted than the control of the external layout. The floorspace and internal layout of new housing is not mentioned within current planning guidance. Planning authorities may, however, exercise such controls over the conversion of former commercial and industrial buildings to housing and the subdivision of houses into multi-occupation.

❏ Second, house builders have to conform to the provisions of the building regulations in respect of a limited range of factors covering health and safety; the conservation of fuel and power, including insulation; and the prevention of the waste, misuse or contamination of water. (For a summary, see Barritt, 1994.) Administrative traditions in Scotland are different and have led, in the past, to a wider range of standards than in England and Wales. For example, the Building Regulations (Scotland) 1972 specified minimum standards over floorspace, external privacy and sunlight. Successive amendments have reduced the scope of control in Scotland. However, the Scottish building regulations continue to specify more detailed requirements for the kitchen and for sleeping accommodation (Williams, 1993).

Conformity to the building regulations is checked in advance, either by the local authority or by an approved private inspector, notably by inspectors employed by an insurance company called the National House Building Council (NHBC). The building regulations are open to less local discretion and less negotiation than the town planning controls.

❏ Third, the NHBC (1995) issues additional performance standards and guidelines on security; the efficiency of central heating, if provided; sound insulation in relation to toilets and living rooms; and the number of power points. Nearly all private builders are registered with the NHBC or with its main competitor, Zurich Municipal, that makes similar requirements. Thus, the standards are relatively simple to enforce, even though they possess no statutory status. However, the main function of the NHBC is to provide a ten year guarantee against structural failure or poor workmanship. The design standards are limited and have been relaxed in the 1990s. In 1992, the NHBC withdrew guidance on the provision of storage space. In 1994, the NHBC withdrew its guidance that a room should only be described as a bedroom if it possessed:

- an overall room size of at least $9\,m^2$ for a double bedroom and at least $4.5\,m^2$ for a single bedroom.
- a principle dimension of at least $2.7\,m$ for a double bedroom and a $1.5\,m$ for a single bedroom.

Guidance is now for builders to provide purchasers with a correctly proportioned and dimensioned plan that indicates the furniture that can be accommodated in the room. Guidance is, of course, not the same as a requirement. Builders may use their discretion whether or not to show furniture in their plans and advertising documents.

The building regulations in Britain are narrowly drawn. In most other European countries, the building regulations cover room size (as in the Scandinavian countries, the Netherlands or Germany) or dwelling size in relation to intended occupancy (as in France); noise protection from the exterior; and disabled persons' access (usually defined in relation to the provision of lifts in blocks of flats, the size of door and stair openings and the provision of level or near level access to the front door) (Björklund, 1994; van der Heijden and Visscher, 1995; MELT, 1992). Moreover, where provisions exist for a ten year consumer guarantee, as in Belgium, France and Italy, the provisions are specified by statute, rather than by the voluntary agreement of the industry (SPAZIDEA, 1992).

To illustrate the scope and level of detail in other European countries, the regulations for room size are shown in Table 3.3.

The variation in standards between different countries begs the question as to whether the European Commission is likely to seek greater harmonisation. There are some precedents. A common framework of standards already exists

Table 3.3 Minimum room sizes in the building regulations of selected countries in western and northern Europe. [The first figure is the minimum room size (m^2), the second figure in brackets is the minimum width (m). Where there is no figure in brackets, the building regulations of that country do not specify a minimum width.]

Country	Kitchen	Living room	Bedroom 1	Bedroom 2	Bedroom 3
Denmark	7	18	7(2.2)	7(2.2)	7(2.2)
Germany	6	14–22(3.5)	13	8	8
Netherlands	5	17–19	5	5	5
Norway	—	(3.6–3.9)*	10(2.7)	6	6
Sweden	(2.4–3.2)*†	18–20(3.6)	12(2.7)	10(2.5)	7(2.1)

Notes: The minimum size of the living room and kitchen may vary by the intended occupancy of the dwelling. In Norway, the standards include those of the National Housing Bank.
* No minimum size is given in the building regulations.
† In Sweden, 1.9 m is specified as the minimum width of a kitchenette.
Sources: Björklund (1994) for Denmark, Norway and Sweden; Heijden and Visscher (1995) for Germany and the Netherlands.

within the European Union for building products and materials and for considerations of safety on the building site. A limited degree of harmonisation also exists for planning control in the form of a requirement that all large projects should be subject to an assessment of the environmental impact. However, there is, at present, no sign that the European Commission wishes to bring forward proposals for the general harmonisation of building and planning controls. Housing is, at present outside the competence of the European Commission and the Council of Ministers. Moreover, house building is not currently central to the achievement of a single European market. It is fashionable to talk of the 'globalisation' of manufacturing industry, but the pace of change in different industries varies. Houses, unlike building materials and building products, cannot be easily moved around and sold in different countries. Prefabricated, timber-framed kit houses are a partial exception, but are as yet expensive and only applicable to detached dwellings. House building is not an international industry in the same way as, say, the car industry or the consumer electronics industry. There are not many multi-national house building firms whose activities would benefit from the harmonisation of building controls.

Harmonisation is, in any case, hindered by continuing large national variations in the organisation of the building industry. Significant variations exist in the techniques of construction, the workings of the labour market, the skills of the work force and the legal responsibilities of different actors (the building contractor, developer and consumer). (Campinos-Dubernet, 1992; SPAZIDEA, 1992). Most likely, if the harmonisation of building and planning controls does proceed, it will be a long-term exercise and will first concern specific issues such as the reduction of energy consumption or the reduction of accidents in the home (Mason, 1995).

The scope of recent debates

The existing framework of controls has achieved much that is taken for granted. Health and safety is no longer a significant source of public concern. Very few people suffer injury or ill-health from the collapse of newly completed dwellings or as a result of any particular type of design. System-built local authority flats provide the only significant exception. Moreover, existing forms of insurance-related control, for example as exercised by the NHBC, have largely overcome popular concern about structural failure.

The absence of popular concern should not encourage complacency amongst private builders. A comparison of building quality in 1990 with that in 1980, undertaken by the Building Research Establishment, reports that house builders are making many of the same mistakes, for example in external walls, roofs and windows, as before. The comparison also suggests that a combination of trends towards more complex elevations, towards higher insulation standards and to the use of more difficult sites (for example, sloping sites or recycled urban sites with a previous use) is giving rise to new types of fault (BRE Information Paper, IP3/93). However, most of those involved in building would argue that the best way forward is through guidance and education rather than regulation.

The scope of regulation now revolves around three main concerns:

❑ consumer protection and the satisfaction of consumer needs;
❑ the needs of disabled people;
❑ the need to save energy and to reduce pollution.

Much of the debate is stimulated by the activities of pressure groups. However, in the case of energy-saving measures, the government also has an economic interest in the introduction of more effective design and building standards.

Consumer protection

The issue of consumer protection came to the fore in the early 1980s in the context of the development of small starter homes. Faced with a sudden slump in housing demand, developers sought to go down-market and to provide dwellings for households who previously would have been dependent on local authority housing. Developers did their best to reduce costs through building very small dwellings, including some of the smallest built in Britain during this century at higher densities on less expensive sites. They also sought to make these dwellings more attractive through the inclusion in the sales price of a 'package' of incentives such as carpets, washing machines and fitted kitchens; free solicitors' fees and moving expenses; 100% mortgages for those eligible; part exchange schemes for those who already owned a house and the chance for first-time buyers to move in while they saved for a deposit (*Which?*, 1984).

The disadvantages of packaged starter homes only became apparent when the original purchasers offered their dwellings for sale. Most new houses possess what estate agents call a 'new house premium' attached to their initial sales price. In the case of starter homes, that premium was enhanced by the existence of incentives that were either a depreciating value (for example, the consumer durables) or non-repeatable (for example, the provision of free solicitors' advice). As a result, owners faced a loss or long delays in resale.

The development of the starter homes led to calls for the strengthening of the building regulations to cover minimum room sizes beyond the level required by the NHBC. (See Housing Centre Trust Seminar, 1983.) In practice, however, the private developers abandoned starter homes in 1982 and 1983 and changed their marketing strategies up-market, before the arguments for stricter controls could have a significant political impact.

Nevertheless, calls for better quality homes, above all larger homes, still persist. Munro and Madigan (1989) have, for example, argued that 'space standards in modern housing are declining' and that the current emphasis on small houses is producing an inflexible built environment incapable of coping with either a tendency for increased home-based work or with the varied demands of different adult members of a household. The assumption of declining floorspace standards is not proven. No statistics exist to show recent trends in the floorspace or other aspects of the detailed design of private housing. However, it is true to say that inadequate size is a frequent cause of complaint amongst house buyers. The report of a survey of a large sample of recently completed owner-occupied dwellings, undertaken by Oseland (1991), states that 'only a third of the respondents considered themselves as having enough space all the time.'

If the point is accepted that dwellings built for sale are too small, the question arises as to the exact form of building control. Oseland (1991) suggests that:

> 'Any future space standards should not be simply based on occupancy and dwelling type but (should) consider how the different parts of the home are to be used and by whom.'

However, Oseland does not explain how such standards are to be defined or enforced. The enforcement of any such standard of use would surely constitute an invasion of privacy. If people wish to use their home for whatever purpose, there is little that can be done. The control of size would surely have to be undertaken on the basis of:

❑ either the overall floorspace in relation to the occupancy, along the lines of the Parker Morris standards and the floorspace standards included in the building regulations in France;

❑ or minimum room sizes as specified in the building regulations in many other European countries.

The strictness of any new standards would depend on the aim of control. If the aim were to endorse existing practice and to ban merely the very worst housing schemes, an overall floorspace standard of at least 75% of Parker Morris might suffice. Karn and Sheridan (1994) have examined the design and layout of a sample of 221 privately-built homes, started between April 1991 and March 1992, and priced less than £100 000. They show that only 3.2% of such dwellings had an average size of less than 75% of the relevant Parker Morris minimum (Karn and Sheridan, 1994, Table 3.8). If the aim were to encourage a major improvement in private housing, a standard of at least 85% of Parker Morris might suffice. The results of Karn and Sheridan's survey suggest that about 24% of new dwellings priced below £100 000 would fail such a test.

There is another possibility. If either the building industry or the government wishes to provide better consumer protection, a more effective way forward might be to broaden the ten year insurance cover provided by the NHBC and other companies. At present, the cover is mainly for structural defects. The cover could be extended to such issues as health in relation to building materials and the ground conditions and safety in use. It might also be possible to introduce a higher standard one year insurance cover of 'perfect completion', much as already exists in France. For this initial year, the purchaser would expect a complete absence of defects in the dwelling and its fittings.

Calls for better consumer protection have, in part, been met through the introduction of the Property Misdescriptions Act 1991. This makes the vendors of property, including private builders, potentially liable to criminal charges if they provide false information to a potential purchaser or if they withhold relevant information in a way that misleads potential purchasers. However, the Property Misdescriptions Act provides no incentive to developers to provide consumers with helpful information. Indeed, in some ways, the Act discourages developers from providing information. The less information is available, the less is the chance of a complaint about 'misdescription'.

Defenders of the status quo would, no doubt, argue that consumers can visit a property or a show house and judge its quality for themselves. However, some aspects of quality, such as energy consumption and noise, are not visible. In any case, a brief visit can only generate an impression. More guidance is necessary. Quality labelling is not common, even in the very limited field of energy consumption where there are established methods for the purpose. In other areas, quality labelling is absent. House builders do not provide an estimate of the overall floorspace of a house and they seldom show the position of furniture in a room, with the furniture drawn to scale.

Access standards for disabled people

The second concern, protecting the interests of disabled people, rests, in part, on the argument that most people are disabled at some point in their lives, through accident or injury or the infirmities of old age. Provision for disabled people is, therefore, not a luxury for the few, but a useful amenity that will be used by most people at some time. In addition, it is argued, designing for disabled people imposes a discipline that results in more spacious, more convenient accommodation for all occupants, irrespective of whether they are disabled. However, the case for access standards is also a question of civil rights. For example, the Access Committee for England (ACE) has argued in favour of access standards 'as a prerequisite for achieving equal opportunities and integration' (ACE, 1992, p. 3).

To say that all people are disabled at some stage in their life might suggest an incentive for private developers to promote 'designed for disability', or some other slogan, as a feature in their marketing strategies. In practice, they do not do so. They may believe that advertising the existence of such features would have a negative impact. The absence of immediate benefit for builders suggests, in turn, the need for explicit public regulations, either through the building regulations, the planning system or both.

Access to public buildings is already covered in the building regulations (Part M in England and Wales). Access to houses is also covered in the building regulations in other European countries. The building regulations would, therefore, seem to offer the best framework for at least a minimum or basic access standard.

The problem is to arrive at a compromise. The house builders generally oppose any new regulation that might increase costs and restrict the market. The representatives of disabled people argue for radical changes that are difficult to implement. The government has considered amending the building regulations to incorporate disabled persons' access since at least 1992. (See DoE, 1992c.) The government has also published draft proposals. However, it has not, as yet, published the results of its consultation.

Most proposals for disabled persons' access derive from the concept of 'mobility housing' as this was first defined in *Housing for People who are Physically Handicapped* (DoE, 1974). Mobility housing is 'ordinary' family housing, designed to Parker Morris standards, with specific features that facilitate use by disabled persons, though not necessarily for people who are wholly dependent on a wheelchair. A standard textbook by Smith (1989, p. 376) lists the following features:

- ❑ access at the front in the form of a ramp (rather than a step);
- ❑ a minimum width of 900 mm for corridors and for doors;
- ❑ in the case of two storey houses, the use of a plan layout that enables the fitting of a chair lift to the stairs.

In Scotland, mobility housing has also been known as 'ambulant disabled housing' (Scottish Homes, 1996b, p. 19).

Mobility housing, as originally conceived, was intended mainly for social housing. It was never taken up by private house builders. In practice, in the context of increasing financial constraints, social housing developers also largely ignored mobility standards until a revived interest in the subject in the 1990s.

In 1992, ACE proposed a revised version of the mobility standard, intended to ensure that disabled persons, including those in wheelchairs, could visit a house in comfort. The new standard of visitable or accessible housing, as it is generally called, mainly differs from the mobility standard in the inclusion of a requirement for an accessible downstairs WC. The new standard comprises the following list of essential criteria (ACE, 1992, p. 11):

'1. Entrances to dwellings should, wherever possible, have a level or gently sloped approach.
2. Where dwellings (usually flats) are accessed by lifts, the lifts should be accessible to wheelchair users.
3. Entrances to dwellings should have flush thresholds and a minimum clear opening door width of 800 mm.
4. Internal doorsets should have a minimum clear opening width of 750 mm.
5. Circulation spaces at entrance level (e.g. halls and corridors) should have a minimum width of 90 mm and allowances should be made so that wheelchair users can turn into rooms and corridors.
6. There should be a WC and living room at entrance level.
7. The entrance level WC should allow for access by a wheelchair user who has sufficient mobility to make either a front, diagonal or lateral transfer to the WC unaided.
8. For dwellings on more than one storey or level, a staircase should be designed to allow for possible future installation of a stairlift.'

In Scotland, the term 'barrier-free' housing is broadly consistent with the ACE concept of accessibility (Scottish Homes, 1996, p. 19).

The ACE suggests that the proposed access standard comprises little more than a series of 'minor design modifications' that 'can be achieved without a significant increase in costs', except at the lower end of the private housing market. It forgets that even the modest requirements of 'mobility housing' require Parker Morris standards if the designs are to possess adequate floorspace for households in the kitchen, dining room and living room on the ground floor. A significant minority of private housing, as well as most social housing schemes, currently fail to meet Parker Morris standards. If the full requirements of wheelchair use are to be met, model layouts prepared by Goldsmith (1975) to a 'wheelchair standard' require between 4.6% and 19.2% additional floorspace compared to the Parker Morris minimum. In houses designed to the Parker Morris minimum, there is inadequate space on the ground floor to accommodate a wheelchair in a WC, with the door closed (Goldsmith, 1984, pp. 423–424).

There is a dissenting viewpoint. The Joseph Rowntree Foundation has proposed a 'lifetime homes' standard, designed for permanent occupation by people at all stages of their life, that is claimed to conform to Parker Morris minimum floorspace standards. The lifetimes homes standard requires all the features of the ACE minimum visitable standards, together with a special disable persons' bathroom; larger room sizes; the inclusion of either a downstairs bedroom or space for an internal lift and sufficient external space to incorporate a larger, disabled persons' parking space. However, conformity to Parker Morris in the lifetimes homes dwelling is only achieved through the abandonment of Parker Morris storage space requirements and the use of a wide-fronted house, rather than the narrow-fronted houses that are usual in social housing. (See the supplement to Trotter's *Innovations in Social Housing*, No. 3, April 1992.)

In practice, standards of new housing generally fall far short of that required for the ACE visitable standard. The survey of house plans undertaken by Karn and Sheridan (1994) in England and Wales found that only a very small proportion of dwellings conformed to this standard. For example, only 4.3% of housing association and 1.6% of private properties had a visitable entrance that avoided such problems as a raised entrance, inadequate standing area or narrow front door. About 45% of properties in both sectors had a ground floor WC. However, because of the size of the compartment and the doorway arrangements only a handful of separate WCs were capable of easy use by a person in a wheelchair.

All this, together with the earlier calculations made by Goldsmith, suggest that the full achievement of the ACE standard as a universal minimum is impractical. In the short term, it is likely that exceptions will have to be made under any new building regulation. Exceptions will have to be made for smaller houses, say under 70 or 75 m^2. Given the expense, it is also likely that an exception would have to be made for the provision of lifts in low-rise flats. The convention in social housing is to provide a lift in a block of six or more storeys. The requirement could be reduced to, say, a flat of four storeys or more, but surely not to all flats. Such a limited interpretation of disabled persons' access is the basis for the building regulations in most European countries, including France, the Netherlands and Germany.

The question arises as to whether planning authorities might also impose standards for disabled persons' access. The position of the government in relation to England and Wales is that disabled persons' access to housing is a national issue and should be incorporated into the building regulations, once the details are worked out. In England, the Department of the Environment has required local planning authorities to exclude or 'water down' any reference to disabled persons' access in their development plans (*Planning*, 7 August 1992). In contrast, Scottish planning guidance, as represented in *Land for Housing*, is more positive in encouraging planning authorities to take into account the physical requirements of people with special needs, including their access to general housing (The Scottish Office, 1996, p. 17).

The potential role of the planning system is to consider local variations. For example, in areas with a high proportion of elderly persons, the planning authority could specify that both private and social housing developers provide a proportion of new housing, say 20% or 30%, to a higher standard than that specified in the building regulations. The result, in the long term, would be to give disabled persons more choice. In addition, the local planning authority could allow exceptions to the provision of level or near level access to the ground floor. The argument in favour of such an exception is that, otherwise, developers would avoid difficult urban sites. This is a planning consideration rather than an issue for the building regulations.

Controls to reduce energy consumption

The area of debate concerns energy efficiency and the environment. Again, the introduction of additional controls is dependent on the scale of ambition. The specification of higher insulation standards is a relatively simple exercise, if undertaken through a series of piecemeal improvements as has been the case in the past decade. Insulation standards in Britain, as progressively modified through the building regulations, are now closer to those in other countries in Northern Europe, though still below what is technically possible. The main question concerns whether building regulations should go beyond insulation and specify standards for solar gain and for controlled ventilation.

The problem with solar gain is its dependence on site layout and orientation. The dwelling has to face south if it is to secure a significant degree of solar gain. Planning authorities could use the scope for solar gain as a factor in judging the acceptability of proposals for new housing. However, the variability of sites means that it would be unwise for public authorities to make a general requirement for solar gain.

Controlled ventilation offers, in some ways, a better candidate for regulation. It reduces heat loss during the winter months when the scope for solar gain is very limited. It is also indifferent to the constraints of site layout. Controlled ventilation, in turn, implies a modification to the building regulations to prevent the front and back door from opening directly into a habitable room. Under such a regulation, the front and back doors would have to open onto a hall, a small 'draught lobby' or a non-habitable room such as a kitchen area. Apart from the small increase in floor area and therefore in development cost, this would encounter few difficulties in its implementation.

Otherwise, controlled ventilation is not an aspect of design that is, at present, suitable for inclusion in the building regulations or planning controls. There are potential objections to the cost of the mechanical ventilation systems that are necessary for the purpose. There are, moreover, uncertainties about the number of air changes per hour that are necessary for health reasons. Inadequate ventilation can promote condensation and internal air pollution. A further uncertainty concerns the techniques available for measuring air changes in different situations. It is possible to measure the 'air-proofing' of a dwelling by comparing the air pressure inside a building with that outside, given certain assumptions about the use of mechanical ventilation. The problem is whether this technique can be used on a routine basis.

The potential for change

Private house builders generally argue that their standards have never been higher and that, for this reason alone, calls for closer public controls are unjustified. They also object to additional controls for fear that this suggests that existing dwellings are somehow inadequate. In addition, private developers object to tighter regulation on grounds of principle. They argue that good design can compensate for low floorspace standards; that consumers are the best judge of quality in housing; and that consumers may well be happy with less space or with low standards in other respects, if this means lower costs.

The arguments of the private builders are unlikely to lead to the removal of the limited forms of control that exist in the building regulations and the town planning system. Though the developers seldom articulate the point, some form of regulation is necessary to maintain the confidence of consumers and mortgage lenders in the quality of new house building. For example, even if the building regulations were abolished, it is most likely that the private builders would continue to rely on regulation by the NHBC or other similar agency.

Despite the rhetoric of the Conservative government in power since 1979, there has been no deregulation, other than to bring the Scottish building regulations broadly in line with those in England. In other European countries, the experience has been similar. There has been no general relaxation of controls (Karn, 1996). On the other hand, the arguments of the private developers in Britain have almost certainly worked against the introduction of additional controls. As in the past, the main rule in private house building remains *caveat emptor*: buyer beware.

Notwithstanding the objection of the private house builders, it is possible to identify the main priorities, if political and economic circumstances were to favour stricter regulation. Any such additional controls should have specific aims, should be relatively simple to implement and should receive the support of the main pressure groups. Two main priorities are apparent:

- ❏ first, the inclusion in the building regulations and possibly the planning controls of new standards for disabled persons' access;
- ❏ second, the inclusion in the building regulations of:
  - ○ a new energy savings requirement that the front and back door of a house should not open directly from any habitable room;
  - ○ a requirement that the total floorspace be published in any advertisement;
  - ○ a requirement that the energy rating of a house be published in any advertisement.

CONTROLS ON REHABILITATION AND REPAIR WORK

The regulatory framework in housing has, from its origins in the nineteenth century to the present, comprised two separate strands dealing with minimum standards for the existing stock and minimum standards for new housing. Standards for rehabilitation may be regarded as an intermediate case. Rehabilitation requires planning permission if it affects the material appearance of a building, involves substantial enlargement or involves the subdivision of a single house into multiple occupation. If planning permission is required, the procedures are similar to those for new housing. In addition, separate controls apply to buildings that are listed as being of architectural merit or historic interest. Such 'listed building consent', as it is called, is required for any works that involve more than mere restoration, including works that affect the interior.

Building extensions and conversion of attics to bedrooms may also require approval under the building regulations in the same way as new housing. However, there are very few regulations or requirements that apply specifically to rehabilitation or repairs work. Most rehabilitation is undertaken by private owners and is subject to minimal control, this being mostly undertaken by a surveyor for the receipt of a building society loan.

The reasons for the lack of control in rehabilitation are obvious enough. Enforcement would be difficult, especially for do-it-yourself work. The older stock is extremely varied. As a result, it is not easy to draft some universal statement of rehabilitation standards.

On the other hand, an extension of building regulations to repair work might have advantages in reducing the incidence of poor quality work. It might be possible to specify minimum standards of workmanship covering such matters as repair work to the roof, the installation of a new damp-proof course and the treatment of external timber. Compliance could be assured by requiring owners to produce a certificate of approval on the sale of the property (Leather and Mackintosh, 1994a, p. 38).

DESIGN CONTROLS IN TOWN PLANNING

Controls exercised through the town planning legislation deserve separate and more detailed consideration. They deal with the design of areas as well as buildings. Moreover, in doing this, they involve a different language. They involve, in particular, the language of 'amenity', meaning the pleasantness of a place, and the language of 'aesthetics', meaning the extent to which any proposal is likely to enhance the character and beauty of a town or city.

The advocates of design controls would say that urban design involves more than amenity and aesthetics. They would say that it involves considerations of cost, safety, convenience for the users, and so forth. This is true. Nevertheless, amenity and aesthetics remain central to urban design. Indeed, in some ways, amenity and aesthetics have become more important. A theme in discussions of post-modern urban life is the way in which aesthetics and visual considerations have come to the fore. The activities of the advertising industry and a proliferation of different life styles have made the city richer in visual signs and symbols (Goodchild, 1991).

The form and role of layout standards

In town planning, judgements of amenity and aesthetics are generally operationalised through a series of pragmatic layout standards and guides to good practice. In Britain, unlike some other European countries, there is no detailed framework of national planning regulations, only a statement of broad principles (as, for example, provided in England by the *Planning Policy Guidance Notes*). Instead, the planning authority has to formulate its own rules to ensure that decisions are made on a consistent basis. Layout standards provide one way of ensuring consistency. These are quantitative statements covering key aspects of layout, notably sunlight and daylight, privacy, noise, car parking and road dimensions. They provide a starting point in negotiation between the planning authority and the developer.

For example, most planning authorities in England and Wales have a policy that, in single and two storey housing schemes, the facing windows of habitable rooms should be no more than 21 m from one another. Even if the standard is not written into a formal policy statement, and even in areas where high land values lead to high densities, 21 m provides a rule of thumb notion of good practice. The standard strengthens the case of the planning authority in attempting to maintain adequate space around the home. Other similar spacing standards might cover:

❑ the space between the flank walls of a house and the side boundary (say 1–2 m;
❑ the space between a flank wall and the windows of a habitable room (say 10 m);
❑ provision of a minimum back garden space, typically of $50 \, m^2$ (or a minimum back garden length of, say, 10 or 11 m);

❑ provision of adequate amenity space for children's play and for open space around blocks of flats.

Standards have to be applied flexibly. Otherwise, they have serious disadvantages.

❑ Standards are often very narrow and selective. For example, the standards for quiet relate to noise from traffic, industry or aircraft, not to noise from children or neighbours. Likewise, the usual standards for privacy refer to the spacing between dwellings or more rarely to the spacing between the front window and a public footpath. Screening, the blocking off of a view by the placing of some obstacle, is sometimes ignored (Woodford *et al.*, about 1974, p. 26).
❑ The achievement of a specific standard may have adverse side-effects. For example, in conversion schemes, an insistence on conventional car parking can have negative environmental side-effects. Such an insistence can lead to an excessive amount of paved areas within a residential area (Llewelyn-Davies, 1994b).

The role of design guidance

Another way to ensure consistency in planning control is through the use of a design guide intended to inform developers about the expectations and requirements of the planning authority. Design guides differ from standards in part in that they provide qualitative as well as quantitative criteria. In addition, they often seek to integrate different aspects of design into a single package or set of illustrative proposals.

The first generation: the Essex Design Guide (1973)

Design guides have existed in town planning since at least the publication of *A Design Guide for Residential Areas* by the County Council of Essex (1973). The Essex design guide (EDG) arose from a fear that new housing was changing the character of Essex in a way that paid no attention to local traditions. It advocated a distinction between a landscape-dominated or rural residential area and a building-dominated or urban residential area. It also suggested that new schemes should conform to one type or the other and not, as in most suburban schemes, to some compromise between the two (Fig. 3.2).

In principle, the distinction between landscape-and building-dominated landscapes could have led to calls for lower densities and for more tree planting in urban areas. In practice, the main aim of the EDG was to increase densities and to ensure that new housing would become more urban in character. The development of landscape-dominated areas is, in any case, constrained by the high land costs of low density areas and the risks of subsidence associated with planting trees close to buildings. The principles of building-dominated areas were the main focus of attention.

Fig. 3.2   The distinction between landscape- and building-dominated streets.

In such building-dominated schemes, the dwellings were to be placed closer to one another at the front, with a longer back garden than is usual under the 21 m rule. The space allocated to front gardens was to be reduced or eliminated, whilst problems of privacy were to be resolved with narrower windows close to the footpath. Dwellings were clustered closely around what the EDG calls a 'mews court' (Fig. 3.3).

Evaluations of the EDG are mixed. One view is that it failed to consider the strengths of the ordinary suburban layout, as revealed in other studies of housing layout. For example, Cooper Marcus and Sarkissian (1986, p. 103) suggest that the existence of a semi-public front garden is important as a means through which residents can personalise their home through planting of small trees and shrubs. The front garden is a display garden, and it may also have advantages for crime prevention in reducing the likelihood of minor theft and vandalism (Poyner and Webb, 1991).

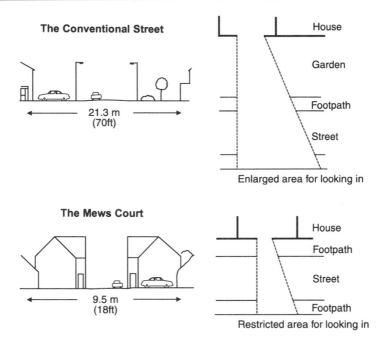

Fig. 3.3 Layout principles of the 'mews court' (adapted from County Council of Essex, 1973).

The contrary view is that the EDG encouraged more co-ordinated urban development. For example, in the case of a town expansion scheme at South Woodham Ferrers, it led, in the view of its supporters, to the creation of 'a new settlement of enhanced character and with a properly planned town centre, industrial and recreational areas and associated infrastructure (Sim, p. 131). In addition, the EDG, 1993, was a force for innovation. Building-dominated streets, with no front garden, have now become more common in new housing, as developers have sought to cope with high land values through higher densities.

Towards a second generation

The preparation of local authority design guides largely ceased in the early and mid 1980s. The Conservative government, elected in 1979, accepted the view of the large private developers that the design guides were an unnecessary constraint on private enterprise. (See DoE, 1980a.) However, by the end of the 1980s, campaigns by influential individuals, notably the Prince of Wales and influential pressure groups, such as the Royal Fine Arts Commission, led to an increased professional interest in what might be called a 'second generation' of design guides.

The difference with practice in the 1980s is that planning authorities can now argue in favour of design controls if these are necessary to control the character of an area. The DoE's *Planning Policy Guidance Note 1* (1992b) (Annex A) indicates the scope of control for planning authorities in England. It encourages planning authorities to set out their design policies in a development plan, focusing on the following broad matters. Italics have been added to clarify the text.

❑ 'scale' (*the overall size of the proposal in relation to its neighbours*);
❑ 'density' (*the intensity of development measured by either the number of units, the number of rooms or the number of single and double bedrooms in a specified area*);
❑ 'height' (*the number of storeys in each building*);
❑ 'massing' (*the relation between the height and width of the elevations*);
❑ 'layout' (*the pattern of buildings and streets in plan form*);
❑ 'landscape' (*the amount and quality of tree and shrub planting, the treatment of external surfaces*);
❑ 'access' (*the link between the proposal and adjoining roads and footpaths*).

In Scotland, *National Planning Policy Guidelines: Land for Housing* provides similar advice. It states that 'The planning system can help to protect and enhance environmental quality. Attention should be directed to the location, siting, form, type and external design of housing' (Scottish Office, 1996, p. 18).

Given that planning authorities may exercise design controls, it makes sense for them to prepare design guides. Hall (1990) provides the fullest account of the possible form and content of the new approach. Whereas the EDG and the other design guides of the 1970s were mostly concerned with the design of individual buildings or small groups of buildings, the new approach is more concerned with the character of areas. Again, whereas the design guides of the 1970s favoured a universal statement of principles, the new approach favours, or at least should favour, different principles in different neighbourhoods and urban districts.

For Hall, seven different levels of control may be distinguished for different areas of a town or city, each distinguished by its degree of strictness or discretion. At one extreme, 'minimum intervention' is the norm. Developers are allowed to develop as they see fit, subject only to controls if the proposals affect other areas subject to stricter controls. At the other extreme, the planning authority imposes a specific form or style and seeks to conserve, in detail, the existing character of an area.

At present, planning practice falls short of the potential. The report of a survey of local authority practice, undertaken in 1990, suggests that most planning authorities 'appear to have few or no formal design policies.' Moreover, this same survey report continues, most design guides remain subject specific, with little attention to strategic issues or to variations between one area and another (Chapman and Houghton, 1991). The subjects most likely to affect housing design are those concerned with house extensions, residential roads, density, crime prevention, car parking and conservation areas.

The absence of comprehensive design guides is open to different explanations. It is possible that resource and skill constraints hinder any improvement to practice. Planning authorities have difficulty in preparing reliable and up-to-date detailed development plans for their area, even without taking on a new responsibility for design guidance. However, resource constraints are not the only possible explanation. Practitioners may wish to retain their discretion in negotiation with architects and developers. Authorities may also be reluctant to confront the opposition of architects and private developers to design controls, even in relation to the relatively broad design controls permitted under current planning guidance.

The views of housing architects and developers are expressed in *Good Design in Housing*, jointly published by the House Builders' Federation and the Royal Institute of British Architects (Davison, 1990). The publication accepts the need for better and more sensitive design. The conclusions list a series of preconditions for good design which involve more flexibility on the part of planning officers and highways engineers. Otherwise, the emphasis is on the role of the architect, the landowners, developers and purchaser working together to achieve better quality. Planning briefs and design guides are most significant by their absence.

Concepts in urban design

The exercise of design controls would be relatively simple, if there were a single notion of good practice. This is not so. There is a potential diversity of different approaches, motivated by different architectural styles and visual images (for example, the historic English town, the planned towns of the eighteenth century, the garden city, the modern American city, and so forth). Indeed, in many ways, it is highly desirable that there is no single definition of good practice. Were design controls to be based on a single notion of good practice, the result would be to promote the standardisation of the urban environment.

The various approaches to urban design may be classified along two dimensions (Ascher, 1995, pp. 232–233; see Fig. 3.4).

❏ One dimension is concerned with the role of planning. It involves a distinction between what might be called 'adaptive planning' that seeks to guide existing processes of urban development, and the 'directive planning' that seeks to anticipate development and mould development into a specific urban form.

❏ The other dimension is concerned with public attitudes towards change. It involves a distinction, first made by Choay (1965) between a 'progressive' or forward-looking, and a 'culturalist' or backward-looking approach. The progressive approach is largely based on the potential of technology and an analysis of user needs. The culturalist approach seeks to humanise the modern city through the adaptation of traditional urban forms.

The dimensions and distinctions are not new. They go back to the first attempts in the late nineteenth century to invent a professional discipline of town planning. The adaptive/directive distinction may, for example, be related to the distinction that emerged before 1914 between Geddes and Howard.

Geddes advocated an organic approach to town planning, based on an understanding of how towns evolve and grow. In contrast, Howard and the garden cities movement advocated the building of new 'social cities' in opposition to the old.

Likewise, the culturalist/progressive distinction may be traced back at least to the publication in 1889 of *Der Städtebau* and the rejection, contained therein, of efforts to modernise the street layouts of historic towns. (For an English translation see Sitte, 1965.) Ellin (1996, pp. 270–279) suggests that the culturalist/progressive distinction overlaps an even older distinction in Western philosophy and art, between romanticism and rationalism. Romanticism favours a search for historical identity and emphasises values, feelings and beliefs. Rationalism favours technology and the use of the scientific method.

The distinctions, though long established, take various forms in different decades. They respond to changing methods of transport and communication (for example the growth, throughout the twentieth century, of private car use and of motor traffic), to changing life styles (for example, the recent growth of single person households) and to a changing economic context (for example, the decline in employment in manufacturing and the increase in services, including financial services).

Directive models generally require a higher degree of public intervention than their adaptive alternatives. They have generally become less ambitious as, in the 1980s and 1990s, planners and designers have increasingly realised the limitations of public investment. Directive models now seek to undertake urban renewal projects, suburban extensions and small settlements, rather than the planning or replanning of a whole city. They are also more likely to involve an appeal for private financing.

In practice, the dimensions become modified. The practical requirements of preparing a plan or design brief means that the purity of one type is invariably muddied by considerations that are related to another type. Virtually no large-scale exercise in town planning can afford to reject either the possibility of progress or the value of tradition. Likewise, virtually no exercise in town planning can credibly either aspire to full mastery of the process of urban development or claim no influence whatsoever. Town planning in any large city is likely to combine different models in different areas and in different ways. No single vision is likely to suffice. The models or archetypes are theoretical constructs that clarify the available choices.

Adaptive/progressive model

This model looks to the dispersed, post-modern city for its inspiration. The image of the post-modern city usually comprises a series of fragmented roads and landmarks, as suggested by Lynch (1960), or a collage of different signs and symbols, as Rowe and Koetter (about 1978) have suggested. A collage is a picture that comprises different photographs that are stuck alongside one another. A collage city is, likewise, a city that comprises different buildings,

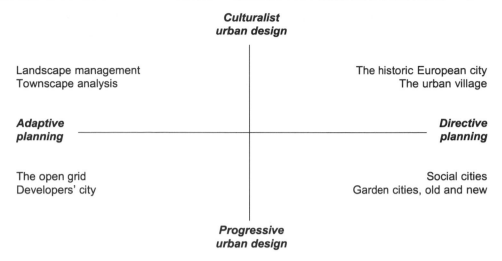

Fig 3.4 The conceptual structure of urban design.

different types of residential layouts and different visual impressions that exist alongside one another, without any direct or immediate sense of connection. It is a city of ethnic pluralism. It is also a city that mixes, in adjacent areas, for example, Georgian calm, Victorian exuberance, busy streets and quiet backwaters. The adaptive model does not seek to change the basic characteristics of the post-modern city. It works with the grain of existing trends to secure social and economic aims.

This emphasis on adaptation encourages, in many cases, a conservative approach to town planning. The adaptive model encourages a devotion to individual choice and economic growth within a loose planning framework. It either uses the grid as a means of generating urban structure or it completely abandons such a concept.

In Britain, the master plan for Milton Keynes, designated in 1967, provides an example. Its aims are summarised as 'Opportunity and freedom of choice', 'Easy movement and access, and good communication', 'Balance and variety', 'An attractive city', 'Public awareness and participation', 'Efficient and imaginative use of resources' (Llewelyn-Davies *et al.*, 1970, p. 13). Urban structure is dictated by the requirements of traffic management and takes the form of an open matrix of car routes. Traffic congestion is reduced through the diffusion of community facilities and employment. Housing is located within the grid to which it is attached by estate roads.

However, Milton Keynes does not provide a pure example of the adaptive/progressive model. The landscape is subject to more intensive shrub and tree planting than would be usual for a private developer.

Moreover, housing development in Milton Keynes has remained subject to detailed controls. A typical housing site brief has usually required a mix of social housing and owner-occupied housing with, amongst the latter, a mixture of different prices. It has also usually included requirements about the choice of materials and colours. The aim has been to ensure a degree of consistency in the visual appearance. A typical design brief has specified a combination of brick walls and tiled roofs, with a preference for dark and unobtrusive colours (light brown, dark brown, dark red) for the woodwork. (See Milton Keynes Development Corporation, 1992, Appendix G, pp. 241–243.)

The adaptive/progressive model is concerned with estate development and the promotion of maximum land values. The model leads to a city characterised by an emphasis on property, products and marketing. Developers strive for the highest densities and the highest building at the centre, where land values are the highest. They accept lower densities on the urban periphery in an attempt to satisfy consumer demands for spaciousness around the home. They identify different sites for each type of land use, such as industry, commercial and housing, and in doing this promote their continued separation into different zones (see Fig. 3.5).

Fig. 3.5 Views of the adaptive/progressive model (adapted from Milton Keynes Development Corporation, 1992).

The London Docklands provides a more radical example than Milton Keynes. It is also more conservative and more market-oriented. The London Docklands Development Corporation, established in 1981, rejected the notion of a master plan such as that used by the Milton Keynes Development Corporation. Design objectives and policies were limited and mostly concerned the protection of notable features, such as the docks and historic churches, within an urban area that had been damaged by industrial decline. Otherwise the aim was to promote private development as quickly as possible and to raise land values to the highest possible (Edwards, 1992).

The result is a disjointed urban landscape that appears to have arisen more by accident than by design. This landscape comprises a loose mixture of existing and new residential areas and estates of contrasting forms and social composition, each separated by water, open space or wasteland. The only focal point comprises distant views of the towers at Canary Wharf or in the City.

Each estate is characterised by different surface materials (concrete, brick or white rendering), by a different height (high rise and low rise), by a different tenure (private, local authority and housing association) and by a different income group. Each estate forms a different territory, occupied by a different social group. There is nothing to stop a pedestrian walking from one estate to another. However, there is little reason why a pedestrian should do so. There is, in any case, no integrated footpath network that might facilitate pedestrian movement.

The adaptive/progressive model is not necessarily conservative. The plan for Milton Keynes had social aims, for example the promotion of participation. It also involved the use of social housing agencies. The plan for Milton Keynes is unusual because it deals with a new town. However, it is also possible to devise adaptive/progressive models that attempt to improve living conditions within urban areas.

The proposal of Le Dantec (1991) provides an example. Le Dantec advocates a revised 'baroque' approach to the design and reconstruction of French cities. Baroque urban design, more than any other historical approach, accepts the existence of multiple points and centres in a city. It is, therefore, not simply an aesthetic but 'an ethic based on the recognition of otherness', an ethic that seeks to express social and cultural differences and diversity. This is, of course, very close to progressive interpretations of post-modernity (see Huyssen, 1984).

Le Dantec explains how a baroque approach to urban design might be undertaken. A grid, say of one kilometre squares, is laid across a map of the urban area. However, the aim is not to standardise urban space and not to create a dispersed American city. Instead, the aim is to bring out the distinctive qualities of each neighbourhood. Sometimes a medical analogy is used to describe such a decentralised approach to urban renewal and planning. The improvements act on specific points in a form of 'urban acupuncture', where selective intervention can ease problems in the broader urban fabric (see Ascher, 1995, pp. 236–237).

The adaptive/progressive model has the advantage of flexibility. Within a grid of main roads or in the London Docklands within an existing urban landscape, the detailed design of streets and houses can take almost any form that meets consumer preferences. The model facilitates innovation in design and requires little or no regulation. The adaptive/progressive model also provides a rich visual experience and a diversity of different types of environment. It allows individuals to create their own sense of coherence through choosing where they live (Werner, 1991, pp. 459–466). The adaptive/progressive model provides, in other words, a framework in which other types of design may co-exist in local improvement, redevelopment and new housing schemes.

The main qualification is that residents actually possess the ability to move around the city and to choose where they live. A criticism of places like Milton Keynes and the London Docklands is that they comprise islands of development within a framework that is better suited to cars than people and that, except in the highest density schemes, they make little allowance for public transport. In the case of the London Docklands, Edwards (1992, pp. 48–49) also criticises the lack of a coherent framework for greenery and landscaping. The so-called baroque approach of Le Dantec provides a means of linking different areas together in a programme of social development, but requires substantial public funding.

Adaptive/culturalist model

This model uses the context of a scheme to generate a layout. It is advocated by those urban geographers, such as Whitehand *et al.* (1992) who advocate a greater emphasis on landscape management in town planning. In urban geography, the centre of attention is the plan form of the urban landscape. This comprises three elements: the forms and patterns of the houses, the size of the plot and the street pattern (Conzen, 1968, p. 117). In architecture, more attention is paid to the facade of the building.

The adaptive/culturalist approach is also advocated by those designers who wish to create a 'street picture'. Cullen's *The Concise Townscape* (1961) is the best example. For Cullen the experience of living and working in towns and cities comprises a series of visual impressions that are influenced by three main factors. These are 'serial vision' which is the unfolding of the townscape as one moves through; 'place' which is the sense of being either inside or outside a clearly defined area; and 'content' which is the material fabric of towns as represented by their colour, texture, scale, style, character, and so on. In principle, these three factors could be used to define the identity of new types of progressive development. In practice, however, Cullen used these categories to analyse the identity of traditional English towns and cities and to defend them from unsympathetic modern development. Townscape analysis, like other culturalist solutions, emphasises enclosure as an aspect of both serial vision and place. In contrast, progressive solutions emphasise spaciousness.

The EDG is an example of the adaptive culturalist model, intended to integrate new housing into the traditional English landscape. Another example is a guide to housing layout prepared by the former Greater London Council (1978). This explains how 'new buildings can maintain the continuity, scale, proportion and harmony of adjacent buildings'. It also explains how new buildings can be combined with existing ones to define urban spaces. The conformity between old and new buildings is mostly about scale relations, massing and layout. It is not generally possible to ensure an exact correspondence, without much care and additional expense.

Both the EDG and the Greater London Council study present similar guidelines relating to the scale and proportion of external spaces. Both recommend between about 1:1 and 1:2.5 for a street and about 1:4 for a square as the appropriate ratio between the height of the houses (to the level of the eaves) and the width across the space (Fig. 3.6). In contrast, for conventional suburban layouts, with a spacing standard of 21 m, the ratio in a typical road is 1:4. For the advocates of enclosure, the conventional suburban road is too open (Colquhoun and Fauset, 1991, p. 241).

Ensuring enclosure

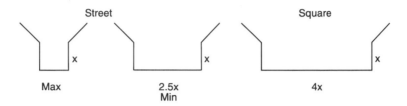

Maintaining consistency in elevations

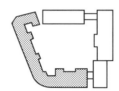

Fig. 3.6 The logic of adaptive/culturalist planning (GLC, 1978).

The adaptive/culturalist model provides a series of guidelines for infill development in or near historic areas. This is its main strength. Its main weakness is to ignore the views of consumers. In emphasising the importance of the street picture, the model takes the standpoint of a tourist rather than a resident. In addition, the model has only limited aims. It is about securing minor changes in the form and character of proposals. It does little to improve an area with serious environmental problems, for example from high traffic levels.

Directive/culturalist model

This model attempts to create a strong visual image that recalls the historic European cities of the past. The image can be created either by a separating barrier or by the adoption of an 'inner organisational principle' (Mulder and van de Meijden, 1991). In Britain, however, the organisational principle predominates. The principle itself is the creation of an 'urban village'.

The key aspects of the urban village, as documented in the Summer 1995 *Newsletter* of the 'Urban Villages Forum' are the advocacy of:

❑ mixed use development;
❑ the provision of affordable property for housing and commercial uses, of a range of costs, types, tenures, and sizes;

❏ human-scaled development;
❏ a high quality of architecture and urban design;
❏ effective civic management;
❏ sustainability, including economic sustainability.

In an urban village, all proposals would be subject to strict regulation. An appendix to another publication, *Urban Villages*, states that separate 'urban codes' would cover infrastructure, urban form, architecture and public space and that these codes would be linked to an environmental action plan (Aldous, 1992, pp. 82–91). The proposed urban form code has 21 articles, including the following:

'(1) In its physical form, the urban village needs to be both simple and subtle; it must be comprehensible wherever you stand, but at the same time have variety and elements of surprise'
'(2) On plan, its form should ideally be rounded and the maximum distance across a walkable 900 metres.'
'(4) Site features should be emphasised and reinforced....'
'(8) Street bocks should decrease in size towards the centre and grow larger towards the perimeter. This ensures a denser but more permeable pattern around the central square.'
'(10) Public open spaces should be planned as a whole – buildings and central space together; should have a strong sense of enclosure and carefully chosen points of focus....'

One version of the urban village, that of Greenville, prepared by Reid and Lyons, resembles the Georgian streets of Bath or Edinburgh (Fig. 3.7). Another version, that of Poundbury, by Leon Krier, has been described as 'an image of baroque interventions into a medieval fabric; (Breheny *et al.*, 1993, p. 128; see also Fig. 3.8).

Both Greenville and Poundbury possess a combination of visual axes, comprising wide streets and boulevards, and focal places comprising squares and monuments. Both possess a high proportion of flats and terraces in their housing stock. The skyline is dominated by churches and public buildings, such as law courts or the town hall, rather than by commercial buildings.

Fig. 3.7 A view of the directive/culturalist model: streets within Greenville (Aldous, 1992).

Fig. 3.8 Examples of schemes consistent with the culturalist model.

The urban village has the advantage of assuming that people and not motor traffic are the most important consideration in town planning. It seeks to humanise the city and to reclaim the streets for pedestrians. It provides a way of building instant nostalgia, an instant conservation area. The urban village also provides a rationale for organising higher density housing of a type that developers increasingly have to build anyway for economic reasons.

The urban village remains vulnerable to the usual culturalist problem of ignoring consumer preferences. The design guidelines are so prescriptive that they are likely to preclude effective consultation with residents. The relatively high density and mixed uses also pose problems in relation to car parking. The urban form code proposes underground car parks but these are expensive to develop and manage.

In addition, the use of traditional, non-standard building materials and non-standard house types is likely to raise development costs in a way that may undermine the commitment to affordable housing. For example, in 1994, the lowest house prices in Poundbury were about £95 000. Poundbury, in common with other urban village schemes, will contain a proportion of social housing and will probably, for this reason, house people who cannot afford or are ineligible to buy a home. However, if high house prices continue, it is unlikely that Poundbury will appeal to lower income owner-occupiers (Turkington, 1994).

The insistence on mixed uses requires clarification. It is possible to argue in favour of mixed uses as a corrective to the usual pattern of land use zoning, as this has emerged in the twentieth century. Town and city centres, in Britain for example, possess fewer mixed use schemes and a lower resident population than the centre of most cities on the European continent. There is a scope for more housing and more mixed use development in town and city centres. However, it is unlikely that mixed uses will ever predominate. Single use schemes are almost certainly inevitable owing to the continued specialisation of economic life and the varied requirements of different types of users. In any case, the meaning of mixed uses is unclear. What uses are to be placed adjacent to other uses? What scale of mixed use is proposed?

Directive/progressive model

This model has evolved from the utopian visions of the past. The history of town planning in Britain is dominated by two main progressive utopias – the horizontal and the vertical garden city. The horizontal garden city dates back to the proposals of Ebenezer Howard (1985/1902). The proposal was for the creation of a series of small, socially-mixed new towns each containing about 22 000 people, laid out in parkland and farmland around a central city. In contrast, the vertical garden, as proposed by the modern movement in architecture, was for a series of tower blocks set either in a park or developed after large-scale slum clearance.

The vision of towers in a landscape persists, to an extent, on the European continent. The results of Europan 2, a Europe-wide architectural competition, contain examples of monumental schemes of high-rise flats, mostly intended to give a new image to derelict waterfront sites (Rebois (ed.), 1991, pp. 82–93). Even in continental Europe, however, most high-rise schemes now follow the traditional street layout. The schemes enhance and modify rather than dominate the existing urban landscape. In Britain, the only recent examples of high-rise flats are in London, especially in the London Docklands. Elsewhere, backward-looking, culturalist solutions similar to the urban village predominate in urban renewal.

The juxtaposition of the terms 'garden' and 'city' provides a rich imagery which has surely not lost its popular appeal. Ward (1992, p. 204) writes:

> 'No-one could seriously claim that Howard's blueprint is still valid in its entirety, but the essence of his proposals retains an enduring lure. Settlements of a manageable size with a sense of identity, the provision of a good living and working environment, a way of dealing with escalating land values.'

In some ways the potential for the garden city is now greater than ever. The initial proposal relied on a non-profit making, voluntary organisation for its implementation. The desire of governments in the 1980s and 1990s to find additional sources of investment favours such an approach.

The garden city has often been criticised for its association with suburbia. The development of Hampstead Garden Suburb, started in 1904 as an example of low density housing and the publication in 1912 of Unwin's *Nothing Gained from Overcrowding!* with its advocacy of a maximum of 12 dwellings to the acre were strong influences on suburban growth in the first half of the century. Suburbia adopts the same horizontal form as the garden city, without of course separating new development from large urban centres. However, the association with suburbia is as much a source of strength as of weakness. Hampstead Garden Suburb remains an attractive place to live, though it is not a socially-balanced community.

The garden city has been taken up by some of the advocates of sustainable development. A density of 12 dwellings to the acre may provide a compromise between the needs of accessibility to local services (a need favouring higher densities) and the minimum necessary for the use of solar energy, recycling and water collection, small-scale sewage treatment and domestic food production (Vale and Vale, 1995, pp. 16–18). However, this is unusual. Most advocates of sustainable development seek higher densities on the grounds that this facilitates public transport and reduces the consumption of greenfield sites.

The American planning literature reveals other interpretations that are less constrained by the burden of history. Calthorpe (1993) has argued in favour of 'transit-oriented development' where housing schemes are arranged around a public transport station, with commercial uses at the core. The aim is to facilitate pedestrian access to urban facilities. Streets are intended to be 'comfortable, interesting and safe to walk along' and which also ensure their safe use for cycling. This rejection of the motor car is a shared feature of most directive models, whether progressive or culturalist. In addition, in contrast to the uniformly low density of the traditional garden city, transit-oriented development provides a gradation of densities and dwelling types, from low-rise flats at the centre to lower densities on the edge.

Detached family houses continue to generate market demand in transit-oriented development. Equally a growth in single person households ensures that small terraces and flats are gaining an increasing proportion of the market share. The minimum density in any residential area is 15 dwellings to the acre.

In addition, Cooper Marcus and Sarkissian (1986) have argued in favour of medium density, to be more precise, low rise/high density or 'clustered housing'. This provides a compact alternative to the typically dispersed American suburb. At the same time, it applies the lessons of numerous consumer surveys that an overwhelming preference exists in the English speaking world for the typical visual and environmental features of a suburban estate. Cooper Marcus and Sarkissian recognise that, in building for the future, planners and designers should reflect consumer wishes, including the wishes of low income households. The design of the home, Cooper Marcus and Sarkissian suggest, should be capable of 'personalisation'. The occupants should, in other words, live in a home of which they should be proud and which also should express their social and personal identity.

In the inner city, clustered housing allows 'people to enjoy a green and quiet environment within easy access to city jobs'. On the city fringes, clustered housing would, 'if repeated often enough increase overall densities and render public transport more economic'. In addition, clustered housing offers the advantages of high-rise flats (privacy, efficient domestic maintenance, the possibility of communal facilities) without their disadvantages (distance from ground, feelings of anonymity). High density/low rise, as conceived by Cooper Marcus and Sarkissian (1986) would be limited to three, or occasionally four storeys.

High density/low rise or 'clustered' housing raises difficult questions about the density limits of low-rise housing. High density/low rise is not easy to design. The concept also raises difficult questions about whether planning authorities should impose minimum density policies in a development plan or other planning document.

In addition, as the authors are aware, the proposal for high density/low rise provides only a selective vision of the future. It is a vision intended for lower income family households, especially single parent households and those households who have no access to a car. The relevance is, in fact, slightly broader than this. High density/low rise may readily be adapted to the design of flats for elderly people. Nevertheless, some households may prefer something different. Younger adult households may prefer a more urban environment. Moderate and upper income families with access to a car may continue to prefer a more suburban life style (Goodchild, 1984).

The different preferences of different age groups reveals a further point. The directive/progressive models of the early part of the twentieth century sought a uniform model for the whole city. The model itself was capable of presentation as a complete ideal city.

In contrast, progressive planning in the late twentieth century generally promotes diverse solutions for different client groups in different situations. The headings of an OECD report *Women in the City* (1995) provide an illustration. The headings include 'Recognising social diversity in the development of cities', 'Planning with a gender perspective', 'Creating liveable environments' and 'Urban services responsive to diverse needs'. This emphasis on diversity means, in turn, the directive/progressive model is no longer capable of a single visual representation.

A mix of house types, housing densities and ownership patterns is the typical characteristic. The local mix will determine the character of each neighbourhood. In suburban extension schemes, the progressive/directive model implies a range of house types capable of appealing to people with different life styles. The overall density of suburban areas would, almost certainly, be significantly higher than the 12 to the acre suggested by the garden city movement before 1914. However, it is not possible to suggest an optimal or maximum density. In the central city and inner city, the directive/progressive model implies a combination of mostly low-rise blocks organised around the existing street layout (See Fig. 3.9).

Fig. 3.9   Residential house types within the progressive/directive model.

CONCLUSIONS

Discussion of the built environment in housing, even if limited to its implications for systems of public regulation, involves an enormously wide range of subjects – about the minimum standards of old and new housing; about public health and aesthetics, about the development process in housing in the public and private sectors, and about the strengths and weaknesses of town planning.

The main points may be summarised.

❑ Standards of fitness and overcrowding invariably lag behind general standards of social acceptability. They focus on basic levels of provision and emphasise the importance of public health as the main consideration in their interpretation. They have to do this owing to financial constraints and the need to minimise objections from those living in poor quality housing. The fitness standard, specified in the Local Government and Housing Act 1989, differs from its predecessors mostly on points of detail.

❏ Problems of fitness and overcrowding have gradually eased over many years from the nineteenth century onwards. However, there are no grounds for complacency. Problems still persist.

❏ The pattern of poor health in British cities is no longer always related to the physical characteristics of the building stock. Surveys of health conditions show that, with a few exceptions, the worst health problems are concentrated in local authority estates and in other areas with a concentration of low income households. This pattern supports the case for a broad view of social policy, one concerned with a combination of housing and other measures to protect and enhance the incomes and living standards of poor people.

❏ In private housing, the process of development is determined by market considerations. Standards of development vary greatly by price and market sector. In social housing, the process of development is determined by the availability of public finance and the rules laid down by the funding and supervisory agencies. Standards in social housing are generally more homogeneous. The minimum standard is closer to the average. In addition, social housing agencies tend to be more concerned with the reduction of long-term maintenance costs. Social housing agencies, unlike private developers, retain ownership after completion.

❏ The emergence of design and build procurement has advantages in reducing the risks of cost overruns for social housing agencies. The main issue in design and build is the degree of detailed control exercised by the housing agencies. House builders, together with some independent building experts, suggest that detailed control, as currently practised by housing associations, inhibits innovation and leads to inefficiencies. A possible way forward is for housing associations to simplify their statement of requirements, whilst using the HAPM or possibly another insurance company to undertake quality control in matters relating to the long-term durability of the scheme.

❏ Full achievement of disabled persons' access is impractical, without a general increase in the size of low cost housing in both the social housing and private sectors. The achievement of visitable standards for the entrance is relatively simple, except for dwellings on sloping sites. Modification of passageways and internal doors to allow negotiation by a wheelchair is also feasible without major modifications. In contrast, the provision of a downstairs WC is a major change for lower priced housing and for housing association housing, especially if the design of the WC is to conform with the requirements of disabled persons' access. The most likely outcome of present debates about disabled persons' access will be a merging of design criteria for disabled persons and those for the general population. The specification of minimum standards for disabled persons' access will provide a general specification of minimum floorspace standards.

❏ A case exists for local planning authorities to prepare more extensive design guidance covering such matters as the scale, density, height, layout, landscape, massing and means of access. The potential of design guides must always be qualified, however, by an awareness:

  o of the resource and staffing constraints on local planning authorities;
  o that piecemeal design controls do little to improve on an area with serious environment problems, such as those linked to traffic or poor standards of street maintenance.

❏ Urban design practice may be classified in relation to whether it is forward looking (progressive) or backward looking (culturalist). It may also be classified by its assumed degree of control over the process of urban development. Each of these distinctions generates a different model of urban design. Culturalist models are especially influential in the 1990s. However, no model is inherently superior to any other. The question is to fuse tradition and modern technology, individual choice and social purpose, giving a different balance in different situations.

Many of the ambiguous and dilemmas in public regulation concern the distinction between standards and quality. Public authorities can specify standards, but they cannot readily ensure the achievement of high quality. This is the responsibility of the developer and raises different questions according to whether the dwelling is built by a private developer or a housing association. For private housing developers, the main priority is to avoid an over-reliance on marketing techniques. Quality in housing includes convenience and flexibility in use, as well as 'kerb appeal'. For housing associations, the main priorities are that a house should be attractive, and that it should provide a home of which the occupants can be proud.

Chapter 4
The renewal of private housing

The achievement of good housing standards means, above, all, the achievement of high standards in the existing stock. Policies to maintain and improve the quality of the existing stock have the potential to cover many more dwellings than policies to promote standards in new housing. If all the relevant policies are counted, for example slum clearance, provision of improvement grants, the renewal of local authority estates, policies for the existing stock are also more important in terms of public expenditure.

Policies to maintain and improve the quality of the existing stock are a means of ensuring that low-income households can live in satisfactory housing. They are also a precondition for the effective management of urban growth. The decay of the existing stock causes people to look elsewhere for their accommodation and so leads to an increasing number of empty properties. This in turn reduces the housing capacity of urban areas. The link between poor housing quality and empty property is documented in successive editions of the English House Condition Survey. The report of the 1991 survey shows, for example, regardless of tenure, that vacant dwellings are more likely to be unfit and more likely to be in poor condition (DoE, 1993, p. 66).

A SUMMARY OF THE HISTORICAL BACKGROUND

How might policies for the existing stock best be pursued?

If the question were asked before 1970 and certainly before 1960, there would have been only one answer – clearance and redevelopment of the older privately owned housing stock. From the 1930s to the early 1970s, the assumptions and working practices of urban renewal and of urban planning are best summarised through the concept of 'cleansweep' planning, as defined by Ravetz (1980). In cleansweep planning, public sector agencies, most notably the local authorities, attempt to create a new urban environment that is totally different from that of the past.

In contrast, subsequent policy from the 1970s onwards is best characterised by another phrase coined by Ravetz, that of 'living with the contradictions'. In this, an acceptance of the wishes of local residents, combined with a greater awareness of the limits of public intervention, leads to a withdrawal of the public sector from large-scale redevelopment. To use the language of urban design, renewal policy has moved from a directive/progressive to a more flexible and more post-modern adaptive/culturalist mode of intervention.

The scale of cleansweep planning may be clarified. Even in its heyday, in the 1930s and again in the 1950s, financial constraints restricted the scope of clearance to the worst unfit dwellings. Indeed, for some critics, cleansweep planning did not go far enough. For example, Bowley (1945, pp. 187–204) argued that housing policy in the inter-war years was preoccupied by narrow 'sanitary' issues. Bowley argued, instead, in favour of 'a general replacement policy' in housing, based on a political guarantee that 'no one shall live below the modern standard'. Nevertheless, even the 'sanitary policy' led to widespread demolition. Between 1933 and 1939 the implementation of a sanitary policy in England and Wales led to the replacement of about 500 000 houses and the provision of a further 300 000 houses in order to combat overcrowding. Moreover, most official statements and most housing experts regarded improvement of the older stock, or 'slum reconditioning' (the derogatory name for improvement before 1939), as a short-term expedient intended to postpone clearance to a later date. (For an account of early improvement policies, see Moore, 1980.)

The largest clearance programmes in Britain, pursued in the most populated cities such as Birmingham, Liverpool and Glasgow, were probably the most extensive ever attempted in Western Europe. In other countries, for example in France, the Netherlands and Sweden, the cleansweep style of planning was generally confined to the development of new towns and suburban extensions. Otherwise, the basic shift in policy is typical of that in other nearby countries in Europe, such as France, the Netherlands and Germany (Lacaze, 1989; Priemus and Metselaar, 1992, p. 11). In these countries, after the mid 1970s, housing renewal and housing policy have also become more concerned with the improvement of the existing stock.

SLUM CLEARANCE

The shift from clearance to improvement started in the late 1960s. The Housing Act 1969 assumed that the problem of unfitness was too extensive to be tackled by clearance alone and that clearance and improvement would have to proceed together. The Housing Act 1974, in contrast, assumed that improvement offered an alternative to clearance. Thereafter, the clearance rate declined rapidly and has not subsequently recovered (Table 4.1). Where clearance is still undertaken, it is concentrated in the cities of the Midlands and the North of England (Mackintosh and Leather, 1993, p. 41).

The question is whether the reaction against clearance has gone too far. Should local authorities be encouraged to undertake an increased rate of clearance? Should additional public funds be made available for this purpose, if necessary at the expense of grant-aided improvement?

Table 4.1 Dwellings demolished or closed in England.

Year	1971	1980/81	1989/90	1990/91
Number of dwellings	72 050	27 153	5913	3352

Notes: From 1980/81 onwards, slum clearance statistics have been collected on a financial year basis. The figures exclude demolition undertaken outside the slum clearance legislation.
Source: The Housing and Construction Statistics.

The experience of clearance in the 1980s

The answer depends partly on local conditions. Some local authorities would argue that they face a backlog of properties in very poor condition (see Case Study 4.1). In addition and probably more importantly, the answer depends on the procedures that on the legal and administrative framework. Local authorities should not expand clearance using existing procedures. Clearance is a slow process that causes much disruption and uncertainty for those affected. In the period before implementation, clearance proposals cause a withdrawal of virtually all investment and effort in building maintenance, street cleaning and similar activities. As properties become vacant, clearance also encourages vandalism, including fire raising. In the longer term, once the residents are rehoused, clearance may lead to better housing conditions. However, for many if not most of those who move, the disruption is not worth the benefits.

The disruption of clearance is a theme of accounts of the mass programmes undertaken in the early 1970s (Gee, 1974). It is also a theme of accounts of the much smaller clearance schemes of the 1980s. Blackaby (1986) reports the results of a survey of a clearance scheme in Birmingham and writes that, among the respondents,

'a clear majority on reflection and having experienced the move and their new home and area would have preferred not to have undergone the process...
'there were many complaints about the way the council had handled the actual rehousing process – clients said they had to wait too long in their old home before being moved, they didn't have enough information about what was happening, and they felt that furniture and belongings had not been removed properly by the council contractors – but far more bad feeling was created by compensation.'

Likewise, information collected by the Birmingham Community Forum, a federation of residents' groups, led Heywood (1992, pp. 14–15) to state that,

'... despite only a small clearance programme, generous priority rehousing to clearance cases and good intentions from some council officers, clearance was still contributing to stress, illness, marital tension and in extreme cases death.'

The complaints about inadequate compensation merit further discussion. Most of the residents in the Birmingham surveys, as in other recent clearance schemes were owner-occupiers before clearance. They were entitled, under the Housing Act 1969 and successive legislation, to compensation for the site value of their property, together with an 'owner-occupier's supplement' that effectively provided for compensation at full market value, plus some additional sums such as home loss payments and disturbance payments. The main condition was that the owner had been an occupier for at least two years before the clearance proposal. However, the level of compensation was still conditioned by the poor quality of the dwellings. Unless the owner could take out a higher mortgage, the level of compensation was inadequate to enable those displaced to buy a decent house elsewhere. Most were forced to become local authority tenants (Heywood and Naz, 1990, p. 105).

In the Birmingham surveys, those who wished to move away and were able to do so were generally happy with the offer they received in compensation. However, most of the residents of the clearance areas were not in this position: they did not want to move. Owner-occupiers at the end of their working life, with no chance of obtaining a mortgage, were the most dissatisfied with their compensation (Heywood and Naz, 1990, p. 103). The use of clearance to provide additional land for commercial and industrial development intensified the sense of dissatisfaction. In these cases, residents felt that their homes had been sacrificed for the sake of big business and their profits.

The rehousing process was also a cause of stress. The residents complained that they were offered properties in areas they did not want and that the properties were often in a poor condition or, in the case of households with children, too small for their needs.

There is a further obstacle to the introduction (or reintroduction) of clearance programmes. Many potential clearance areas are now home to Asian households who have a particularly strong attachment to home ownership, who wish to remain together and who have established grassroots organisations capable of representing their interests. The campaigns of local Asian groups are a theme in the case studies provided by the Birmingham Community Forum (Heywood and Naz, 1990). They have also been documented in a case study of renewal in Leicester (Stoker and Brindley, 1985).

The surveys of clearance in Birmingham tell a depressing story. Accounts of community-based clearance schemes in Liverpool, the schemes that led to the creation of co-operatives at Weller Street and elsewhere are more encouraging. These schemes have been praised for the high degree of control exercised by residents, for the diversity of the internal and external layout and for the high quality of the completed schemes (see McDonald, 1986; Sim, 1993, pp. 161–164). However, the Liverpool co-operatives are not a typical example of clearance. The cleared houses mostly comprised rented, rather than owner-occupied property. Moreover, the co-operatives received additional financial support from the Department of the Environment to cover the additional costs of higher standards in the replacement schemes.

The reform of the rules for compensation

If clearance is to be encouraged, the legal and administrative procedures will have to be reformed. The terms of compensation are now more favourable than previously. The Local Government and Housing Act 1989 has made market value the relevant criterion for all compulsory purchase and abolished the previous rule that landlords were only entitled to site value. Also, the Planning and Compensation Act 1991 has abandoned the previous maximum of £1000 for home loss payments payable as a result of compulsory purchase. In addition to receiving market value for the purchase of their homes, owner-occupiers (but not tenants) are entitled to a home loss payment calculated at a rate of 10% of the market value of the property up to a maximum of £15 000.

The terms of compensation for the residents of clearance areas still pose problems, however. The abolition of the site value rule is not relevant to the owner-occupiers who comprise the majority of residents in clearance areas. The increase in home loss payments is mostly relevant to middle class owner-occupiers who face compulsory purchase for road building and other public works schemes. It is very unlikely that home owners in a proposed slum clearance will own a house that is worth £150 000 and will gain any sum that either comes close to the £15 000 (i.e. 10% of £150 000) maximum or allows the purchase of a good quality house elsewhere.

In any case, the philosophy of the Planning and Compensation Act is open to dispute. It is not clear why compensation for home loss should be tied to market value of a property. Surely the concept of home loss implies that compensation is worked out either on a flat-rate basis or possibly in a way that is related to length of residence.

The priority is to find some way of increasing the owners' limited purchasing power. Grant aid for the developer, for example the old City grant available under the Inner City policy, fails to provide a full answer. Grant aid to the developer merely provides a means of encouraging private developers to build on economically marginal sites. It is not intended to lead to a substantial reduction in house prices. The need is for grant aid payable to the occupier or mortgage lender.

Another possibility is shared ownership with a housing association. Shared ownership schemes are subsidised through Housing Association grants in a similar way, though not to the same extent as Housing Association build for rent. However, the occupiers pay a mixture of rent and mortgage repayment and have the right to buy out the housing association if they are able and willing to do so. Shared ownership may not, of course, be as attractive as full home-ownership. It may require explanation and 'selling' to local residents. However, this is probably not an insuperable problem.

More significant is a lack of measures to co-ordinate building for shared ownership with the requirements of slum clearance. Administrative criteria have made it difficult to use publicly funded shared ownership schemes to rehouse people from slum clearance. The cost limits have favoured one and two bedroom dwellings rather than the family dwellings which are necessary to rehouse households from many clearance areas, notably those with a predominantly Asian population (Morris, 1992, p. 139). Moreover, housing associations are generally obliged to offer the property to a first time buyer.

A few local authorities have attempted to use what they initially called a 'rebuilding grant'. In 1986, for example, Rochdale District Council used the so-called 'conversion clauses' of the Housing Act 1985 to undertake the replacement, on the same site, of 14 dilapidated, unfit terraced houses by the same number of new homes, all occupied by the original owners most of whom were elderly (Chadwick, 1988). Likewise, from 1990 onwards, Birmingham Metropolitan District Council proposed various versions of a rebuilding grant, using finance available under the urban programme. Later, the Housing Grants, Construction and Regeneration Act 1996 introduced a discretionary procedure whereby the local authority could make a relocation grant available to owner-occupiers.

The Rochdale and Birmingham experiments encountered difficulty. The Rochdale procedure is of doubtful legality and has not been repeated. The Birmingham initiative was initially rendered impractical by a condition, imposed by the Department of the Environment, that a building society should hold an average 30% stake in the scheme. Morris (1992, p. 142) reports that most building societies showed no interest in participating in slum redevelopment and that even the most sympathetic building society was not prepared to hold an average stake of 30%.

However, a later pilot scheme went ahead in Birmingham in 1992 using a combination of different sources of finance – the conventional home loss payment, an additional means tested grant and a deferred ownership arrangement in which the local authority retained ownership of the site of the property after completion. These different measures enabled the residents to purchase 70% of the value of the house (though not, of course, the land on which the house stands), with the remaining equity held by the housing association in a privately-financed shared ownership initiative (Karn and Lucas, 1995).

The legal and financial arrangements of the Birmingham initiatives are too complex to provide a model for the future. The initiative remains of interest, however. It shows that the level and size of a relocation grant is crucial to whether residents can actually undertake the purchase of a new home. The initiative is also of interest as a test of the extent to which the provision of grant aid is likely to make clearance more acceptable to residents. Karn and Lucas (1995) have compared the views of a small number of people (16 respondents) who received additional grant aid with another group (35 respondents) who experienced conventional clearance. Those who experienced conventional clearance were far more negative in their views of clearance. However, improvement remained the more popular option for owner-occupiers, despite the availability of additional grant aid.

Other reforms

The provision of additional grant aid would ease the burden of rehousing, as more residents would be able to rehouse themselves independently. This, in turn, might reduce the cost of clearance. However, the various studies that were stimulated by the clearance debate of the early 1970s, as well as by the experience of clearance in Birmingham in the 1980s, have identified many other problems.

In part, the components of reform comprise a series of detailed measures intended to meet previous criticisms. For example:

❑ The complaints of local community groups about blight may be met by the specification of small, relatively easily implemented clearance areas. Such complaints may also be met by the specification of a strict timetable for action.

❑ The complaints about the lack of information and consultation may be met by the employment of community workers to represent the interests of local residents; and by the use of local site offices or caravans to provide a contact point with the local authority.

❑ Finally, residents may be persuaded on the long-term benefits through the provision of good quality replacement housing in a desirable location and, possibly, through participation in design. For example, residents are less likely to welcome clearance if they are only offered the possibility of moving to a barely acceptable local authority property built in the 1920s or 1930s.

The problem is whether local authorities can actually implement a reformed clearance programme. There is no guarantee, for example, that local authorities will be able to undertake clearance to a fixed timetable, given financial uncertainties. Likewise, there is no guarantee that local authorities will be able to afford community workers. Finally, given other pressures on the local authority housing stock, there is no guarantee that a local authority will be able to rehouse those displaced in the highest quality housing.

The reform of clearance involves more than the acceptance of a series of detailed measures. It also involves the acceptance of a broader concept of housing quality. The report of the Birmingham Community Forum survey notes that local authorities undertake clearance on the basis of only one criterion, the physical condition of the building fabric, as expressed through the unfitness standard and the degree of disrepair (Heywood and Naz, 1990). In contrast, local residents judge the quality of their housing according to four other factors:

❑ adequate floorspace;
❑ location;
❑ cost;
❑ a sense of personal control.

Building condition may sometimes be so poor that residents accept the need for clearance. In the future, it is possible that a deteriorating housing stock will lead those affected to accept, more willingly, the likelihood of and the need for clearance. However, to meet the wishes of residents, the local authority will also have to accept that residents are rehoused in dwellings that are at least as satisfactory in respect of these other factors.

THE ASSESSMENT OF RENEWAL OPTIONS

The question remains as to whether local authorities should be encouraged to undertake more clearance. The advocates of clearance typically suggest that this is necessary to avoid the ageing of the national housing stock. For example, Perry (1991) of the Institute of Housing has argued that the clearance rate is now so low that 'the average house standing now will have to last thousands of years'.

So what? It is not realistic to make policy decisions on the basis of the consequences over a time span of five hundred or a thousand years or more. In any case, age is, of itself, not a reliable measure of quality. Some of the oldest dwellings in Britain are the most valuable. Houses do not live and die like biological organisms. They have a variable life according to whether it is in the interests of their owner to undertake repairs and modernisation when and where this is needed.

Likewise, any building, in whatever bad condition, can be saved. If necessary, a building in a very dilapidated condition can be completely reconstructed. The crucial test is whether the increased costs of demolition and replacement are justified in any given place and at any given time. How might one conduct such a test? How might one assess the conditions in which the added costs of new housing are justified? There are only three methods:

(1)   the least cost test, as exemplified by Needleman's formula;
(2)   the cost/value test;
(3)   hybrid tests that use a combination of costs and values and, in some versions, provide separate evaluations for different interest groups.

Needleman's formula: the least cost test

The first attempt to lay down assessment guidelines was the economic formula set out by Needleman (1965, p. 201). This may be described in the most simple terms as follows: (Italics have been added to the quote by the author to clarify the text.)

> 'modernisation (*an expression which may be understood as equivalent to either improvement or repair or a combination of improvement and repair*), is worthwhile if the cost of rebuilding' (*meaning the combined cost of demolition and the construction of replacement housing*) 'exceeds the sum of the cost of modernisation, the present value of the cost of rebuilding in λ years' time (*an arbitrary time span that has to be fixed during the analysis*) and the present value of the difference in the annual repairs cost.'

A later formulation included an additional factor, that of quality of the building as measured by an estimate of the increased rent that people would be prepared to pay for a new rather than a modernised dwelling. This additional rent, together with the likely difference in maintenance costs, were treated as deductions from the cost of redevelopment (Needleman, 1969).

Needleman's formula attempts to assess the savings caused by delayed rebuilding. The key variables are:

❑ the relative costs of building and modernisation;
❑ the expected life of the dwelling;
❑ the discount rate, meaning the extent to which the future value of an investment or its future cost is discounted compared to its present value or cost.

The latter concept may be explained in more detail. Discounting is an attempt to measure the value of time. It assumes that, irrespective of inflation, the value of future investments and future benefits is less than an equivalent sum of money made available now. Discount factors are easily calculated once the rate is known. For example, the discount factors for various years at a rate of 5% and a 30 year life are:

End year	1	2	3	4	5	10	20	30
Approximate discount factor	0.95	0.91	0.86	0.82	0.78	0.61	0.38	0.23

This means that an investment of £1 in 30 years' time is worth only 23 pence at its present value.

The preferred option is the one that costs least in the long term. For example, Needleman calculates that, in the case of a modernised dwelling with an expected life of 15 years, the maximum expenditure that can be justified for modernisation is 40% of the cost of redevelopment at a discount rate of 4%; and 60% of the cost of redevelopment at a discount rate of 7%. If the discount rate is 8% and the expected life is 30 years, and this is a more common situation, the maximum expenditure that can be justified on modernisation is 86% of the cost of redevelopment. The higher the discount rate and the longer the expected life of the dwellings, the more attractive is the choice of modernisation.

Needleman's formula was used for many years as a means of justifying compulsory purchase for clearance and was only made obsolete by the publication of new advice in 1990 in the circulars linked to the Housing and Local Government Act 1989. The main difference in comparison with Needleman's previous formulation was in the treatment of housing quality. Whereas Needleman had used an estimate of the rent levels as a measure of quality, local authority practice was to use a subjective assessment.

Publication of Needleman's formula led to an extensive, though ultimately inconclusive, debate within the academic journals. The choice of appropriate discount rates raised particularly difficult issues. Needleman treated the discount rate as equivalent to the interest rate and, as a result, suggested that improvement becomes more economically justified as interest rates rise. Official advice was based on the Treasury discount rate that also varies according to inflation. Appendix B of Circular 65/69 uses the then recommended Treasury discount rate of 8% (MHLG, 1969). In 1973 the Department of the Environment provided further economic advice that used an updated Treasury rate of 10% (cited by Moore, 1980, p. 141).

In contrast, others preferred lower discount rates that favour clearance and redevelopment. For example, Brookes and Hughes (1975) argued that the discount rate should be equivalent to the real rate of interest, excluding inflation and should be calculated as a function of the long-term difference between the rate of inflation and the bank interest rate. When Brookes and Hughes modified Needleman's formula for use in two case studies in Cardiff, they used a rate of 5%. Merrett (1979, p. 298) went further and suggested that, so long as inflation is under control, say in the range of 3% to 5% per annum, a zero discount rate should be used. However, this was and remains an extreme position. The economic orthodoxy is that the use of a zero discount would distort the results.

Inflation in the 1990s is lower than in the previous two decades. In the spring of 1994, the Treasury recommended that the discount rate was 6%. Nevertheless, the old questions remain. Should the evaluation of renewal options be determined by national trends in inflation? Should investment in housing be treated as a social good and be assessed at a relatively low rate of interest?

There are other weaknesses.

❑ There is no simple or fully satisfactory way of assessing variations in quality on completion. Treating quality as an expression of rent levels ignores the way in which rents in the private sector have a scarcity value that is not significantly influenced by quality. In addition, the use of a subjective assessment is likely to lead to arbitrary results.
❑ Though sometimes described as a method of cost/benefit analysis, there is no measure of benefit.
❑ Finally, the cost of land or property acquisition is excluded from the calculation of costs in Needleman's formula. The reason is, in part, one of theory. The cost of land acquisition is a transfer payment between different owners, rather than an economic burden on the community as a whole. However, the omission of land acquisition costs is also a product of specific historic circumstances which have now changed. In the 1960s, unfit dwellings were bought by the local authority at site value only. Subsequent legislative changes now make market price the usual criterion for valuation purposes, irrespective of condition. To say that acquisition costs are zero is no longer realistic.

The cost/value test

By the late 1970s, dissatisfaction with Needleman's formula led to a search for an alternative method of evaluation. In *The Economic Assessment of Housing Renewal Schemes* (1978) the Department of the Environment advised local authorities to calculate the economic merits of a renewal option solely in terms of the difference between the cost of the works (including the cost of borrowing and the costs attributable to a loss of revenues during completion of the work) and the resulting enhancement to market values. This is the cost/value test. It is similar in principle to the discounted cash flow analysis or net present value techniques used by commercial developers. (See, for example, Ratcliffe and Stubbs, 1996, p. 249.)

The key difference with Needleman's formula is that the cost/value test ignores differences in quality and in life expectancy. The assumption is that these could be subsumed within any difference in value. In the words of the report (DoE, 1978, p. 15).

> 'The value set on the dwelling by the market can ... be regarded as an expression in present value form of the stream of advantages and disadvantages which would flow to any prospective occupant over the future life of the building including the discounted residual value of the site at the end of its life.'

The test involves an exercise in discounting during the period of implementation. The usual rate is the commercial bank interest rate. The test avoids long-term discounting exercises.

The implications were worked out in detail through a case study of a typical area of poor, but not unfit, two and three storey privately owned pre-1919 terraces. Five renewal strategies were evaluated:

❏ local authority acquisition and improvement;
❏ private sector improvement;
❏ improvement area declaration, with the provision of grant aid;
❏ redevelopment;
❏ minimum public action.

The latter option provided a base line against which the others were tested.

The preferred option was the minimum public action. In all the other options, costs exceeded benefits. Indeed the more public money spent on the area, the less favourable was the relation between costs and values. Redevelopment was the least preferred option. The higher capital costs of redevelopment was one factor that worked against this option. Other factors were that the lower density of the completed scheme led to reduced future rental income and that the existence of a delay between clearance and completion left a period of time during which the cleared site generated no income.

In comparison to Needleman's formula, the cost/value test has various advantages. It enables the incorporation of a 'do-nothing' option. It enables a better appreciation of the importance of phasing a programme of redevelopment so that revenues are generated quickly before full completion of the scheme. Finally, in including a measure of property values, it enables an assessment of benefits as well as costs. Changes in property values provide an indication of changing public perception. If, for example, prices rise, this may be considered as an indication that the property, and most likely the area in which the property is located, has become more attractive to the community.

The difficulty is that the cost/value test invariably suffers a tendency towards negative results in which the costs of a publicly funded renewal programme exceed the likely enhancement in property values. This is not surprising. The test involves a contradiction between a theoretical reliance on market values and an application of such values to areas and situations where the market has failed. If the market were to provide a satisfactory solution in urban renewal, one might argue, there would be no need for public intervention.

Local authorities have very seldom used the cost/value test to assess renewal options, even though they were given the discretion to do so in 1982. Heywood and Naz (1990, p. 225) quote an unpublished study to the effect that no local authority ever used this method to present a case to a public inquiry for compulsory purchase for slum clearance. In part, local authorities may have avoided the cost/value test on the grounds that it involves more data collection and more calculation than Needleman's formula. More likely, local authorities may have avoided the cost/value test on the grounds that the results are generally even less favourable to clearance than Needleman's formula.

Hybrid tests

The most recent official advice is contained in a circular that the Department of Environment published to guide local authorities in their interpretation of the powers available under the Housing Act 1989 (DoE, 1990). The circular outlines a new procedure of neighbourhood renewal assessment and, in this context, specifies a method of economic evaluation that reworks Needleman and the cost/value test, without superseding them. In addition, unlike previous techniques, the circular recommends the use of a separate socio-environmental evaluation.

The recommended method is often called a net present value (NPV) analysis. However, it is a heavily modified NPV analysis compared to the usual approach in commercial valuations. The recommended method is better understood as a hybrid between the least cost test and the cost/value test. The method has similarities to Needleman's formula in that local authorities assess costs over a 30 year period and base costs for year 30 on a further major decision on the future of the area. The method reinstates 'life' as a consideration and allows a longer term evaluation than is possible under the cost/value test. In doing this, the method reinstates long-term discounting. Equally, the new method has similarities to a cost/value test in that the costs of property acquisition are taken into account. Like the cost/value test, the main indicator of benefit is the enhancement in property values. Quality is not treated as a separate item.

A major advantage of the hybrid method is that it allows the disaggregation of costs and benefits to different interest groups. Karn and Lucas (1995) show how this might be done. They make a separate assessment for the government (local and central combined), for housing associations where relevant and for residents. The benefits of increased property values under this approach are attributed to the owner (for example, the owner-occupier in the case of an improvement scheme, or the housing association in the case of a scheme involving housing association acquisition). The costs of repairs are allocated to whoever is legally responsible. Government costs include the cost of grant aid for improvement or compensation for clearance.

A disaggregated test aims to show who benefits and who loses. Options that are beneficial to the owner, for example, may pass on additional costs to government or to the developer and vice versa. The test shows, for example, that the provision of compensation for compulsory purchase, together with the existence of a subsidised right-to-buy for local authority housing, means that clearance may have financial advantages for residents, despite its high costs to government (see Table 4.2).

Table 4.2   A simplified disaggregated net present value analysis.

Option	Government		Housing Association		Residents		Total	
	NPV	R	NPV	R	NPV	R	NPV	R
Option 1: Individual grant aid with good repair thereafter	600 000	2	n/a	n/a	600 000	3	1 200 000	2
Option 2: Group repair	200 000	1	n/a	n/a	900 000	4	1 100 000	1
Option 3: Clearance, no rehousing, with good repair thereafter	1 500 000	3	n/a	n/a	300 000	2	1 800 000	3
Option 4: Clearance with rebuilding grant	1 700 000	4	70 000	n/a	150 000	1	1 920 000	4

NPV: cost as revealed by an analysis of a modified net present value analysis.
R: rank.
Source: adapted and simplified from Karn and Lucas (1995).

The worked example of Karn and Lucas also shows that, in most schemes, the financial implications for government are generally greater than those for residents or the housing associations. If the costs and benefits are simply added together, the lower costs of improvement continue to predominate.

The outcome of assessments

The technical difficulties of evaluation mostly affect the evaluation of the form and standard of rehabilitation and the procedure used to promote rehabilitation. They do not generally change the choice between clearance and improvement. Whatever technique is used, clearance and redevelopment is generally shown as an option that government should only use as a last resort. The main qualifications are that:

❑ The test follows the economic orthodoxy and uses a discount rate of at least 5%.

❑ The test recognises all the relevant costs, including administrative costs in local and central government, the costs of property acquisition and the loss of income during the period of works.

❑ The test uses the existing definitions of the fitness and subtolerable standards as the main trigger for public intervention. If these revised standards were to include a minimum standard of energy efficiency, the assessment would be more likely to favour redevelopment (DoE, 1996).

❑ Finally, the test applies to an area that is likely to remain in residential use, at about the same density, after redevelopment. If redevelopment results in the displacement of housing by industry or if it results in higher densities with significantly more houses on the same site, the assessment would again be more likely to favour clearance.

A full estimate of the need for clearance can only be made at the local level, after the economic test are applied to concrete cases. Moreover, the social and environmental implications must also be considered. To say that clearance should only be used as a last resort does not preclude the possibility that clearance rates are currently too low. To say that clearance is a last resort does, however, suggest a degree of scepticism about the case for more clearance.

THE IMPLEMENTATION OF LOCAL RENEWAL STRATEGIES

Given the expense and other problems of clearance, improvement is likely to remain the principal means, perhaps the only practical means of renewing the older housing stock. How might this best be achieved? What is the experience of the improvement policies of the recent past?

Gradual renewal and comprehensive improvement

At first, in the early 1970s, the abandonment of comprehensive slum clearance was conceptualised in terms of an alternative policy of 'gradual' or 'cellular' renewal. This was first elaborated by McKie (1971; 1974) and then endorsed by the government in the circulars sent to local authorities to explain the implications of the Housing Act 1974. Comprehensive clearance tackled large areas at one time through a single policy measure and it relied on a single agency, the local authority, for its implementation. Gradual renewal was the precise opposite. It tackled small areas or 'cells' of housing, in some cases as small as an individual dwelling; it proceeded through a mixture of rehabilitation and minor rebuilding; and it attempted to protect the economic and social functions of the older housing stock, notably its function of providing low cost accommodation for lower income groups. Finally, though this is an aspect that was stressed more in the writings of McKie than in the government circulars, gradual renewal promoted private investment. It encouraged local builders to use vacant sites and involved environmental improvements that attempted to lift the status of the neighbourhood within the town.

Gradual renewal was not the only way forward. In 1966, the Denington committee argued that local authorities in England and Wales should adopt a comprehensive approach to renewal. They should review the condition of the housing stock and draw up plans for different types of area action, namely clearance, minimal improvement with the provision of basic sanitary facilities and full improvement to a relatively high '19 point' standard that included, among other things, requirements for a satisfactory environment, a good state of repair and the provision of modern sanitary facilities and adequate heating and lighting (CHAC, 1966, p. 29). In 1981, the Royal Town Planning Institute (RTPI) suggested a similar strategic approach. As a reaction against the slow progress of gradual renewal in the 1970s, the RTPI suggested that local authorities should make a distinction between areas that could be treated through clearance, areas that could be tackled through comprehensive improvement to a basic standard, and areas that were best tackled through comprehensive improvement to a high standard.

The choice between gradual renewal and comprehensive improvement was never fully resolved. Instead, by the end of the 1970s, both concepts started to wither away in the face of financial constraints. By this time, the improvement programme had become too piecemeal and too disjointed to merit the description of either gradual renewal or comprehensive improvement.

The lack of resources applied most obviously as a constraint for comprehensive improvement. The sheer scale of poor quality older housing made proposals for comprehensive improvement largely unrealistic, except for limited areas. The 19 point improvement standard of the Denington Committee was never implemented. The 19 point standard became a simplified '10 point' standard, with no environmental requirements. Like earlier target standards, the 10 point standard became a criterion for individual improvement work and was seldom applied as a universal standard for area-based programmes.

Later, in the 1970s, the high cost of improvement work led to criticisms that an insistence on high standards was discouraging owners from applying for grant aid and was also limiting the number of houses that could be treated through grant aid. To this end, the Housing Act 1980 reduced the required level of repair under the target standard from 'good' to 'reasonable' and enabled local authorities to provide grant aid merely to ensure that the dwelling conforms to the minimum fitness or tolerable standard.

Comprehensive improvement was, in some ways, a throw-back to the type of cleansweep planning that Ravetz (1980) criticised for its lack of sensitivity and realism. Such improvement to a high standard was likely to rely more heavily on the use of mandatory measures and risked, as a result, causing hardship for those on low incomes. In a dissenting report to the Denington committee, Cullingworth argued against the enforcement of high rehabilitation standards for exactly this reason.

In addition, though not said at the time, in relying on mandatory measures, comprehensive improvement to a high standard can provide an obstacle to effective public consultation. For example, Ambrose (1994) reports that, in Denmark, the quality standard for renovation is the same as for new housing and that this has hindered the involvement of young people. Young people have sought cheaper forms of renovation, with shared bathrooms and kitchens.

Gradual renewal was, and remains, more flexible to economic constraints and the demands of different user groups. In practice, however, it also proved demanding in terms of capital investment and local authority staff resources. Thomas (1986, pp. 120–121) comments that by the end of the 1970s,

> 'Despite circular guidance, the type of fine-grained approach ... anticipated by McKie ... had rarely been implemented. The reasons for this seem to have been largely practical. To prepare and continually revise detailed proposals implied a substantial resource input.'

Not only were resources unavailable but, Thomas added, many 'questioned whether such an individualised approach was a feasible response to the scale of housing problems.' The identification of different 'cells' within a residential area was time-consuming. Moreover, the slow pace of renewal work, combined with the usual mixture of small-scale improvement and new housing had the disadvantage of turning some residential areas into perpetual building sites.

Area-based improvement in England and Wales

Gradual renewal and comprehensive improvement originated as a successor to slum clearance. In some places, local authorities implemented the new improvement policies in areas that had previously been subject to clearance orders, even that had been partially cleared. Slum clearance took the form of an area-based programme. Improvement followed suit.

Piecemeal area-based improvement

The Housing Act 1974 provided two main types of improvement area, each covering about 200 dwellings. The General Improvement Area (GIA) continued largely as already established under the Housing Act 1969. It relied exclusively on improvement grants for its implementation; it provided grant aid at 60% of anticipated improvement and repair costs, rather than 50% that was the rule elsewhere and was essentially aimed at areas consisting predominantly of owner-occupiers and containing fundamentally sound houses.

The Housing Action Area (HAA), newly established under the Housing Act 1974, raised grant aid private owners to 75%, or in the case of individual hardship, to 90% of anticipated improvement and repair costs; it also attracted additional finance through subsidies, provided by central government, to housing associations to purchase privately rented dwellings and undertake improvement for rent. The HAA was intended to tackle the poorer areas and it possessed an explicit social objective of securing 'the well-being of existing residents'. It also gave local authorities additional powers of compulsory purchase and compulsory improvement for houses that were in a particularly poor condition.

The inclusion of additional finance for housing associations was the main way in which the Housing Act 1974, introduced by a Labour government, differed from its Conservative predecessor, the Housing Bill 1973, which envisaged a greater role for private landlords. The Labour government had no confidence that private landlords would undertake improvement. However, it did not wish to expand the role of local authorities in inner city areas for fear that this would result in a monopoly in rented housing. Instead, in a major departure from previous practice, the government encouraged the establishment of housing associations.

The Housing Act 1974 specified another type of improvement area, the priority neighbourhood. This was intended for areas that possessed a high proportion of poor quality rented accommodation, but were not yet in the local authority's HAA programme. It gave the local authority additional powers to undertake compulsory purchase and compulsory improvement, but provided no additional grant aid for private owners to undertake improvement work. In practice, very few priority neighbourhoods were declared, almost certainly less than five. Local authorities did not want the additional responsibility of managing such areas, without the financial instruments and resources necessary to secure improvement work. Priority neighbourhoods were abolished in the Housing Act 1980.

The area-based programmes of the 1970s were an innovation and were, for this reason, subject to detailed policy evaluation. Critics argued that improvement was a short-term palliative and could not offer a satisfactory, long-term alternative to the clearance and replacement of older housing. Berry (1974, pp. 206–207) declared, for example that 'the commitment to a rehabilitation policy is a vast exercise in putting off the evil day and not putting it off for very long.' Moreover, the critics argued, grant aid was likely to be misused for property speculation and would encourage middle class households to move into poorer areas. In London, the inner areas had already started to acquire an increasing proportion of middle class households in the 1960s. Glass (1964) coined the term 'gentrification' to describe social change in inner London. The introduction of the first improvement areas in 1969, the critics maintained, sustained and increased gentrification.

The extent of physical improvement in HAAs and GIAs was reviewed in the publications of the 1981 English House Condition Survey. The report of survey shows that the programmes succeeded in stopping a further slide into disrepair and unfitness in the designated areas and they also ensured that more dwellings possessed standard amenities such as hot water and a fixed bath. However, progress was invariably slow. Disrepair remained common. In any case, the limited successes of individual HAAs and GIAs were offset by a failure to designate sufficient numbers of such areas. Less than a quarter of the houses in potential HAAs and GIAs were located in designated areas or in areas that the local authority planned to designate. In these undeclared areas, there had been an increase in poor housing conditions (DoE, 1983a, pp. 24–25).

Though the report does not say so, the main problem was a lack of resources. The compulsory powers available in HAAs were cumbersome and seldom used. Grant-aided improvement was the main method of implementation, supplemented by housing association investment. Spending on the older private sector stock in England in the late 1970s was well below that considered necessary for most of the 1980s (see Table 4.3).

Table 4.3 Expenditure on the renovation and clearance of private housing in England, 1978–1991 (in £ million).

(a)

Year	78–79	79–80	80–81	81–82	82–83	83–84
Annual expenditure	151	192	204	274	507	815
Real value %	31	34	31	38	62	100

(b)

Year	82–83	83–84	84–85	85–86	86–87	87–88	88–89	89–90	90–91
Annual expenditure (changed definition)	573	1064	891	581	519	535	512	521	495
Real value (%)	177	314	259	159	138	136	123	117	100

Notes: Annual expenditure is based on the cash outturns included in successive editions of *The Government's Expenditure Programme*, with real values estimated from the retail price index and expressed as a proportion of the figure for 1983(a) and 1990(b) as appropriate. The retail price index for each year is based on the figure for the month of September, this being the mid-point of the financial year.

The social aspects of the HAA programme were reviewed by Niner and Forrest (1982) through a survey of the residents of six areas five years after designation. The interviews produced some ambiguous results. The improvement to the older stock did not lead to a measurable increase in the satisfaction of residents with their housing. This, Niner and Forrest (p. 120) suggested, was due to higher expectations. 'Better housing may not lead to fewer complaints from occupants, but different complaints.'

Otherwise, the results of the social survey were favourable. The programme successfully met popular demands to avoid clearance and, in addition, secured the long-term future of the dwellings in these areas. Residents continued to believe in the existence of a local community, perhaps surprisingly so given that the survey also revealed a high level of population turnover.

Finally, the HAAs largely avoided gentrification. Population turnover meant that the programme had not and could not achieve the aim of the Housing Act 1974, namely 'to benefit the majority of residents who live in these areas at the time of declaration'. By the time the survey was conducted, over half the original households had moved away. However, the areas continued to provide relatively low cost accommodation to lower income households.

Though Niner and Forrest do not explain the point, the HAAs avoided gentrification partly owing to the intervention of housing associations which provided subsidised rented accommodation in the improved dwellings. In the six areas, housing associations were responsible for the improvement of 37% of all houses. Housing associations were particularly important in London (see, for example, Tickell and Hughes, 1979). Here the pressure for gentrification was and remains intense owing to the growth of professional employment. In other cities in England, another, equally important constraint on gentrification was that the local authorities only designated HAAs in the worst areas that were largely unattractive to middle class households. Indeed the Department of the Environment required local authorities to do this and used statistical indicators largely drawn from the census to ensure the zones were targeted on areas in the greatest need.

The designation of GIAs was subject to less stringent guidelines. However, in practice and contrary to the initial intention at the time of the Housing Act 1974, GIAs were also designated in areas of need. Despite initial fears about gentrification, area-based improvement programmes retained and fulfilled important social objectives throughout the 1970s.

The GIA and HAA programme continued until the Local Government and Housing Act 1989 came into force in 1990. The principle of area-based action persists in the concept of the Renewal Area, established under the latter Act. The main differences is that the Renewal Area is larger, covering at least 300 dwellings, so that it may also include commercial property and that designation must follow an analysis of the renewal options. Otherwise, the Renewal Area is little more than a simplification and name change to the previous HAA and GIA programme. There are no published evaluations of the impact of the Renewal Areas as a national programme. At a local level the impact is varied, with progress in some places being hindered by financial constraints (see case studies 4.1 and 4.2 at the end of this chapter). Housing association acquisition for improvement is now less common than before.

The principle of area-based programmes also persists in other urban regeneration initiatives such as City Challenge and the Single Regeneration Budget. However, since 1980, area-based improvement programmes have become less controversial and subject to less evaluation and research. The view of improvement as a short-term palliative is no longer credible.

Enveloping and group repair

Though the declaration of an HAA provided higher levels of grant aid than elsewhere, improvement was usually slow. In Birmingham, particular difficulties were encountered. By 1977, the local authority realised that the improvement programme was not only lagging behind expectations but was actually failing to establish confidence in the designated areas. Also, substantial financial input in the form of publicity campaigns and environmental improvement had little effect in stimulating anything more than a superficial effort by residents (Brunt, 1982).

Birmingham City Council could have undertaken compulsory purchase for redevelopment or improvement. But compulsory purchase would have reduced the numbers of owner-occupiers in the inner city in a way that would have contradicted the political priorities of the Conservative group then in control of the City Council. It would, in any case, have generated opposition from local residents, many of whom had successfully opposed compulsory purchase for clearance in the early 1970s (Karn and Whittle, 1978).

The solution was for the local authority to repair, free of charge, the external fabric or 'envelope' of the house – hence the name enveloping. The programme started in 1978 and by September 1981 had involved the completion of 1700 dwellings (Mitchell, 1982). It continued to be used in Birmingham's inner city throughout the 1980s, often in areas with a high proportion of Asian households. After 1982 enveloping was also used in HAAs of other local authorities, mainly in the Midlands and the North of England.

However, the programme ceased after the introduction of means testing in the Local Government and Housing Act 1989. Local authorities completed the last schemes in 1991. Thereafter, the closest equivalent to enveloping has been a 'group repair' procedure that involves a cost limit on the grant aid available to each owner.

Enveloping had significant advantages (Thomas, 1986, pp. 125–134). It:

❑ enabled the improvement programme to be concentrated on areas which, most likely, would not have otherwise experienced improvement;
❑ enabled the programme to be securely implemented on a street by street basis;
❑ enabled economies of scale in repairs work and produced a more favourable ratio between administrative costs and work completed;
❑ was cheaper and quicker than either slum clearance or the acquisition and improvement of privately owned dwellings by public sector agencies;
❑ ensured the comprehensive treatment of the fabric of the dwelling (door frames, window frames, chimneys, roofs, rain-water goods and brickwork) and so achieved higher standards of work than is generally possible through voluntary grant take-up;
❑ ensured better visual coherence than the piecemeal efforts of individual owners.

Interviews with residents confirmed the advantages of enveloping. A survey of completed enveloping schemes in Birmingham found that 92% of those interviewed 'thought it was a good idea' and that 77% were either satisfied or very satisfied with the scheme. Moreover, residents of the enveloped areas showed a greater degree of optimism about the future of these areas than the residents of the HAAs interviewed in the earlier survey undertaken by Niner and Forrest (McCarthy and Buckley, 1982). In Sheffield, in the late 1980s, enveloping was similarly welcomed by the residents of inner city neighbourhoods, such as Abbeydale, Darnall and Tinsley, as the only effective means of reversing long-term decline.

Enveloping had limitations as a renewal strategy:

❑ It was not suited to areas where a large number of owners had already used grant aid to undertake selective improvement. In such areas, the specification of works could become complex and time-consuming.

❑ In addition, enveloping did nothing to improve the interior and was, for this reason, unsuited to multi-occupied dwellings (Birmingham Community Forum, 1983).

❑ Finally, like nearly all improvement programmes, success depended crucially on the quality of implementation. Problems of workmanship still arose in some schemes. Moreover, contractors sometimes used people's homes like a builder's yard, so causing much disruption while the work was in progress.

Beyond these limitations, enveloping raised some political objections. It was more expensive to the public purse than voluntary grant aid, for example two or three times more expensive for each dwelling. In addition, enveloping involved no means testing. Even those owners who might have been able to pay for improvement and repairs made no financial contribution.

As a result of all this, central government only allowed local authorities to undertake enveloping programmes under strict conditions. Local authorities could only implement enveloping programmes in HAAs and could only do this after prior approval. The need for prior approval often resulted in delays of six months or more.

In many ways, the full potential of enveloping was never realised. Enveloping has had a visible and permanent impact on the areas in which it was implemented. It proved an effective way of improving the poorest owner-occupied property, whilst enabling the owners to remain in their home.

For central government, the main issue in relation to enveloping was whether it was possible to stimulate the improvement of the worst areas, whilst still asking owners for a financial contribution. The Green Paper *Home Improvement – A new approach* (DoE, 1985, p. 12) which first advocated the abolition of enveloping argued that local authorities had been able to secure contributions from owners and to bundle these in a single contract for groups of dwellings. In fact, the use of 'block repair' or 'block grants', as this previous procedure was called, never worked as well as enveloping and was never used on a large scale. Moore (1992, p. 108) writes of the experience in Sheffield that,

'the need for owners' contribution (of 10% or 25% to the cost of works) reduced the scale of operations. Intensive effort was required to secure a high enough level of participation to make schemes viable and owners tended to constantly renegotiate scheme content and contribution level. Small renovation contracts based on single terraces were the norm.'

In any case, the use of block repair grants as a supplement to enveloping, for example in areas with fewer problems, is quite different to the complete abolition of enveloping.

Though the experience varies from one local authority to another, anecdotal reports suggest that the introduction of a means test in 1990, together with the association reduction in grant aid, has greatly reduced the willingness of households to agree to improvement. The regulations for the use of group repair have proved an additional complication. The regulations discourage their use for flats and state that they should be only used where 'the scheme makes a significant impact on the visual amenity of an area or where there are likely to be useful economies of scale' (DoE, 1996, p. 133). Before the Housing Grants, Construction and Regeneration Act 1996, the requirements were even more stringent and included cost limits that have precluded their use for larger properties. The government justifies detailed control on the grounds that the level of exchequer control is higher for group repair than for other forms of grant aid. Surely it is possible to design a simpler system.

Social and private approaches in Scotland

The rehabilitation of the older stock has taken a distinct form in Scotland. Since the Housing Act (Scotland) 1974, the main policy instrument has been a HAA, as in England and Wales. However, the Scottish HAA is distinctive. It may be used for clearance as well as improvement, though in practice improvement has remained the usual method of treatment. It also permits public acquisition for improvement and rent.

The distinctiveness of renewal policy lies in the marked features of the pre-1919 urban housing stock in Scotland.

❑ First, the predominance of four storey tenements, rather than the two storey terraces usual in England, makes improvement more difficult. The improvement of tenements frequently raises problems of multiple ownership and of joint responsibility for the common elements of the building such as the roof, the structure, the entrance, stairs and the back courts.
❑ Second, in the early 1970s, these problems of multiple ownership were exacerbated by the small size of individual units and by the way in which modern amenities, notably the provision of an internal WC and bathroom, could generally only be achieved through reducing the total number of units in a block and moving the occupants elsewhere.
❑ Third, in the early 1970s, property values were mostly low and there were only limited opportunities for owner-occupation. At this time, the great majority of dwellings were owned by private landlords.

In the cities of the East of Scotland, especially Edinburgh and Aberdeen, the property market was never so depressed as to preclude any improvement by private owners. Local authorities used a combination of common repairs grants and enforcement notices to encourage and require private owners to undertake improvement. In contrast, in Glasgow and the West of Scotland, the local authorities sought to change tenure patterns in favour of social ownership (Robertson and Bailey, 1996). Political differences were also relevant. The Labour-controlled local authorities in Glasgow and other towns in the West of Scotland were more sceptical of the value of private ownership than those elsewhere.

The most ambitious and best documented renewal programme was in Glasgow. At first, improvement proceeded through the compulsory purchase of blocks by Glasgow City Council. The procedures were similar to those used in slum clearance and, like the clearance procedures, they proved unacceptable to the majority of residents. Compulsory purchase orders were contested, public inquiries had to be held and the programme became greatly delayed (see Duncan, 1976; Rogerson, 1979). Later, after the Housing (Scotland) Act 1974, Glasgow City Council handed over the bulk of the improvement programme to a number of small, 'community-based' housing associations, each with a clearly defined territory covering between about 1000 and 2000 dwellings in need of rehabilitation. Previous experiments by a voluntary group, ASSIST, had shown that a combination of a decentralised administrative structure (giving site managers and architects the ability to make important decisions), a commitment to voluntary improvement for most owner-occupiers (no compulsory purchase) and a commitment to local rehousing could succeed in securing rehabilitation at a time when local authority action was delayed by protest action (Armstrong, about 1985).

The impact of housing rehabilitation in Glasgow has been reviewed by Maclennan (1983; 1987). By the time Maclennan undertook his research, the programme of rehabilitation in Glasgow had become the largest in Britain and one of the largest in Europe. About 11 000 dwellings had been rehabilitated by 1983, mostly by 25 community-based housing associations, with the rehabilitation of a further 9000 dwellings planned for the next few years. The programme had achieved much:

❑ The quality of individual dwellings was markedly better, with the removal of previous problems such as leaking roofs and insanitary toilets.
❑ The quality of the surrounding areas was improved as a result of the cleaning and treatment of the stone tenements.
❑ Existing residents had been mostly retained. Gentrification was not widespread.
❑ Property values of unimproved dwellings in the locality had risen and this had, in turn, caused an increase in private investment.
❑ Jobs had been created in the city's construction industry.

The main drawback was one of cost. A combination of the low income of existing residents, the high improvement standards and the poor condition of the tenements meant that the programme had to be heavily subsidised. In 1982 subsidies amounted to 95% of a total cost of about £25 000 per unit, this comprising building costs of about £20 000 and acquisition costs of a further £5000. For this reason alone, the Glasgow model of urban renewal is not capable of wide application.

A general evaluation of Scottish HAAs, including both the social and more privately oriented approaches, has been undertaken by Robertson and Bailey (1996). The evaluation shows residents had a very favourable opinion of the area, irrespective of approach. However, there were important differences between the areas subject to the different approaches. Where social landlords had brought about improvement, there was more social diversity in the completed renewal areas. There was a higher proportion of households with children and of low income households. In contrast, areas that had been improved by private owners had experienced a shift in population towards younger, more affluent households. In Edinburgh, in particular, the improved dwellings came to be inhabited by a relatively uniform population of young people.

The involvement of social landlords had, in other words, prevented or slowed down processes of gentrification, much as had been the experience of improvement areas in London in the 1970s. The involvement of social landlords also had other effects. It strengthened community organisation and facilitated the establishment of preventative repairs programmes for the communal elements of the blocks (notably the roof, stairwell and external fabric). Where community-based housing associations were absent, the maintenance and repair of the communal elements of the block remained a potential problem for the future.

The role of area-based programmes

Concepts of gradual renewal and comprehensive improvement have now largely disappeared from the housing literature. However, their main means of implementation, the improvement area, still persists. What is its current validity and role?

The advantages of area-based programmes may be listed:

❑ Declaration allows the local authority to make a political commitment to residents and property owners.
❑ Area-based programmes provide a means of co-ordinating house improvement with environmental improvement, for example, measures to treat vacant and backland sites, the renewal of pavements, the rearrangement of car-parking and traffic calming.
❑ Area-based programmes provide a means of ensuring that staff resources are concentrated on places with a concentration of poor properties. They allow the local authority to open a local office where residents can go for advice.
❑ Finally, area-based programmes provide an effective way of organising the building work for enveloping or similar 'block-by-block' programmes of housing improvement.

Area-based programmes are also advocated as a means of enhancing local economic regeneration. Broadbent (1993, p. 51), one time Assistant Director of Housing at Bolton, summarises the view from a local government perspective.

'Area based regeneration produces confidence which enables homeowners to buy, sell and improve; it sows the seeds for the developments of community spirit and has strong links to local employment opportunities.'

There is an obvious truth in saying that the housing market, as interpreted by professional valuers and by most house buyers, comprises a patchwork of different areas of varied attractiveness, rather than a mass of individual properties. (For a survey of the search patterns of home buyers, see Canter and Brown, 1978.) There is also an obvious truth in saying that the improvement of one, two or more houses in an area may encourage the owners of neighbouring properties to undertake improvement. The value of a dwelling depends, in part, on the value of adjoining properties. Thus, the outcome of investment in a dwelling is likely to depend, in part, on investment made in other dwellings in the area.

The question is to quantify the scale of such effects. The experience of the HAA programme in the 1970s and early 1980s provides a means of testing the impact on housing investment. The experience is that area-based intervention can sometimes stop private disinvestment. The HAA programme, together with other forms of intervention, may have stopped the abandonment of run-down neighbourhoods in the way that has occurred in the United States (see Andersen, 1995). The declaration of an area-based initiative can at least give an indication to private owners that the area has a future. However, the poor quality of improvement within completed HAAs also suggests that area-based intervention has little effect in encouraging additional investment from private landlords or from low-income owner-occupiers.

The later experience of the Neighbourhood Revitalisation Service (NRS) again suggests that area declaration is only likely to have a small impact in increasing investment amongst owners. The NRS was a privately managed improvement programme that was started by the National Home Improvement Council (NHIC) in four areas in 1984 and later expanded with government support in 1985 to include a total of 25 areas for a fixed experimental period from 1985 to the financial year 1991/92. The NRS was targeted on areas of older housing where, it was believed, a significant number of households had sufficient personal and financial resources to raise a building society loan. These were not the poorest areas. Nevertheless, the results were disappointing. The NRS depended heavily on public grant aid to secure improvement and typically generated a gearing ratio of public to private investment of less than 1:1 (Carley, 1990, pp. 44–45; Mackintosh and Leather, 1992b, p. 212).

Housing rehabilitation in Glasgow provides more encouraging results. Here the rehabilitation of tenements in the late 1970s and early 1980s not only stopped further private disinvestment and possible abandonment. It also paved the way for a transformation in the image of the entire inner city. However, the Glasgow experience is best regarded as an exceptional product of a particularly ambitious and well-financed programme that went beyond housing to include environmental measures, the provision of cultural facilities and commercial property development. In any case, the extent of the economic recovery in Glasgow has been disputed. Robertson and Sim (1991, p. 10) state that the economic base of Glasgow's inner city and, even more so its outer estates, remains weak and that earlier enthusiastic support for housing-led programmes of urban regeneration were misleading. It is not easy to show that housing improvement promotes job creation beyond its short-term impact on the building industry.

There is a hidden dilemma in relation to seeking to promote further private investment. Is the aim to stimulate private investment in a run-down area whilst leaving unchanged its social composition? If so, the effectiveness of any such policy is likely to be constrained by the low income of the owners or, in the case of rented property, the low rents that tenants can afford. Or is the aim to attract private investment through changing the social composition of area, through attempting to push a run-down area 'up-market'. If so, the area-based programme will, by definition, not improve the housing conditions of those most in need.

The critics of area-based programmes point to other limitations. Area-based programmes, the critics argue,

❏ have often resulted in programmes that only help a minority of households living in poor quality accommodation;
❏ can easily lead to the unfair situation in which two households living in identical dwellings, say on the opposite side of a street, find themselves entitled to different levels of financial assistance;
❏ in areas outside the improvement area, discourage private investment while the owners delay work in anticipation of declaration.

For example, Leather and Reid (1989, pp. 53–54) write, on the basis of the experience in Bristol, that the improvement grant programme should generally seek,

> 'to improve conditions for individual households who cannot afford to do so, rather than to protect or enhance the general level of conditions in particular areas.'

The criticisms of area-based programmes are well taken. The improvement of conditions for individual occupiers and their households is usually the main aim of renewal policy. Improvement areas are more of a means to an end, rather than end in their own right. Nevertheless, area-based programmes have a valid role in renewal programmes if poor quality dwellings are concentrated in specific places, if house improvement depends on broader environmental improvement or if, for some other reason, the local housing market has collapsed.

Continuity and change in policy in England and Wales

A Conservative government, like that in power in Britain from 1979–1997, might have been expected to reduce the scale of intervention in the older housing stock as part of broader policies to promote free enterprise and reduce public expenditure. Indeed, some official statements suggest exactly this type of policy. For example, A Green Paper (essentially a discussion paper) *Home Improvement – a new approach* (DoE, 1985) declared that

'the primary responsibility for maintaining and improving private housing rests with the owners.'

At the same time, the government's commitment to the promotion of low cost home ownership meant a continuation of grant aid for those who could not otherwise afford the work. The commitment to reduce public expenditure and the commitment to promote home ownership cancelled each other out and ensured a degree of continuity in policy. In Scotland, the framework of renewal areas established under the Housing Act 1974 remains largely intact. In England and Wales, the government has introduced a series of detailed legislative changes in an effort to make improvement grants more flexible and more targeted on dwellings and people in need.

Policy change in the 1980s

The first Conservative Housing Act, that of 1980, was introduced against the background of complaints amongst practitioners and independent observers about an over-emphasis on area-based programmes. The Act treated the dwelling rather than the area as the main focus of improvement policy and, as part of this, it ensured that grant aid was available on the same terms outside GIAs and HAAs as within them. The Act made repairs grants available on a discretionary basis to all poor quality dwellings and raised the level of grant aid for all priority dwellings to 75% of total improvement and repair costs or 90% in the case of hardship. In addition, the Act

❑ abolished a previous requirement that the grant be repaid if the dwelling is sold within five years;
❑ abolished the Priority Neighbourhood;
❑ introduced a new grant to enable the adaptation of dwellings for disabled people.

The increased level of aid available under the Housing Act 1980 encouraged more households to apply for improvement and repairs grants and enabled the government to promote an improvement grant boom in the financial years 1982–83 and 1983–4. In England, the number of grants given to private owners increased from 68 941 in 1981 to 229 107 in 1984 and then declined to 136 412 in 1985.

The initial aim was to provide a short-term boost to the building industry at a time of recession. However, the programme was subsequently extended in response to the disappointing results of the English House Condition Survey 1981, notably to the way in which this revealed little or no reduction in the numbers of unfit dwellings. Electoral conditions may also have been relevant.

The improvement grant programme was expanded in the run-up to the General Election of 1983 and then reduced.

The 1989 Act and subsequent debates

The Local Government and Housing Act 1989 was the second Conservative Housing Act to deal specifically with the renewal of private housing. The Act sought to focus improvement grants more clearly on households in need and, in the pursuit of this, introduced new means-testing procedures. In addition, it sought a simpler and more flexible regime for administration of improvement grants for different types of property. It widened the rules of eligibility for mandatory grant aid for owner-occupiers to cover all the work necessary to bring a dwelling up to a revised minimum standard of fitness; strengthened local authority powers for provision of grants for disabled persons; and introduced new discretionary grants for small works (under £1000 in 1990, adjusted for inflation thereafter), and for the common parts of flats and multi-occupied dwellings.

The introduction of means-testing was the most controversial aspect of the Act. This stemmed, in part, from the experience of the improvement grant boom of the early 1980s. Internal research undertaken by the Department of the Environment officials in 1983 suggested that 'as many as a third of those eligible for grants ... could in fact afford to finance from their own resources all the work which is needed...' (Smith, 1989, p. 323). In addition, independent observers realised that the only feasible way of making 100% grants available was for these to be means-tested. For example, in 1981, the RTPI argued that 'grant rates should be made more flexible with a basic grant entitlement, together with an extra allowance of up to 100% of costs which *would be dependent on income.*' (Italics have been added by the author for emphasis.) (*Planning*, 15 November 1985).

In the immediate aftermath of the Act, in 1990 and 1991, critical attention mostly focused on the means-testing criteria. Few critics went as far as to advocate the abolition of means-testing. This would almost certainly have led to rationing by the length of the waiting list as happened in the early 1980s or, perhaps by the selective declaration of improvement areas, as occurred in the 1970s. Rather the critics typically made two points:

- ❏ that the means-testing of grants for the provision of facilities for disabled persons should be abandoned on the grounds that it is a necessary part of community care politics and is essential to the health and well-being of occupants;
- ❏ that, in order to respond better to the realities of low-income households, the means-testing criteria for conventional improvement grants, should be made more generous for those on limited incomes.

Later, from about 1992, concern turned to the scale of investment. In the first two years of operation, demand for improvement grants under the 1989 Act was manageable. In contrast, by the financial year 1992/93, demand started to exceed the resources made available. Moreover, because the Act gave owner-occupiers a right to a means-tested grant, local authorities encountered difficulty in deferring applicants from coming forward.

Part of the problem was the absence of an upper limit for grant aid. In April 1993, the government introduced a ceiling of £50 000. After 1994, the ceiling became £20 000 (£24 000 in Wales). £20 000 is, of course, not a large sum to improve properties in the worst condition.

However, pressure on resources continued. Local authorities started to discourage application for grant aid, even in a few cases maintaining an informed waiting list; they required a test of resources before inspecting the property; and they confined grant aid to mandatory grants, with little or no provision for the type of discretionary grant and involved in area based programmes, in the minor works grant for elderly people or in the grants for the common parts of flats and for dwellings in multiple occupation. In the financial year 1992/1993, 90% of expenditure on the renovation of private housing was spent on mandatory grants for unfit houses, a figure that significantly exceeded a target of 70% that the Department of the Environment had anticipated when the new system was first established (DoE, 1992a, p. 95).

The simplest response would have been to increase public expenditure to cope with increased demand. However, the usual assumption of government policy in housing is that the available resources will be determined by broader policies for public expenditure. Instead, under the Housing Grants, Construction and Regeneration Act 1996, grant aid for owner-occupiers is now only available at the discretion of the local authority. The effect is to return the system back to that in existence before 1989, though with the inclusion of means-testing and with the continued possibility of using grant aid for the common parts of a property. The system remains far more flexible than in the 1980s. In addition, the Act involves marginal changes to the disabled persons grant and minor works grant.

An earlier White Paper, *Our Future Homes* (HM Government, 1995) justified the new measures as a means of encouraging local authorities to develop renewal strategies that aim at the renovation of whole areas or that focus on special problems. However, there is no suggestion that more funds will be made available to implement a strategic approach. The election in 1997 of a Labour government is unlikely to make a significant difference in the short term.

The underlying issues are not easily resolved. Any review of the improvement grant system clearly has to consider the financial interests of central and local government and their desire to reduce public expenditure, or at least to make public expenditure as cost-effective as possible. However, a review of the improvement grant system must also consider the very different views of:

❏   the technical officers in the local authority (Environmental Health, Surveying and Planning Officers) who generally emphasise matters relating to physical condition and who frequently express a preference for area-based programmes

❏ the various pressure groups who represent elderly people and other low income households and who emphasise the rights of individual households.

The aims of the policy review must also be considered. The system established under the 1989 Act was criticised for reasons of equity, that it fails to help those in need, and of efficiency, that it hinders the management of renewal programmes. It is unlikely, given current resource limitations, that any renewal strategy will satisfy both criticisms.

Leather and Mackintosh (1994a) have attempted to bridge the differences through the concept of a 'sustainable' housing renewal policy that 'tackles the full range of current and future house conditions problems'. Sustainability in this context means a policy that protects the existing stock against decay, supports and encourages owners to care for their property and, in addition, avoids an unrealistic dependence on public funds. Sustainability is now a *leitmotif* in renewal policy, much as was gradual renewal in the 1970s. However, sustainability is an ambiguous concept. It does not, of itself, resolve the difference between equity and efficiency.

OVERCOMING SPECIFIC CONSTRAINTS

The renewal of the private housing stock is usually examined in terms of the aims, effectiveness and history of government initiatives. Another way is to examine the process of private housing improvement in an attempt to identify ways of countering the failures of the market.

Analysis of the process of rehabilitation in turn requires an initial point of clarification. Unlike new housing, and unlike the rehabilitation of commercial property, housing rehabilitation in Britain is almost entirely undertaken by owners or in the case of the privately rented sector by small private companies. Private developers are significant by their absence. The main exception is where rehabilitation is linked to more complex schemes that involve the creation of additional dwelling units on a site (for example, through the subdivision of a house into flats or where rehabilitation is linked to the development of new dwellings in the garden space or a large property).

The existence of a so-called 'valuation gap' is one constraint on the activities of private developers. This is where the value of a property after improvement is about the same or even less than the cumulative cost of the improvement and repairs works and initial acquisition. The valuation gaps is also, almost certainly, a deterrent on improvement by private landlords. It means that there is literally not financial incentive for landlords to improve except with grant aid. In addition, the existence of differential VAT rates is a constraint on the involvement of private developers. In comparison to new housing, the cost of rehabilitation works is increased by 17.5% owing to its liability for VAT (Llewelyn-Davies 1994a). Otherwise, the main constraints lie in the owner-occupied sector. They comprise:

❏ the lack of demand for improvement amongst low income and elderly home owners;

❏ the lack of suitable private funding arrangements for low income and elderly home owners.

The lack of demand amongst poor and elderly home owners

The five yearly reports of the English House Condition Survey provide the most reliable and detailed information of the maintenance and improvement activities of owner-occupiers. The reports typically show that grant aid only accounts for a small proportion of investment in the home. Leather and Mackintosh (1997, p. 142) cite data from the 1986 survey that grant aid only accounts for 7% of private investment on essential repairs and improvements (excluding such improvements as new kitchens, double-glazing and extensions). To this extent, to be realistic, housing renewal policies must always start with the principles of self-help and personal responsibility.

Equally, the reports show a degree of resistance to investment amongst those living in poor conditions. The report of the 1976 survey provides the most detailed account. It shows that the occupants of poor quality dwellings have a consistently more favourable view of the state of repair of their home than that of professional surveyors. A lack of technical knowledge is one reason for the relatively favourable views of residents. The residents are sometimes not aware of the problems. However, elderly households and other long established households are also more likely to tolerate conditions which professional surveyors considered inadequate.

The report (DoE, 1979) concludes,

> 'Only a small minority of households who occupied dwellings in poor condition were sufficiently dissatisfied either to seek improvements ... or to move to better accommodation ... as householders grow older and become settled in their homes they become less willing to recognise its defects or to tolerate the disturbance caused by repairs or improvements.'

The reports of the 1981, 1986 and 1991 surveys contain consistent information.

The reports of the English House Condition Survey are also significant for their omissions. The survey makes no mention of any tendency for households to reject investment in repairs in favour of inappropriate cosmetic works such as double-glazing or stone cladding. The main problem for poor quality dwellings is a lack of any form of investment.

The evaluation of HAAs, undertaken by Niner and Forrest (1982, pp. 113–115), provides a slightly different perspective on the reluctance of elderly owner-occupiers to undertake improvement. Niner and Forrest place more emphasis on the problems which the elderly experience in finding reliable building contractors. They give examples of people who had completed improvement work and who complained about the excessive time of the building work and the poor standard of the finished product. The resistance to improvement is not simply a result of apathy or the passive acceptance of poor conditions. It may also reflect a rational assessment that the apparent long-term advantages are not worth the time, trouble or money.

What is the best way forward? The complaints about building work suggest a need for a system of quality labelling for contractors who undertake improvement and repair on the older stock. Local authorities could, for example, bar unsatisfactory builders from a list of approved contractore that may undertake work in receipt of grant aid. Some local authorities, for example Leicester, already do this. Another possibility is for existing trade organisations, such as the Federation of Master Builders, to undertake more inspection work and to disseminate good practice. Such quality labelling would probably not eliminate all the disruption of improvement and repairs. However, it would increase the confidence of the owner that the work would be of a good standard. It could also be linked to the introduction of a warranty that gives more protection in the case of any subsequent defect.

Otherwise, the most commonly cited way forward is to establish a network of advice centres, variously called 'care and repair agencies' or 'home improvement agencies', which can provide impartial counselling and information on all aspects of improvement and repair, including how to obtain grant aid or a building society mortgage, how to select a reputable builder and how to supervise the work. The full number of such centres is not known. However, Leather and Mackintosh (1994) have stated that the government provides funding for more than 100 schemes in England.

Agency services provide a way of managing grant-aided work and of encouraging owners to finance work from their own funds. So long as they target their activities on priority cases, they can also meet housing needs. An early review, undertaken by Wheeler (1985) of six centres over a three year period from 1981 to 1984, provides numerous examples of elderly households who benefited from the project and who received help in obtaining a grant or a building society loan. Moreover, a follow-up survey, undertaken by Mackintosh and Leather (1992c) shows that most of those who received help from staying put projects in the early 1980s enjoyed long-term benefits.

The main weakness is that large numbers of people in need still do not come forward. Moreover, of those that do, many enquiries do not lead to improvement or repairs. A high proportion of owners discontinue their enquiries once they realise the potential complexities and costs. For example, in Wheeler's study of staying put in the early 1980s, about 70% of clients failed to go ahead and undertake the work.

Agency services can charge a fee for their work and, since the Local Government and Housing Act 1989, this fee may be incorporated into the overall costs that are eligible for grant aid. It is unlikely, however, that many will ever become self-financing. Their continued existence remains dependent on a combination of public and voluntary funds, as well as their income from private fees.

Agency services, like most policy initiatives in renewal, have been primarily concerned with promoting relatively large investments to bring property up to either the fitness standard or a higher standard. In Leicester, the local authority has pursued a policy to encourage owner-occupiers to undertake regular maintenance after improvement (Leicester City Council, 1995). In four areas of the inner city, the local authority offers a series of maintenance services including:

- ❏ free advice;
- ❏ small-scale demonstration schemes;
- ❏ the provision of a maintenance officer to people who are disabled or single;
- ❏ small-scale grant aid;
- ❏ the selective provision of at cost or free repairs using training agencies or private contractors;
- ❏ the provision of tower scaffold or ladders for DIY work.

The policy raises questions about the extent to which local residents can and should pay for these services. However, it is surely worth of wider application.

The lack of suitable funding arrangements

With the exception of very minor, preventative work, house improvements and repairs involve substantial sums of money that owners on moderate or low incomes find difficult to finance from their weekly or monthly salary. Some method has to be found of smoothing out payment over a number of years. In principle, there are three main methods:

- ❏ a loan offered by a private lending agency such as a building society or a bank;
- ❏ a loan offered by a public agency, such as a local authority, usually under slightly more generous terms;
- ❏ an insurance policy or sinking fund that provides finance for the work in advance.

The role of private lending agencies

The availability of private finance is a prerequisite for the implementation of renewal programmes and is now widely recognised as such. Renewal, it is said, should proceed through a partnership of the private and public sectors. The partnership has not been easy to sustain, however. Private lending agencies, whether building societies, banks or insurance companies, have their own interests and preoccupations.

The involvement of private lenders in housing renewal started with the end of mass clearance in the early 1970s. At this time, the main problem was the absence of the building societies from the inner city. The building societies believed that most inner city residents had an insufficiently reliable income to satisfy the conditions for a loan and they wanted to avoid areas that might be the subject of possible clearance schemes. Some so-called 'redlined' areas were considered completely unsuitable for loans. Elsewhere, particular types of property were considered unsuitable, for example, houses with no front garden, houses of three or more storeys, converted flats and property in mixed residential and commercial use. Even if loans were offered, the terms were often less advantageous than for conventional family houses in the suburbs.

The shortage of building society loans in inner city areas was so marked that in 1974 and 1975 the implementation of the HAA programme relied on local authority mortgages. The Labour government then in power anticipated that building societies would not lend in such areas and it encouraged local authorities to provide alternative finance. Although local authorities did not lend at the very bottom of the market, they still had a better record compared to building societies in lending on older property and in giving more effective help by granting higher percentage loans. However, the number and value of loans was small in comparison with those of the building societies and, from 1976 onwards, the local authorities withdrew from mortgage lending on the older privately owned stock.

The response of the government to the decline of local authority lending was to introduce the 'support lending scheme' in which the building societies reserved a proportion of their funds for local authority nominees. The scheme was undertaken on a small scale and made relatively weak demands on the building societies. Local authority referrals could be turned down in a way that undermined the purpose of the scheme (Karn, 1978). The scheme continues to the present, but receives little publicity and little policy discussion. In the 1980s, the scheme gradually became less important as increased competition between the building societies, and between the building societies and banks, ensured that loans became more readily available in inner city areas. Low income applicants approached building societies directly, rather than through the intermediary of the local authority.

Nevertheless, the support lending scheme did have an effect in broadening the interest of the building societies in renewal work. Building society managers met officials of central and local government and came to realise the potential importance of schemes to help low income owner-occupiers. Cumming, one time Chairman of the Building Societies Association, explained the point in evidence to the House of Commons Environment Committee (1983, p. 40).

'The real significance of the support scheme would be that up until that point building societies were, and were encouraged to be, only money lenders. That was the first occasion that anyone ever encouraged us to take an interest in housing.'

The 'Home Improvement Low Payment Plan', introduced by the Halifax Building Society in the early 1980s, provides an example of the new initiatives. In this, the capital value (or 'equity') of the dwelling can be used as security for a loan to undertake repairs and improvement (House of Commons Environment Committee, 1983, p. 11). Owner-occupiers can borrow up to 100% of the value of the property in its improved condition. The society is then prepared to accept interest only payments until either the property is sold or the owner dies when full payment is required.

Insurance companies have also developed financial packages to help older owner-occupiers. Davey (1996) distinguishes between two types: mortgage and annuity schemes, and home reversions.

'In the former (also referred to as home income plans), a mortgage is taken out against the client's property and used to purchase a life-long annuity.... In reversion plans, houses are sold at a discount to the investor, either wholly or partly, but the resident retains occupancy rights for life.'

However, the new financial packages have still not resolved the problems at the lower end of the market. A review by Mackintosh *et al.* (1990, p. 49) states that the numbers of interest-only mortgages,

'is believed to be very small and the average elderly borrower approaching the average lender would have to be very persistent to find out, let alone obtain one.'

The general impression is of a market that is small, but stable and with limited potential for expansion. Potential clients and their advisers generally remain suspicious of the financial packages. They are aware that major capital assets may be put at risk. They worry about indebtedness and also want to leave some assets to the next generation (Davey, 1996). From the viewpoint of the lender, the schemes are labour intensive. Taking on additional staff to promote equity release schemes would reduce their competitiveness in comparison with other building societies or banks.

In any case, much of the effort in promoting equity release has not been aimed specifically at home improvement. Equity release schemes are essentially personal loans, guaranteed by the value of the house on sale at the death of the owner, that provide additional capital or income for whatever purpose the resident wishes. Davey (1996) summarises the results of a recent survey of equity release as:

'The predominant use ... at all levels, was to pay for everyday expenses, sometimes expressed as "to live better" or "to pay bills' ...
'Use for house related expenditure was much less prominent. This was mainly used for decorating, with repairs and improvements much less common.'

Building societies and banks have another potential role in ensuring improvement. When providing loans for purchase, they can make retentions and impose conditions relating to required work. In the past, the use of retentions and required conditions was a means through which building societies avoided lending in inner city areas. In contrast, in the 1990s, it is possible that lenders place too little emphasis on the need for repairs and improvements. Lenders do not encourage prospective owners to take a long-term view. Leather and Mackintosh (1994a), p. 37) note that few purchasers commission a structural survey. They also state that:

'conditions are used infrequently and only at the outset of a new loan... A more interventionist role for lenders could be introduced by requiring the properties should be kept in a reasonable condition as a loan requirement. Conditions of this kind would have to be imposed on all lenders as most are unlikely to be willing to impose them on a voluntary basis.'

The proposal would only apply to new loans and would therefore have a relatively slow impact on house conditions. It is not without its risks. Measures to limit loans to sound property might lead to a withdrawal of private investment from the inner city, as happened before 1975.

Local authority equity sharing schemes

The limitations of private lenders have, in turn, led to proposals for local authorities or possibly some other public agency to offer an improvement loan. The most common proposal has been for the owner to give up a proportion of the value (or 'equity') of the property as a condition for the receipt of financial aid. The local authority would share the financial benefits that arise from rising house prices, but would not require the recipient of the loan to make interest payments.

The proposal originated in the 1985 Green Paper, *Home Improvement – A new approach*, in which the government suggested that, apart from grant aid to make dwellings conform to the fitness standard, the only form of public assistance should be interest-free, equity-sharing loans. The proposal was to work as follows. If, for example, improvement involved £3000 of public funds and the dwelling was worth £30 000 after improvement, the local authority would lay a charge of 10% against the value of the property, payable either on the sale of the dwelling or the death of the owner.

The original proposal, as conceived in the 1985 Green Paper, encountered numerous objections and never reached legislation. Equity sharing would have been expensive in the short term, before the local authority received cash receipts at the time of sale of the improved dwellings. It would have almost certainly hindered the ability of local authorities to target grant aid on dwellings which, though fit, were in a state of disrepair. It was inappropriate for areas such as those in the North of England where property values were and remain relatively low and where, as a result, the proportion of the equity shared by the local authority would, in many cases, exceed 50% (*Planning*, 15 November 1985).

The objections were mostly directed against the use of equity sharing loans as a replacement to grant aid. The use of equity sharing loans as a top-up alongside mandatory and discretionary improvement grants would have made better sense. However, even the use of an improvement loan as a top-up would have had disadvantages. It would not have satisfied those who object to equity sharing loans on the grounds of its short-term public expense. In any case, the proposal for equity sharing loans as a supplement to improvement grant is very similar to the type of scheme that is already available from some insurance companies and other private institutions. Private lending institutions have not been able to generate a substantial demand for their product. It is unclear whether local authorities would be able to achieve a significantly improved response.

Insurance schemes and savings for repairs

Another alternative is to encourage or possibly require owners to contribute towards some form of insurance or sinking fund that can be used to finance repairs when these are necessary. The National Home Improvement Council (1985) has argued that building societies or, in some versions of the proposal, local authorities should create a 'repairs bond', to which those in receipt of a mortgage would contribute through an annual subscription. The Institute of Housing (IoH) (1992, p. 19) has suggested that building societies should, as a condition of a loan, require owners to take out an insurance policy to finance building repairs. Finally, Leather and Mackintosh (1994, pp. 38–39) have suggested the possibility of introducing a 'compulsory sinking fund for all privately owned houses', intended to ensure that resources would be available for essential repair work, including work necessary after a property was sold. Such measures, it is suggested, would reduce the price of older housing to a more realistic level. It would make owners more aware of the real long-term costs of home ownership. In the long term, it might also make owners more aware of the importance of routine, preventative maintenance.

Proposals for a sinking fund or for enhanced insurance cover are, in some ways, an extension of existing practice. A few specialist firms, such as Rentokil, offer insurance against specific aspects of building decay. Rentokil offers owners insurance against rising damp, penetrating damp, wet rot and dry rot on condition that the owner agrees to a detailed survey and agrees, in addition, to undertaking the works specified in the survey. The problem, as always, is one of cost. The survey charge, the works necessary to satisfy the requirements of the insurer and the annual charges are likely to prove substantial for older property. Unless countervailing measures are introduced, the introduction of compulsory insurance could easily exacerbate inequalities in the housing market. The requirement would probably have its heaviest financial effect on lower income households living in the least expensive property in the worst condition.

CONCLUSIONS

Tackling problems of disrepair and poor maintenance has now become the main preoccupation of measures to renew the older, privately owned housing stock. Earlier clearance programmes tackled dwellings and residential areas that had been poorly designed at the outset. Earlier improvement programmes tackled the problem of dwellings that lacked an internal bath, an internal WC and other standard amenities. Failure to maintain property is almost certainly the main cause of unfitness or, in Scotland, the main cause of subtolerable housing in the private sector. Disrepair is, moreover, not a static problem with a fixed number of dwellings in poor condition. It is an on-going problem that results from a natural process of decay and that needs constant attention and investment, if it is not to increase in size.

Tackling problems of disrepair and poor maintenance requires, in part, the establishment of educational and confidence-building measures amongst low income and elderly home owners. Older and low income home owners should have confidence that building contractors undertake the work to a high standard. Possible ways forward include the preparation of a list of reputable builders, as is the practice of many local authorities and, possibly for the future, the establishment of a national quality labelling system for building contractors involved in repair work and the introduction of some system of warranties or guarantees.

In addition, older owner-occupiers should be able to secure various types of practical help. They should be able to go to an advice centre that can provide information about how to raise finance and organise the work. For simple, small-scale repairs, they should be able to go to a local do-it-yourself school or similar service that will help them develop the necessary skills. Many local authorities already possess a housing advice service for elderly people, though the coverage remains patchy. Very few local authorities offer support with do-it-yourself.

Advice alone is inadequate. Advice must, in turn, be strengthened by the selective use of compulsory powers. Under existing legislation, local authorities can serve a repairs notice or a compulsory purchase order. The serving of such an order is particularly useful if a local authority faces problems of abandoned, unoccupied properties. The mere threat of compulsory purchase is sometimes sufficient for the owner to undertake remedial work. Likewise, the threat of compulsion may be the only way to encourage private landlords to maintain their property.

The scope for compulsion is limited, however. Compulsion is a potential intrusion into a person's privacy. Existing compulsory measures only deal with the very worst properties and are, in any case, subject to lengthy and complex legal procedures.

It is possible to imagine a wide variety of extended compulsory measures, including comprehensive compulsory insurance, laying down new requirements on the vendor of old property and laying down new requirements on a private lender at the time of sale. The introduction of additional compulsory measures is probably the most important theme in recent attempts, notably by Leather and Mackintosh (1994a), to work out a low cost 'sustainable' housing renewal strategy. The measures would almost certainly have little political appeal. There are no electoral advantages in proposing to increase the costs of home ownership. Moreover, even if implemented, the results could easily prove counterproductive and actually increase public expenditure. The long-term impact of extended compulsory measures would probably be to limit the scale of low income home ownership. Who would house the sector of the market now displaced? What would happen to the housing stock that previously was home to low income home owners?

There remains a continuing case, therefore, for direct public intervention and direct public investment in the older housing stock. Public finance and investment is crucial in obvious ways:

❏ in the form of grant aid, as a means of enabling low income owner occupiers to afford the cost of improvement and repair work;
❏ as an incentive for private landlords or housing associations to repair or improve the older housing stock without raising the rent or, in the case of private landlords, without selling the completed dwelling into owner-occupation;
❏ as a subsidy for local authorities or possibly some other agency to undertake clearance in a way that permits low income households to afford the rent or the purchase price of the replacement dwellings.

The availability of public finance is crucial in another, less obvious way. Attempts to use private sources of capital finance have proved of only limited success. The attempts of private lenders to promote voluntary improvement by elderly and low income owner-occupiers have foundered,

❏ either on their ability and unwillingness to employ additional specialist staff;
❏ or on the tendency of the occupiers of unsatisfactory housing to under-estimate the need for repairs and improvements;
❏ or on the suspicions of elderly owner-occupiers of equity release schemes;
❏ or on the inability of lower income households (those just above the threshold for help under either the improvement grant regime or the DSS regulations) to afford additional outgoings on a loan or repairs insurance policy;
❏ or on some combination of constraints.

If public finance is made available for housing renewal, the question arises about how it is best used. The experience of renewal policies during the past two decades suggest a series of lessons.

❏ In comparison to the renewal policies of the 1970s, current practice is exceptionally dependent on improvement grants. The priority must surely be to reintroduce enveloping and other methods of public action, such as local authority or housing association acquisition for improvement, that can tackle the very worst housing. Housing association improvement also has the advantages that, in high priced areas, it can stop gentrification and bring private finance into housing renewal.
❏ Local authorities should take particular care before starting even a selective, small-scale clearance programme. Clearance requires that adequate resources are more or less guaranteed in advance. Otherwise, delays and uncertainties will cause much disruption and hardship among residents. If clearance is to be pursued, the compensation available to owners should be improved. The use of a relocation grant provides a possible way forward. This is a grant that helps the displaced owner to purchase a good quality

dwelling of a similar size elsewhere. However, much will depend on the value of the grant and the terms under which it is made available. Another possibility is through the increased use of shared ownership schemes.

❑ Area-based renewal programmes only have a small effect in promoting private investment amongst existing residents. They should not be used as a rationing device in the distribution of grant aid. There are, nevertheless, various justifications for the pursuit of area-based programmes:

    ○ as a means of increasing the demand for improvement grants in places with a concentration of houses in poor condition;

    ○ as a means of co-ordinating house improvement with environmental improvements and with the improvement of community services;

    ○ as a means of countering the risk of local (at the scale of a neighbourhood) collapses in the housing market.

❑ Finally, removal of VAT liability for improvement and repairs, given that house building is exempt, would correct an anomaly that is felt keenly within the building industry. It would probably encourage more rehabilitation by private developers and private landlords, and might also discourage 'cowboy' contractors who are prepared to offer consumers VAT-free bills. Making exemptions to VAT is subject to European Community constraints. However, even if the exemptions were introduced, the savings in improvement costs are not necessarily sufficiently large to help lower income owner-occupiers who have to undertake a wide range of remedial and improvement work.

The dilemmas and complexities of housing renewal discourage governments from introducing large changes in policy. For the immediate future, policy is likely to change through a process of piecemeal adaptation, much as it has changed in the late 1970s and throughout the 1980s. The policy changes that led to the abandonment of mass clearance in the early 1970s were more substantial. However, these were associated with a much broader change in the conception of town planning and urban policy.

Case study 4.1: Burngreave Renewal Area, Sheffield

Burngreave Renewal Area provides an example of the difficulties faced by local authorities in promoting private renewal in depressed inner city areas, without significant levels of public investment. It shows the dependence of housing improvement on public investment. It also shows the importance of relating housing investment to other programmes as a means of promoting the confidence of residents.

Burngreave Renewal Area is one of three inner city priority areas declared in 1991 in response to the Local Government and Housing Act 1989. The Renewal Area contained, at the time of declaration, 1843 houses in one of the poorest areas of Sheffield, with a high proportion of single parent households, households in receipt of some type of benefit and ethnic minority households. Burngreave itself covers local authority estates as well as private housing. However, to conform with government regulations, the boundaries of the Renewal Areas excluded the local authority estates.

The local authority linked the declaration of the Renewal Area to a participation exercise and an evaluation of different renewal options. Different user groups, local residents in the North and South of the area, local traders. Pakistani men and women and Afro-Caribbean people were asked to attend a focus group meeting where they were asked 'What would make Burngreave a better place to live in?' The answers showed that the residents' priorities were to keep the area clean and tidy, and to improve security and safety, as well as improving the housing. Residents also came up with a wide range of ideas for improving community services, the improvement of education, the creation of jobs and improving the environment. In addition, the local authority undertook, as it is required to do under government guidance, an economic evaluation. The results showed that 'wholesale improvement' was more cost-effective than either extensive or piecemeal clearance.

The implementation of the renewal programme has proceeded slowly. Investment has been very much lower than expected. For the three Renewal Areas, the City Council initially proposed to spend about £36 million. Actual spending has been less than £5 million. Spending on environmental improvement and on other social and economic initiatives has virtually ceased. The momentum brought about through the initial consultation exercises has been lost. It is possible that most residents would not now even know they live in a priority area.

Group repair has brought about a significant improvement for a few blocks. However, it has proved difficult to organise and has not tackled the property in the very worst condition. The area contains a number of properties in serious disrepair for which demolition and replacement may now prove the only realistic solution. It also contains examples of blocks where previous individual house improvements have resulted in a poor visual appearance.

Source: Sheffield City Council (1991); *Burngreave Renewal Area* Committee report to a sub-committee of the Housing Committee, 19 June 1996; Interview with a local renewal officer.

(a)

(b)

Fig. 4.1   (a) Vacant and poor quality housing in the Burngreave area of Sheffield. (b) The results of group repair schemes in Sheffield.

Case study 4.2: Renewal Areas in the inner area of Leicester

Leicester City Council provides an example of a local authority that has managed to pursue a strong and varied area-based improvement throughout the 1990s. Leicester's *Area Renewal and Home Improvement Strategy* comprises:

❑ six statutory Renewal Areas, covering a total of 4322 houses, characterised by a concentration of poor quality housing and poverty, where the local authority undertakes a combination of group repair and environmental improvements;

❑ a 'Grant Priority Area', covering 631 houses, characterised by a lower concentration of poor quality housing where the local authority promotes improvement, but undertakes no group repair schemes;

❑ four 'Urban Management Areas', mostly comprising former improvement areas, where the local authority encourages home maintenance and undertakes other minor works, including street maintenance and the provision of home energy grants.

The local authority also pursues city-wide improvement strategies. These include an 'Empty Property Strategy' that involves the selective serving of compulsory purchase notices and a 'Home Energy Strategy' that attempts to tackle fuel poverty. In addition to all this, in some of the Renewal Areas, the local authority works in partnership with a separate urban regeneration programme undertaken under the government's City Challenge initiative.

The various renewal strategies have been mostly applied to a mixture of small and large terraces. In some streets, factories and workshops co-exist with the houses in a way that, under the planning orthodoxy of the 1950s and 1960s, would have probably led to clearance. Some of the results are impressive. Elsewhere, the improvement remains unfinished. It remains possible to find examples of derelict properties. In one area, the take-up of grant aid has been hindered by a high proportion of private renting and multiple occupation.

By April 1995, over half of the city's pre-1919 stock had received grant aid since the commencement of the improvement programme in 1975. The stock has been saved from extensive demolition. However, the local authority would admit that much still needs to be done. The annual rate at which the local authority has made properties fit remains relatively small. For example, in the financial year 1995/96, the *Annual Review* estimates that the local authority and local housing associations made 379 properties fit, against a background of about 15 700 unfit privately owned properties. Of course, even as the local authority makes some properties fit, others fall into decay. Leicester shows that the improvement of the older, poor quality housing stock is a long-term, probably permanent public responsibility.

Source: The Housing Department, Leicester City Council (1995): *18th Annual Review of Leicester's Area Renewal and Improvement Strategy*; Various internal committee reports; interviews with local renewal officers.

(a)

(b)

(c)

Fig. 4.2   (a) A typical street scene in Leicester's renewal area. (b) Unimproved housing, and (c) improved housing in Leicester.

Chapter 5
The renewal of 'problem' estates

The idea of renewal means a process of upgrading the physical condition of the housing stock. The physical condition of the local authority stock, as measured by the standards of disrepair or unfitness, is about the same as that of the owner-occupied stock. In 1991, 6.9% of dwellings owned by local authorities were unfit, according to the English House Condition Survey (DoE, 1993, p. 66). The equivalent proportion for owner-occupied housing was 5.5%, the difference with the local authority housing stock being within the margin of error of the survey. For housing associations, the proportion was 6.7%.

However, the standards of disrepair and unfitness do not tell the full story. These standards exclude the more subjective aspects of environmental quality – aspects such as the attractiveness of the architecture and the estate layout; the absence or presence of vandalism and the care and maintenance of external spaces. Some local authority estates are plainly a problem in terms of these latter aspects of quality.

Moreover, variations in the proportion of residents who state that they are dissatisfied with their housing are larger than variations in unfitness. For example, the social surveys undertaken alongside the English House Condition Survey show that, in 1991, about 11% of local authority tenants were dissatisfied with their home and that about 13% were dissatisfied with their 'immediate environment'. Equivalent proportions for owner-occupiers are about 3% and 4% (DoE, 1993, p. 122).

DEFINITION OF THE PROBLEM

The character and cause of the 'problem' estate is open to discussion. The usual explanation is that the problem of local authority estates is caused by a double process of 'residualisation'. This comprises:

❑ an increasing impoverishment of local authority housing in comparison with owner-occupied housing;
❑ an increasing differentiation between estates in the local authority sector.

In addition, an alternative explanation exists in the form of labelling theory. This does not dispute the existence of residualisation or polarisation as possible statistical trends. Rather it qualifies the significance of these trends and assumes that they should only be assessed to the extent to which they contribute to the perception of an estate as desirable or undesirable.

Residualisation

Willmott and Murie (1988, p. 1) provide a good example of those who emphasise residualisation. They contrast a former situation in which 'Council housing was ... a marvellous jewel in the crown of civil enterprise' and the present situation in which,

> 'Council housing as a whole has become more and more the preserver of poor people ... and within the council sector the poorest and most disadvantaged have more and more had to live in the worst estates.'

In support, the authors cite evidence from successive editions of the General Household Survey and other evidence showing how local authority housing has increasingly become a residual tenure in the sense that its tenants have, on average, become older and poorer. They show how the 'right to buy' has concentrated an increasing proportion of economically and socially disadvantaged households within those estates that are least attractive to potential purchasers. Finally, they explain how housing allocation practices maintain social segregation and force the most vulnerable households into the least attractive accommodation. Those in the worst housing conditions are the least able to wait for the right house. Their urgent need for rehousing increases the pressure on them to choose an unpopular estate.

The concept of residualisation shows how local authority estate are now outside the mainstream of British society. The concept also helps explain why most people in Britain would prefer to own a home, rather than rent if they have a choice. However, the concept still raises some unanswered questions.

For example, does the concept of residualisation imply that renting from a local authority is unpopular with tenants? Surely not. Under the Housing Act 1988 local authority tenants have the right to choose another landlord, either a housing association or private landlord. The experience of the ballots undertaken under this Act suggest that tenants need some persuading before a majority is prepared to vote for transfer. The experience of the Housing Action Trust (HAT) illustrates the point. The HAT is a device whereby an independent body takes control of a local authority estate before undertaking improvement and modernisation work. The initial proposals for HATs, made in 1988, led to widespread resistance from tenants who asked why the money could not be made available to local authorities. HATs only proved acceptable once government started to work with the relevant local authorities and gave tenants various guarantees about their future. (See Dennis, 1990; Gregory and Hainsworth, 1993; PIC – Peat Marwick McLintock, 1989, p. 31).

Again, does the concept of 'residualisation' suggest that trends within the housing market are the only factor that encourages social segregation. Again, surely not. Segregation is also influenced by trends within the labour market. The city of Sheffield provides an example. Between 1981 and 1991 unemployment in Sheffield almost doubled, especially amongst those who had formerly worked in manual occupations. The middle class suburbs of the west of the city were less affected by increased unemployment than the poorer areas of the inner city that include, according to the official definition, local authority estates near to the city centre, the east and north. Other cities have experienced similar tendencies as a result of a decline in the availability of semi-skilled and unskilled work (Atkins *et al.*, 1996, pp. 38–40). The contrast between rich and poor areas, between the affluent middle class areas and the deprived inner city has become starker, but for reasons which are largely independent of housing policy.

Labelling theory

Reade (1982) provides a good account of the alternative theory, based on labelling processes. For Reade, problem estates are merely the negative, mirror image of the large detached house in a prosperous middle class suburb. In the same way as the detached house provides a symbol and material representation of success, so the problem estates provide a symbol and material representation of the relative 'failure' of those who live within them. A competitive society needs a system of rewards and deterrents. The problem estate, together with other equivalent low status areas, provides the housing equivalent of a deterrent.

An advantage of labelling theory is to provide a link between environmental perception and housing policy. Labelling theory admits visual considerations are important in determining whether an estate is desirable as a place to live. It recognises that signs of vandalism, litter and poor maintenance make an estate undesirable. A further advantage is that labelling theory acknowledges that the media, and especially the local newspapers, influence the perception of estates. The media generally claim that they seek to reflect public opinion and are not responsible for the problems that they report. Yet, the repetition of problems in the media can go beyond factual reporting and create a self-sustaining labelling process that greatly amplifies public awareness of problems (Cohen and Young, 1981, p. 425–440; Goodchild, 1987).

Finally, labelling theory helps explain the distinctiveness of housing association housing. Residualisation also applies to the tenants of housing associations. The incomes and other social characteristics of housing association tenants are not significantly different from those of local authorities. Moreover, the average incomes of housing association tenants has declined relative to the national average in the 1980s. The difference is, however, that housing associations have few large estates that are easily stigmatised.

However, as with the concept of residualisation, clarification is necessary. Does labelling theory imply that local authority estates be split up in favour of a diversity of different housing providers? Is such a break-up of estates likely to diminish the likelihood of stigmatisation? The answer is a qualified 'No'. Breaking up an estate sometimes has the potential of ensuring greater democracy in the provision of social housing. It may allow local residents to take control. However, stigmatisation applies as much to areas as to the type of housing provider. Unpopular estates exist in other European countries, such as France and the Netherlands, where the social housing stock and larger social housing estates have long been characterised by greater diversity than in Britain. Indeed, the housing literature in these other countries shows that diversity is sometimes a disadvantage rather than a strength. For example, Béhar and Rosenberg (1990) argue that the existence of a number of social housing agencies in a neighbourhood reduces the ability of a local authority to implement a co-ordinated allocations policy and it encourages a tendency towards the specialisation and segregation of different residential areas.

Relationship between the theories

The distinction between explanations based on labelling theory and those based on residualisation may, in part, be understood in terms of their relation to history. The concept of residualisation emphasises the distinctive features of housing policy and social housing provision in the 1980s and 1990s. In contrast, labelling theory suggests that undesirable, stigmatised residential areas are likely to occur in an unequal society, whatever the institutional framework in housing. Labelling theory is more general, less historically specific.

In addition, the distinction between the two approaches concerns whether the problem is located in the estate or elsewhere. For the concept of residualisation, the problem lies in the characteristics of the estate and its occupants. In part, residualisation refers to the physical standards of the estate. These standards are said to have declined in problem estates in comparison both to other local authority estates and to the owner-occupied housing stock. Residualisation therefore implies a strategy based on the improvement of living conditions. In addition, it treats the poverty of the residents as a material cause. In doing this, residualisation suggests a case for wide-ranging anti-poverty strategies, including strategies that promote local employment.

In contrast, labelling theory pays more attention to causes outside the estate, in the perception of significant others. The assumption is that when society defines a certain group or certain estate as deviant or undesirable, that group or estate tends to become excluded or estranged and starts to develop its own subculture and sense of deprivation. Labelling theory suggests the need to change the image of an estate and to counter the fear of crime amongst residents.

The two approaches have a different emphasis. However, they are best regarded as complementary explanations of the same problem.

THE DIFFERENT DIMENSIONS OF ACTION

The problem estate is often subject to complaints from local residents who demand that something should be done; it is a potential source of disorder; it offers an affront to notions of social justice. As a result, governments of all political persuasions are more or less obliged to prevent problems from becoming too bad, even though the persistence of social and economic inequality ensures, as labelling theory insists, that the contrast between good and bad estates cannot be fully eliminated.

A variety of measures are available. An early guide *Tackling Priority Estates* (DoE, 1983b), lists seven dimensions of intervention. These are:

❏ improving security;
❏ physical improvement;
❏ local allocations;
❏ administrative decentralisation;
❏ estate budgets;
❏ tenant participation in management;
❏ the promotion of sales to the private sector.

However, the list is too long, too complex and too out-of-date. It needs simplification and updating.

'Local allocations', administrative decentralisation', 'estate budgets', and tenant participation' are all aspects of housing management. They may be discussed under this heading. 'Local allocations' must, in addition, be read in conjunction with the views of Page (1993) that high child densities are a cause of the problem of unpopular housing association estates.

'The promotion of sales to the private sector' is now absorbed into broader measures to promote the local economy and has largely ceased as a separate measure. Since the passing of the Housing Act 1988, local authorities have largely preferred transfer of the stock to housing associations rather than sale to private individuals or developers. Housing associations use a substantial proportion of private finance in their investment programmes, say between 40 and 55% of total costs. However, they have an explicit social ethos and are, for this reason, more likely to be sympathetic to calls to support the rehabilitation of a deprived estate.

The reference to 'physical improvement' requires further clarification. It means rectifying basic problems of building disrepair and dampness, and installing modern kitchen and bathroom fittings. In the case of estates with a high proportion of flats or estates built to an excessively high density, physical improvement may also mean the rectification of design errors. For estates with problems of serious disrepair or serious design faults, physical improvement is likely to involve a choice between clearance and improvement. The rules for making such a choice are similar to those used to determine renewal options in the private sector. The rules involve a trade-off between short-term costs and long-term savings on repair and management. Moreover, the choice must also consider the likely effects on property values of any proposal and their social and environmental implications.

Physical improvement is a technical exercise that may be understood as a precondition for action. However, the renewal of problem estates is more than this. It is essentially about changing its image and social conditions. A revised list of measures is as follows:

- ❏ improving security;
- ❏ reducing child densities;
- ❏ improving housing management.

IMPROVING SECURITY

In many estates, crime prevention and the improvement of security are key priorities. Crime, and the fear of crime, are of concern for most people, but particularly for women, old people and households with children. Crime also has economic implications. Vandalism, criminal damage, arson and abandonment of estates are a threat to the integrity of the building fabric of a housing estate. They require huge sums of money for their rectification. They also encourage local businesses to move away.

The distribution of crime

Crime, and the fear of crime is, of course, not confined to problem estates. Crime rates increased rapidly throughout Britain in the 1980s. However, problem estates are amongst the most insecure, crime-ridden places. The 1992 British Crime Survey classifies residential areas into 11 neighbourhood types according to their demographic, employment and housing characteristics. In England and Wales, people living in 'the poorest council estates' are more likely to report some experience of crime than nearly anywhere else. They are almost three times as likely to experience a crime as the national average. People living in 'less well-off council estates' also experience an above-average risk of crime, especially for burglary attempts (see Mayhew *et al.*, 1993). In Scotland, less information is available, though the pattern is probably similar. For example, in Edinburgh, with the exception of the town centre, recorded incidents of crime are concentrated in deprived local authority estates on the urban periphery (Wester Hailes Partnership, 1996).

In some problem estates the incidence of crime, especially of burglary, is very high. Reynolds (1986) cites survey evidence to the effect that 55% of the residents of 'Omega Estate' (the pseudonym for a real estate) were victims of some crime in two years in the mid 1980s. Likewise, Bright (1986, p. 129) states that on one estate in Hackney in East London, a total of 58 break-ins to five tower blocks were reported to the area repair base in the first four months of 1984, a rate of offending which means that each tenant of the tower blocks had a more than 1-in-4 chance of being burgled each year.

Council tenants are not just more likely to be victims of crime. They are also more likely to offend. Much 'naïve' crime, such as vandalism and burglary, is undertaken within a short radius of the offender's home and is perpetrated against neighbours or near neighbours (Baldwin and Bottoms, 1976; Bottoms and Xanthos, 1981). Consequently, much of the geographical variation in crime rates reflects the local social composition, with the incidence highest in low income areas with a high proportion of adolescents and young adults. Young males are the most frequent offenders.

Methods of estate-based crime prevention

Estate-based measures may, in part, be understood as resting on a 'situational' or 'opportunity' model of crime prevention. Such models assume that crime is not wholly caused by deep-seated social and economic processes or by individual, psychological deficiencies. It is also caused by the existence of opportunities for crime in the immediate situation. Situational measures either encourage potential offenders to 'think again', for example through increased public surveillance or the mobilisation of neighbourhood watch activities, or they manipulate the environment so that opportunities do not arise, for example through obscuring opportunities from view. Situational models have the advantage, according to their supporters, that they are adaptable to different circumstances and offer solutions that are relatively inexpensive in comparison with the solutions offered by the criminal justice system (Hough, 1980; Hope and Shaw, 1988, p. 23).

In addition, the situational model of crime prevention overlaps the so-called 'broken windows' theory of crime and crime prevention (Wilson and Kelling, 1982; Skogan, 1988). This theory involves a spiral of community decline that starts with minor signs of 'incivilities', (evidence of vandalism, litter, dilapidated buildings or undesirable people on the street such as gangs of teenagers) and ends up with the neighbourhood sliding out of control. As incivilities proliferate in a run-down area, residents lose confidence in the future of their area and in the effectiveness of both formal (police) and informal social controls. As residents become more fearful and minor lawbreaking goes unpunished, more serious crime increases. This, in turn, leads to increasing fear of crime and a reduction in the commitment of residents to that area. Thereafter the spiral of decline is likely to continue unchecked, unless countered by positive measures to promote the confidence of residents (for example, through community development and the formation of a tenants group); to stabilise population turnover (for example, through changed allocation practices); and to remove signs of incivilities (for example, through effective estate cleaning and maintenance).

However, neither the situational model nor the broken windows theory provide a full rationale for the various crime prevention measures undertaken in local estates. The principle of surveillance, emphasised in the situational model, is likely to extend to only a very limited area immediately around a home. Moreover, informal controls, exercised by tenants' groups and other exercises in community development, tend to have little influence on the behaviour of young people (Foster and Hope, 1994, p. 92). Reaching young people requires educational, self-help and recreational programmes that can promote their self-confidence, divert their energy into worthwhile activities and increase their chances of obtaining work.

The approach of the Safe Neighbourhoods Unit gives an indication of the range of measures that might be applied to a large estate. Bright (1987) summarises a typical security package as including the following:

❑ strengthening doors, frames, locks;
❑ improving lighting and garaging areas;
❑ external landscaping and the provision of private gardens;
❑ the provision of phone entry systems;
❑ the removal of walkways and the remodelling of blocks;
❑ improved management and maintenance;
❑ the provision of a receptionist for each block;
❑ the improvement of play and youth facilities;
❑ enhanced co-operation with the police and other agencies to respond to racial crime;
❑ better home beat policing.

Some aspects of this list, notably the installation of strengthened doors, frames and locks, and the provision of phone entry systems, are now standard practice. A more recent list of security measures would almost certainly include other items, for example:

❑ traffic calming devices, mostly in the form of road humps, intended to protect pedestrians from speeding cars;
❑ legal remedies such as injunctions against individuals and repossession orders against persistent offenders.

The philosophy of the Safe Neighbourhoods Unit is a search for a balance between target hardening measures such as strengthening door frames or the introduction of entry-phones and other measures intended to promote local community life and the confidence of residents. Target hardening measures, it is said, are useful, but only if linked to a system of intensive management and the promotion of community involvement. Target hardening can, in any case, create fire hazards, restrict access to emergency service and create a 'fortress mentality' where people lock themselves up in an atmosphere of mutual suspicion (Stollard *et al.*, 1989, p. 11). Target hardening is, therefore, not to be pursued in isolation.

The Safe Neighbourhoods Unit is not the only agency to offer advice on crime prevention. The Priority Estates Project (PEP), and various design theorists, notably Coleman (1985) and Hillier *et al.* (1987) have also contributed advice. However, both the Priority Estates Project and the design theorists are relatively narrow in their approach. The PEP emphasises the importance of housing management in maintaining a good appearance in an estate. It also promotes tenant involvement in housing management in a way that may facilitate the emergency of a community identity and the growth of informal social controls. Finally, it emphasises the speedy allocation of empty homes that could otherwise be vandalised or squatted. The speedy allocation of vacant property is a com-

mon theme in official advice (see, for example, DoE, 1983b). The design theorists focus, for the most part, on the principle of 'natural' or passive surveillance
that results from the existence of pedestrians in a street or from the use of streets
and footpaths that are overlooked by nearby houses and flats.

It is possible that a crime prevention programme could include aspects of all
the different measures. In practice this is rare. Measures are selected as appropriate for particular problems of an area. A Home Office publication, *Targeted
Crime Reduction*, has explained how this should be done (Shapland *et al.*,
1994). The publication was prepared for the Police Research Group, but in
principle is applicable to any other agency that wishes to organise a local crime
prevention initiative.

The process of selection starts with an analysis of crime patterns in a particular
area as revealed, for example, by police statistics and the distribution of different
types of offence in various places. This stage presupposes that the police are able
and willing to present information about recorded crime in adequate detail. The
process of selection proceeds through a process of consultation with the various
statutory and other agencies that are involved in an area. It includes measures to
involve local people, either through public meetings, group discussions or face-
to-face interviews. The aim is to agree priorities and, in the case of large projects,
to secure the agreement of heads of agencies for the necessary finance.

The problem of evaluation

A major problem with all these measures is to evaluate their impact. In part, the
problem is a lack of resources to undertake evaluation. There are few resources
specifically set aside by government for funding community-based crime prevention initiatives. If local authorities want to implement anti-crime measures,
they generally have to use investment programmes principally directed towards
other objectives. The Estates Action programme is, for example, principally
concerned with the improvement of housing conditions. The main measures of
success and the efforts of policy evaluation may therefore not be directly related
to crime or vandalism.

In addition, and more significantly, there are numerous pitfalls in assessing the
effectiveness of any particular measure. Most research into crime prevention
depends on the interpretation of patterns of incidence. The research seeks to
explain why some places suffer an above average or a below average level of
crime. In doing this, the research seeks to identify those factors that a social
housing agency or a developer might use to reduce crime. However the validity
of the interpretation depends crucially on the accuracy of the crime statistics.
Therein lies a problem.

❏   Local police forces generally collect statistics of reported crime at the level of
    a 'beat area', meaning the area patrolled by a single police officer or by a
    team of police officers. This is sufficiently small to monitor trends in an
    estate, if the boundaries of the beat area and the estate are reasonably

consistent with one another. However, police statistics only show reported crime and may provide an incomplete record. The victims of crime may regard the offence as too trivial to count as a crime or they may think that the police would not be able or willing to take effective action. For example, people generally have to report theft, if they wish to make an insurance claim. However, if the stolen goods are uninsured or of low value, people may not bother. Moreover, the willingness of people to report crimes can vary substantially from place to place and over time. For example, an increasing number of criminal incidents does not necessarily indicate the failure of an estate-based initiative. The persistence of crime and vandalism might be caused by a greater willingness of local residents to report incidents.

❏ The limitations of official statistics have led researchers to use so-called 'victimisation' surveys that ask residents whether they have been the victim of any form of crime during the previous six moths or year. Victimisation surveys are usually considered more accurate than police crime statistics. They form the basis of the British Crime Survey. Good practice in evaluation studies is to use a combination of victimisation surveys and police statistics. However, victimisaion surveys may also be vulnerable to under-reporting. Respondents may be unwilling to disclose full information to a stranger.

Even if the statistics are accurate, the interpretation of any pattern requires the exclusion of 'extraneous' factors that might distort the results. In particular, it is not sufficient to show a correlation between a specific design feature, say a lack of defensible space or other feature of one or more estates and the incidence of crime and vandalism. Correlation is best regarded as a preliminary exercise. It is not the same as causation. The pattern of crime and vandalism is too easily influenced by variations in the social composition of different areas, by variations in local subcultures or by variations in local patterns of pedestrian movement. Streets with a large volume of pedestrians may, for example, be characterised by higher crime rates, almost irrespective of the design of the houses.

'Before and after' studies are potentially more reliable. These assess the incidence of crime before and after an intervention and, in doing this, enable a more precise test of the impact. However, before and after studies raise other difficulties.

❏ First, the social composition of an estate is not always stable over even a one year period. It is possible that an apparent reduction in crime is caused by the arrest of local offenders. A small number of individuals can commit a large number of crimes in a short period if time and account for a high proportion of the crimes on an estate (Osborn, 1993, p. 29). Conversely, the allocation practices of the local authority might change in a way that leads to an increased concentration of people who are most likely to offend.

❏ Second, an analysis of local crime trends may ignore the displacement of the problem elsewhere. For example, the use of a security camera at the entrance to a block of flats or in a car park may drive offenders to other blocks of sites out of range of the cameras. In addition, though this is seldom discussed in the literature, the introduction of a specific anti-crime measure may lead to displacement by type of crime. For example, an offender who has specialised in car theft may, on the introduction of CCTV, turn to mugging.

❑ Third, local crime trends may vary as a result of the so-called 'Hawthorne effect' in which the presence of the researchers distorts the behaviour of those being observed. Local housing managers and community workers may be so eager to demonstrate the success of a scheme that they undertake additional work during the course of the research. Once the researchers withdraw, the estate managers and community workers may be less conscientious.

❑ Finally, large projects of estate renewal may take two or three years or longer to implement. The pursuit of a research programme for such a long time is not always feasible. In response, researchers sometimes use a 'retrospective' before and after study in which residents are asked their experience after completion of the works. The validity of retrospective before and after studies, in turn, depends on how well local people remember former conditions.

The pitfalls in evaluating crime initiatives might be interpreted as suggesting that local studies are not worth the effort. Equally, however, the difficulties have another implication. They suggest that virtually any research method, including those used in the most expensive national studies, have disadvantages as well as advantages. This being so, reliable conclusions in the field of local crime prevention are only likely to arise from a wide variety of different studies, including those undertaken to assess the local impact of specific initiatives.

The results of evaluation

Despite the difficulties of evaluation, some estate-based initiatives have clearly been highly successful. For example, Young (1992) documents the example of Hilldrop estate in North London. Here a combination of neighbourhood action better policing, the provision of social facilities and estate regeneration led over a four year period from 1986 to 1990 to a 14% reduction in burglary, an 80% reduction in vehicle theft and a 40% reduction in street robbery.

The question is to identify what type of initiative is most likely to work. Osborn (1993) has undertaken the most thorough review of estate-based crime prevention measures. Osborn was able to locate 31 different studies whose methodology was sufficiently sound to merit serious consideration. Of these 31 studies, ten provided a strong case in favour of a reduction in local crime problems. Successful schemes were generally those that had been carefully planned in advance and were:

❑ led by housing management initiatives rather than, say, architects or designers;

❑ part of a co-ordinated effort to improve local living conditions in a way that extends beyond housing management;
❑ subject to intervention by an independent, voluntary agency (such as the Priority Estates Project or the Safe Neighbourhoods Unit) that, in the case of dispute, can mediate between the residents and such official organisations as the police and the local housing department;
❑ orientated towards a range of different problems and various solutions;
❑ based on a wide process of consultation and a commitment to resident participation;
❑ based on ring-fenced budgets that protect the schemes from competing demands on public resources.

Crime prevention programmes that relied only on design and physical improvements generally provided little more than anecdotal evidence in their support. The most successful schemes were those that combined a package of measures, including management initiatives, community development and measures to improve physical living conditions. (Also see the case studies of Wester Hailes, Edinburgh (5.1) and the Holly Street estate, Hackney (5.2).

The achievements of even the most successful schemes remains subject to qualifications. There is no simple formula for success. There are some unsuccessful schemes with all or some of these same features. Moreover, there are doubts about the long-term future of even the most successful schemes. These local interventions are invariably unable to influence broader socio-economic conditions, and are usually unable to influence the policies and practices of local welfare or housing agencies in a way that would enable local people to manage their own affairs (Osborn, 1993, pp. 162–164).

Though Osborn does not say so, there is another limitation. Estate-based initiatives of crime prevention cannot easily tackle violence committed within the home by members of the same households. Despite the fear of many women and others about darkly lit streets and impersonal estates, the home is the place that poses the highest risk of attack.

Nevertheless, irrespective of the limitations, the various anti-crime and anti-vandalism measures generally receive support from local housing managers, the police and residents' groups. They provide a means of removing obvious crime opportunities and offer a starting point for local discussions. They are generally cost-effective, if only for the reason that they are not generally pursued within pre-existing or dedicated anti-crime expenditure programmes.

Moreover, even if doubts exist about the impact on the actual incidence of crime and vandalism, the various measures may still be justified as a means of raising the confidence of residents, of reducing the fear of crime and so improving the quality of life. The fear of crime is not always closely associated with its incidence. It is often associated, as the Safe Neighbourhood Unit assumes, with a generalised dissatisfaction with the appearance of an area if, for example, it looks neglected, and a generalised dissatisfaction with its services, fabric and facilities (Bright, 1986).

THE REDUCTION OF CHILD DENSITIES

Modernisation and improvement schemes, including anti-crime measures, are unlikely to succeed in improving living conditions if residents face the vandalism, noise, wear and tear caused by large numbers of children living in the vicinity. Reducing child densities may not reduce the rate of vandalism per child. Vandalism is caused by so many factors, including the quality of recreational facilities and the socio-economic characteristics of the population, that the evidence is unclear on this point. In addition, vandalism is often confused with accidental damage that arises during children's play. However, a reduction in child densities lessens the impact of crime and vandalism on residents, reduces the problems of housing management and reduces problems of noise and nuisance for residents.

A Department of the Environment guide suggests on the basis of previous research the problems of vandalism increase when there are more than 5 children per 10 dwellings or when the total number of children in a block exceeds 20 (Estate Action, 1991, p. 35). However, such a guideline must be treated with a degree of caution. It is, at best, no more than a simple rule of thumb.

The application to flatted estates

Policies to reduce child densities apply mostly to flats, especially high flats. Problems of child densities, such as noise and vandalism, are more acute in and are more clearly documented for flatted estates (see Westminster City Council, 1980; Wilson, 1980). Moreover, it is generally desirable for reasons of child welfare to reduce the number of families with children living in flats. Very few families with children wish to live in flats if they have a choice. Living in a flat places additional pressures on parents in child-rearing. It also diminishes the opportunities for outdoor play amongst children and increases the risk of accidental death and injury from falls (Littlewood and Tinker, 1981).

In some other countries in Western Europe, for example Germany, the Netherlands and Scandinavia, living in a flat appears to cause fewer problems for children. In these countries, where social housing agencies own unpopular flatted estates, they are more prepared to improve the blocks as family accommodation. In contrast, in Britain, families with children have such an entrenched dislike of flats that the reduction of child densities is a usual prerequisite for improvement, wherever this is possible.

In Britain, nearly all local authorities would now accept that it is not desirable to allocate flats, especially high flats, to households with children. However, those local authorities with large numbers of high-rise blocks also accept that they have no choice but to let at least a proportion of these flats to households with children. Clarke (1992) has reported the results of a survey undertaken by the National Tower Blocks Network, an organisation that aims to improve the quality of life in high-rise blocks. The report of the first national survey of tower blocks, undertaken in 1987, showed that many local authorities were pursuing special lettings policies for families such as 'no children in blocks' or 'no children at a height'. These earlier policies have now largely been abandoned.

A major constraint is a lack of finance for modernisation. It is generally not feasible to reduce child densities through the piecemeal allocation of flats to childless households. Piecemeal allocation encounters the difficulty that those who move in first live in a block with continuing problems. Elderly households experience particular difficulties and are sometimes at risk of harassment if they live in blocks with high child densities. Also, they should not be mixed with larger families (Estate Action, 1991, p. 35).

However, lack of finance is not the only constraint. Equally important is that many local authorities, especially those in London and the big cities, possess an insufficient number of houses with gardens. The right to buy legislation has led to a disproportionate loss of houses with gardens. Moreover, this loss has not been adequately countered by the building programmes of housing associations.

The growth of homeless households is another factor that has perpetuated the allocation of flats to households with children. Households accepted by local authorities as homeless have little choice but to accept whatever is offered. As a result, they often have to move into unpopular blocks that have the highest turnover of tenants. Local authorities are more likely to accept households with children or with pregnant women as homeless due to the risk which home-lessness poses for children. To do otherwise would lead to children living in even worse conditions in bed and breakfast or temporary accommodation. The result is a constant supply of new households with children living in flats (Goodchild, 1987).

The scale of housing needs means that significant numbers of children are likely to continue living in local authority flats for the foreseeable future. The concentration of flats in inner London and some other big cities is likely to have the same effect. This being so, it is even more important to promote intensive housing management, including the use of a resident caretaker. In addition, social housing agencies and other relevant public agencies could improve the blocks to a particularly high level in an effort to compensate children for the disadvantages of living in a flat. Typical measures of improvement might include the enlargement of units (reducing the number on each floor from say, three to two, or five to four); the enlargement of entrances and hallways; the creation of day care facilities, kitchens and common rooms for communal activities on the ground floor; and the improvement of external landscaping.

Where local authorities in Britain have managed to reduce child densities, the most popular solution is conversion for old people. The ground floor is usually easily adapted for communal space. If the aim is to create sheltered accommodation, part of the ground floor may be set aside by a warden. Turnover of tenancies is relatively low amongst old people. Moreover, old people are less likely than other age groups to make noise or act in a way that might annoy neighbours.

In the 1980s, local authorities also undertook the conversion of flats for use by colleges, private businesses or for more expensive, up-market accommodation.

The experience of such schemes indicates few problems (see Anderson *et al.*, 1985). In contrast, it has sometimes proved difficult to manage high flats that possess a high proportion of unemployed young people and young people on low incomes. Foster and Hope (1994) report a case in Hull where the allocation of flats to homeless young people, mostly young men, helped promote a 'subterranean' youth culture characterised by noise, criminal activities and the destruction of council property. The problems caused by young people may be countered by the presence of a caretaker in the flat, if this is not too expensive. However, the problems are sufficient to show that the reduction of child densities is no panacea.

The application to low-rise estates

In older, low-rise local authority estates, child densities are tempered by what housing managers call 'under-occupation'. This means that children have left home and that many family homes are now occupied only by older adults. Local authorities have not built new estates of family houses since the mid 1980s.

The pattern of development is different for housing associations. Page (1993, pp. 16–19, 52–59) has shown how, in the 1990s, housing associations have built a relatively high proportion of family houses and that this has resulted in estates with high local child densities. Page studied nine estates with management difficulties. For all housing association schemes, the average ratio of children to adults was about one child to four adults. (This is a ratio of about 20%.) For the nine case study estates, the average ratio was 54%, meaning that there were more children than adults.

High child densities may have caused management problems in specific housing association estates, as Page suggests. However, this does not mean that problems of high child densities are common in housing association estates. Housing associations seldom build estates at all, mostly a series of small infill schemes. A national survey of housing associations schemes in the period from 1 April 1992 to 31 March 1995 suggests that almost two thirds of sites accommodated 23 dwellings or less and that 85% of sites were in urban areas (Farthing *et al.*, 1996). In such schemes, even if schemes mostly comprise family houses, they do not lead to high child densities in a street or a neighbourhood.

IMPROVING HOUSING MANAGEMENT

Effective housing management is generally recognised as a precondition for crime prevention in problem estates. It is also an important means of mitigating the impact of high child densities. However, the achievement of effective housing management is easier said than done. Housing management is subject to pressures for economy and cost savings. It is also embedded into organisations that, especially in the past, have proved bureaucratic and inflexible in the face of change.

Many of the measures to improve housing management stem from the experience of the Priority Estates Project which was established in 1979 as an experiment in a small number of estates in England. The supporters of the PEP draw on the ideas and work of the nineteenth century housing reformer, Octavia Hill, who advocated intensive housing management as a technique of urban renewal and who remains an influence on the organisation of some London housing associations such as Octavia Hill and Rowe, and Richmond Churches. Power (1987) is the leading theorist and advocate. For Power, effective estate management can only be achieved if two conditions are met:

❑ the dwellings are owned by a small, flexible housing agency such as a small housing association or by larger agencies organised in the form of small, autonomous units;
❑ the dwellings are managed by a 'generic' housing worker who, within a small patch, deals with all aspects of service delivery such as the supervision of rent collection, the resolution of neighbour complaints and the ordering of repairs.

However, the PEP has not been the only advocate of small-scale, locally-accountable housing management. In Scotland, the community-based housing associations, established in the 1970s for the renewal of private housing, offered an alternative model. Moreover, throughout Britain, tenants' groups, pressure groups within the Labour and Liberal parties and some chief housing officers have independently called for more participation and decentralisation in local authority housing management, as well as more investment in the local authority stock (Hambleton and Hoggett, 1987).

Participation and decentralisation

The campaigns of the PEP, combined with the desire of local authorities to make their housing service more effective and more democratic, have led to significant change. Local authorities now routinely call public meetings to discuss proposals for the physical improvement of estates. Most have appointed staff whose sole responsibility is to support tenants' groups and most have also provided a degree of financial assistance in the form of rent free meeting places and small grants to cover postage and other running costs of tenant groups in selected estates. A survey cited by the Department of the Environment (1992e, p. 6) in a consultation paper *Tenant Involvement and the Right to Manage* suggests that about 70% of English local authorities report the existence of at least one tenant participation initiative, ranging from joint decision-making bodies at estate level to tenant representatives on the housing committee. In contrast, an earlier survey undertaken by the Institute of Housing in 1980, found that 21% of local authorities in Britain had any form of arrangement that amounted to more than 'irregular discussions' with tenant representatives (Ash, 1982, p. 139).

Professional housing managers have also shown more interest in participation: it features regularly in conference programmes and the housing journals. In addition, a variety of agencies, including local and central government and the voluntary sector, have funded training courses for tenants and helped establish the Tenants Participation Advisory Service, to promote and give advice on the subject.

Most larger local authorities have also decentralised their housing service and, as part of this, opened local offices for estates and groupings of estates. They have not, however, generally followed the precise line of the PEP. Decentralised housing management, as understood by local authorities, has usually covered larger areas, say more than 2000 dwellings, while the PEP estate offices have usually covered less than 1000. Local authority decentralisation has also been more limited. It has, for example, generally excluded building maintenance and local allocations.

In some of the larger local authorities, such as Sheffield, Bristol and Tower Hamlets, local authority decentralisation and the PEP model of decentralisation have proceeded together. Local authority decentralisation has attempted to improve service delivery for all tenants, whilst PEP decentralisation has focused on the worst estates.

There are a variety of reasons why local authorities have generally not adopted the PEP model of decentralisation.

❑ In relation to the size of the management area, the cost implications are one constraint. Some of the early statements in favour of the PEP approach suggest that the cost of intensive housing management is more than out-weighed by the financial benefits, notably by a reduction in the number of empty houses and a reduction in rent arrears. (See Polly Toynbee, *The Guardian*, Friday 19 February 1982). In contrast, local authorities have assumed that the costs of establishing and staffing local offices, including the increased training costs, are likely to be higher than any increase in revenues. They would also argue that their more limited form of decentralisation can be made to work effectively. In any case, the claim that intensive housing management leads to reduce rent arrears is open to doubt. Rent arrears are mostly influenced by economic and financial factors (trends in the local unemployment rate, the level of social security and housing benefit pay-ments) which are beyond the control of a housing agency.

❑ In relation to the organisation of building work, small teams are generally considered less efficient than larger, more specialised teams serving a larger area. Efficiency in building maintenance involves economies of scale in tendering, in the ordering of materials and in the organisation of skilled labour such as plasterers and electricians.

❑ Finally, the introduction of local allocations has been hindered by the desire of most local authorities to pursue district-wide or borough-wide policies. Many councillors would argue that residents living on different estates should all have the same likelihood of obtaining a home and that any local variations are potentially unfair. The fear is also sometimes expressed that the delegation of housing allocations might lead to a situation in which applicants for a house would be judged on the basis of a 'beauty contest', rather than in terms of their needs. Where local allocations policies do exist, they apply to small areas characterised either by a high turnover of tenants or by low demand. In such areas, local allocations have the advantage of giving priority to people who actually want to live there (Griffiths *et al.*, 1996). They also enable the social housing agency to slow down the turnover of tenants and to re-establish a sense of local community (see the case study of Holly Street estate, Hackney (5.2)).

Alongside decentralisation and participation, the Department of the Environment argued, in the early 1980s, for local budgets. The aim was to provide a full statement of the expenditure and income of each estate and, in doing this, to provide an assessment of their relative financial performance. However, very few, if any local authorities established such budgets. The reasons were varied. Estate budgets had no clear relevance to the typical demands of tenants for a better housing service. They also had disadvantages. Large-scale and expensive changes were needed in the accounting procedures as these were (and remain) based on rent pooling across the whole of the local authority housing stock. Furthermore, housing officers believed the establishment of estate budgets would publicise and so call into question existing arrangements for cross-subsidies between trouble-free estates and those with the highest rent arrears, vacancy levels and management problems (see Kirby *et al.*, 1988).

After 1985, the publications of the Priority Estates Project and of the Department of the Environment hardly mention estate budgets. So it is unlikely that many local authorities have favoured their creation after this date. Admittedly local authorities have introduced estate improvement budgets which local managers and residents can spend as they see fit. However, these are not full estate budgets of the type envisaged by the Priority Estates Project in the early 1980s. They do not, for example, depend on rental income or attempt to match rent income and outgoings on improvements and other forms of estate expenditure.

In any case, the context of housing management has now changed with the requirement, introduced into England in 1995, that local authorities should put their management services out to competitive tender. Competitive tendering and estate budgets have some similarities. Competitive tendering requires a clearer accounting system than local authorities have usually used. In the case of the larger local authority, competitive tendering also requires a subdivision of the housing stock into smaller, more manageable units. Moreover, some local authorities took the advantage of competitive tendering to restructure their housing service.

However, the differences are also significant. Whereas the management initiatives favoured by the PEP stress the collective rights of tenants, competitive tendering stresses their individual rights as consumers. Competitive tendering does not, for example, permit participation at the level of an estate, though tenants may participate in the setting of performance standards. Competitive tendering incorporates a more market-oriented strategy of reform, with a greater emphasis on cost reduction, than the measures pursued by the Priority Estates Project.

The desire to reduce, or at least not to increase, management costs is probably the single most important constraint on decentralisation. The decentralisation measures of the 1980s, though still intact, have not been followed by a further wave of more radical measures. Anecdotal reports suggest that some local authorities have recently reduced staffing levels within local offices. Discussion of participation still persist, however. Housing management has not returned to its previous complacency.

Co-operatives and related initiatives

The limitations of local authority decentralisation and, to some extent, of estate budgets have led to a search for other, more radical means of changing housing management. Co-operatives provide perhaps the most participatory form of social housing. They combine in a single body the different interests of tenant and landlord and, according to their supporters, they create a sense of local community. Moreover, the supporters note, the tenants of co-operatives are aware of these advantages. A national survey of co-operatives in England, undertaken in 1986 and 1987 by McCafferty (1989, p. iii) states that,

> 'when asked why they chose to live in a co-op, tenants frequently mentioned specifically wanting to live in a co-op and having a say in how their property was managed.'

Co-operatives are not without their disadvantages, however. Their small size means that they are vulnerable to adverse financial circumstances. For example, if a relatively large housing association or local authority identifies a need for expensive repairs on an estate, it can draw on extensive resources to tackle the problem. If, in contrast, a small co-operative finds that its stock needs expensive repairs, it may face bankruptcy. A further disadvantage is that co-operatives are generally unable to employ a wide range of specialised professional staff, able to anticipate opportunities and problems. In any case, setting-up and running a co-operative thereafter is a time-consuming task that requires substantial personal commitment and skills amongst its members.

The limitations of co-operatives have, in turn, led the Priority Estates Project to develop a new model of tenant participation, called the Estate Management Board (EMB), in which the local authority remains the major landlord. The EMB comprises a management agreement between the local authority and the tenants of an estate. It ensures a degree of local autonomy, but does not load sole responsibility onto the tenants as in a co-operative (see Bell *et al.*, 1990; Zipfel, 1989). From the tenants' viewpoint, therefore, the board involves fewer financial risks than a co-operative and offers the possibility of more administrative and technical support.

A review of the first eight pilot projects suggests that the concept of the Estate Management Board is potentially popular with tenants; that it can succeed in areas with no previous experience of tenant participation; and that it permits a continued involvement from local councillors. On the other hand, it has limitations. It is poorly adapted to areas where the local authority stock is scattered; it requires the full support of the local authority to go ahead and also requires the availability of resources to tackle any significant capital repairs or design deficiencies (Bell, 1991). Finally, it is unsuited to estates with a high turnover of tenants. In such areas, the composition of the board may prove unstable.

The case for tenant participation was recognised in the Leasehold Reform, Housing the Urban Development Act 1993. This gives tenants a statutory right to manage their home. However, the regulations for tenant housing management preclude the secondment of local authority staff. The tenants now have to pay for any professional advice or help. The right to manage, at least in its present form, offers less practical support to tenants than the original concept of the Estate Management Board and is, for this reason, likely to prove less popular.

The establishment of co-operatives and Estate Management Boards has, in any case, proceede only slowly. Between 1990 and 1992, 62 tenant management organisations were established in England. At the end of this period, in 1992, tenant management organisations only accounted for a very small proportion of the housing stock, just over 2% of the total Council stock in 1992, even if planned as well as completed initiatives are included in the calculation (DoE, 1992e, pp. 6–7). Co-operatives and Estate Management Boards, like earlier initiatives, have now largely disappeared from the specialist journals. It is unlikely therefore that a large number of such organisations have gone ahead since 1992.

Estate agreements

As an alternative to both co-operatives and Estate Management Boards, the supporters of participation in housing management have advocated Estate Agreements. In the words of Steele *et al.* (1995):

> '(Estate agreements) represent a negotiated agreement between landlords and tenants of a particular area concerning the standards of service to be provided, and mutually agreed priorities for action for the coming years.'

Estate Agreements are consistent with the 'contract climate' of local government, as represented in competitive tendering, though they are not contracts in the sense of legally binding documents. The agreements are more like statements of intent.

The main advantage of Estate Agreements is their flexibility. They may be applied to estates of different sizes and may be adapted to meet specific local circumstances. They may be formal or informal, depending on the wishes of the parties; they permit varying degrees of tenant control; varying degrees of intensive housing management; and a varying involvement from other local authority services if necessary. They may also be used in estates in multiple ownership by different social housing agencies.

Local authorities have introduced Estate Agreements in Camden, York and Lancaster. Initial evaluations suggest that these Agreements have potential for development in the future. The main disadvantages are similar to those experienced in virtually all exercises in tenant participation. They comprise the costs of setting up the agreement; the possibility of stimulating unrealistic demands amongst tenants; the possibility of an over-bureaucratic approach in which tenants are overwhelmed by paperwork and meetings; and the possibility of an unsympathetic response from agencies and contractors that are mostly concerned with the achievement of financial targets (see Cole and Smith, 1995; Roe, 1995; Steele *et al.*, 1995).

An assessment of local management initiatives

Local management initiatives generally receive a favourable review. There is almost complete agreement that improved housing management, involving the tenants, is usually necessary in the improvement of unpopular estates. There is less agreement about whether improved housing management is sufficient or about whether the intensive, small area models of the Priority Estates Project invariably provide the best results.

Some evaluations of intensive housing management provide unqualified support.

❑ Power (1984) has reviewed the experience of the first 20 projects, as revealed in a survey in 1982 after two or three years of action. She noted improvement in all cases, but more so in low-rise 'cottage' estates than in the mid-and high-rise blocks built in the 1960s and 1970s. Improvements included a cleaner environment, achieved by the provision of rubbish skips for the use of local residents, by a combination of paid and voluntary clean-up campaigns and a variety of other techniques; a better and quicker repairs service, at least achieved in those projects which had involved the decentralisation of the repairs service; and a reduction in the number of empty dwellings.

❑ The Association of Metropolitan Authorities (1986, p. 20) has given an equally favourable review of estate-based initiatives.

> 'Schemes such as these go a long way in improving the lives of tenants: repairs are carried out more quickly and efficiently, management staff are more aware of specific problems or characteristics of the estate on which they work and there is greater opportunity for people who live on estates to become involved in the way that their homes are managed.'

❑ Finally, Glennerster and Turner (1993) have provided a favourable evaluation, based on the comparison of the progress over three years of two experimental Priority Estates Project initiatives and two other 'control' estates where no such initiative was implemented. The researchers used a combination of

    ○ two questionnaire surveys, before and after the changes;

o   physical surveys of the standards of maintenance of external areas;
o   interviews with staff.

They concluded that

> 'the decentralisation of housing management and maintenance functions to an estate level did succeed in improving the standard of most aspects of the housing service, most notably short term repairs, and raised tenant satisfaction. It was also associated with a reduced level of property damage and nuisance.'

In contrast, other studies provide more qualified support.

❏   Power's later reports, based on revisits to the estates in 1988 and 1994, place greater emphasis on the constraints. Poverty and social tensions continued in the estates. Indeed, in some cases, the incidence of poverty, unemployment, lone parenthood and, in the London estates, the proportion of black households had increased (Power, 1995). Decentralisation had not proceeded far enough; problems of poor physical condition had not been fully resolved; concern about crime and social breakdown had increased.

❏   Llewelyn-Davies (1994b) have surveyed the environmental quality of 50 residential areas in London, including both improved and unimproved social housing estates. They used professional surveyors to rate the quality of estates. They also interviewed representatives of the organisations involved in the design and implementation of improvements. The report of the survey notes 'the positive improvement made through the ... Estate Action programme'. However, it also lists the limitations of recent initiatives (1994b, pp. 9–10).

> '– despite physical improvements both improved and unimproved estates still tend to suffer from a harsh, unfriendly, monotonous and noisy environment;
> – the importance of after care and maintenance in sustaining the quality of improvements was not always recognised;
> – estates cannot be separated from their surrounding environment. The most successful estate improvements are those which are set within a wider programme of economic development and environmental improvement.'

To an extent, the observations of Llewelyn-Davies have been accepted in recent initiatives. The improvement of local authority estates is now more likely than in the 1980s to be tied into broader regeneration programmes undertaken, in England, within the framework of the City Challenge and Single Regeneration Budget initiatives. In Scotland, the Regeneration Partnerships, established in 1988, also provide a broad framework for estate improvement.

❏   Finally, much depends on the quality of implementation. The Home Office has undertaken an independent evaluation of intensive housing management to determine its impact on crime and anti-social behaviour. The study was based on the same estates as that undertaken by Glennerster and Turner, but used a slightly different research method. Questionnaire surveys were supplemented by participant observation, for example attending resident meetings and attempting to develop local social contacts through informal discussions. The report gives the example of an estate where the goodwill of local residents was lost at the start by the unsympathetic approach of the first team leader. Thereafter, the second team leader had a difficult fight to make up a loss of confidence. Moreover, the demoralisation of tenants was heightened by the temporary withdrawal of the Priority Estates Project consultants and by the loss of a popular home beat policeman. In this particular case, intensive housing management on the project model was less effective than in the nearby 'control' estate that had benefited from an independent, though less radical, local authority decentralisation initiative (Foster and Hope, 1994, pp. 84–85). Clearly, local authority decentralisation can be made to work at least as well as small-scale intensive management on the Priority Estates Project model.

The evaluation of intensive housing management presupposes an evaluation of the significance of participation. The advocates of management initiatives typically assume that the only way to reverse the decline of estates is 'through harnessing the energy and goodwill of residents and workers' (Power, 1984, pp. 1–2). Such statements ignore the extent to which the success of community-based initiatives depends on pre-existing resources for self-organisation.

The pattern of community organisation varies from place to place. Some local authority estates possess a strong tradition of tenant organisations and leadership. On other estates there may be no tenants' groups, whilst elsewhere the tenants' groups may comprise no more than two or three committed individuals. Moreover, the groups are often short-lived. They grow in response to some problem or threat or as a result of a community development initiative and then decline in strength as the initial impetus fades away. There is nothing unusual in this. Middle class residential areas are also often lacking in community organisations unless faced by some external threat such as a proposal for a road.

There has to be an incentive for even the most community-minded resident to spend their time in lengthy and sometimes complex negotiations with local authorities and other agencies. In many cases, the incentive is provided by the promise of modernisation or rehabilitation. The report of the Priority Estates Project follow-up survey (Power, 1991, p. 93), undertaken in 1988, states that,

'physical improvements were particularly effective in winning tenants' support and involvement, and in developing much more positive attitudes towards the estate.'

What is less widely recognised, at least in the PEP and community development literature, is that there is no guarantee that the tenants' group will continue on completion of the modernisation works.

There is another reason why the potential of tenants' groups has to be qualified. The work involved in first starting a group and then in keeping the group running creates, as Donnison (1991, p. 62) has noted, 'strong personal bonds and a power structure in which newcomers with new ideas may not be welcome'.

There is a risk of some form of discrimination. Indeed, this is a reason why local authorities are sometimes reluctant to establish local allocations for different estates. In addition, local rivalries and personality disputes may also encourage a defensive, inward-looking attitude amongst community leaders. Consequently, it is essential that the local authority, or possibly some other agency, retains the ability to supervise the activities of tenants' groups and to ensure that they organise their procedures on a democratic basis.

SOCIAL BALANCE

Policies for estate renewal have a significant omission. Accounts of unpopular estates frequently link their problems to patterns of social segregation. For example, Power (1984, p. 11) writes that,

> '... concentrations of vulnerable households ... not only intensify the families' isolation and compound the impact of poverty on the life of the community, but also feed the image of deprivation and therefore the unpopularity of an estate.'

In addition, it is sometimes said, segregation encourages the emergence of a British 'underclass'. This is a group of people characterised not simply by poverty but by a dependent culture and various forms of anti-social behaviour, such as an inability or unwillingness to participate in paid employment and an involvement in crime and drug use. Social segregation, it is argued, intensifies the trend towards an underclass. It removes those sources of community leadership, support and control that would otherwise keep deviant and criminal activities in check (see Foster and Hope, 1994, p. 9).

Social balance is the opposite of segregation. It may be understood as a situation in which a representative cross-section of different social groups, ethnic groups and family types live in the same place. For those who see social segregation as a cause of problem estates, social balance is a logical starting point for estate regeneration.

Practical and ethical constraints

With a few exceptions, mostly concerned with the reduction of child densities, local authorities seldom attempt to upgrade estates through local allocations policies or the promotion of social balance. Local authorities may promote social balance either through changing their allocation practices or through selling houses and blocks of houses into owner-occupation. Neither is easy to implement.

Constraints within social housing

The residual role of local authorities within the housing market is arguably the most significant constraint on the achievement of social balance within an estate.

Local authorities no longer house a cross-section of the community. They only house people in need and unable to buy.

In addition, local authorities are required to accept whoever will live on an unpopular estate by the emphasis that most local councillors and most independent advisers, including the Priority Estates Project, place on the speedy allocation of empty dwellings. The achievement of social balance requires that vacant dwellings remain vacant until a household with the appropriate economic and demographic characteristics declare a desire to move in. Vacant, boarded-up houses are an eyesore. They attract vandalism and squatting.

Housing associations encounter similar constraints. They are undertaking active programmes of new house building in a way that local authorities are not. They may, therefore, seek to locate new housing schemes in relatively attractive owner-occupied areas. However, housing associations are not free agents. They have to develop where land is available at not too high a price, for example in or near existing local authority estates. Moreover, nearly all housing associations are required, by virtue of nomination and other agreements made with local authorities, with the Housing Corporation and other funding agencies, to house the poor and the homeless. These agreements cannot be easily broken or altered in a way that might permit housing associations to move up-market.

Even if local authorities and housing associations were able to pursue policies for social balance, it does not necessarily follow that they should do so. The implementation of such policies generally requires a local housing manager or possibly some other person to make a judgement on whether the history and social characteristics of the members of a household are of the correct type for each estate. If the household members are of the wrong type, they are turned away. In France, social housing agencies sometimes refuse to house people if their social and economic characteristics fail to promote the social balance. Such practices would almost certainly prove incompatible with the social ethos of housing associations and local authorities in Britain.

There are, moreover, special objections if the promotion of social balance involves the dispersal of ethnic minority households into predominantly white residential areas. Policies for ethnic balance amount to less favourable treatment of ethnic minorities, if they are not pursued on a voluntary basis. Thus they can easily break the Race Relations Acts 1968 and 1976 which forbid racial discrimination in housing (MacEwan, 1991, p. 180, pp. 230–232, p. 410).

Social balance policies also raise a series of practical questions. At what level of concentration do the problems of poverty become exacerbated to the point that action is necessary? What types of person should be prevented from moving in? What effects would such policies have on other areas and other local authority estates? What effects would such policies have on the housing rights and housing opportunities of those turned away?

Constraints on the sale of social housing

The sale of social housing into owner-occupation encounters other constraints. The sale of occupied housing under the provisions of the Right-to-Buy legislation

does not promote social balance, as it involves no change in the social composition of an estate. Indeed, the Right-to-Buy has been criticised as exacerbating
existing divisions between 'good' and 'bad' estates. To achieve social balance,
sale has to be aimed at outsiders, to buyers who would not have otherwise
moved into such an area. The radical Conservative government of the early
1980s encouraged such a policy. The guide *Tackling Priority Estates* cites
various advantages. The sale of the local authority stock brings empty dwellings
back into use; it provides extended opportunities for low-cost owner-
occupation; it generates capital receipts for the local authority; and finally it
saves the capital investment of repairs and improvement (DoE, 1983b).

The policy proceeded at first through a so-called 'homesteading' initiative in
which the local authority sold houses to individuals to make improvements and
repairs as appropriate. The initiative assumed the existence of large numbers of
'surplus' local authority properties that were more or less suitable for immediate
occupation. In practice, the numbers were always limited and became increasingly so as local authorities faced a growing problem of homelessness. Many
vacant properties were empty owing to building defects and delays in local
authority modernisation schemes. Others were located in high-rise blocks or in
run-down areas that were unattractive to potential purchasers, even with a
discount of say 20 or 30%. Still others were merely vacant between lettings and
were required to meet the local authority's own housing obligations. The total
number of voluntary sales is not recorded. However, Littlewood and Mason
(1984, p. 25) state that, by March 1984, about 6700 houses had been sold by
local authorities and new towns to individuals through the homesteading
initiatives. Thereafter, the sale of individual Council dwellings disappeared as a
national policy for estate regeneration.

The limitations of individual sales soon led the Conservative government in
power in the 1980s to promote the disposal of local authority dwellings to
private developers. The assumption was that developers would undertake
modernisation schemes before sale to the eventual occupier. However, the
numbers again remained very small. In 1985 only 0.1% of the local authority
stock had been sold in this way (Duncan, 1988, p. 7).

Ideological opposition from Labour-controlled local authorities was one
reason for the small number of sales, especially in the early 1980s. These
authorities sometimes took the view that the promotion of sales to private
developers was motivated purely by the ideology of the Conservative government and would not help their tenants. However, even where local authorities
were prepared to sell, they encountered numerous obstacles. Developers were
sceptical of the profitability of the schemes and doubted whether the high cost of
repairs and environmental improvements could be adequately covered by the
low house prices which, apart from inner London, are usual in areas of predominant local authority housing. As a result, developers did not come forward
to buy estates or they offered prices that the local authorities regarded as too
low. Local authorities doubted the feasibility of emptying blocks in a way which
would, simultaneously, meet the demands of tenants for suitable accommodation elsewhere and the desire of developers for a strict timetable. Organised

protests from local residents, the difficulty of moving residents who had exercised their Right-to-Buy and the vandalism of empty dwellings during the rehousing process were other worries.

Completed disposal schemes have been generally satisfactory (Glendinning *et al.*, 1989). They have generally provided better housing for those who have moved in (mainly because the schemes have been mostly offered to first-time buyers) and better housing for those who have moved elsewhere (partly because local authorities have been sensitive to the wishes of tenants and additionally because the property was invariably in need of modernisation before sale). They have also improved the immediate environment. The disposal of empty blocks of flats or vacant sites within local authority estates persists as a selective measure. However, it is unlikely that local authorities could repeat the early successes, were they to undertake the mass disposal of property. The simultaneous requirement of finding better accommodation for those who move out, of meeting the needs of those eligible for Council housing and of attracting owner-occupiers to low status estates implies an extremely expensive housing programme.

Examples of social balance initiatives

The case for social balance deserves a closer scrutiny. The promotion of social balance has a long history in progressive thought in the late nineteenth and twentieth centuries. It was an aspect of the garden city movement before the First World War and was later adopted in the housing and new town programmes of the 1945 Labour government. Aneurin Bevan was a particular advocate of social balance. Bevan deleted the term working class from the provision of local authority housing and sought to ensure that local authorities built for all. Bevan was scathing about the inter-war and earlier patterns of urban development. These he regarded as 'castrated communities'. Instead, he wished to build 'the living tapestry of a mixed community' similar to the long established English and Welsh village (Foot, 1975, pp. 75–76).

The promotion of social balance disappeared as a deliberate policy initiative in the 1950s. It foundered on the growth of owner-occupation and the persistence of quality variations within the local authority housing stock. In the meantime, the implementation of the policies for social balance stimulated a series of evaluation studies. This was probably the first time that social researchers had sought to evaluate a planning policy. The conclusions were generally sceptical. They suggested that physical and social distance is largely independent of one another; that social balance, defined as the existence of a cross-section of social and economic groups in the same estate, does not promote social interaction, and may even promote disputes between neighbours; and that, if given the choice, most people would prefer to have neighbours of a similar background to themselves (Orlans, 1952, pp. 81–95; Kuper, 1953; Carey and Mapes, 1972).

A recent survey, undertaken by Cole (1996) in four housing association estates in Yorkshire, comes to similar conclusions. In one relatively deprived estate, for example,

> 'Many residents said they valued living near people in similar circumstances to their own, not least because of opportunities to develop informal networks (around child care, for example) when formal provision was inaccessible or too expensive.'

The survey also included a series of focus group discussions where residents discussed their ideal estate. Social balance was not a major concern. When asked about an ideal estate, residents spoke, amongst other things, about the need for adequate resources to support the integration of different groups, about the need for suitable and affordable facilities and about the need for some kinds of 'community contract' to mitigate neighbour conflicts.

The results of the post-war surveys have, in turn, led Evans to suggest a more or less natural process of 'social agglomeration' in which the movement of individual households creates areas of a relatively uniform social composition. Evans (1973) states:

> 'If people in a given income group prefer to interact with others who are in the same group it is plausible to assume that they will prefer to live in the same area as the others and that, *ceteris paribus*, the greater the number in the same group in that area, the greater advantage of living in that area will be.'

The argument is purely theoretical. Evans assumes that social homogeneity arises from the desire of people to interact with neighbours. If social homogeneity arises from a desire to avoid problems with neighbours, the possibility remains of some combination of fine grained segregation at, say the level of a series of streets, within the context of social balance at the level of a neighbourhood. It may also be possible to build small social housing estates, in respectable areas or to build new communities, with a mix of tenures.

There is no universal tendency towards greater social agglomeration. It is possible to find examples of areas, for example, in inner London, where the degree of social balance has increased as a result of an influx of middle class people into a previously poor or working class area. Such gentrification leads to a reduction in the housing opportunities for low income people, unless countered by low cost housing provision elsewhere. However, it does not necessarily lead to an increase in tensions within the local community (see Bridge, 1990).

The main implication of the post-war surveys is to weaken the idea of social balance as an antidote to the British underclass. The distinction between physical distance and social distance suggests that, even in a mixed or socially balanced community, families and individuals will often retain distinct life styles, including deviant life styles. The concept of the underclass is, in any case, subject to other criticisms. The underclass considers poverty as a cultural process. It blames poor people for their predicament and ignores the economic causes of poverty.

The promotion of ethnic and racial balance was not a significant theme in town planning and housing policy in the 1940s and 1950s. The number of ethnic minority people, though growing in the 1950s, was relatively small. However, it is possible to find a few later examples. For instance, in the early 1970s the London Borough of Lewisham and Birmingham City Council used a slum clearance programme to break up concentrations of Afro-Caribbean and Asian people. In practice, however, as was demonstrated by research undertaken by the Community Relations Council and later reported by Flett (1984), dispersal had disadvantages. Dispersal did not promote racial harmony. White hostility was just as widespread in areas with a low concentration of black people as in high concentration areas. Moreover, black people and Asians did not share the negative image of their community as a 'ghetto'. They valued the support and amenities available from living amongst people with a similar life style and when rehoused as a result of slum clearance, they frequently insisted that they were not relocated far from their previous residence. Fear of violence and of racial attacks were other factors that deterred minority households from moving away. Most likely, for a variety of reasons, the trend towards 'social agglomeration', to use Evans' term, is stronger among ethnic minority households than among income groups within the white population.

Planned dispersal and social balance in inner London

The debate about social balance takes a slightly different form in inner London. Here, the *Final Report of the Lambeth Inner Area Study* suggests that social balance is the only practical way of tackling inner city housing problems (Shankland *et al.*, 1977). Owner-occupiers are able to move out of inner London, the report notes, if they so wish. The low income tenants of local authorities and of private landlords generally have no such choice, even though a substantial proportion would almost certainly wish to do so and any such move would improve living conditions in inner London. Balanced dispersal would reduce child densities and overcrowding in the inner city and would also enable the replacement of flats by family houses.

To an extent, the recent pattern of housing association development has followed that recommended in the Lambeth Inner Area Study. For reasons of cost and land availability, housing associations have purchased existing properties and undertaken development in the London suburbs and beyond, and have rehoused people from inner London. Building costs and land costs are higher in inner London than elsewhere in England and are recognised as such in the annual cost allowances (the system of Total Cost Indicators) prepared by the Housing Corporation. Development in inner London is also often more complex than elsewhere. It is in the interests of those involved in social housing to avoid development in inner London. Moreover, where local authorities and housing associations undertake the redevelopment of older estates to provide more low-rise family housing, the result is generally lower densities.

However, the recommendations of the Lambeth Inner Area Study have never been implemented on a co-ordinated basis. Since the abolition of the Greater London Council in 1986 there has been no strategic housing and planning authority for Greater London. Indeed, even before the abolition of the Greater London Council, the possibility of a co-ordinated dispersal, policy was restricted by a combination of the opposition of the Conservative controlled suburban boroughs and the weaknesses of the Council's powers (Young and Kramer, 1978).

The recommendations of the Lambeth Inner Area Study are, in some ways, the exception that proves the rule.They remain distinct in supporting social balance as desirable for environmental reasons and as a means of promoting housing choice. They avoid any suggestion of social engineering, of reducing social segregation as a means of controlling the underclass.

However, even the apparently benign recommendations of the Lambeth Inner Area Study raise numerous questions and practical difficulties. Let us, for the moment, assume that the original diagnosis holds true and that large numbers of low income households still want to move out of inner London. How much investment should be allocated to dispersal and how much to reducing poverty and improving living conditions in the exporting area? What are the likely effects of dispersal on the economy of the exporting area? Would dispersal, as was widely argued in the 1970s, precipitate further economic decline in the inner city?

The answers to these questions are troubling. It is obvious that any large-scale dispersion programme, even if phased in over a number of years, risks damaging the economy of the exporting area. The only exception is if the exporting area is experiencing rapid population growth. In such circumstances, however, the achievement of social balance would be a superfluous aim. Dispersal would be justified merely as a means of meeting housing needs.

CONCLUSIONS

The assessment of public policies towards problem estates depends crucially on the level of prior expectations. If estate upgrading is expected to resolve all problems on a permanent, once and for all basis, the results are often disappointing. Even after ten years of effort or longer, there are still numerous examples of unpopular local authority estates. Even some of the early pilot PEP schemes which have received sustained long-term attention continue to possess a poor social reputation and an increasing proportion of poor and otherwise vulnerable households (Power, 1995).

The evaluations undertaken within the framework of the Priority Estates Project are open to criticism that they are only concerned with the impact of management measures. Improved housing management cannot resolve all the problems caused by building disrepair or a poor design, let alone the problems caused by unemployment and poverty. However, a similar impression of fragility is also in other renewal exercises. The same impression is evident in the evaluation of crime prevention measures and in the evaluation of large-scale multi-agency regeneration partnerships such as the Wester Hailes regeneration partnership in Edinburgh (see Case Study 5.1). In the latter case, the evaluations of progress have still expressed concern about the persistence of unemployment, the tendency of the housing allocation systems to bring in unemployed people from elsewhere and the need to develop management and other measures that might cope with the withdrawal of the funding programmes.

If, in contrast, estate upgrading is viewed as a modest exercise in maintaining living standards, a more positive evaluation is possible. Estate-based measures may lessen the impact of inequality, reduce stigmatisation and, in doing all this, improve the quality of life of residents. Where the original conditions are very poor, improvement and redevelopment is also likely to improve the health of residents.

Local authority housing is not simply a collection of problem estates. The English House Condition Survey shows that most tenants are satisfied with their home, even if the proportion is not as high as in the owner-occupied sector. Estate upgrading helps to maintain tenant satisfaction.

In relation to the experience of specific measures, it is possible to specify various lessons.

❑ As is widely recognised, crime prevention is crucial to the outcome. Indeed, in the poorest and most stigmatised estates, crime prevention is often the most important measure of all. Moreover, measures to reduce the fear of crime are as important as the reduction of its incidence. The most successful anti-crime initiatives are those that:
  ○ include a variety of measures that are selected pragmatically according to an analysis of the types of problem and the priorities of residents;
  ○ are supported by measures to improve social and economic conditions;
  ○ involve measures, say training or recreational programmes, that reach young people.
❑ There is no single way forward in the provision of good quality housing management. There is a variety of different ways, for example limited decentralisation, radical decentralisation, the establishment of co-operatives and estate management boards, and the introduction of estate agreements, each of which makes different demands on tenants, officers and local councillors and is better suited to different situations. Moreover, much depends on the quality and commitment of staff.
❑ Local or estate-based allocations may be justified as an exceptional measure to reduce the turnover of tenants in areas of low demand. However, broader policies to promote social balance should be treated with caution, as their aims may not accord with residents' priorities. The achievement of social balance may involve people in need being turned away and may, as a result, lead to discrimination against particular types of household and ethnic groups.

Case study: Wester Hailes, Edinburgh

The Wester Hailes Partnership is an example of a well-funded, multi-agency attempt to renew a large, deprived local authority estate. Wester Hailes is one of four Partnerships announced by the Scottish Office in 1988. An interim evaluation is available in the Partnership's Progress Report, published in 1994 and in an independent report prepared by McGregor *et al.* (1995).

Wester Hailes, located on the western periphery of Edinburgh, was developed between 1969 and 1975. The housing stock on completion comprised a mixture of tenements and high rise. By the time the Partnership began, Wester Hailes possessed a declining population of about 12 000, with a high proportion of single parent and low income households, high unemployment and a high turnover of tenancies. Wester Hailes was not the most deprived area in Edinburgh. However, it was clearly in need of renewal.

Renewal has proceeded through overlapping initiatives covering housing and environmental improvement, the improvement of social facilities, the provision of training opportunities and the promotion of community activities and community involvement. Housing and environmental improvements have accounted for most of the expenditure. Crime prevention was not a stated aim of the initial renewal strategy. However, many of the initiatives have had a role in crime prevention. For example, the housing and environmental improvements have involved the creation of defensible space: the community initiatives have promoted neighbourhood watch and have given young people recreational opportunities.

The Partnership has had a mixed success. The housing and environmental improvements have had a visible impact. Most of the old, unpopular high-rise blocks have been demolished. New low-rise estates have been developed. Areas of tenement housing have been improved, as has satisfaction with housing. Privately-funded improvement has taken place in the town centre. Some indicators of crime, notably burglary, have shown a relatively fast rate of decline. On the other hand, unemployment levels remain high compared to the Edinburgh average.

The estate remains predominantly in the ownership of the local authority whose allocations practices continue to bring a high proportion of unemployed and single parent households to the estate. Allocations practices in the Wester Hailes Community Housing Association, established after the Housing (Scotland) Act 1988, have much the same effect. The local housing agencies cannot change their allocation priorities, without abandoning their commitment to house those in need.

The main question now is whether recent improvements will prove sustainable, once the funding largely ceases in 1999. Much will depend on the extent to which population turnover declines, and on the quality and effectiveness of estate management. Finally, much will depend on the effectiveness of local educational and training centres.

(a)

(b)

(c)

Fig. 5.1 (a) Unimproved tenements, (b) improved tenements, and (c) new housing in Wester Hailes.

Case study: the Holly Street estate, Hackney

The experience of the Holly Street estate illustrates, in an extreme form, the processes of decline and regeneration in social housing (Fig. 5.2). Holly Street features in Harrison's *Inside the Inner City* (1983). Harrison explains how the estate declined from a model to a 'sink' within five years of its completion in 1971. The estate, in the words of Harrison, 'typifies the expensive problems that past errors have left for present generations to suffer and revolt' (p. 227). In the 1990s, in contrast, Holly Street has been the subject of an ambitious initiative, led by the Hackney Borough Council. An initial evaluation of the first phase has been made by Woodin *et al.*, 1996.

The estate comprised, at the time of completion, 1187 dwellings in four tower blocks and a series of five storey blocks laid around grassy quadrangles. The external environment of the estate was, and where not demolished, remains no worse than many other local authority estates of the same date. The main source of problem, from the outset, was the interior conditions of the flats, especially the five storey blocks. The homes in the blocks have long suffered from problems of noise and insect infestation. The blocks have also proved expensive to repair and have suffered from persistent problems of squatting. Above all, the internal corridors are long, dark and grim, with numerous signs of graffiti.

Hackney Borough Council made various attempts to rectify the problems in the 1980s, but these were frustrated by a lack of finance. The present attempt started in 1991 with the announcement of the Hackney 'Comprehensive Estate Initiative', covering five large system-built estates. It is due for completion in the year 2000 or 2001 and is linked to another renewal programme, a City Challenge initiative, that focuses on the commercial area of Dalston. The regeneration of Holly Street is organised around a partnership that includes the local authority, tenants' representatives, five housing associations and a construction company, Laing Homes.

The initiative combines the redevelopment and improvement of the estate, with training programmes for young people, measures for community development and community art. In Holly Street, community art measures have had a striking visual impact. They include a temporary mural on the fence around the building site and a series of mysterious footpath signs.

The redevelopment aims to replace the system-built estate with traditional housing, organised around a traditional street layout. On completion, the estate will possess a mixture of family and single person housing and a mixture of local authority, housing association and owner-occupied. The total number of units will be reduced to about 960. In part, the programme is intended to promote the stability of the community. For the social housing, the local housing manager operates a rule of rehousing at least 65% of original tenants in the completed houses on the scheme.

The training initiatives will take many years to evaluate. The evaluation of the initial phase of completed new houses has revealed very encouraging results; residents feel safer and report less crime; they express a greater sense of personal well-being and report a lower dependence on the local health services.

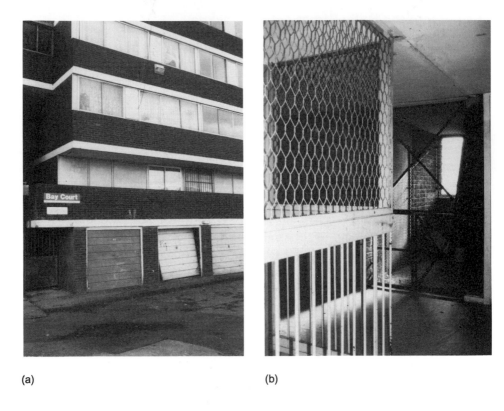

(a)   (b)

(c)

Fig. 5.2   (a) External and (b) internal conditions in the old Holly Street estate. (c) The first phase of completed houses at Holly Street.

Chapter 6
The management of urban growth

The renewal of older urban areas often requires a combination of housing renewal and measures to promote the development of vacant sites. However, the sources of potential housing sites are diverse and include not just sites within residential areas, but also those in abandoned industrial areas, surplus hospital and school sites (so-called windfall sites that arise from the continuous process of economic development), and greenfield sites that are beyond the built-up area. The diversity of competing housing sites means that it is necessary to relate the development of individual sites to the general pattern of urban growth and development, including the balance between urban and rural sites in the provision of new housing.

There are particular reasons for a broad view of urban growth. In 1995 and 1996, demographic forecasts suggested the existence of a huge backlog of unmet housing demand. Holmans (1995) has suggested, for example, the need for over 4.7 million new homes in England in the period between 1991 and 2011. The figures may be exaggerated. They may represent a projection of the number of people who would like to set up an independent home, rather than an estimate of the number who will be able to do so. However, the projections have concentrated the minds of the major planning pressure groups and the government on where the additional households will go. (Also see Breheny and Hall, 1996.)

THE COMPACT CITY AS AN AIM OF PUBLIC POLICY

The general aims of public policy may be summarised. The conventional wisdom in Britain is in favour of what might be called 'the compact city', meaning a city that counters tendencies towards dispersed or fragmented urban growth. Endorsement of the compact city is implicit in concepts of urban renewal and urban regeneration. Urban renewal implies the development within the existing bounds of a built-up area. Endorsement of the compact city is also stated explicitly in the guidance that central government offers to local authorities in the use of their planning powers. In England, for example, *Planning Policy Guidance: Housing* states that 'it is important that full and effective use is made of land within urban areas' (DoE, 1992c, revised, para. 15). Likewise, *Planning Policy Guidance: The Countryside and the Rural Economy* states that

'Expansion of villages and towns must avoid creating ribbon development or a fragmented pattern of development' (DoE, 1992d, para. 2.17).

The compact city encompasses the long-standing aim, dating back at least to the 1940s, of town planning as urban containment. The main aims of urban containment are to protect the countryside and to maintain a sharp boundary between town and country. In addition, the compact city expresses recent concerns with sustainable development, the minimisation of motor traffic and the reduction of pollution. The compact city promotes an urban form that, according to its supporters,

❑ is better suited to pedestrian movement;
❑ encourages the substitution of public for private transport.

The advantages of the compact city for public transport have, moreover, been supported by ECOTEC in a study undertaken for the Department of the Environment (Bozeat *et al.*, 1992). This study compared travelling patterns in eight case study areas and sought to assess the impact on travelling patterns of variations in population density, the degree of centralisation of economic activities and the degree of land use mix. The authors report that,

'– Variations in the amount of car travel between areas are mainly accounted for by differences in population density and car ownership; ...
– Differences between areas in the use of public transport for journey to work are remarkably well explained (some 90%) by a positive association with centralisation and density; ...'

The advantages of the compact city have to be qualified. The compact city can easily degenerate into a naive, backward-looking culturalist solution. It is not convincing to talk of a return to 'traditional' urban forms in the context of existing patterns of large scale urban growth.

In addition, the development of a compact city may encounter a degree of consumer resistance. The report of the national *Housing Attitudes Survey* suggests, in England, an inverse relationship between population density and residents' satisfaction with the area in which they live. Residents are more likely to be satisfied if they live in an area with a low population density and less likely to be satisfied if they live in an area with a high population density (Hedges and Clemens, 1994, p. 134).

The qualifications are not fatal. The compact city implies the intensification of urban land uses, rather than any particular pattern of urban form. It is possible, within a compact city, to retain a diversity of types of external space and neighbourhoods with a different character.

Moreover, the pattern revealed in the *Housing Attitudes Survey* does not necessarily suggest a popular dislike of high densities per se. Local authority areas with a high population density are generally characterised by an older housing stock and a higher proportion of local authority housing. These other characteristics may cause higher levels of dissatisfaction amongst the residents of higher density areas The lesson is to undertake new housing schemes in such a way that residents are protected from broader urban problems. Equally, the lesson is to combine new housing with measures to improve the older stock and its surroundings.

THE DEVELOPMENT OF URBAN SITES

Responsibility for town and country planning usually rests with a local authority. In England and Wales, the planning authority, as the responsible body is called, is usually either a District or a Borough Council, though in some parts of England County Councils also become involved in strategic issues. In Scotland, since April 1996, town and country planning has become the responsibility of Unitary Authorities. National Parks, Urban Development Corporations and New Town Development Corporations are also planning authorities where they exist.

From the viewpoint of a developer, the main role of a planning authority is to consider applications for planning permission. However, planning authorities do not make decisions on a wholly *ad hoc* basis. The planning legislation, as represented in England and Wales by Section 70(2) of the Town and Country Planning Act 1990, requires decision-makers to 'have regard to the development plan ... and to any other material considerations in determining planning applications'. The provisions of a development plan are the first factors to be considered and are not to be lightly dismissed.

The form of the development plan varies from place to place. It comprises *either* a combination of a Local Plan (a detailed land use plan) and a Structure Plan (a broader strategic policy statement) *or* a Unitary Development Plan that combines both local and strategic considerations. Whatever the precise form, however, the development plan provides an authoritative statement of the planning authority's views and is subject to a formal procedure of consultation that culminates in a public inquiry. Most plans cover a time scale of between about five and ten years and are revised every five years or so.

Preparation of a development plan requires the planning authority to estimate, in consultation with interested parties, the housing potential of sites within urban areas. Planning authorities have to do this to estimate the balance between greenfield and urban sites. The ultimate housing potential is not easy to estimate, however. The calculations made by the planning authority become quickly out-of-date and are generally sensitive to different judgements about their environmental suitability, likely development costs and market attractiveness.

To an extent, the planning authority can adapt and update its estimates through interim and non-statutory policy statements outside the development plan. However, uncertainties still remain. The estimates of the local authorities are seldom fully accepted by the pressure groups who have an interest in the outcome. The private house builders, who want as wide a choice as possible of development sites in greenfield areas, generally reduce the estimates to a bare minimum. The Council for the Preservation of Rural England and other related groups generally argue that more housing could be built within urban areas, if only developers were encouraged or required to do so.

The different interest groups make their estimate of land availability on different assumptions and ask very different questions. The private developers are concerned with short-term land availability. They ask the question: How much urban land has all the necessary preconditions for housing development, but is not developed? The answer in most cities is 'not much'.

In contrast, the local planning authorities are mostly interested in the estimation of trends. They attempt to estimate the stocks of land at varying stages in the housing development process. They ask: how much land is in the process of acquiring the preconditions for housing development?

Finally, rural conservation and environmental groups ask: How much urban land could be developed in the future given a commitment to do so? The answer is potentially very large, especially if all under-used open space and vacant non-residential land is used for housing. For example, Llewelyn-Davies (1994a) suggest that, in a typical English urban area, up to 90% more housing land can be identified than is possible under the conventional criteria of most planning authorities. In practice, however, only a proportion of this will ever be developed, depending on the extent of demand and the actual policy measures used to encourage such development.

The process of private house building in the inner city

The difficulty of making a reliable quantitative assessment of potential housing gain has meant that research into urban house building has mostly focused on a qualitative assessment of the constraints on development. Much of the research was stimulated by the inner city policies of the 1970s and 1980s. They have a social and economic emphasis, rather than the environmental emphasis that characterises more recent discussions. An *Inquiry into Planning for Housing*, prepared by The Joseph Rowntree Foundation (1994), lists the advantages of bringing housing to the inner city, defined, as has been usual, as an area of concentrated social and economic deprivation.

> 'New or refurbished housing in towns and cities can bring employment to the area, help stabilise existing communities and ensure that local businesses and services remain viable.'

Many of the arguments in favour of new house building apply to both private and social house building. In the mid 1980s, for example, the Labour Party campaigned for increased local authority house building as a job creation measure. However, the efforts of local authorities have focused mostly on private house building. In the 1990s, private house building has accounted for about 80% of all house completions in Britain. Moreover, private house building has a series of specific advantages in urban renewal (Goodchild *et al.*, 1984; Maclennan *et al.*, 1987). It can,

- add to the quantity and variety of the existing stock and meet new demands from younger owner-occupiers who wish to live near the city centre;
- help satisfy a demand for owner-occupation in areas where the owner-occupied stock is often small;
- help correct the population imbalances which result from the emigration of economically active households to the suburbs.

The main constraints

The first, and in many ways still the most systematic study of private house building in the inner city, is that undertaken by Nicholls *et al.* (1981) in Nottingham. It comprises a detailed assessment of the suitability of vacant sites in two sample areas, one in the inner city and another on the periphery, followed by two questionnaire surveys of the majority of private house builders active in the city. The first aspect deals with their general attitudes to the inner city, that is to the older areas where most vacant land is located, while the second deals with their attitude to specific sites.

The study found that most of the vacant land in the inner city was owned by the local authority. The main obstacles to development were land prices; a scarcity of available land caused mainly by the refusal of the Labour-controlled authority to sell; and a lack of knowledge of potential sites amongst developers. If the local authority released more land, Nicholls *et al.* (1981, p. iii) concluded,

> 'the prospects for inner city residential development are considerably brighter than might be expected.'

The study's conclusions were accepted by central government and by the Building Societies Association as confirming their belief that private developers were willing and able to build in urban areas if land was available. They are also consistent with the provisions of the Local Government, Land and Planning Act 1980 which requires local authorities to prepare and maintain registers of vacant land in public ownership in order to alert private developers to investment opportunities in the inner city.

In fact, the conclusions of the study were at variance with much of the detail. Nicholls *et al.* (1981, p. 65) also state that,

> 'the kind of inner city site most likely to attract residential development is one which is situated in an area of the city, preferably non-industrialised, separated from local authority housing developments and terraced housing, which is not populated by and identified with immigrant communities and which is large enough to accommodate at least 30 units.'

Private developers who declared an interest in principle in the inner city became less interested when confronted with the reality of particular sites.

Virtually all the experience from the mid 1980s onwards suggests that public land ownership is not the prime obstacle to private house building in the inner city. The experience of the vacant land registers is illustrative. The House Builders Federation stated in evidence to the House of Commons

Environment Committee (1984, p. 211) that at this time only about 11% of registered land could be used for private housing. A longer and more thorough analysis by the House Builders Federation (1987, p. 5) came to similar conclusions.

In any case, local authority land holdings are now less extensive and less significant as a development constraint. Sample surveys of derelict sites undertaken by the Civic Trust (1988, p. 20), a pressure group that is concerned with urban design and the urban landscape, suggests that 'public bodies are not the only or even the chief problem'. In 1988, at the time of the Civic Trust survey, only about 28% of derelict sites were in the ownership of the local authority. The Joseph Rowntree Foundation (1994) does not even mention local authority land holding as a constraint.

Development in the inner city presents a combination of difficulties for private house building and these difficulties are largely independent of whether the land is publicly or privately owned (Goodchild *et al.*, 1984, p. 21).

(1)   First, the development strategies of private house builders are very sensitive to the likely price of a scheme on completion. Other than in inner London and in a few attractive areas in provincial cities, developers are aware that newly completed houses in the inner city command relatively low prices. The demand in most inner areas comes from lower income groups, often first-time purchasers, who are searching for less expensive property. In such areas new dwellings generally have to compete with modernised pre-1919 dwellings that provide better value for money in terms of the relationship between price of the dwelling and its size.

(2)   Second, development costs are less predictable with many sites that are small or awkwardly shaped or have other difficulties such as old foundations and poor ground conditions. The development costs of greenfield sites can also vary, of course. However, so long as land availability is not severely restricted by town planning controls or some other factor, the choice of greenfield sites is invariably larger than that in the inner city. As a result, developers find it generally easier to find sites that fit their requirements.

(3)   Third, land acquisition costs are uncertain owing to competition from industrial and commercial developers. Even in the most depressed areas, costs are inflated by 'hope values', where the owner's perception of value is based on an optimistic expectation, sometimes an over-optimistic expectation of economic expansion at some future date. Moreover, buying land from the local authority often encounters the same difficulty of high prices as local authorities are constrained in the sale of publicly owned land by the Local Government Act 1972 and subsequent legislation which requires them to sell land for 'the best consideration'. The latter phrase is not very clear and can be qualified by clearly defined social or other policy considerations. However, in the case of sale to private developers, local authorities generally interpret this phrase as 'the best price'.

Progress in private house building in the inner city

The constraints on inner city house building have to be qualified. For some property journalists and urban planners, the most significant aspect of recent house building patterns is the revival of interest in city centre and inner city sites. A report in the Property Section of the *Guardian Weekend* (7 August, 1993) is typical. The report carries the headline 'life returns to the inner city' and it details the experience in the centre of Manchester, where in the five years from 1988 to 1993, some 2300 new homes had been built or were planned. Moreover, this article continues, these city centre and inner city sites 'are recording lively sales in an otherwise indifferent ... property market'.

Waterfront sites overlooking a river, canal or harbour have proved especially popular with private developers, especially for more up-market schemes. The London Docklands provides the best known example. Other smaller versions exist in many medium-sized and large English cities, for example in the old Bristol docks and along the River Aire in Leeds. These are mostly prestige, 'flagship' schemes that are intended to sell the benefits of inner city living (Fig. 6.1).

The form and type of housing varies. In some places, inner city housing is similar to that in suburban areas. For sites close to town and city centres, a combination of higher land values and the requirements of the planning authority have led to more urban-looking schemes that mostly comprise low-rise flats (Fig. 6.2).

In the 1970s and early 1980s, doubts had been expressed as to whether owner-occupiers wished to live in the inner city. An early review, undertaken by the National Economic Development Office (1971), even involved a national opinion poll to determine the existence of a demand for owner-occupied housing in former slum clearance areas. Now it is usually accepted that a demand exists, so long as the price is not too high. Two particular groups of consumer have been identified as wishing to live in the inner city. These are:

❑ existing residents who want to move to better quality homes within the area that they already know well;
❑ younger households, often first-time buyers, who are geographically and socially mobile and who wish to live close to their work and to the facilities available in the city centre (Cullen and Turner, 1982).

However, the demand remains relatively limited amongst middle and upper income groups who already live in the suburbs. Research Associates (Stone) (1988) have assessed the demand for inner city housing through a combination of group discussions and interviews with 742 adults from social classes A, B and C1. The report of the survey states that most people would not want to move to inner-city areas. The main drawbacks were a lack of greenery and the possibility of high noise levels and parking problems. Developments by water were considered attractive, but were not suitable for children. The desire of households with children to want good schools in the locality was a further constraint.

(a)

(b)

Fig. 6.1   Waterside housing in (a) London Docklands, (b) Leeds.

Fig. 6.2   Inner city housing in Edinburgh.

The limited scale of demand, combined with a lack of easily developed sites, ensures that most private house building takes place either on greenfield sites or on small infill and redevelopment sites in relatively affluent suburban areas. The latter count as 'brownfield' under the official definition, but are not in the inner city. In Sheffield, even at the height of the short-living building boom of the late 1980s, in 1987 and early 1988, only about 5% of private sector schemes were located in the area eligible for assistance under the government's urban programme (Squire, 1988).

Studies of population trends also suggest that renewal measures have only had a limited impact. The trend for many years has been, for the higher density urban areas, notably the big cities, to lose population to their lower density periphery, to smaller, free-standing towns and to rural and seaside retirement areas. In the period between 1981 and 1991, the last period for which accurate census data is available, the trend towards dispersal and decentralisation continued, though at a slower rate. (Champion and Dorling, 1944; Atkins *et al.*, 1996, pp. 8–9). The population of both the inner areas and the outer areas of the largest cities in England declined. Migration was the main component of population change, rather than the balance of deaths and births. Moreover, migration from the cities mostly involved a movement within owner-occupied housing or from renting into owner-occupation.

During the period 1981–1991, Greater London was an exception. This has been characterised by a growth of professional work and, to a greater extent than other British cities, by immigration from overseas. In Greater London, the population increased by about 1% (Champion and Dorling, 1994). However, the most recent estimates show a continued decline in Greater London, as well as in all the other large metropolitan areas (*Financial Times*, 6 December 1996).

Population decline has, in many cities, taken place against the background of declining employment opportunities. However, population has declined even in the two large provincial centres, Bristol and Leeds, that have recorded a significant increase in inner city employment in the 1980s. The most likely explanation is that a decline in the occupancy rate in the existing housing stock, caused by a decline in household size, has outweighed trends towards urban house building. The decline in household size is simultaneously the main source of housing demand, the main source of housing pressures on greenfield sites and a major cause of urban decline and decentralisation.

Measures to promote more private urban house building

The amount of house building in urban areas may, in principle, be increased through maintaining and strengthening existing policies for urban containment, such as the Green Belts. Studies of private house building have repeatedly shown that urban containment policies are a prerequisite for any policy which promotes house building in urban areas. The study of house building in Nottingham undertaken by Nicholls *et al.* (1981, p. 65) noted that private sector interest even in the 'better' inner city sites was partly dependent on planning controls that precluded the development of greenfield sites.

> 'Given a choice most developers would perceive a greater demand for houses in attractive suburban locations and would adjust their development programmes accordingly.'

Again, a later study of urban house building, undertaken by Llewelyn-Davies (1994a) in Lewisham, Cheltenham and Newcastle, states that:

> 'So long as there is an expectation that greenfield sites can be developed there is unlikely to be much interest in derelict ones, even if they are allocated in local plans or are likely to attract grants.'

Likewise, a survey of house building in Scotland, undertaken by Gibb *et al.* (1995, p. 45) states that 'everyone wants greenfield sites because of the problems inherent with brownfield'.

Urban containment is limited as a policy measure, however. It is essentially negative. It cannot ensure that development will be undertaken in a specific place. Development has to be shown to be profitable before private investors risk their capital. Given the various economic and other constraints in the inner city, that prospect remains uncertain.

Including measures that could require new legislation, there are four main ways in which local authorities and other public agencies may encourage private developers to use more sites in urban areas. These are:

- the provision of adequate information;
- the provision of grant aid;
- the public acquisition of land;
- the use of development charges or 'impact fees', intended to give a disincentive for greenfield development.

The provision of adequate information is another prerequisite for private development and has been widely recognised as such. Inner city development opportunities are not always obvious. Pacione (1990, p. 227) has even argued in favour of a 'regularly-updated comprehensive geo-coded computer based register of both publicly and privately owned sites in the city'. Most local authorities would say that they take some action to provide information to private developers. However, few local authorities possess the resources to establish or to maintain an up-to-date computerised database of vacant sites.

The identification of possible sites may still not lead to development if the financial calculations of the developer suggest that it is not profitable to do so. In such circumstances, the local authority or possibly another agency may wish to consider the provision of grant aid. The rationale has been explained by N. Falk, Director of a firm of economic planning consultants 'URBED'. In 1983 in evidence to the House of Commons Environment Committee (Session 1983/84), Falk argued that,

> 'it seems a basically sensible system to have some kind of discretionary money that can be used to entice development. The key is operating on projects that are at the margin where demand is reasonably promising, but the costs are uncertain.' (Report, p. 90.)

Between 1982 and 1990, 10 063 homes, nearly all intended for sale, were completed in England with the benefit of grant aid under the government's inner city initiatives (DoE, 1990b, p. 24).

The provision of grant aid for private housing is an accepted aspect of urban regenerations. It also continues to receive support from private builders (see Llewelyn-Davies, 1994a). However, its cost-effectiveness is not fully established. Price Waterhouse (1993) have argued that grant aid is effective in the double sense that,

- it has enabled development to take place where it would not otherwise have occurred in the short-to medium-term future;
- the rules for the receipt of grant aid give priority to the most depressed sites and exclude those where development would have taken place anyway.

Llewelyn-Davies (1996) provide a similar positive evaluation of the experience of grant aid in Clydebank, but suggest that it may also result in 'landowners receiving more than the land is worth'.

Coopers Lybrand and Associates (1986, p. 37) are more critical. They suggest that, for most types of housing and especially for low cost housing, the availability of grant aid in the inner city will have little effect on the demand for greenfield sites. Grant aid in England has been mostly used to promote low income owner-occupation. The effect has been to redistribute existing demand within the inner city and, in particular, to reduce demand for older property. In other words, grant-aided development facilitates trends towards lower occupancy rates amongst existing inner city owner-occupiers. The use of grant aid to promote up-market schemes in better urban locations is more cost-effective in diverting housing demand away from greenfield sites. However, the use of grant aid for up-market schemes runs counter to the usual social aims of inner city policy. In Scotland, grant aid has also been available to promote privately rented housing. Again, this is unlikely to have a significant impact on the demand for housing on greenfield sites.

For sites affected by ownership constraints, public land acquisition offers another way forward. A study of housing land availability in Leicester, Salford and St Albans, undertaken by the School of Land and Building Studies at the former Leicester Polytechnic (SLABS, 1987) explains the rationale as follows:

> 'In each of the three areas the attitudes of land owners and problems of land assembly are significant constraints to the development ...
> Adjacent plots of land may individually be unsuited for housing development because of the quality of the immediate environment. Atomistic decision making, individual decisions taken in isolation, will fail to produce housing in such circumstances and a co-ordinated approach to site assembly is necessary.' (p. 88)

At present, only the Urban Development Corporations undertake land purchase on a large scale. Local authorities possess roughly equivalent powers under the Town and Country Planning Act 1991. However, apart from schemes intended to promote commercial and industrial development, they seldom use their powers. The main reason has been a political climate in which successive Conservative governments have sought to reduce the role of local authorities in urban renewal.

Even if local authorities were encouraged to take a more active role, it is unclear whether they would wish, for financial reasons, to undertake a substantial programme of public acquisition. In the long term, say after five years, the authority is likely to recoup the initial cost, so long as the land is bought with a degree of care and entrepreneurial skill. Depending on the aims of policy, the local authority may even enjoy a substantial capital gain. However, in the short term, the expenditure may be difficult to justify if, at the same time, the authority is facing financial pressures in other areas of public expenditure, say the social services, recreation or environmental health.

The cost of land acquisition may be reduced if the local authority was able to purchase at below the market value. This has sometimes been proposed within Labour party circles and amongst radical planners. However, any such proposal would prove potentially disruptive to the property industry, for example to developers who have already bought land at full market value. In addition, it would create a two-tier market in housing land acquisition, unless the local authority takes responsibility for the provision of all land for private developers. Owners would find that the sales price was less if they sell to the local authority rather than to another agency. They would object to this and would probably withdraw their co-operation. Compensation for compulsory purchase would almost certainly have to remain at market values. Moreover, public land acquisition would have to be limited to a selective exercise that focuses on key sites.

There is another, more cost-effective way forward. The planning authority could impose some form of financial disincentive or penalty to ensure that the actions of developers conform to those of public policy. For example, developers who build in greenfield sites could pay some form of charge or 'impact fee' to the planning authority for doing so. The introduction of impact fees differs from other measures because it would almost certainly require legislation. Its introduction without legislation, say within the development plans, would lead to a confusing proliferation of different charges in different local authority areas (Goodchild *et al.*, 1996). Proposals for impact fees have not been adopted in the policy statements of any major national political party. However, they have been widely discussed in the professional planning literature (see Delafons, 1991; Grant, 1991; Purdue *et al.*, 1992). Moreover, impact fee systems already exist in France and the United States, and in the fees that developers pay to the regional water companies.

The justification of impact fees is that greenfield development generally imposes higher costs on public services than development in urban areas, certainly more than infill development on small sites within existing urban areas. The introduction of impact fees would therefore require private developers to 'internalise', to use economic jargon, the costs that development causes for the provision of public services. It would not act as a tax on greenfield development, such as is sometimes advocated by countryside protection groups. It would instead avoid hidden subsidies in favour of greenfield development and would, moreover, provide a formal framework for collaboration between developers and local authorities, and ensure that developers are more certain about infrastructure constraints.

Developers may already make contributions to infrastructure through planning agreements made under Section 106 of the Town and Country Planning Act 1991 (Section 50 of the Town and Country Planning (Scotland) Act). The terminology is potentially confusing. In the past, planning agreements were said to generate 'planning gain', that is to say some benefit for the community. An amendment to the Town and Country Planning Act in 1991 substituted 'planning obligations' for 'planning gain' on the assumption that an obligation was more likely to be closely related to the development (DoE, 1991b). However, the change in terminology has not led to any change in practice, and planning authorities still use Section 106 agreements to maximise the gain for the community.

More significant is that contributions made under Section 106 have been subject to numerous criticisms, that they are negotiated on an *ad hoc* basis and lack a strategic dimension; that the negotiations are undertaken in secret; that they often delay development proposals; that the whole system fails to give guidance to developers in advance; and, finally, that it amounts to little more than a device for 'selling off' planning permissions to the highest bidder.

The main objection to impact fees is that they would act as an additional cost for developers which would be passed on to consumers, including, of course, those who are buying or renting their home. Impact fees, it is suggested, would allow planning authorities to impose a wider range and higher level of charges. However, any tendency for the charge to increase consumer costs would only be in the short term. In the longer term and so long as the fee rate is not too high, the charge would be absorbed into the cost of the land. Even under existing practice, it is usually the landowner who pays for any additional costs that arise from the application of planning agreements to residential development (Gibb *et al.*, 1995, p. 45; Grant, 1991, p. 81). Moreover, any adverse effects on low cost housing can be overcome through making the charge payable on a per unit floorspace basis, rather than per dwelling, as well as by weighting the charge so that more profitable types of development, such as retailing and office, pay a higher charge.

The Joseph Rowntree Foundation *Inquiry into Planning for Housing* (1994) argues against impact fees on the grounds that these do not offer much scope for the additional provision of low cost housing. The objection is valid enough, but misses the main point. Impact fees have a potentially useful role in managing the pattern and location of housing development.

The various ways of promoting urban house building each have their limitations, strengths and weaknesses. The implementation of policies for urban renewal does not generally involve a choice between one measure and another. Implementation depends, instead, on a co-ordinated approach that combines greenfield restraint with the promotion of vacant sites, the use of grant aid, selective public land purchase and, where appropriate, the charging of infrastructure costs for greenfield development.

The provision of low cost housing

Private housing has numerous advantages in urban renewal. However, it has a crucial weakness of failing to meet the needs of those who, for reasons of age, low ages or unemployment, cannot afford to buy or fail to satisfy the requirements of lending agencies. Moreover, if private developers seek to go down-market to appeal to low income families, they risk building poor quality accommodation that fails to hold its value.

In the social housing sector, there is a similar dilemma. The provision of subsidies and grant aid ensures that local authorities and housing associations can better meet housing needs. However, local authorities and housing associations must also respect cost constraints.

Licensing and partnership schemes

Housing developers, whether in the private or social housing sectors, can reduce their development costs if they can obtain low cost land. This was the approach favoured in the low cost home ownership initiatives announced by the first Thatcher government in 1981. Local authorities were encouraged to enter into a partnership or licensing agreement with private developers so that they might sell houses at a discount to purchasers who fell within certain defined categories, for example existing Council tenants or those meeting the requirements of waiting list registration. Under this procedure, the local authority licenses the developer to occupy a site and to build. Land ownership remains with the authority and the freehold is sold directly to the occupant, with conditions applied to resale within a defined time limit, usually five years, to discourage speculative purchase.

The licensing schemes of the early 1980s enabled a slight shift down-market. They enabled some people to buy who would not otherwise have been able to do so (Reeves, 1986). They did not provide a full replacement for Council housing, however. A large section of the population remained too poor to buy or was otherwise not eligible to receive a mortgage.

Moreover, the provision of cheap land took the form of a 'once-and-for-all' capital subsidy that benefited the first purchaser, but was not passed onto the subsequent buyer. After the initial sale, the dwellings were sold on the open-market at the maximum that the vendors could obtain. Local authorities made no attempt to control prices in the long term. They believed that any such control would prove difficult and perhaps impossible from an administrative and legal viewpoint.

There is an exception, where a local authority has sought to control prices on resale. Ashford Borough Council has used a procedure called a 'Trust for Sale' in which the local authority retains an interest in the property in perpetuity (Driver, 1994). However, this procedure is not commonly used and seems not to have been used at all in the context of policies for urban renewal.

In many inner city areas, the low price of the existing stock also discouraged the use of partnership or licensing schemes. In the financial year 1980/81, during the heyday of the licensing initiatives, 59% of all sales of houses built under partnership schemes in England and Wales were built by new town development corporations that generally had large landholdings purchased at a low price some years earlier and were therefore in a good position to offer discounts. In this year, only 12% of partnership schemes were undertaken in the area of local authorities designated as a priority under the government's inner city pro-gramme (Crook, 1984).

The development of social housing

After about 1985, policy gradually shifted away from building for sale to the promotion of housing building by housing associations. The promotion of private house building has not disappeared as an aspect of urban renewal. However, the limitations of owner-occupation are more widely appreciated.

House building by housing associations has increased since 1988 and now exceeds that of local authorities. Compared to private developers, housing associations are less constrained by the uncertainties and additional costs in inner city house building. The framework of grant aid provides additional subsidies for building in high cost areas, such as inner London, or building high cost types of development, such as disabled persons' accommodation. Moreover, housing associations are not constrained by the low price of owner-occupied housing in many inner city areas. However, the total level of completions in the social housing sector (local authorities and housing associations combined) remains relatively low by the comparison of the 1970s or earlier decades and much lower than that of private house builders (Fig. 6.3).

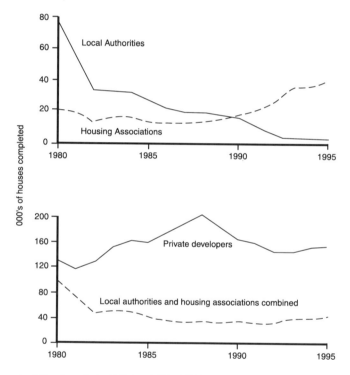

Fig. 6.3 House building trends in Britain, 1969–1993.

House completions are not the only way that social housing agencies can increase the number of homes available for people in need. Other methods include giving tenants a financial incentive to move out of their existing homes into owner-occupation, acquiring existing satisfactory dwellings, and acquiring older dwellings for improvement. These other methods are often cheaper than building new houses and are particularly appropriate for places where development sites are either expensive or unavailable. They are, moreover, undertaken on a large scale. A Joseph Rowntree Foundation publication *Housing*

Review 1996/97 shows that, in England in 1995, all the various methods, including new house building, created about 70 000 homes within the social housing sector. In contrast, social house building only resulted in 31 880 completions (Wilcox, 1996, pp. 10, 100).

Yet, even if all the various sources of new social housing provision are considered, doubts persist about their adequacy. Holmans (1995, 1996) provides the most reliable and informative assessment. It is unlikely, Holmans suggests, that owner-occupation will continue to grow amongst younger households. Higher incomes might encourage owner-occupation, but this will be offset by more job instability and a reduction in tax relief. Expected housing needs amongst low income and unemployed households will have to be met by increased social housing. Moreover, given the continuing loss of social housing through sales to sitting tenants and through selective demolition, the rate of increase will have to be about 90 000 units each year in England, rather than about 70 000 units as has occurred in the period between 1992 and 1995.

Calculations of housing need are theoretical exercises that make numerous assumptions. Of more significance is that, as Holmans (1996) shows, a shortage of social housing has already led to an increasing number of low income and unemployed households living in the privately rented sector. Meeting housing needs in the privately rented sector has disadvantages. Continued growth in the numbers of privately rented dwellings is uncertain. In relation to housing people in need, continued growth is probably dependent on the availability of sufficiently generous, publicly funded housing benefit payments. This is not a cheap option for the public purse. Moreover, the quality of housing in the privately rented sector is generally lower than a local authority or housing association tenant could expect. Successive editions of the English House Condition Survey show that, compared to either local authorities or housing associations, the privately rented sector has a higher concentration of property that is either in poor condition or is difficult to heat, or both.

Self-build and individual development

The difficult character of inner city sites has occasionally led to suggestions in favour of self-build as an alternative method of housing provision. Self-build is more flexible in its application to small sites. It is also less expensive than conventional build, sometimes by as much as 30% and, in the views of its proponents, has generally resulted in schemes that are well built and well designed. Ward (1976) has, in particular, championed the case of self-build as a means of liberating the individual from developer's housing.

Self-build has, moreover, potential social advantages for deprived individuals and households. It promotes self-help and self-sufficiency amongst its members. It makes use of the labour power, the so-called 'sweat equity' of young men and is, for this reason, especially well adapted to a declining urban economy characterised by structural unemployment, diminishing real incomes and increased free time.

There are some examples of low income self-build schemes. The Zenzele project, completed in Bristol in 1988 by a black self-build group, is possibly the best known. Moreover, the Walter Segal Self Build Trust (named after an architect who pioneered self-build) has promoted a prefabricated timber frame system for use by low income groups.

However, most self-build is not what it seems. Most self-build is not self-build in the sense that the owner or future occupant undertakes the work. Most is best described as individual development or owner-build in which the owner contracts out most of the building work. Such owner-build is definitely not a method of inner city regeneration. It is generally undertaken by existing owner-occupiers and often results in expensive, up-market houses in villages or countryside locations. It enables individuals to obtain their 'dream house'. Most likely, in the absence of effective planning controls in the countryside, increased individual development would lead to a greater dispersal of housing development. This is certainly the experience in France where individual development grew rapidly in the 1970s and remains more common than in Britain.

There are numerous constraints on self-build by low income households.

(1) The rationale for low income self-build underestimates the limitations of unskilled labour. It is true that unskilled labour can undertake heavy building work, for example digging trenches, pouring concrete, moving heavy loads around a site. Other aspects of construction, for example plastering or bricklaying, may be undertaken by unskilled labour, but only slowly and under supervision. Further tasks, for example the installation of a central heating or electrical system, require specialist skills.

(2) Low income self-build is undertaken by small groups of individuals. The organisation of the group is inherently a difficult task that involves arranging and finding suitable finance and a suitable site, arranging suitable training, arranging experienced and knowledgeable professional help, whilst maintaining the morale of the members over the long period (say five years) from inception to completion. Completion requires a determined membership and effective leadership.

(3) In addition, the difficulties of group self-build have been exacerbated by limitations in the financial and administrative context.

     ❏ Building societies and banks generally refuse mortgages for group self-build on the grounds of insufficient security and the difficulty of selling half-completed dwellings.

     ❏ The Department of Social Security has ruled that unemployed self-builders are ineligible for unemployment benefit on the grounds that they are not actively seeking employment (*Inside Housing*, 12 June 1992, p. 7). To escape this trap, the members of self-build groups generally have to demonstrate that they are receiving training in a building trade from an accredited training agency.

     ❏ The procedure for obtaining grant aid is complex. The usual procedure is that self-build groups have to choose and work with a sponsoring housing association that applies to the Housing Corporation for grant aid on their behalf. Housing associations find that the administrative costs of self-build are relatively high. They therefore have no financial incentive to help self-build groups.

High land values in inner city areas are another potential constraint. They reduce the value of labour as a proportion of total development cost and increase the capital that a group has to obtain before work starts. However, high land values are less important than the other considerations. If low income groups can satisfy the requirements of public and private funding agencies, they have generally been able to obtain low cost local authority land.

There are no published statistics for the number of completions by low income self-build groups. Most likely, the number throughout Britain is less than 100 each year. If low income self-build is to become more common, the housing associations or possibly some other agency may have to adopt a more active and more prescriptive role. They may have to organise the groups, selecting those members with experience in the building trade. They may also have to use subcontractors to reduce the element of self-build work to a more realistic level. The problem is that the more an outside agency takes the lead, the less is the distinctiveness of low income self-build.

Much depends on the role of the training programme in the building industry. Low income group self-build is clearly valuable if its associated training programme is of sufficient quality to ensure that the participants can gain permanent employment on completion. In the context of a depressed building industry and intense competition for jobs, as in the mid 1990s, this is not easy. Low income group self-build is a worthwhile activity for those who participate and bring the schemes to completion, but is unlikely to make a significant quantitative contribution to urban regeneration.

THE SEARCH FOR HIGHER DENSITIES

The compact city implies the intensification of urban land uses, including the intensification of housing density. To what extent, one might ask, can and should such intensification be pursued? How far can and should densities be raised in new development and existing residential areas? What is the best policy response?

Definitions and forms of density

Discussion of density requires, in turn, a brief digression to explain how it is measured. Research into the relationship between transport patterns and urban form is mostly concerned with general population density of local authority districts. The report of the *Housing Attitudes Survey* (Hedges and Clemens, 1994) is also concerned with general population density. This is a broad measure that is influenced by other factors apart from the character of a residential area. Population density is influenced by the degree of population scatter and by the amount of countryside within a local authority area. In addition, population density is influenced by the occupancy rate in the existing housing stock.

Other measures are available to indicate the density of residential areas and comprise:

❏ net residential density, based on an area that comprises the dwelling, the garden, incidental open space, incidental car-parking and road access;
❏ gross residential density containing all the components of net density, together with local community facilities, neighbourhood parks and local shops.

The most widely used measure is net density. The process of urban development is usually too disjointed, with each estate too small, to allow the planning of a neighbourhood with community facilities.

For both gross and net densities, the unit of measurement varies. This unit can refer to:

❏ dwellings;
❏ habitable rooms (meaning all rooms in a house other than the kitchen area, bathroom, toilet and storage room);
❏ bedspaces (meaning the number of double and single bedrooms);
❏ persons (generally meaning the intended maximum occupancy of a scheme rather than the actual occupancy after completion).

Measures of bedspaces and persons are generally interchangeable in the architectural literature. Otherwise each measure cannot be converted to the rest with any precision, unless the scheme details are known. In town planning, the most common unit of measurement refers to habitable rooms per acre (hra) or hectare (hrh).

Density trends

Assessment of the scope for higher densities implies, in turn, an evaluation of recent trends in the density of new housing. The most reliable source comes from map updates undertaken by the Ordnance Survey and from analyses undertaken by the Department of the Environment of the number of houses on sites with planning permission for housing. A summary of these sources, undertaken by Bibby and Shepherd (1997) state that 'at county level, both sources agree on an average density of residential development of between 22 and 23 dwellings to the hectare (say between 88 and 155 hrh)'. Other than in London, where densities were significantly higher, the average did not vary greatly between different countries and regions. Moreover, there was little shift in density in the study period from 1985 to 1992.

The Report of the English House Condition Survey 1991 gives information that is relevant to a longer term assessment of change. The survey does not provide information on density as such. Instead, it gives data on the proportion of dwellings built as flats and the plot size of houses (excluding flats) according to the date of construction (1993, Tables A3.1, A3.8). This data may be considered a proxy for density. The proportion of dwellings built as flats provides little recent evidence of change. The proportion of dwellings built as flats was 26% between 1965 and 1980 and 24% after 1980. (Calculated from DoE, 1993, Table A3.1.) However, this apparent stability almost certainly conceals a shift within private house building in favour of low-rise flats.

At the same time, the plot size of houses with gardens has diminished. The average plot size of houses built after 1980 is 333 m^2, compared with an average size of 357 m^2 for those built between 1965 and 1980, and 411 m^2 for those built between 1945 and 1964. In other words, the average plot size of houses built after 1980 is:

❑ about 13% less than those built between 1965 And 1980
❑ about 19% less than those built between 1945 and 1964.

This same survey report also shows that the average plot size for houses built after 1980 is virtually identical as that for houses built between 1900 and 1918, before the growth of private car ownership. The implication is, therefore, that the density of recently completed dwellings is relatively high by historical standards.

A survey of floorplans undertaken by Karn and Sheridan also shows the small size of gardens in recently completed houses.They suggest that in the financial year 1991/92 about 37% of housing association houses and about 17% of private houses with a price of less than £100 000 had gardens of less than 50 m^2. The latter figure may be defined as a functional minimum that is necessary for the typical activities (drying clothes, sunbathing, children's play and hobbies) that take place in a back garden. (See Cheshire County Council, 1976.)

Awareness of the declining size of house plots has, in turn, led some critics, notably Hall *et al.* (1973, pp. 394–405) and Evans (1987), to argue that residential densities are already too high and that more land should be made available to housing developers in the hope that this will reduce land prices. The critics would argue that the declining plot size is mostly a response to increased land prices which are caused by restrictive planning controls in the countryside. The assumption is that, as incomes rise, consumers generally want a larger house with a bigger garden. For plot sizes to have decreased, consumer demand must have been frustrated.

The assumption is oversimplified. There is no simple relation between land availability, land prices and density. In the short term, even if planning authorities were to release more land for development, this may not lead to a significant reduction in either land prices or residential densities. Land owners might make windfall profits and keep prices much as before. Even if prices were to fall, developers might attempt to use the savings to reduce the price of dwellings and to appeal to a new low income market. Developers might also use the savings in lower land costs to provide dwellings that have a larger floor area or that have higher internal fittings.

Nevertheless, the question remains as to the extent to which the higher density of recently completed schemes actually meets consumer preferences. The most thorough answer is provided in the report of a survey undertaken by Winter *et al.* (1993) in six estates built by private developers in the South of England and South Wales between 1985 and 1989, and designed at a variety of densities in the range of 28 to 48 dwellings per hectare, say, between 120 and 240 hrh. The report of the survey suggests that the residents were not generally dissatisfied with their new home and that their main concerns were with the internal characteristics of the dwelling, its cost and location. There were, however, specific problems with privacy in the back garden, with adequate or poorly located car-parking and with the provision of children's play space.

Though this is not the authors' interpretation, the most significant implication of the survey is to suggest that smaller plot sizes have not reduced consumer satisfaction. The survey results do not, therefore, provide a strong case for either the release of more housing land or for a deliberate policy in favour of lower densities. Low density housing is, in any case, not a panacea in ensuring environmental quality. Numerous examples exist of low density local authority estates where the occupants have proved either unwilling or unable to maintain the gardens and which, as a result, look dilapidated.

Density policy and density limits

Few planning authorities pursue a general density policy. Though there is no recently published survey, the planning literature contains little discussion of residential densities and makes few references to planning authorities that operate density policies. Most planning authorities rely, instead, on detailed spacing standards, for example the 21 m standard, or site-specific factors, such as a requirement to retain existing trees and shrubs, to protect against over-development.

Greater London as a special case

The main exception is amongst the London boroughs. Density policies in London originated in the 1940s as a means of managing the overspill of housing and population from the inner area to the suburbs and beyond. They have persisted as a means of providing an additional rationale for control in the face of extreme development pressures. Density policies have aided developers in providing an indication of the capacity of a site. They have also helped planning authorities defend the refusal of planning permission at appeal (Llewelyn-Davies, 1994b, p. 11).

The Greater London Development Plan, approved in 1976, provides the starting point for the density policies currently in force. The plan sought to even out densities between inner and outer London. It sought to make the best use of the sites available in outer London, whilst simultaneously limiting housing densities in inner London. It therefore proposed a uniform band of minimum and maximum densities with, in particular, a maximum density of 85 hra (about 210 hrh) for schemes consisting predominantly of family houses. In contrast, earlier government advice had supported densities of up to 200 hra or 494 hrh) in an effort to encourage the development of high flats (Hebbert, 1978).

The abolition of the Greater London Council in 1986 enabled individual boroughs to pursue their own planning policies subject to relatively loose city-wide guidance. The London Planning Advisory Committee (LPAC), the successor to the GLC planning committee, recommended a similar range of minimum and maximum densities in 1994, again with a maximum for family housing of 210 hrh and a further maximum of 250 hrh for non-family housing. A survey of planning practice in London, undertaken by LPAC in 1995, shows that, at this time, most of the inner London Boroughs used similar density guidelines. There were exceptions, however. At the time of the LPAC survey, four outer London Boroughs, together with the City of London, had no density policy. A further five Boroughs had a maximum density for new family housing, but no minimum. Others had adopted maximum densities below the LPAC guideline of 210 hrh. In addition, two Boroughs, Croydon and Camden, had worked out different policies for different zones within their area.

The variety of different policies suggest a need for clarification. First, the aim of the density minimum is to ensure the efficient use of housing sites. Economic factors in the form of high land prices already do this in Greater London. However, the use of a minimum density standard may still be justified as a way in which the local authority can guide developers about likely trends. A density minimum also provides a means of controlling exceptional schemes. The choice of a specific density minimum level is best related to the existing character of an area and to local development pressures.

Second, the status of a density maximum requires a separate analysis for family and non-family housing. The LPAC guideline of 210 hrh for family housing may be justified as a practical or desirable maximum for an estate of two storey dwellings whose layout complies to the long established spacing standard of 21 metres. It is the practical desirable minimum, given the likely existence of site constraints such as access difficulties and slopes and, in addition, given the likely wish of developers and planning authorities to avoid long, unbroken rows of terraces. (MHLG, 1952; Llewelyn-Davies, 1994a, p. 9.) It is perhaps slightly high. However, the calculation of density maxima is not a subject where precision is easy. On the other hand, the minimum is easily exceeded if designers and developers use three storey terraced housing, or if they reduce the spacing standard below 21 m, or if they use a mix of family houses and low-rise flats. (See Fig. 6.4.)

The maximum of 210 hrh for family housing is also consistent with the results of a series of satisfaction surveys undertaken in the 1960s and 1970s. Smith and Burbidge (1973, p. i) have summarised the results of a series of five surveys covering 68 different schemes. Though the survey used bedspaces rather than

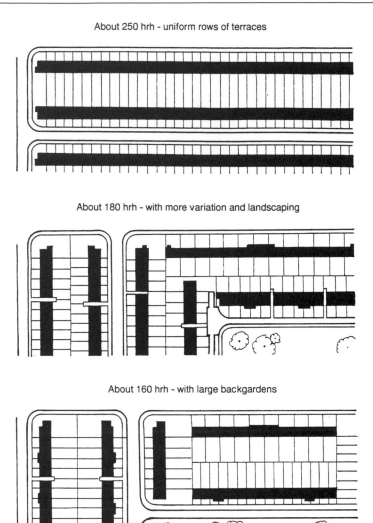

About 250 hrh - uniform rows of terraces

About 180 hrh - with more variation and landscaping

About 160 hrh - with large backgardens

Fig. 6.4   Maximising the density of low-rise housing (adapted from MHLG, 1952).

habitable rooms to measure density, the results clearly showed that high density low-rise schemes were less satisfactory for tenants. The authors state that,

> 'Low rise schemes below 80 bedspaces per acre' (*198 bedspaces per hectare*) 'achieved high levels of satisfaction. For low rise schemes above this density, satisfaction levels were distinctly lower.' (italics added)

On the other hand, more recent interpretations of user response in housing suggest that:

❑   Child density is a more precise indicator of satisfaction than general building density (Westminster City Council, 1980).

❑   Notions of social acceptability are essentially local and particular. The issue is not the absolute density, but the relative density in comparison to respectable housing nearby and, in particular, whether the scheme stands out as unusual or easily stigmatised (Cooper Marcus and Sarkissian, 1986, pp. 33, 51–52).

All this suggests that:

❑ Resolution of the problems of excessive densities in central London continues to depend on the ability of social housing agencies to rehouse households with children in the suburbs or elsewhere.
❑ Acceptable densities for households with children vary between central London and elsewhere. In central London, nearly everyone of whatever income has to live in a flat developed to a high density.

For non-family housing, it is again likely that the acceptability of different types of scheme depends on their context. Llewelyn-Davies (1994b) have used professional surveyors to assess the quality of estates built to varying density levels. They suggest that

'high quality residential environments can be created at densities well above 250 hrh. However, this requires high quality design and either a reduction in car parking requirements or the provision of car parking underground.' (p. 154)

The most likely direction of density policy in London is for more differentiation, with limits determined by the characteristics of the neighbourhood. The zoning policies pursued in Camden and Croydon provide an example. However, even within each zone, it is likely that planning authorities will take other factors into account. The LPAC survey of practice (1995, unpublished) shows numerous examples where local authorities accept higher densities, for example, 'adjacent to major roads or where there is no established residential character', 'higher on small infill development (less than 10 units)', 'higher within 400 m of Public Open Space'. The survey also shows that local authorities may apply lower density levels in sensitive areas. The idea of a uniform density policy, first proposed in the 1970s in the Greater London Development Plan, is surely obsolete.

Density policy outside London

If it is difficult and probably impossible to establish a uniform density policy for Greater London, it is likely to prove equally difficult to attempt a uniform density policy for the country as a whole. Conditions in different towns, cities and in different regions are too diverse. The views of conservationists on one hand, and house builders and consumer interests on the other are, moreover, too divergent to enable easy agreement. Planning authorities should, in any case, resist any attempts to increase the density of new family housing. Densities are already high by historical standards.

It is possible that planning authorities could be required to introduce density policies as a result of a policy commitment to build a high proportion (say 50%

or more) of new houses on urban sites. The experience of planning in Greater London suggests that individual local authorities could work out a flexible policy, based on a combination of general density zones, each with a different minimum and possibly a different maximum related to the surrounding area or a comparable type of scheme. Moreover, any such model would probably involve a recognition that about 210 hrh provides a realistic maximum for family housing that is developed with a conventional street layout and conventional spacing standards. Otherwise, increased densities should be achieved through the use of a higher proportion of flats.

Even if an explicit density policy is unnecessary, planning authorities still have to make assumptions about densities when preparing an estimate of land requirements. It is necessary to make a density assumption to convert an estimate of housing requirements into an estimate of land requirements. These assumptions should be explicitly stated in the development plan.

Urban intensification and the problem of car parking

The trend towards increased densities raises particular issues if it proceeds through the piecemeal development of existing residential areas. Such 'urban intensification', as it is called, is a common process, especially in the South East of England in those areas where land values and the financial gains are relatively high. Whitehand *et al* (1992, p. 226) suggest that, by 1987, over 50% of the original plots on the residential fringe of North London had been affected by some change leading to the provision of more houses or flats.

The outcome is subject to mixed evaluations. Crockett (1990) and Munro and Lane (1990) suggest that, at least in outer London, there is now a popular backlash against what they call 'town cramming'. However, the economic pressures are so strong and the strategic planning arguments, related to the compact city, are so persuasive that it is not possible to reject urban intensification out of hand. Whitehand *et al.* (1992) provide a more balanced assessment. They suggest that intensification is not undesirable per se, but requires sensitive management. This means minimising the problems caused by intensification, whilst retaining the character and most attractive features of an area. The problems have been listed by Llewelyn-Davies (1994a, p. 16):

'– hard surfacing of front gardens;
– loss of front garden walls;
– loss of street trees and shrubbery;
– proliferation of crossovers;
– proliferation of rear extensions;
– excessive alterations to attractive buildings;
– addition of incongruous features such as bin stores, meter boxes;
– on-street car parking competition.'

In the conversion of family houses to flats, car parking is the single most important constraint. Many local authorities attempt to reduce on-street car parking competition through requiring additional car parking spaces, sometimes a separate car parking space for each flat. Except in areas that contain large detached houses with extensive plots, the result is either to preclude conversion to flats, or to limit the number of flats that are permitted, or to cause the garden area to be paved over in a way that leads to a loss of greenery. Clearly, such a policy is open to criticism. It is hardly sensible for a planning authority to insist on a condition that may lead to a loss of environmental quality. Moreover, parking in a street can sometimes slow down traffic. It is not necessarily less safe for pedestrians.

There is a complication. It is possible that the owner or occupants of the flats could make their own parking places. There is usually a strong desire amongst residents for secure car parking arrangements. Moreover, planning control is generally ineffective in stopping residents using their front garden as a car park. However, it is open to doubt whether such home-made car parking conversions are more likely after the subdivision of a family house into flats. Llewelyn-Davies (1994b, pp. 159–161) suggest that, in Greater London, converting houses into flats may not lead to an increased demand for car parking, at least not on the scale implied by the planning policy. Car parking demand is related to the number of adults in a property and to their income level, rather than to the number of households. For example, the car parking demand amongst three or four students may be less than in an affluent family with two adults. The difficulty of providing car parking in older and higher density areas is not confined to conversion schemes. The appearance of high density terraced estates also suffers if every resident wants a separate car parking space (Fig. 6.5).

The difficulties, in turn, raise the possibility of what might be called 'car-free' housing. Many towns and cities possess car-free shopping centres. Why not extend this principle to residential areas? Every house in a car-free area would still have to be accessible from a lane or narrow street capable of use by ambulances, removal vans, refuse lorries and so forth, but there would be no need for wide two lane roads, plus space for car parking. The streets could be designed to complement and enhance those of historic areas. Moreover, without cars, the area would be quieter and cleaner. (See, for example, Wolmar and Arlidge, *The Independent*, 5 September 1995.)

As in other exercises to restrain car use, the proposal has limitations.

❑ For social housing, restrictions on the use of a car could be written into the tenancy agreements. For owner-occupied housing, it is unclear whether residents' use of a car could be subject to general restrictions, or whether the restrictions could only apply to parking and use within the confines of the scheme. Otherwise, the use of a car would have to be discouraged by general traffic regulations, such as car parking restrictions.

❑ The demand for car-free housing is uncertain. Perhaps only a small minority of households would accept the limitations. Moreover, some of those who accept the restrictions at the outset might change their minds later.

❑ Car-free housing has had a poor social image. Estates with inadequate car parking are usually social housing estates in which the residents are assumed

(a)

(b)

Fig. 6.5 High density car parking problems. (a) Front garden paved over for car parking. (b) Minimal frontage in a high density terrace.

not to own a car. For a car-free zone to avoid the poor image of such estates, its residents should actively choose to live in such a place.

❏ Car-free housing almost certainly has strict locational requirements. People living in such housing require easy access to urban services and public transport. The best location is near a city centre.

Nevertheless, even if the application is limited, a car-free area would provide a supplement to existing models of urban design.

THE PROMOTION OF MIXED USE DEVELOPMENT

Most proposals for new housing assume a continued separation of residential land use from areas of industry, offices and commerce. Such land use zoning, as it is called, has obvious validity in protecting the amenity of residential areas. For example, zoning is routinely applied by local planning authorities as a means of avoiding the entry of heavy goods vehicles into narrow residential access roads or of avoiding future problems of industrial noise. Zoning is, in any case, often justified on economic grounds. Some sites and locations are better suited to one particular type of land use, for example industry, than others.

The rationale for housing in town and city centres

At the same time, new opportunities now exist for mixed use development that include an element of housing. In part, the opportunities arise from the changing pattern of commercial and industrial activities. The growth of out-of-town centres has led to a decline in the value of town centre and city retailing premises. In addition, new opportunities have arisen as a result of changes in the organisation of commercial activity amongst established town and city centre users. The growth of 'just-in-time' ordering has reduced the need for storage space above shops. The growth of information technology and the emergence of new forms of less hierarchical, more co-operative working practices has ensured that older office buildings are increasingly obsolete (see Ratcliffe and Stubbs, 1996, pp. 402–441). Finally, a preference of manufacturing industry for large open sites near to the motorway network has reduced demand for older industrial sites in the vicinity of towns and city centres.

The case for housing in town and city centres is, moreover, strengthened by its policy advantages. The development of town and city centre housing is unlikely to revive shopping centres that have completely lost their market. Compared to the broad catchment area of a typical city shopping centre, the potential number of new housing units is insignificant. However, housing development can at least counter dereliction and improve the local environment.

Moreover, the development of housing in town and city centres has advantages in crime prevention. The presence of 'eyes on the street', whether the eyes of other pedestrians or the eyes of local residents, may promote personal safety in the street and so help reduce the fear of crime amongst passers-by. This is an extension of the argument in favour of situational methods of crime prevention in which the aim is to remove the opportunities for wrong-doing and to encourage potential offenders to think again. Likewise, the presence of 'ears in a building' may deter burglary in the shop below. Burglary is invariably a noisy exercise, especially if the burglars set off an alarm.

Crime prevention measures are not easy to evaluate. However, a series of case studies undertaken by Goodchild *et al.* (1997) suggests that virtually all local police officers and housing association managers agree that the principle of housing over shops has some advantages, though not dramatic advantages, in crime prevention. Likewise, statements made by young offenders suggest unoccupied property (or more accurately property with no visible evidence of occupation) is more attractive as a potential target for burglary. The main qualification is that the scope for passive surveillance is limited by design factors (the position and outlook of windows, the general street labour) and by a lack of contact between residents and the occupiers of local commercial property.

This same study by Goodchild *et al.* also suggests that most residents of town and city centre flats find their present home about as safe or safer than their previous one. Housing in town and city centres is best suited to single adults and childless households. It is less suited to family households or elderly people. However, this is as much an advantage as a weakness. Younger single person households and childless couples account for a growing proportion of housing demand.

The provision of housing in town and city centres

The problem, as in other aspects of urban renewal, is to ensure that developers and property owners grasp the opportunities for housing in town and city centres. It is not possible to make a quantitative estimate of the housing potential in town and city centres or, indeed, of mixed development schemes elsewhere. There is an absence of detailed survey work. Moreover, much depends on the changing balance of economic advantage. The basic economic constraints are similar to those that limit private house building in the inner city. In other words, development is constrained either separately or in combination by a lack of demand for owner-occupied property, by high or uncertain repair and construction costs and by high acquisition costs.

New mixed use schemes

The most distinctive feature of mixed use development is its complexity. Providing housing in town and city centres, like other exercises in mixed use development, generally involves a multitude of different commercial users who have little formal contact with one another. These different users have to be brought together. The Urban Villages Forum has promoted mixed use in the context of a campaign in favour of good urban design. The Urban Villages *Newsletter*, Summer 1995, has argued that,

> 'The people who have real influence over the planning, design and development process represent a wide range of interest, experience, attitudes and expectations. Significant change depends on helping them recognise common interests, widen their experience, and acquire new attitudes and expectations.'

Private developers in Britain have less experience than those in other European countries in providing mixed use schemes. They also dislike the additional complexity of schemes with various uses on different floors, as this increases the cost of managing the investment. Developers may accept the case for mixed development in principle, but object to its application to their site. From the viewpoint of the planning authority, the main task is to negotiate with commercial developers for the inclusion of as much accommodation as possible.

A particular question is whether a policy of 'micro-zoning' might be desirable. The promotion of housing is not the only way a planning authority may promote the regeneration of a city centre. The promotion of leisure, including the promotion of night-clubs, are other alternatives. Moreover, these other alternatives are not necessarily consistent with housing. For example, the existence of a noisy night-club may cause complaints from residents. Planning authorities could identify those streets and areas that are most suitable for mixed use development. Quiet streets, with low levels of traffic, on the edge of the main shopping area (and without substantial commercial pressures) provide the best possibilities.

The promotion of new housing schemes is also complicated by a tendency for many town and city centres to be classified as conservation areas. As a result, planning control is exercised more strictly than elsewhere and has the specific aim of enhancing and protecting the character of an area. Expensive materials (stone or antique bricks) and unusual architectural detailing may be required. The protection of a conservation area is clearly an important policy priority. However, planning authorities might consider whether the advantages of mixed use development justify the relaxation of some architectural requirements.

Housing over shops

City centre housing may also be provided through the reoccupation of empty floorspace above shops. Again there is no reliable estimate of the potential at the national level. However, Petherick and Fraser (1992, p. 3) report the results of some local surveys that 'between 33% and 90%' of the upper floorspace in shopping streets is vacant. The ultimate potential is therefore substantial.

The reoccupation of vacant floorspace in commercial buildings is of obvious financial benefit for owners if this enhances the value of a property or provides a rental income. So long as the building fabric is in good repair and the flats possess separate means of access, the capital costs of reoccupation are low. In some cases, the only requirement is to undertake redecoration and to install modern kitchen equipment and heating.

However, there are countervailing factors that discourage reoccupation.

❑ In the highest value areas, the economic logic favours the use of upper floorspace for office use. Indeed, in some places. economic advantages of office use may encourage the conversion of existing flats over shops into offices. In such places, planning control has an important function in preventing the loss of housing to other uses.

❑ Conversion for housing may restrict flexibility in the subsequent use of retailing property. It may, for example, restrict the use of upper floors for intermittent storage or may reduce marketability in the event of a property sale. As a result, conversion can adversely affect the capital value attributable to the premises as a whole (Junior RICS, 1993). In response, owners usually prefer the use of a short-lease, say between 5 and 15 years, and avoid a sale of the property into owner-occupation.

❑ Much high street property is owned by large financial institutions as part of an investment portfolio. The standard lease used by these institutions will often prohibit the retailer from sub-letting the upper floors for residential purposes (Junior RICS, 1993).

❑ Finally, a minority of commercial property occupiers worry about the security implications of people living over their premises. This minority sees housing over shops as a mixed blessing for the security of their property. They may require the housing association or estate agent not to let the property to people in receipt of social security payments. Insurance companies have a similar ambivalent view of housing over shops. Insurance companies recognise that empty property is more at risk of burglary, criminal damage and accidental damage than occupied property. However, they are sometimes suspicious of letting housing over shops to people in receipt of social security payments (Goodchild *et al.*, 1997).

In Greater London, privately funded housing over shops is common. Here, the larger chains of retailers, such as Boots the Chemists, Threshers (off-licences) and Ladbrokes (betting offices) have undertaken their own schemes. Elsewhere, development is more dependent on the activities of housing associations or on other local initiatives that offer some form of financial subsidy for the repairs and building works. The assumption is that these initial subsidised schemes will demonstrate the viability of housing over shops and will encourage other privately funded schemes. In practice, though there are no reliable statistics, anecdotal reports suggest that in most provincial centres the demonstration effect is small. Progress remains largely dependent on the availability of public funds.

The scale of the housing association activity is itself relatively small, however. Unpublished data collected by the Department of the Environment suggests that, in the three year period between the financial years 1992/93 and 1994/95, the Flats over Shops initiative (funded by the Department of the Environment) and the Social Housing over Shops initiative (funded by the Housing Corporation) had together led to the approval of 1795 homes. Since 1995 the numbers have almost certainly declined as a result of policy changes.

The cost-effectiveness of recently completed flats over shops schemes compares favourably to conventional rehabilitation (Chamberlain and Goodchild, 1994). Indeed, the costs of flats over shops schemes have to compare favourably to conventional rehabilitation or new housing schemes. The primary focus of social housing is to meet housing needs. Planning and environmental benefits are a mere by-product. The main constraint on housing associations is to find sites that are simultaneously suitable for reoccupation and available for occupation. Negotiations with owners are slow, time-consuming and often involve abortive work.

To an extent, housing associations have learnt from experience. They have learnt which properties and which types of landlord offer the best potential. Housing associations appear able to sustain an output at roughly the present level, say 400 flats each year. However, they would almost certainly encounter difficulties if they were asked, say, to double the output within one or two years.

The conversion of empty offices and warehouses to housing

A third and final way of providing housing in town and city centres is through the conversion of vacant offices and warehouses. The housing potential of such blocks is substantial. Barlow and Gann (1993a) have undertaken a detailed review of the housing potential of offices, based on a postal questionnaire of planning authorities and interviews with developers. They state that,

> 'older, technically obsolete, office buildings currently account for 806,000 m^2 (*square metres*) of floorspace in central London. The conversion of this stock could create between 10–20,000 new flats. (The national figure could be three times as much.)'

The problem, as always, is one of realisation. The extent of interest in conversion seems well ahead of the number of completions. Barlow and Gann (1993b, p. 4) conclude that 'in the short-term, it is likely that only a handful of conversion schemes will be initiated'.

The process of conversion is almost certainly highly sensitive to the ups-and-downs of the office market in different locations. Conversion to housing is only likely if the owners believe that the long-term site value for offices or for other commercial use is uncertain or less than that for housing; that, in addition, the block is unsuited to easy modernisation; and that the cost of conversion for housing is not prohibitive in terms of likely rents or selling prices.

The conversion of empty offices and warehouses encounters a series of constraints. Most were never designed for residential use. They generally possess fewer services for the supply and disposal of water acts than would be usual in a residential block of the same size. In addition, and especially in the larger deeper blocks constructed in the 1960s and 1970s, the interior spaces are much larger than in flats over shops. Natural daylight in these blocks is also poor by residential standards, at least towards the centre of the block. Likewise, standards of acoustic insulation in the partition walls are often poor in comparison with those generally considered necessary for the separation of one flat from another.

As a result of all this, and unless the block is already designed for relatively small, self-contained units, the conversion of offices and warehouses often favours larger than average apartments, of at least 100 square metres, with large areas of undivided floorspace. These apartments are sometimes called 'lofts', after the first schemes that were undertaken in New York in the 1960s and 1970s. Their unusually spacious internal layouts can sometimes result in attractive and unusual living accommodation. In London, lofts are now a fashionable form of accommodation for young professionals and executives. However, their large size and unusual design generally leads to high fitting-out costs (*Weekend Telegraph*, 1 July 1995, p. 15).

The conversion of offices is also more likely than either housing over shops or new schemes to encounter planning objections. Some schemes are adversely affected by the desire of the local planning authority to retain potential employment. If the developer can show that use for offices is unlikely in the foreseeable future, this particular objection can be overcome. Other sites are affected by objections that the density of the blocks is too high for residential use or that the amenities are deficient in other ways. However, planning authorities are often willing to promote conversion so as to retain a resident population in or near to town and city centres. The task for the developer is to find a suitable site.

The development of housing in older industrial areas

The development of new housing in industrial areas raises separate and distinctive difficulties. Older industrial areas often comprise a patchwork of small vacant sites and multi-storey premises of a type that is unsuited to modern industrial processes and that contain a substantial amount of vacant floorspace. Could or should the local planning authority encourage the rezoning of older industrial areas for other uses, including housing?

The potential for rezoning varies from place to place, according to local conditions. However, the general rule is that older industrial areas are very difficult to rezone, either in whole or in part.

Constraints within the planning system

One constraint concerns uncertainties about the amount of industrial land that will be needed in the future. Industrial land and buildings that are vacant at the trough of a recession may be needed to satisfy demand at a later date. Many local authorities argue that a degree of 'excess' industrial land allocation is necessary to maintain the competitive position of their area in comparison with that of other local authorities.

For example, a study of land availability in Nottingham (Hillier Parker 1991), recommended that the City Council undertook the redevelopment of older industrial areas for industry and warehousing as a means of avoiding a shortfall of industrial land in the future. The fact that the city of Nottingham was also likely to experience a shortage of housing land – evidently a major change since the survey undertaken in 1979 in the same city by Nicholls *et al.* was beside the point. The allocation of adequate industrial land was the main priority, as this was so closely linked to the city's future economic prospects (Lockwood, 1992, personal communication).

In the past, the development of housing in industrial areas has also been hindered by a lack of precision in the development controls available under the town planning legislation. Some local authorities, such as Sheffield City Council, have been reluctant to grant planning permission for housing in or near industrial areas for fear that, even if environmental conditions were acceptable at the time of application, any new housing would be at risk from the intensification of industrial use, against which the town planning controls give little effective protection.

The town planning legislation is now clearer. The Town and Country Planning Use Classes Order 1987 introduced a new business use class (B1) which specifies those types of commercial and industrial activities that may be carried out within a residential area without detriment to the amenity of residents. If an operator were to intensify industrial activities in such a way that the amenity of residents is adversely affected, planning permission is now required. At the same time, the Planning and Compensation Act 1991 has strengthened the enforcement of planning control and enables a planning authority to seek an injunction to restrain a breach or an apprehended breach of planning control.

The planning controls still possess limitations. They permit mixed residential/business development only for particular types of business activities. They do not cover cases where housing is proposed adjacent to sites and where the intensification of industrial processes is permitted by virtue of existing use rights. If an industrial activity exists on a site, it is said to enjoy existing use rights and these permit a degree of intensification. These rights also exist for a time after an industrial activity has ceased. The law of nuisance provides a partial answer for an aggrieved resident, but is cumbersome and expensive to use.

In any case, to use a well-worn phrase, the prevention of problems is always better than a cure. The separation of housing from areas of existing industry avoids possible disputes between householders and industrial firms and also avoids the use of strict forms of administrative regulation. Mixed industrial/housing land uses remain much more difficult to achieve than mixed commercial/housing areas.

The problem of contaminated land

Another constraint concerns land contamination by industrial waste. Most cases of land contamination can be treated through the replacement of the topsoil and land fill. The usual test is whether the site is safe for its end use. However, the standards required for housing are higher than for most other uses. Use for car parking, for example, requires little more than the laying of tarmac. As a result, development costs for housing are often high and prohibitive in their effect on the economic viability or development.

The insurance implications of contamination are especially complex. Cover is generally not provided by the National House Building Council within the framework of their ten year guarantee. The NHBC guarantee mostly covers the risk of structural failure rather than the risk of pollution. Moreover, it is practically impossible for a developer or consumer to obtain cover from another insurance company if there is a risk of industrial pollution. Even for sites without known problems insurance costs are high.

The high cost or unavailability of insurance is partly a result of the losses that insurance companies have experienced in the United States. It is also a result of a lack of a certain policy framework. There is, at present, no definitive list or register of sites showing the actual degree of contamination. Moreover, for reasons of cost and time, it is unlikely that local authorities will be required to prepare a definitive register in the near future. In 1989, the Department of the Environment estimated that it would cost about £15 000 per hectare (about £6000 per acre) just to investigate potential contaminated sites (*Innovations in Social Housing*, No. 6, December 1993).

A register was planned to come into existence in April 1994 under the Environmental Protection Act 1990. However, this was merely a register of sites on which 'contaminative uses' had existed in the past. The register did not include all the potential sources of contamination and provided no procedure whereby sites could be removed on clean-up. The government abandoned the register in 1993 after objections from the property industry who feared that it would depress land values.

Planning authorities can still assess sites on an ad hoc basis. They can use their internal records to identify sites at risk and undertake further tests to determine whether the risk is acceptable. The tests generally possess a margin of error, however. The assessment of risk and the need for remedial action still involves an element of subjective and qualitative judgements (Graham, *Planning Week*, 9 January 1997).

If a site is unsuitable, who should pay for the clean-up? The main principle in environmental policy is that the 'polluter pays'. Under English law, at least since the judgement in the House of Lords in December 1993 of *Cambridge Water Company v. Eastern Counties Leather PLC*, the rule of polluter pays has also prevailed, though the rule is qualified by a requirement that any damage arising from pollution must be foreseeable at the time. In practice, however, in the case of contaminated land, the polluter does not pay. The polluter is usually either out-of-business or able to claim that the consequences could not be foreseen at the time. As a result, either the developer, the owner or the public sector has to pay.

The answer of many in the property industry is for more public grant aid. They argue that there is no other practical way forward; that, without grant, development will not take place and that, as a result, consumers will suffer. For badly contaminated sites, there may indeed be no other way forward. However, the private sector will also have to carry the financial burden. Much of the problem is that, until the early 1990s, the property industry was insufficiently aware of the risks of contamination. Owners expected too high a price and developers paid too much. Owners and developers now have to adjust their expectations, at least if the site is to be used for housing.

Commercial development as a measure in estate regeneration

Mixed use development may also proceed through the development of commercial activity in residential areas. In particular, the development of commercial activities – shopping, leisure or small-scale industry – has advantages in the renewal of 'problem' estates. Commercial development may break the sense of isolation of such estates, bringing in visitors from elsewhere. It may also provide local employment opportunities, though this latter advantage must be qualified. The size of new sources of employment may be small in comparison with the scale of local unemployment. Moreover, unemployed residents are likely to have to compete for local jobs with other people from a wide area around the estate.

Within an estate, commercial premises can be provided by a variety of means. Estate Action (1991, p. 12) suggests the following possibilities.

> 'Vacant shop units,
> Disused communal garages,
> Space beneath decks or walkways which could be enclosed,
> Disused or unused land within estates which could provide sites for new build or pre-fabricated premises.'

One problem, as Estate Action also notes, is that the development of business premises is not always appropriate. Development for commercial use is always in competition with development for other uses, for example for community use, for open space or, in some cases, for conversion to housing. In inner London, for example, housing land is in such short supply that its conversion to industry or commerce is difficult to justify. Sometimes commercial activities cause environmental problems, for example from increased noise or increased traffic. For this reason, the most suitable businesses are likely to be workshops or small business premises rather than factories or supermarkets. Sometimes, notably in the case of proposals to convert garages or empty blocks of flats, business use is precluded by building and fire regulations.

Even if business use is appropriate, developers may not be interested. Problem estates often possess a high incidence of burglaries and have a poor image. For shopping development, the poverty of the residents is another constraint, especially in relatively isolated peripheral estates. Unless the proposed scheme can cater for a broad catchment area, retailers will almost certainly prefer areas where residents have a relatively high disposable income. This being so, some form of grant aid is often necessary to encourage commercial development. Otherwise, development will only proceed if sites are not available elsewhere.

PLANNING FOR URBAN GROWTH

The question remains about the likely extent of achieving the compact city. Two alternative policies are possible.

❏ Either, urban decentralisation ceases completely and new housing is only provided within existing urban areas. This is the interpretation of the European Commission in the *Green Paper on the Urban Environment* (1990).

❏ Or, decentralisation is managed to ensure that the built-up area is continuous, with no breaks other than those required for parks and other planned open spaces. Urban decentralisation continues, but in a compact or ordered way and not through dispersal or fragmentation.

The balance between brownfield and greenfield development

In practice, other than in towns and cities characterised by little or no house building, 'planned' or 'managed' decentralisation is more realistic than no decentralisation at all. Statistics, collected by the Ordnance Survey during map revision suggest that, in 1992, the last date for which data is available, about 57% of house building in England took place on what are sometimes called 'brownfield' sites – 47% of house building took place on 'recycled' land that had previously been developed for some other purpose, and a further 10% took place on previously undeveloped land within urban areas (*The Planner*, 1 June 1995, p. 8). In 1985, the proportion of housing on recycled land was 38% and, in 1989, the equivalent proportion was 42%. The Ordnance Survey statistics suggest, *in other words*, a gradual shift away from greenfield sites.

Future trends are uncertain. The White Paper *Our Future Homes*, published by a Conservative government, states that the aim of the government is to ensure that half of all new housing is built on 're-used sites' (1995, p. 47). Some later Ministerial announcements suggested an even more ambitious target of 60% (*Planning Week*, 28 November 1996).

However, it is also possible that the trend towards urban and re-used sites has now reached its limit. House building rates in the early 1990s were low by historical standards. The proportion of development on urban and re-used sites may decline if the rate of house building expands. In an expanding building programme, developers may encounter more difficulties in finding a sufficient number of such sites. The best sites may, in any case, have already been developed. The Town and Country Planning Association (1996) suggests that, in the next few years, the 'high costs of reclaiming the remaining land, and questions of absolute land supply, may reduce this figure to 30 to 40 per cent'. Moreover, political support for radical targets has been uncertain.

Much also depends on the regional pattern of development. Places with relatively low levels of demand, such as south Yorkshire and south Lancashire, generally have the largest areas of vacant sites. In contrast, places with high levels of demand, such as Surrey or Cambridgeshire, have the least. Achievement of a target of 50% or more of urban house building may require a diversion of demand from areas of growth to those of decline.

Variations in the pattern of demand suggest, in turn, that it is not possible to apply a universal target to all local authorities. It is not possible for the government to issue planning guidance that requires each local authority to ensure that 50% (or whatever target is desired) of all new dwellings are completed on urban sites. Some local authorities will meet such a target easily. Others will fail to meet the target. It will be necessary to establish a series of local targets.

The form of urban development

The implication is that house building will, for the foreseeable future, involve a mixture of greenfield, urban and re-used sites. How is greenfield development best organised and planned? The main choice is similar to the distinction between adaptive and directive planning. Planning authorities may choose between a fixed settlement pattern and a more flexible approach. In addition, if planning authorities are able and wish to pursue a fixed settlement strategy, they may choose between a series of development options: planned suburban expansion, the growth of key villages and the development of new towns and new settlements.

A fixed settlement strategy or adaptive planning?

The compact city implies a precise form of how human settlements should grow. It implies that a city grows evenly from a centre in a series of rings and retains a rounded shape. For most planning authorities, the rigidities of compact urban forms are impractical. Planning authorities must consider previous policy commitments. They must also consider other factors that are site specific.

For example, the compact city is, in principle, consistent with long-standing policy commitments in favour of Green Belts. The aim of the Green Belt policy, from its formal acceptance as a national policy in 1954 through to *Planning Policy Guidance: Green Belts*, has been, among other things, 'to check the unrestricted sprawl of large urban areas' (DoE, 1995, revised para. 1.5). The very concept of 'sprawl' implies a spreading formless pattern of growth that should be avoided in favour of more compact forms.

However, the Green Belt, as currently defined in most British cities, preserves heavily indented urban edges and sometimes even isolated islands of undeveloped sites within the built-up area. The Green Belt actually promotes fragmentation of the built-up area. Not that such fragmentation is disliked by the public. Undeveloped areas within the urban fabric often have a significant visual impact and possess a symbolic value for many urban residents. They may also contain footpaths that local people use for exercising themselves and their dogs. Moreover, areas of abandoned land within the built-up area have sometimes proved to possess a surprisingly varied and abundant natural habitat for rare plants and for wildlife.

The pattern of water supply and drainage is another constraint on the achievement of neat or simple urban forms. Sustainable development in relation to water supply and drainage is concerned with such issues as minimising the risk of flooding to new development, protecting the catchment area of water supplies from pollution and respecting the capacity of existing water treatment and supply facilities. Since the privatisation of the water industry in England in 1989 and the water supply problems of the drought year of 1995, the protection of water catchment and supply facilities has been of increased importance as a planning constraint.

Water supply and sewage disposal are also important as a cost consideration in housing development. The water companies charge for connection to the main services (as well as making another charge for the general infrastructure implications). As a result, it is in the interests of a developer for housing sites to be located close to existing services.

The existence of water supply and drainage constraints, together with other constraints, implies no particular pattern of land uses. They imply instead the use of a 'sieve-map' or overlap technique of plan generation. In this, each type of constraint, for example, existing built-up areas, the existing pattern of Green Belts areas, the location of sites of scientific interest, areas of steep slopes or excessive height and the location of water catchment areas, is mapped. The separate maps are then aggregated to identify those sites where there are no constraints. The process literally 'sieves' out those sites that are unsuitable.

New towns or suburban expansion?

In some places, the pattern of constraints may narrow the choice to specific sites and locations. Elsewhere, especially if development is expected to take place on a large scale, a wider range of choice is possible, including piecemeal suburban expansion and the development of a new town. Planning authorities have generally preferred the solution of gradual expansion as this is more flexible. Developers have likewise favoured some form of piecemeal development as this minimises infrastructure costs. The basic unit of development for private developers has been the estate rather than a neighbourhood or community.

In the 1980s, however, some private developers sought a more radical and ambitious approach. In 1985, a consortium of larger private house builders formed Consortium Developments Limited (CDL) to submit planning applications for a series of new settlements, mostly in the South East of England. The most notable examples were at Tillingham Hall, Essex, Stone Bassett, Oxfordshire and Foxley Wood, Hampshire. In the late 1980s, individual developers and other independent consortia also prepared proposals for new settlements. The development of a new settlement offered a selling point to consumers and, in addition, enabled a greatly increased land allocation for housing development.

The proposals for new settlements were mostly at variance with the development plans prepared by the local authorities. None of the original proposals of Consortium Developments succeeded in receiving approval. The usual grounds for refusal were the significant visual impact of the proposal, the ecological and environmental harm caused by such large scale development in their location and, in some cases, the likely growth of traffic problems. Tillingham Hall suffered the additional problem that it was located in the Green Belt (see Ratcliffe and Stubbs, 1996, pp. 486–488).

The proposals were, nevertheless, of sufficient importance for the government to sponsor a review of how best to accommodate urban growth. The review, undertaken by Breheny *et al.* (1993, pp. 50–51), provides the most detailed and most widely quoted assessment of the case for new settlements. The review suggests that, in principle and ignoring the vagaries of different sites, the size of the new settlement is the crucial factor that determines whether it should go ahead. The size of the settlement determines its critical mass in relation to the provision of facilities and so determines its degree of self-sufficiency.

> 'First, that the minimum viable size of a new settlement would be that, in a given county, would support a primary school (variously 750–1,500 dwellings)
> 'Second, greater emphasis on social and environmental considerations, suggests that it would be preferable if new settlements were large enough to support a secondary school and sufficient employment to offer most of the residents of working age the choice of employment in the community (this would suggest a size in the range of 3,000–5,000 dwellings (7,500–12,500 population) at least).'

Finally, Breheny *et al.* suggest that if full consideration is given to the requirements of sustainability, 'the size should be sufficient to minimise the need for car-borne journeys ... for employment, facilities and amenities'. Such a size would point to the desirability of new market towns accommodating up to 10 000 dwellings (25 000 population). Small new settlements score badly on infrastructure costs, access to social facilities and dependence on private transport. Large new settlements score better because they are more likely to contain a mixture of employment and housing and provide a wider range of facilities.

The detailed logic of Breheny *et al.* almost certainly places too much emphasis on the advantages of large new settlements. Unless developed in places of large-scale dereliction, such as former airfields or other military establishments, large new settlements have the disadvantage of consuming greenfield sites in exactly the same way as smaller new settlements. The rate of consumption of greenfield sites is determined by the density of new housing and the possibilities of urban intensification. The location of new housing estates is largely irrelevant. Moreover, suburban expansion invariably has the advantage of enmeshing the individual in a larger labour market that can be achieved in even the largest new town.

Breheny *et al.* (p. 33) also suggest that new settlements have advantages in promoting combined heat and power schemes. These are schemes that use the waste heat from power stations to heat nearby housing and therefore save energy consumption within the home. New settlements, it is said, provide economies of scale in the installation of combined heat and power. Moreover, installation is invariably easier and less expensive on greenfield sites.

However, it would surely seem strange to build a new settlement merely to allow the provision of a combined heat and power system. Similar district heating systems in social housing have proved unpopular with tenants. The acceptability of combined heat and power to consumers remains largely unknown. Satisfactory low energy design can be achieved merely through a combination of high insulation and controlled ventilation, perhaps through high insulation alone. Moreover, the use of combined heat and power is only likely to prove feasible with higher than usual residential densities. Of course, if higher densities are used in large suburban schemes, these can also be adapted to combined heat and power.

Even supposing that large new settlements represent a valid planning solution in principle, the question arises whether they are desirable or feasible in relation to a particular site. *Planning Policy Guidance: Housing* states that planning authorities should only 'contemplate' such a proposal where 'the net effect of a new settlement will either enhance the environment or cause only modest environmental impact' (DoE, 1992c, paras. 32–34). Even a relatively modest new settlement will consume a large area, say 200–250 hectares, yet, to qualify as a new settlement, it must, as *Planning Policy Guidance: Housing* also states, be separate from existing built-up areas. It must also avoid protected land, such as Green Belts and the best quality agricultural land. Planning guidance in Wales states that:

> 'New settlements on greenfield sites are unlikely to be appropriate ... and should only be proposed where such development would offer significant environmental, social and economical advantages....'

The Scottish guidelines are more positive in noting the advantages of new settlements 'to improve standards of layout, sensitive siting and innovative design' and, in addition, to achieve energy conservation. However, the Scottish guidelines also make the additional requirement that the new settlement should make positive provision for public transport (Scottish Office, 1996, p. 13).

There are numerous reasons, therefore, for refusing planning permission for a new settlement. Given the likely opposition of local residents to the loss of greenfield sites, progress in finding sites has invariably proved slow. In Cambridgeshire, for example, the site selection process took ten years before the local authority finally gave planning permission for a new settlement of 3000 dwellings (plus a large industrial estate) eight miles west of Cambridge (Hussell, 1994).

Large new settlements are not easy to develop. They are only feasible

❏ if developers, acting either alone or in a consortium,
    ○ can predict, with a degree of certainty, a high level of housing demand for a number of years, say five years, ahead;
    ○ can stand the initial infrastructure costs and are able to guarantee a stable supply of finance for the period of development;

    o are able to purchase the required land according to a suitable timetable and a reasonable price.

❑ if planning authorities are able and willing to stop competing schemes that might divert demand into other localities. The development of large new settlements generally contradicts the usual piecemeal procedures of local planning.

Even if large new settlements are feasible in the long term, their development risks short-term teething problems and delays. In the first phases of development, large new settlements are little more than badly planned small settlements characterised by a scattered built-up area and a lack of facilities. The risk is that these early stages may persist for many years if economic circumstances mean that private development is unprofitable. Developers are, of course, aware of the practical difficulties of developing large new settlements. Breheny *et al.* (1993, pp. 80–81 and Appendix 1) list the characteristics of 184 new settlements proposed by private developers between 1980 and 1992. With the exception of one scheme, the size is in the range of 350 to 5500 dwellings, with most under 1000 dwellings.

The need for a range of solutions

What are the implications? The Town and Country Planning Association (1996) suggests that it might be necessary to review Green Belt boundaries and that, in addition, a range or 'portfolio' of solutions offers the best way forward. No single approach will suffice. Instead,

> 'a portfolio approach will be needed, where different elements – peripheral extensions, infilling, selected new communities at different scales – are combined and adapted to local circumstances. Where rail corridors exist, or could be re-opened, they should be considered as the basis for a series of clustered developments.'

The call for a range of solutions is surely right. However, unless the government allows relatively small schemes, it is unlikely that many new settlements will actually be developed in the next few years. The suite of solutions will mostly comprise suburban extensions, infilling and clustered development around existing railway stations, with much of the detail determined by a sieve map analysis of constraints.

The estimation of housing land requirements

The planning of urban expansion is made more complex by uncertainties about the possible scale of new development. In plan preparation there are, in principle, two main methods of estimating the requirements for housing development. These are:

❑ demographic forecasts that seek to estimate the number of households in a district or county at the end of the plan period;

❑ forecasts of the rate of construction in the private and social housing sector.

Demographic forecasts are typically the most important consideration. In Scotland, the National Planning Guidelines state that 'the demographic calculation of overall housing need has for many years provided a cornerstone in assessing the requirements for housing land'. (Scottish Office, 1996, p. 7.) In England, planning authorities can use either method. However, they must consider regional forecasts of population and housing prepared, largely on the basis of demographic data, by the Department of the Environment.

Though the technical details vary, demographic forecasts have a series of shared features. They involve an estimate of natural growth as an outcome of the balance between the death and birth rates in the existing population; they make assumptions about migration trends; and they assess the extent to which the population is likely to divide into separate households. It is likely, for example, that even in a town or city with a static population, a continuing trend towards smaller households will cause an overall increase in housing needs. The growth of single person adult households is now the main component of increased housing demand at a national level.

Demographic forecasts involve numerous uncertainties. At a local level, the migration assumptions are sensitive to the prosperity of the local economy, on whether local firms close down or new firms move in. This aspect of the projection takes the form of a professional judgement rather than a statistical calculation. Even at a national level, estimates of immigration from overseas are subject to uncertainties.

Likewise, the rates of household formation are more uncertain than they might seem. Most projections are little more than an extension of previous trends into the future. In practice, actual rates of household formation are influenced by unemployment levels, the ratio between house prices and income level and the availability of low cost rented property. Relatively high prices, increased unemployment and a lack of affordable rented accommodation reduce the likelihood that young people will leave the parental home and set up an independent household either alone or with a partner. If they do leave home, they are more likely to live in relatively crowded, privately rented housing (Di Salvo *et al.*, 1995; Holmans, 1996).

Finally, in attractive rural areas subject to pressures for in-migration, the projections tend towards circularity. In such areas, the rate of population growth is restrained by a lack of available sites and by a consequent failure of house builders to meet demand. As a result, the estimate of future land requirements will merely serve to project the policies of the present and the recent past into the future.

Projections of house building rates involve fewer calculations. They assume that about the same number of dwellings will be built each year in the near future as in the immediate past. However, projections of house building also raise difficulties. Projections of social house building are sensitive to national priorities and public spending constraints. Projections of private house building are sensitive to the ups and downs of the market. Projections made at the time of an upturn in the house building cycle give very different results to those made during the depths of a depression. Moreover, projections of house building suffer, like local demographic projections, from problems of circularity caused by restrictive planning policies in attractive areas.

To an extent, the technical deficiencies of each approach would not raise insuperable problems of there was a degree of consistency in their forecasts. However, this is seldom so. In the mid 1980s, especially in the counties of southern England, the rate of house building exceeded expectations. In contrast, in the 1990s, house building and new social housing provision in England has run below projections of trends in household formation. Holmans (1995) estimates that, in England in the period between 1991 and 2001, private house builders need to provide about 155 000 new dwellings per year. In fact, house completions in the period between 1991 and 1995 have only been, on average, 122 448 per year (Wilcox, 1996, p. 100). The difference in any single year is not massive but it is leading to a progressive backlog of need.

The gap between demographic projections and building rates raises a dilemma. Should planning authorities now allocate more land to anticipate a growth in the number of households? If planning authorities do this, they risk undermining policies for urban renewal and urban house building. Or should planning authorities hold back and wait to determine trends in house building? If they do this, they may fail to provide an adequate supply of land for building and may, in the long term, increase land costs and house prices.

Attempts to quantify the financial costs of greenfield planning controls show that these may not be large. To this extent, one might argue that a cautious approach to land supply is justified. For example, Cheshire and Sheppard (1989) have compared house prices in a town subject to a strict policy of urban containment (Reading) to another (Darlington) with a more liberal planning regime, the two towns being chosen because they match each other in their size and socio-economic composition. They conclude that the scarcity costs of urban containment are between about 6 to 8% of average house prices (or 3 to 5% if an allowance is made for the increased plot size in a relaxed planning regime). Moreover, measures to abolish the price difference would lead to a substantial increase in the size of the built-up area of the South East of England from 19 to 28% of the total land area. Likewise, Bramley (1993, pp. 14–16) has estimated, on the basis of a financial model of the house building industry, that increases of 75% in the rate of land release would only reduce prices by 7.5%, so enabling an extra 3 or 4% of households to buy their own home. Ever more draconian measures of land release such as using the Green Belt, Bramley argues, would only have a marginal effect on these price reductions.

On the other hand, even a small increase in house prices is best avoided, if possible. Moreover, it is possible that, in the long term or in conditions of growing housing demand, restrictive land supply conditions could have a more dramatic impact.

The essential problem is that over the usual five year or ten year time period of a development plan, neither a single forecasting method nor even a combination of methods can provide a guaranteed reliability. The development plan has to become more flexible. How is this to be achieved? One possibility, suggested by the Joseph Rowntree Foundation Inquiry *Planning for Housing* (1994), is that strategic plans should be reviewed every two years. Such a proposal has staffing implications for planning authorities. Plan preparation is a staff intensive process. In addition and more importantly, it is largely inconsistent with existing procedures for public consultation. A two year rolling developing plan would be no more than a bureaucratic device. It would lack the authority that comes from extensive public debate.

Another possibility, more in keeping with current planning practice, is for the development plan to incorporate a clear framework for phasing. The planning authority might consider current demographic forecasts as a long-term possibility, but still require developers to use, in the first place, a limited range of sites, probably vacant and under-used sites. The Town and Country Planning Association (1996) has argued, for example, that plans might contain a combination of 'short-term allocations and longer term contingent policies'.

A phasing policy would not insist on a specific date for the completion of a scheme. The timing of development would have to remain a matter of commercial judgement, in the light of market conditions. Phasing would merely indicate the order in which development would take place. The phasing policy would say to developers that, for example, sites within an urban area or sites within another designated area would have to be developed first before sites elsewhere. It would enable planning authorities to satisfy the needs of a growing number of households, if this trend becomes a reality, whilst maintaining pressure on private developers to use urban sites.

The difficulty from the viewpoint of a local planning authority is that, once a site is allocated as suitable for housing even in the long term, developers might seek its immediate release. The principle of phasing is long established in town planning. However, developers would probably object to a phasing policy if this were to lead to a further restriction on their choice of sites.

ALLOCATING LAND FOR LOCAL NEEDS

A peculiarity of the town planning system is that forecasts of housing land requirements are mostly indifferent to whether housing is provided by the market or by social housing agencies. 'Need', defined as the need for social housing, constitutes the main interest of local authorities in the preparation of housing strategy statements and housing investment programmes. In contrast, for the local authority in its role as a town planning agency, the main interest is the total estimate of housing land requirements, including both private and social housing.

Therein lies a problem. Not all housing consumers have the same weight or buying power. In conditions of scarcity, those consumers with the least buying power are at a disadvantage. They may have to pay more than they would wish. They may, in extreme circumstances, find that developers are providing no homes for their needs. The problem is especially acute in attractive rural areas subject to high demand from commuters or from retired households. In such areas, the allocation of more land for housing development will not assist the provision of low cost housing. It will merely result in the development of more high priced housing for in-migrants. However, the problem also arises in some urban areas of high demand. The former Greater London Council (1985, pp. 31–33) argued, for example, that it was necessary to allocate land separately to social housing agencies. Otherwise, private developers could take all the available sites and prevent their use for households in priority need.

The use of planning agreements

Planning authorities have long been aware of the problem. In the 1970s, for example, many County Councils included a reference to housing for local needs in their draft Structure Plans. In practice, however, the references mostly comprised a declaration of intent and lacked effective mechanisms for enforcement. Planning authorities could say that they had long exercised controls over the occupancy of agricultural dwellings in the Green Belt. They had granted planning permission to dwellings in the Green Belt on condition that they were occupied by agricultural workers. However, there was uncertainty whether such controls could or should be extended to 'ordinary' housing in the countryside. Enforcement would have extended planning control to the type of occupant rather than, as is usual, to the type of scheme. The definition of 'local' in the context of relatively large housing markets and journey to work areas was another problem.

In the early 1980s, the Conservative government adopted a particularly hostile view of local needs policies. In nearly all cases, references to local needs in development plans were deleted or significantly amended when the plans were submitted to the Secretary of State for approval. The view of the government in the early 1980s rested on a series of propositions; that private enterprise should be freed from unnecessary state interference; that the planning system should attempt to encourage private house building by releasing more land; and that the planning system should deal only with land use and the environment and not with the social characteristics of occupants.

There is no published record of the internal debate within the government. However, in February 1989, the government reversed its earlier decision and announced that, henceforth, planning authorities could come to an agreement with developers, under Section 52 (now Section 106) of the Town and Country Planning Act, to secure the provision of low cost housing for local needs on land that, otherwise, would not have received planing permission for housing (DoE, 1989). In return for such an 'exceptional' planning permission, land owners were expected to make their land available at a relatively low price.

Subsequent surveys of planning practice suggest that authorities have taken considerable care in the implementation of their new powers. For example, a survey of planning practice in Yorkshire, Humberside and Derbyshire, undertaken in the spring of 1990, suggests that planning authorities sought to measure housing need as a preliminary to their policy; that they adopted a definition of local connection which covered multiple criteria and not merely the fact of local residence; that they treated dwellings covered by the local occupancy condition as an addition to projected house building requirements (as they were in fact required by the DoE); and that, as a result, they avoided any risk of pushing up house prices (Goodchild, 1992, p. 50). Moreover, local planning authorities were sufficiently sensitive in their choice of sites to avoid widespread protests from local residents. The report of a national survey states that 'there is no evidence that the exceptions initiative has, in any way, undermined existing local plan policies' (Williams and Bell (1992, p. 143).

By 1991, officials and ministers were sufficiently encouraged by the success of the rural exceptions initiative to introduce a general policy to encourage the use of planning agreements to provide social housing. In England, *Planning Policy Guidance: Housing* (DoE, 1992c) states that, where local authorities have identified a need for low cost housing, the willingness of a developer to include an element of affordable housing is a material consideration that the planning authority should take into account in deciding whether to grant planning permission. The implication is that any proposal, certainly any larger housing proposal, will be treated more favourably if it includes a mix of private and social housing. In Wales and Scotland, the equivalent statements of planning guidance, both entitled *Land for Housing*, have similar implications (see Scottish Office, 1996).

The various housing pressure groups, representing both the private and the public sectors, have supported the local needs policy. Planning agreements are almost certainly a more effective route to the provision of low cost housing than the simple release of more housing land through the town planning system (Bramley, 1993). Moreover, as was the intention, they have the advantage for private builders of allowing the use of sites that would otherwise not be available for development. The Institute of Housing and the House Builders Federation have, for example, jointly published a guide to good practice in planning for housing that endorses the use of the planning system to obtain land for social housing (Dunmore, 1992).

The main qualifications, from the viewpoint of social housing providers, are that:

❏ The saving in land cost is not sufficient to allow a reduction in the rents of completed housing association schemes. The rents are generally not low cost in relation to existing local authority and housing association schemes (Williams and Bell, 1992).

❏ Planning agreements are time-consuming and complex to negotiate (Farthing and Lambert, 1996). Negotiation must consider the suitability of the site for the proposed number of dwellings. It is also invariably limited by the commercial judgements of the developer.

❏ The complexity of negotiation means that planning agreements are only used for a small proportion of housing association build for rent schemes. In England, in the period from the beginning of the financial year 1992/93 to the end of the financial year 1994/95, about 9% of housing association sites were provided through a planning agreement or condition for an element of affordable housing on a private scheme. About 4% of housing association sites were rural exception sites (Farthing and Lambert, 1996).

❑ Negotiation is most likely to yield additional sites in rural areas, rather than where housing is most needed, in the inner city (Mullins *et al.*, 1993). Other than in rural areas, it is unlikely that the use of planning agreements will ever make a substantial impact on housing need.

For planning authorities, the affordable housing policies raise other difficulties.

❑ First, what is the definition of low cost or affordable housing? Does this refer only to rented housing allocated by a social housing agency to persons in need? Or does low cost and affordable housing incorporate low priced housing built for sale?

❑ Second, environmental pressure groups and many practising planners still fear that the use of planning agreements to achieve social and financial benefits will undermine public control and accountability. For example, the Royal Town Planning Institute (RTPI) has criticised the 'exceptions' policy for encouraging inappropriate and environmentally damaging development in rural areas (*The Planner*, 17 July 1992).

❑ Third, it is not easy to apply local needs policies to specific sites. The *Planning Policy Guidance: Housing* encourages planning authorities to specify targets for the proportion of social housing throughout a plan area, based on evidence of need. However, they are also encouraged to avoid quotas that are applied rigidly to each site.

❑ Fourth, the formal policy statements are limited in their application. *Planning Policy Guidance: Housing* only refers to the provision of affordable housing as a means of ensuring a reasonable mix and balance of house types and sizes (DoE, 1992c, para. 38). The policy is evidently not intended for implementation in areas where there is a predominance of smaller or less expensive housing.

There is surely a case for the better integration of planning and housing policies. The local development plan should discuss explicitly the balance between social housing and private housing. However, planning agreements are not a proper vehicle for this. Planning agreements are merely a device through which local planning authorities can undertake, ad hoc, negotiations to improve the marginal acceptability of a proposal.

Proposals for a low cost housing use class

The limitations of the affordable housing initiatives have led to a search for some other way of ensuring that the provision of such housing remains a proper planning consideration. In particular, some rural pressure groups, notably the Council for the Preservation of Rural England (CPRE) and Action with Communities in Rural England (ACRE) have called for the creation of a new low cost housing category within the Use Classes Order (*Planning*, 10 February 1989). At present, there is only one class of residential use in the Use Classes Order (excluding the sub-class that covers hotels and hostels).

The creation of a low cost housing use class would probably require planning any change from low cost to medium or high cost housing permission. As is current practice in respect of most planning agreements, the low cost use class would have to refer to social housing as a tenure rather than low cost as an economic category. Rents, house prices and the income levels are not easily incorporated with planning controls.

The creation of a low cost housing use class would formalise the provision of affordable housing within the town planning legislation. It could open the way for the explicit consideration of tenure issues within a development plan. To subject tenure change to planning control is going too far, however. It would interfere with the right to buy and similar rights of local authority and housing association tenants.

Otherwise, the proposed low cost or Social Housing Use Class would have few, if any, advantages in comparison to existing practice based on the use of Section 106 agreements. Sometimes it is said that the low cost housing use class would protect potential social housing sites from competitive purchase from private developers and would therefore allow housing associations to purchase land at a reduced value. However, much would depend on the expectation of owners and their willingness to sell. It is possible, for example, that owners could refuse to sell at a price less than for private housing. Housing associations have no means of undertaking compulsory purchase. Local authorities have such powers, but would be required to purchase the land at market values.

CONCLUSIONS

The management of urban growth starts with a simple view of the compact city as a counter to urban dispersal. It is reasonable to assume that dispersed development in the countryside, unrelated either to jobs or services, will damage the countryside and is likely to stimulate the use of the private car. In practice, however, the scope for creating a compact city is limited by consumer preferences for places with relatively low population densities, by the difficulty of promoting urban house building in the face of economic constraints and by a general and steady decline in household size and housing occupancy rates. It is not easy for cities to increase the size of their housing stock. Measures to promote urban house building, though worthwhile, are generally insufficient to counter population loss caused by a decline in occupancy rates. The population of most urban areas continues to decline, even in places that have experienced employment growth in the 1980s and 1990s.

The limitations of the compact city mean that policies to promote urban house building have to be accompanied by an acceptance of continued urban expansion. Nevertheless, existing measures of urban containment should not be relaxed. A degree of caution is justified by the relatively modest rate of private housing building in the 1990s and by the possibility that the excessive allocation of housing development sites will undermine urban renewal. Development may be phased so that developers are required to use vacant and under-used sites first.

In the planning of new development, the task is to apply different solutions such as infill development, suburban extension, development around railway stations in a way that promotes pedestrian access to facilities; that makes best use of the existing infrastructure (public transport, roads, sewers and schools); and that avoids development constraints such as steeply sloping sites, areas liable to flooding, and so forth.

Planning the compact city also raises a series of specific issues, mostly related to the method of implementation.

❑ There are five main ways of promoting urban house building. These are greenfield restraint, the promotion of vacant sites, the provision of selective grant aid, selective public land purchase and, though this remains unusual at present, the charging of infrastructure costs for greenfield development. In addition, for former industrial sites, publicly funded remedial works are often necessary. The various ways of promoting urban house building each have their limitations, strengths and weaknesses. The implementation of policies for urban renewal does not generally involve a choice between one measure and another. Implementation depends, instead, on a co-ordinated approach that combines the various measures together.

❑ The promotion of urban house building implies the intensification of existing residential areas. Here the main constraint is the level of car parking requirements. The rigid application of generous car parking standards, for example, one space for each unit, hinders the subdivision of houses into flats and damages the environment. Housing developers and planning authorities should consider the possibility of car-free housing.

❑ The anticipated growth of single person and two person adult households favours the development of housing in town and city centres. Local authorities can encourage commercial developers to include a proportion of housing in new schemes in town and city centres. Outside Greater London, however, the conversion or reoccupation of existing town centre property for housing mostly requires some form of grant aid or other subsidy.

❑ The successful implementation of complex schemes, both new housing and renewal schemes, often involves the use of Section 106 agreements. These enable the planning authority to place a financial or similar obligation on a developer and, in doing this, to secure additional community benefits, from roads to leisure facilities and including the provision of social housing.

Planning agreements do not, however, lead to a significant increase in social housing provision, except possibly in the context of small villages. The provision of social housing still depends on the availability of direct public subsidies.

Chapter 7
Homes for today and the future

Virtually all those involved in housing and planning would accept the desirability of looking ahead. The ability to look ahead is a necessary aspect of preparing plans and strategies. It is, in any case, the only way to minimise the risks and seize the opportunities of change.

THE STRATEGIES OF 'FUTURE RESEARCH'

Forecasting the future may seem a daunting exercise. The future is, in principle, unknowable until it arrives. The various factors that influence events are too diverse, too complex, too delicately balanced and too dependent on chance to allow a complete knowledge of their workings. Yet partial forecasting is possible so long as the analysis is not too ambitious and so long as any prediction is limited in its scope. Even if the prediction turns out to be flawed, the very process of forecasting the future can be valuable in identifying possibilities.

There are many different methods of forecasting. Gordon (1992) argues that 'futures research', to use an American term, has at least 19 methods and that these methods may be classified by the double criteria of whether they are:

- ❑ 'quantitative' or 'qualitative'
- ❑ 'normative' or 'exploratory'.

However, forecasting in housing and urban planning is not as well developed as in business studies, the defence industry or in other fields that have been the primary focus of future research. The range of methods is less. Moreover, in housing and town planning, there is less of a sharp distinction between different categories of forecasting. It would, for example, be difficult to prepare a forecast of the future in a way that completely ignores normative considerations or that wholly concentrates on quantitative rather than qualitative considerations.

In practice, in housing and town planning, two overlapping forecasting methods are of particular relevance. These are:

- ❑ trend impact studies, concerned with the impact of new technologies and of changing social patterns;

❑ scenario analysis, concerned with the implications of a political or social value or of some policy initiative.

TREND IMPACT ANALYSIS

The analysis of trends proceeds through the identification of a series of headings and the identification, under each heading, of trends that might have a significant impact. A possible starting point is the distinction between:

❑ technical innovations in house construction;
❑ the life styles of the occupants and the use of the building after construction.

The distinction refers, in part, to the difference between the production of a good, the 'home' and its consumption. However, a degree of caution is necessary. The use of a dwelling often involves time-consuming and demanding activities. In particular, raising a child is a demanding exercise that is more than mere 'consumption'. Moreover, the difference between the production of a good and its consumption sometimes breaks down within the home. The home is sometimes the site for the small-scale production of goods and services.

Technical innovations in house construction

Assessment of the impact of technical innovation requires, in turn, a brief explanation of the economic logic of housing development. In a competitive market, the main driving force for change is to reduce costs and improve efficiency. In the development of social housing, contractors compete with one another for tenders and, in doing this, they try to demonstrate the best value for money, with the quality of the schemes specified in detail in a statement of employer's requirements or similar statement. In the development of housing for sale, developers market their products to potential house buyers as offering the best value for money.

The key words are value for money. This is more than mere cost-effectiveness measured as the cost per dwelling unit or the cost per unit floorspace. Value for money is the cost for a given level of quality, understood in broad terms that includes build quality (durability), floorspace, comfort, economy in use and appearance. Increased value for money may be accomplished either through the achievement of higher quality at previous costs or through a reduction in costs at a previous level of quality.

Competition amongst house builders might be thought to lead to rapid technical innovation. In practice, innovation is invariably slow. Firms generally give a low priority to research and development or no priority at all. Any innovation in design has to succeed almost immediately, say within one or two years, if it is to be introduced at all. In addition, even within this short period of, say, one, two or three years, any innovation has to avoid a significant increase in costs if the firm's competitive advantage is not to be eroded (see, for example, Gibb *et al.*, 1995, p. 73).

The small size of construction firms, especially in the field of rehabilitation, is another constraint. Rolfe and Leather (1995) have undertaken interviews with 80 small-scale builders working mainly on repair and maintenance in the private sector in and around Bristol. The interviews revealed that most firms operating in this sector comprise single individuals or firms with less than six staff. Such small firms have few resources to try out risky new techniques.

The prevalence of subcontracting also limits innovation. Since 1980, the subcontracting of building work has expanded and now accounts for about 60% of all construction industry employment (Clarke and Wall, 1996). Subcontracting promotes flexibility in the construction. It means that the principal contractor can shed labour at the time of a down-turn, without trade union opposition and without legal constraints. However, flexibility is usually at the cost of either a stable workforce or a workforce that can be trained easily in new techniques. Subcontracting only works if each contractor is already familiar with the construction techniques.

Skill shortages are now of increasing concern within the construction industry. (See, for example, *Building*, 26 April 1996). It is possible that contractors will again start recruiting and training their own workforce in an effort to increase quality (*Building*, 19 April 1996). Tax changes that have reduced the financial advantage of self-employment and the relative weakness of the trade unions are other factors that have led contractors to reconsider their reliance on subcontracting. However, increased in-house training will not, of itself, lead to more innovation in construction. The building contractors are mostly concerned with training for existing crafts, notably for bricklayers, joiners and, to some extent, plasterers.

In social housing, the organisation of the development process is a further constraint. Individual housing associations are mostly concerned with short-term responses to the annual priorities of the government. They have no incentive to adopt a long-term view and mostly rely on their employer's agent for technical advice. However, the employer's agent is mainly concerned with controlling cost and with ensuring conformity with the statement of employer's requirements. The activities of the employer's agent in turn restrict the ability of the contractor to innovate (see Winch and Campagnac, 1995, p. 9).

Innovation in social house building invariably causes difficulties in tendering and increases costs. Even if there are benefits in the long term, it is not in the interests of any single housing association to experiment. Local authorities have not undertaken significant levels of house building in the past five years. In the past, they complained that cost constraints were too tight to permit innovation.

The constraints on innovation in social house building are more amenable to modification than those in private housing. The government can use housing associations or local authorities to undertake experimental or demonstration building programmes. There are examples of such experimental programmes in France, mostly led by an agency called *Plan, Construction et Architecture*. In contrast, for many years in Britain, the overwhelming emphasis in social housing development has been on the reduction of costs.

However, it is unlikely that even an experimental programme will lead to rapid technical innovations in construction methods or materials. The most common building materials are timber, brick and concrete. They have unequalled advantages of value for money, durability and flexibility to different designs. They are, moreover, unlikely to face supply problems in the near future.

Timber, brick and concrete are used in various proportions in different types of construction and in different European countries. Once established, national building traditions persist because they provide an integrated package that is familiar to consumers and well understood by contractors, that has stood the test of time and is, as a result, subject to favourable risk assessments by the main insurance companies. Brick and block, with a cavity wall dominates construction in Britain, accounting for over 90% of output (*Building Homes*, A supplement to *Building*, March 1996, p. 24). Phippen (1982), an architect with experience in both private and public sector housing, writes of this method.

> 'The low capital and maintenance cost of brick walls and tiled roofs, combined with standard windows of modest size, constitute a well understood design vocabulary, simple and quick to employ ... It thereby satisfies, at modest cost, requirements of function, appearance and climate, giving reasonable standards of lighting, insulation and privacy. Cost in housing is possibly the most finely tuned of all building types – carefully balanced between all components which represent "best buys". Opportunities for changes are minimal, except where there are special circumstances, aesthetic or functional, or where cost limits are higher than normal.'

Innovation is not absent from British house building. Numerous examples may be given of specific innovations during the past 20 years: for example, concrete floors, insulation block linings to cavity walls, standardised timber frames, timber roof trusses (joined by connectors instead of craftsmanship), plasterboard rather than plastered block partition walls, chipboard floors rather than floorboards, rationalised plumbing units, plastic windows and door frames, epoxy resin-based materials for repairing and fixing brick and concrete. In addition, portable mechanical tools such as drills, cutters and hammers have become increasingly common on building sites. They are available from local hire shops and, as a result, are used by the smallest building contractors. Though figures are not available, the number of workers on a site has almost certainly greatly declined over the past 10 or 15 years.

In the future, it is possible to identify other technical innovations. Rudlin and Falk (1995) suggest that traditional forms of cavity wall construction are obsolete. They state that traditional methods of cavity wall construction are 'irrational' as they involve a 'Russian doll approach of two structures one inside the other' (p. 42). They also involve technical constraints in the design and use of the wall ties that link the two walls together. Instead of cavity walls, Rudlin and Falk suggest two other possibilities. These are prefabricated timber frame construction, as used in Scandinavia, and 'rationalised' masonry construction with a solid wall and external insulation. Yet, as Rudlin and Falk also recognise, these are mostly theoretical possibilities. The building industry remains highly conservative.

The form of new dwellings is a potential influence on the type of construction. The use of brick and block methods of construction, including rationalised masonry construction, is well adapted to low-rise housing forms such as terraces, semi's and detached houses. Timber-frame methods of construction are also well adapted to such low-rise dwelling forms. In the development of mid-rise and high-rise flats, say of five storeys or more, prefabricated concrete panels and concrete cast in situ offer a competitive and generally quicker alternative. If developers build more mid-rise and high-rise flats in Britain, the pressures will surely increase for the use of concrete as a construction material.

In Britain, concrete is distrusted mainly as a result of the poor quality of the industrialised schemes completed in the 1960s. In contrast, concrete is widely used in Germany, the Netherlands and other European countries with no apparent loss of value-for-money (Clarke and Wall, 1996). In Germany, for example, Daubner (1994) has advocated the continued use of large prefabricated panels as a means of coping with urgent housing shortages. Concrete is strong and durable if used correctly. The worst that can be said of concrete is that it requires extensive insulation and, a minor detail, that it is more difficult to hang pictures on concrete walls.

To summarise the discussion: radical innovation is unlikely for typical low-rise housing. The main case for innovation arises in the development of higher density, mid-and high-rise dwellings for which traditional brick and block are not best suited. For such development, it might be wise for public agencies to encourage the use of building methods, mostly based on concrete, that have been used in the Netherlands and Germany.

Trends in the use of the home

Forecasting trends in the use of the home requires a conceptual framework. Previous exercises in forecasting provide some guidance. Hole and Attenburrow (1966) identify:

- 'changes in the family"
- 'women's work in the home and elsewhere';
- 'changes in spending patterns'

as the main influences on design trends in British housing. Maheu (1989, p. 8) identifies:

- 'the breaking up of the traditional family unit into various "domestic groups"'
- 'new relationships between home/work'
- 'development of new forms of communication and consumption'

as the principal cause of innovation in housing design at a European level.

Finally, Rudlin and Falk (1995, p. 19) have discussed the various aspects of 'comfort' as an influence on design and building technology, and have identified 'changing household composition' and increased paid home working as future trends.

These previous exercises in forecasting were prepared at different times and different contexts. Hole and Attenburrow's analysis was prepared as a response to the post-war house building programme. It involves a reflection on social changes in the 1950s and early 1960s and a projection of these trends into the immediate future. Maheu's analysis is a means of clarifying and classifying the contributions to a European architectural competition called EUROPAN. This analysis reflects the preoccupations of innovative young European architects in the late 1980s. Finally, Rudlin and Falk's analysis is a call for innovation in housing design in Britain in the mid 1990s.

Despite the differences in their date of publication and purpose, the various analyses have common features. They suggest essentially that change is organised around three overlapping, but distinct, processes that are concerned respectively with:

(1)   personal consumption, identity and comfort (including changes in spending patterns);
(2)   the structure of families and households;
(3)   new relations between home and work.

Personal consumption, identity and comfort

In the past, forecasts of trends in housing design have assumed continued economic growth and have suggested that this would lead to increased size in new dwellings and an increased demand for quality. A report *The Prospect for Housing* (1971) prepared by Colin Buchanan and Partners for the Nationwide Building Society provides an example. In the future, the report argued, as levels of income and mobility rose and as people became better educated and more leisured, demand for an improved environment would become the driving force in the demand for new housing. Since much of the existing stock was obsolete either in terms of size and amenities, or in terms of its broader environment, demand for new houses would continue to be high and would mostly take the form of large family houses, of more than $100\,m^2$ on the American model. New houses would be designed to provide a greater separation of household activities, more individual privacy and a larger number of habitable rooms.

The search for more space and more comfort is also a theme in the analyses undertaken for EUROPAN. Ragone (1989, pp. 104–107) distinguishes three new requirements of the home:

❏   a growing concern with health and the body beautiful, and a demand for bathrooms that are larger than the functional minimum;
❏   a desire for 'sociability', to meet, to get to know, to exchange experiences

with others and therefore a demand for additional space for receiving visitors;

❏ a desire for self-sufficiency, independence and protection from crime, resulting in a demand for more storage space and space to accommodate household gadgets.

The possibility of a better environment has, indeed, become an important motivating factor in house purchase, as Buchanan and Partners predicted in 1971. For example, a leading firm of property consultants, Savills (1992, p. 25), have argued that, other than for those individuals and households who have to move for reasons of relationship breakdown or for reasons of employment, most people buy new houses for aspirational reasons, rather than out of pure necessity. Likewise, a market research company, Research Associates (1988, p. 8), have suggested that people mostly buy a new house in order to 'move up' to a better location, or to a more spacious property, sometimes as a result of increased income or capital becoming available to them.

In contrast, the pattern in relation to dwelling size provides only partial support for the views of Buchanan and Partners, and Ragone. In all countries in Northern and Western Europe, the available living space has increased in the sense that average household size and the occupancy rate of the existing stock has declined. In Britain, where the increase is probably slower than elsewhere, the report of the English House Condition Survey 1991 shows that the average floorspace available to each member of a household increased in the 1980s, by about one square metre between 1986 and 1991 (DoE, 1993, p. 132).

In some countries the actual size of dwellings has also increased. In France, as a result of a combination of house building and the conversion of enlargement of the existing stock, the average habitable floorspace of principal dwellings (excluding secondary and holiday homes) increased from $68\,m^2$ in 1970 to $85\,m^2$ in 1988 (Mormiche, 1993). However, in Britain, the trend towards larger houses has not materialised. The report of the English House Condition Survey 1991 suggests that houses built after 1980 possess a slightly smaller average floor area than those built between 1965 and 1980. Whereas the former, the more recently completed dwellings, have an average overall floor area of $73\,m^2$, the equivalent figure in the latter is $78\,m^2$ (DoE, 1993, Table A3.4).

The variation between trends in Britain and elsewhere in Europe has no single explanation. The relatively high cost of development sites in Britain is, almost certainly, a relevant factor. It may be the single most important consideration. Another consideration is the existence in most European countries of more generous space standards in social housing and the inclusion of minimum room sizes or minimum overall dwelling sizes in the building regulations.

The possibility exists that increased wealth and higher expectations will make the older housing stock obsolete. This was certainly a theme in *The Prospect for Housing*. In fact, the older housing stock remains popular. Brown and Steadman (1991a, p. 279) state, on the basis of a detailed review of architectural form, that,

'The 19th-century terrace is probably the classic example of successful adaptation... Though far too cramped to be acceptable today for housing large families as originally intended, the standard terrace is well suited to couples and small families and through upgrading, through increased accommodation and improved sanitation, has ensured a reasonable fit to middle class needs... It is the staple "first-time buy" of the estate agents window'.

The typical 'semi' built by private developers during the 1920s and 1930s is also adaptable to different uses. The inter-war 'semi' generally contains a through hall and so provides independent access to all the main rooms; it generally provides separate living rooms at the front and back on the ground floor (unless these have been knocked into one large through living room); and it is easily extended through a single storey back projection (see Brown and Steadman, 1987, p. 431).

The existing stock, especially the older pre-1919 stock, has other advantages. It is generally less isolated than new housing, more accessible to social and cultural facilities and to public transport. The existing stock is, therefore, better adapted to those households and social groups, including old people, without access to a private car. Moreover, the older housing stock may combine the advantage of greater accessibility with other advantages that arise from the existence of larger gardens and more space around the home. The occupier of an older property is likely to face higher repair bills and higher heating charges. However, these disadvantages are not so great that they lead to a steady depreciation in the value of the older housing stock, unless the house is located in an area that is blighted for some other reason (for example, the closure of local industry or a reputation for crime).

The local authority housing stock, including the stock that has been sold to housing associations and other agencies, is often less adaptable than that in the private sector. The local authority stock contains a higher proportion of high-rise flats and a higher proportion of unusual, high density estates. For these reasons, the local authority stock is more liable to become obsolete and is therefore more vulnerable to demolition. This is likely to persist for the immediate future, at least until the present backlog of problems is tackled through public action.

The structure of families and households

Increased living standards also has implications for the structure of households. They enable the younger members of a household to move out to an independent home. However, increased living standards is not the only force for change. The gradual ageing of the population is leading to increased numbers of single person and childless households. Those aged over 60 years now account for about 20% of the total population. National population projections suggest an increase to about 25% by 2021.

The network family

In addition and most importantly, the family itself has changed. The basic trend may be summarised as a move towards the 'network family'. Amphoux (1989, pp. 70–74), another contributor to the debates in *EUROPAN*, describes the move as follows:

> 'the family, today, is becoming uncertain and improbable. No one marries for life any more, but for an undetermined period. One cohabits, but stays independent... One divorces but stays in touch, close to the children whose custody is shared. The young leave their parental home, but hold onto a pied-à-terre there. The old get close to their children without as much as invading their home.
>
> 'To the "pyramid family", founded on the home and the succession of generations and heritages, is added, and in part substituted the "network family"...'

The emergence of this new network family reinforces other tendencies towards larger homes. It implies that family houses should allow for greater privacy and independence amongst its members. The family house should allow the retention of a *pied à terre*. Otherwise, the network family implies, at least, in principle, an increased demand and an increased need for affordable housing that is suitable for a diverse mixture of single adults, childless couples and single parent families.

Recent demographic forecasts clarify the likely impact. The forecasts invariably suggest that the future growth of households will almost entirely comprise single persons and, to an extent, childless couples. Increased demand for non-family housing implies, in turn, an increased demand for flats and, apart from older households, an increased demand for housing in central locations. However, the forecasts do not necessarily suggest the emergency of new or different house types, except possibly for the most affluent, style conscious groups. The lesson of the housing market is the continuing popularity of two bedroom and three bedroom terraces and semis. Small one bedroom homes lack flexibility in use and have not provided a growth market. Indeed some reports suggest that mortgage lenders have started to refuse loans on one bedroom houses and flats for fear that they are 'no longer considered desirable by a large part of the first-time buyer market' (*The Times, Weekend Money*, Saturday 1 June 1996).

A further limitation is that young adults may lack purchasing power to influence trends within the private housing market. If they have to leave the parental home, say for job-related reasons, they may have to accept shared accommodation in the existing stock or even in hostel accommodation because they cannot afford separate accommodation. Housing associations and local authorities have sometimes provided new or renovated shared housing schemes for young people. However, the numbers, though not published, remain small. Shared housing is often difficult to manage, owing to the desire of tenants to select their house partners. Where housing associations have built for single adults and childless couples, they have mostly provided independent accommodation.

Private developers have not developed shared housing. They are, moreover, unlikely to do so unless they can build for private landlords. There are legal and management complications in shared home ownership for couples of groups of people who are unrelated to one another.

Housing for the elderly

In the past, debates about housing for old people have generally assumed that they require some form of specialist accommodation. In the 1970s and early 1980s, 'sheltered housing', provided with warden support, appeared almost as a panacea. Completed sheltered housing schemes proved easy to let and the occupants expressed very high levels of satisfaction with their new accommodation (see, for example, Fennell, 1986). Moreover, from the early 1980s onwards, specialist private house builders, notably McCarthy and Stone and Anglia Secure Homes, followed suit with a closely related concept of 'retirement homes'.

Sheltered housing is now less fashionable in social housing. At present, there is little desire on the part of either the government or the housing and social services pressure groups to encourage elderly people to live in any form of institutional care, whether publicly or privately financed. The current emphasis is on 'community care' and the pursuit of a policy that enables older people to live at home and to retain their independence as long as possible.

Most elderly persons would, no doubt, agree with this. Aspinall *et al.* (1995, p. 17) have analysed the results of a Scottish survey that suggests that only about 24% of the elderly might be prepared to move 'in some circumstances'. Ground floor accommodation, either as a bungalow or a ground floor flat, was the most popular choice amongst those who were to consider moving.

The shift in policy emphasis has paralleled a shift in demand. In the social housing sector, older sheltered housing schemes and those in less favourable locations, usually those away from urban facilities, have sometimes become difficult to let. In the private sector, the depression in the housing market in the 1990s has reduced demand. When service charges, ground rents and other costs are considered, the financial outgoings involved in a retirement home are potentially substantial and certainly higher than living in conventional accommodation.

Nevertheless, retirement homes are likely to remain a 'niche' market for private developers, especially high quality, high cost retirement homes, perhaps provided with leisure facilities (Williams, 1990). Of course, if retirement homes remain a niche market in private housing, it is also likely that they have a specialist role in the social housing sector. The existence of sheltered housing provides a degree of choice for elderly tenants, even if, as the surveys show, they only appeal to a minority.

Health experts in Britain and the United States have argued that old age is currently undergoing a process of redefinition. (See Warnes, 1994.) Increased affluence and better health care is leading to an increased number of active elderly people. These are people who are in the early years of retirement and who wish to enjoy life to the full. These people may move to a new or different house located in a pleasant location, in the countryside or near the centre of a small country town, but they do not necessarily want to move to some form of collective accommodation such as a retirement home.

Later in life, elderly people enter a period of life characterised by restrictions on activity and increased dependency. However, the needs of this later period of life also do not necessarily imply a case for sheltered housing or a private retirement home. This later stage implies either care in the community, including the provision of home adaptations for the elderly, or care in a nursing home, with a high level of personal support.

It is possible to envisage new forms of housing that offer accommodation for both stages of life for the elderly. Such accommodation is called a 'continuing care retirement community' in the United States. So long as older people can afford the initial costs of entry, they can live full and active lives in the security that, within the context of a privately funded health system, increased care will be provided when required at either no additional cost or a reduced cost (Cassel, 1993).

In Britain, the development of a continuing care retirement community is a novelty that poses risks for private developers. Hitherto, only the Joseph Rowntree Housing Trust has persevered with the idea. The Trust has proposed to build a modified version on the outskirts of York. If the scheme succeeds, others will surely follow. The model provides a way in which private developers can appeal to a new, affluent (though probably small) market. The cost to prospective purchasers will be substantial.

New relations between home and work

The emergence of the network family presupposes a change in the role of women. Women are now more likely to go out to work than at any point in the present century. Though women are still under-represented at the highest levels in the professions and in management, they are more likely to occupy senior positions than in the past. In the future, one might reasonably assume a continuation of the same trend. Women are likely to gain more and more economic independence. As a result, they will expect that the design and the organisation of the home are more conducive to their varied needs as carer, mother, earner and pensioner.

The growth of women's professional employment means a greater pressure on time management. It means that women and increasingly men will have to juggle working and running a home. The traditional role of women has been in the home. The process of juggling work and household duties is still mainly a problem for women. However, if women gain greater economic independence, this traditional role will surely become less dominant. In family households, men will surely gain new domestic responsibilities and will also face new pressures of time management.

The pressures of time management
There is, of course, nothing new about married women going out to work. Hole and Attenburrow (1966, p. 57) note that, even in 1950, 40% of all employed

women were married. Though Hole and Attenburrow do not say so, a proportion of these working married women surely had children.

There is, moreover, nothing new in women demanding changes in the design of houses. In the past, for virtually the whole of the twentieth century, a driving force for increased housing standards has been the demand of women's groups and of women consumers for easy-to-run homes that reduce the burden of housework. In part, the demand for higher standards has expressed itself in political action. The women's movement was prominent in demanding good quality, easy-to-run housing at the end of the First World War. In addition, the demand has expressed itself through the market. House builders have realised that making a house attractive to women is important in securing its quick sale. Likewise, the manufacturers of domestic equipment have realised the market advantages of offering new labour-saving devices.

The result has been a long list of technical innovations, many of which are now taken for granted (see Ravetz, 1995, pp. 118–148). In the years between 1900 and 1939, the main innovations were:

❑   the replacement of coal-fired cooking ranges by gas cookers;
❑   the general installation of electric lights;
❑   the installation, first in new middle class housing and then, in the 1920s and 1930s in new Council housing, of a fixed bath, an internal WC and of new heating and plumbing systems for the transport of hot water.

In addition, between 1945 and the present day, there was a second wave of innovation comprising:

❑   the installation of electrical circuits that could support labour-saving domestic appliances such as washing machines, refrigerators, dishwashers and vacuum cleaners;
❑   the replacement of coal fires by a combination of gas fires, electric fires and gas or oil-fired central heating;
❑   the upgrading of the pre-1919 housing stock to include a bathroom, internal WC and new plumbing systems.

The various labour-saving devices have reduced the drudgery of housework for working class women. In 1919 a women's advisory group stated that:

> 'When the house and water supply are heated and the lighting and cookery done by electricity, half the domestic work now necessary will become unnecessary.' (Ministry of Reconstruction, p. 5.)

The labour-saving devices have also enabled middle class women to avoid a dependence on resident servants, as was the practice before 1918.

However, the labour-saving devices have not led to changes in the division of labour within the home and have not necessarily reduced the time involved in running a home. They are not an answer to the more radical calls for women's liberation. Gershuny has reviewed a series of time budget studies that, over the past 35 years, various organisations have undertaken in Britain for market research purposes. These studies show that most women now spend less time on cooking and housework, but more time on shopping, more time on travel linked to domestic activities (going to the shops, taking children to school and so forth) and much more time on child care (*The Independent on Sunday*, 19 December 1996; also see Berk, 1988).

Innovation in labour-saving technology continues in the form of proposals for home automation, 'smart housing' or 'domotics' (domestic robotics) as it is variously called. This is where computer technology permits the automatic control of the electrical systems within a home. A fully automated home would undertake the independent control of the heating, ventilation, air conditioning and security. It might also allow the occupants to exercise remote control over household appliances from outside the home, for example from the workplace or a car. (See Schofield, 1995.) Other innovations appear in the specialist journals such as the self-build journal *Built It* and at exhibitions such as the annual *Ideal Home Exhibition*. An example is the central vacuum system in which a hose is plugged into the skirting board.

However, compared to the innovations of the past, the gains in labour saving are likely to be relatively small. Computerising a house does not, for example, ease the task of cleaning. Perhaps for this reason, automated housing has not, as yet, caught the imagination of either housing developers or consumers. In the 1990s, the most widely used innovations in labour-saving devices have arisen through the provision of new services such as pre-cooked foods available from a supermarket or by fast food ordered over the telephone and brought to the house. (McCrae, *The Independent*, 24 March, 1994.)

Reductions in the burden of housework have not been merely caused by improvements in technology. The reduction in overcrowding and improved kitchen design are other factors. This latter trend towards improved and larger kitchens may continue. Feminist architects sometimes argue for larger and more open 'family' kitchens where the adult members of a household can gather and share in the domestic responsibilities (Peatross and Hasell, 1992). On the other hand, the growth of convenience foods and the small size of new houses in Britain might suggest that, in smaller single and two person homes, the kitchen may become absorbed into the living area of the home. The kitchen may cease to be a separate room, becoming only a corner of a relatively large living area. The arrangement already exists in some small flats, but may become more common.

Increased pressure of time management may also lead to changes in the spatial pattern of housing demand. The conventional suburban family house is essentially a solution for the nuclear family, in which the women stay at home to rear the children and the male partner commutes to work. The suburban family house isolates the housewife and mother, but at least provides a pleasant spacious environment. In contrast, the dual career family, the household with two principal earners, may have different, more urban locational requirements. The dual career family is likely to require accessibility to as wide a range of potential sources of employment as possible, as well as accessibility to the shops, nursery schools, child-minders and social networks that permit a mother to work on a part-time or full-time basis. Dual career families are therefore likely to demand more urban, more central locations. They are likely to want to reduce the time spent in domestic travel.

There is a complication, however. Studies in the Netherlands show that the locational and housing preferences of dual career families are influenced by other social and economic factors such as the income of the household and the age of its members. Dual career families, like other households, vary in their purchasing power. Good quality urban housing in a safe, pleasant location is scarce and expensive. Those dual career families that involve a double professional income are relatively wealthy. They are therefore able to seek the best of both worlds; they can afford to buy or rent a generously proportioned property with a garden in an urban location. Other families are less fortunate. Working class and lower middle class families generally have to make a choice between home and work, particularly if they wish to raise children. The typical solution remains for the male partner to retain the traditional role of the main bread-winner, while the woman arranges her paid work around a combination of unpaid housework and child-rearing. These working class and lower middle class families continue to live in the suburbs (Bootsma, 1995; Drooglever Fortuyn, 1993). Likewise, dual earner households with unequal incomes amongst the partners or where one partner works part-time and the other full-time are more suburban-oriented in their housing preferences (Kruythoff, 1993).

Some feminists seek more radical solutions. They suggest the end of independent family houses in favour of new styles of communal living. An American feminist, Friedan (1981, p. 287) puts the point most clearly:

> '... in the first stage of modern ... feminism, house-work and home only figured as something feminists wanted liberation *from*....
> 'The second stage, I'm convinced, has to focus on a domestic revolution within the home and extending, in effect, the concept of home. We have to take new control of our home life, as well as work life, with not only new sharing of roles by women and men, but physical, spatial design of new kinds of housing and neighbourhoods that take into account the changing, shifting needs of women and men, in couples or singly, with or without children, over time, with mortgage financing and building codes and zoning that encourage the new combinations of private space and shared communal spaces and services...

This is a broad agenda. The desire to combine private space and communal living can take a variety of different forms, mostly distinguished by the extent of communal aspiration. Horelli and Vepsä (1994) have, for example, distinguished five separate levels in a ladder of communal living. To simplify the account, these levels include:

❏ a minimal form of co-operation, defined as 'well-functioning housing area' (ordinary housing with the possibility of communal eating at a local club and an active residents' association);

❏ an intermediate level of 'a dwelling collective' or 'big family' (where members

live in the same house and share most or all the tasks of cooking, cleaning up and building maintenance);
❑ at a collective extreme 'a working community' (where members share their income).

Communal housing for women has not been subject to many independent evaluations. A search in the database of the British Library has failed to reveal any independent satisfaction survey or post-occupancy survey in Britain. Moreover, the wider European literature is inconclusive in its implications. The publications of EUROPAN include a sceptical evaluation of communal housing schemes in Germany, undertaken by Schneider (1989, pp. 152–155). Living in communal housing, the author suggests, had some advantages for its women residents. It facilitated the supervision of children and the organisation of crèches. It also provided moral support for the occupants. There was always someone to talk to and to share daily problems. On the other hand, communal living did nothing to reduce the burden of housework or to encourage men to undertake greater responsibilities for housework. Indeed, the inclusion of communal facilities in the schemes actually increased housework. Communal housing also led to a loss of privacy. Women talked of a feeling of social control, of being surveyed by other members of the community, even of being used. In contrast, Horelli and Vepsä (1994) provide a more positive account, based on the experience in Scandinavia. They suggest that the sharing of housework in communal schemes has expanded the roles of men and women and has encouraged men to learn how to cook and undertake domestic chores.

The growth of paid home work

The growth of female employment encourages more paid home working. This may be the only way that many women with children can participate in paid employment. Other factors are leading in the same direction. Financial and competitive pressures are leading the manufacturing industry to place more emphasis on just-in-time delivery and flexible production. Home workers are more flexible because they can be easily hired and fired, with a minimum of fuss. In addition, the growth of telecommunications and of information technology is enabling new types of clerical and professional work to be undertaken at home, including work undertaken by men.

As a result of all this, the sharp distinction between workplace and the home is likely to become more flexible. For those involved in paid home working, the distinction becomes based more on the organisation of time rather than the organisation of urban space. The growth of paid home working, in turn, raises the possibility that residential areas will change their character. In some cases, the growth of paid home working might, for example, lead to more visitors and more delivery vehicles going to private residences. Any such tendency may, in turn, lead to calls for planning authorities to stop the conversion of houses to commercial premises. Hitherto, however, most paid home working has been practically invisible, without significant implications for neighbours.

The impact of telecommunication and information new technology has been the main pre-occupation of futures research, both in the newspapers and in professional publications such as those of EUROPAN. Teleworking, as this new type of work is called, has potential advantages for both the employee and employer. The employee avoids the stress, time and cost of commuting. The employer can reduce the size of an office and also reduce such overheads as heating and lighting (see *The Independent*, 6 June 1994). So, it is assumed, teleworking will inevitably grow in the future.

However, teleworking is not without disadvantages that might hinder its growth. Teleworking equipment remains expensive to install and to run. Employers and management experts worry that home-working might reduce their control over day-to-day activities. They also worry that the efficiency of the workers will decline in the absence of social contact. The trade unions worry about health and safety issues and the possibility of the workers incurring additional cost such as heating, lighting and insurance (Hillman, 1994, pp. 21–22).

The potential scale of teleworking remains subject to wildly different estimates. A report prepared on behalf of the European Foundation for the Improvement of Living and Working Conditions suggests that up to half of the jobs in Britain could be undertaken either in whole or in part through teleworking (Hillman, 1994). However, this is just an ultimate or maximum estimate. The actual number of teleworkers is low. Richardson *et al.* (1995, pp. 82–84) cite research undertaken by the Department of Employment that only 0.5% of the working population is engaged in telework, if this is defined as those who spend at least 50% of their working week at home. If the definition is relaxed to include those who spend at least one day a week working at home, the proportion increases, according to Richardson *et al.*, to between about 2.2% and 2.5% of the working population.

Were teleworking to increase in popularity, the question arises as to its locational implications. The apparent flexibility of teleworking might suggest the possibility of an exodus of urban workers to the countryside. Teleworking gives people more freedom to live in pleasant surroundings in the countryside if they wish. In fact, most teleworking in Britain takes place in London, the South East of England and East Anglia (Richardson *et al.*, 1995, p. 83). Teleworking in remote places in the North of Scotland and elsewhere is the exception rather than the rule. In other words, the existing distribution is in areas of economic growth, including areas within commuting distance of London. Ascher (1995, pp. 57–60) has argued, mostly on the basis of experience of France, that such a metropolitan distribution of teleworking is likely to persist. Ascher draws a parallel between the emergency of teleworking and history of the telegraph and telephone in the late nineteenth centuries. These innovations also allowed communications at a distance, but did not do away with the need for conventional forms of personal transport. The same is almost certainly true of telework. Most teleworkers will still need to maintain regular face-to-face contact with their employers and colleagues.

Whatever the impact of teleworking, the relation between home and work will remain, as at present, conditioned by the socio-economic circumstances of the household. Given a continuation of recent economic trends, one might imagine a new geography of homework (Sassen, 1991, p. 255). The homes of the professional middle classes will increasingly become places with a combination of:

❏ paid housework (cleaning women who come once or twice a week, together with nannies to look after children in the most affluent households);
❏ paid work (word processing, freelance professional work).

In contrast, the homes of low-income households, including immigrants, will remain places of unpaid housework and poorly paid subcontracting work. The latter will remain the most common type of paid homework and will be undertaken in dwellings that are relatively small and poorly adapted for use as a workplace. Home-working, for all its apparent flexibility, will not therefore necessarily lead to an improvement in living conditions.

SCENARIO ANALYSIS

It is easy to get lost in the specifics of different trends. The main alternative method, that of scenario analysis, enables these different trends to be brought together. Scenarios deal with basic values and basic choices about the future of society and so reveal the implications of political ideology in a way that is impossible through the analysis of trends. Nevertheless, the analysis of scenarios is like the analysis of trends in the sense that it seeks a degree of realism. A scenario is only useful if it is relevant to existing policy issues or existing trends.

The status and selection of scenarios

The analysis of scenarios overlaps the long-standing concern of town planning with ideal cities. Planning has to adopt or to assume some scenario if it is to provide direction for urban development. A development plan may, for example, be regarded as a distinct type of scenario whose form and content is bound by its legal requirement of providing guidance for the control of development. The preparation of a development plan generally involves a prediction of what will happen without public intervention, combined with a judgement of the extent to which existing trends can be modified to achieve desirable aims and objectives. However, the preparation of a development plan merely involves a choice between scenarios of land use and the physical environment. In housing, scenarios must combine social and physical factors.

Scenario analysis is not a scientific exercise, at least it is not a scientific exercise in the usual meaning of a body of theory that is capable of testing against reality. Social change cannot be projected in the total sense implied by a scenario, except through imagination. The value of scenario analysis is to import values from the future into the present, so clarifying present choices and giving a moral dimension to planning and policy making. Scenario analysis admits the possibility of a continuation of the status quo. It also recognises that, at any time, it is likely that several images of the desired future, of the possible future, will co-exist with one another.

The possible scope of scenarios in housing may be illustrated through the contributions to a story that appeared in the journal *Housing* in June 1995. The story was entitled 'Cities of the future: what will they be like?' and consisted of eight different contributions by housing practitioners, politicians and experts. It provides a broadly representative and up-to-date cross-section of the views of informed public opinion.

Paul Jenks, the Housing Chair of the Association of District Councils, foresaw the possibility of an improved city. The future city would be:

'like the best European cities of today, with good quality rented housing occupied by all income groups and ages, tree-lined broad avenues, cycle paths and parking areas, pedestrian squares with open air cafes, excellent public transport and lots of water.'

In contrast, Peter Malpass, Professor of Housing Studies at the University of the West of England, adopted a more pessimistic viewpoint:

'increasing international competition will have a damaging long term effect on the British economy, leading to greater income inequality and social polarisation, as the better off seek to shore up their living standards at the expense of the marginalised poor.'

Likewise, David Cowans, Director of Housing for the City of Birmingham, stated that:

'The future will be as was portrayed in *Blade Runner* — a mix of new high tech structures and services combined with road works, congestion, poverty and decay.'

The question is to pull such views into a coherent framework. One way forward is to adapt the four scenarios identified by Robertson (1986; 1990) in the context of a discussion of the future of work. Robertson's framework allows for the both pessimistic and optimistic views of the future. However, it also allows a more differentiated future, with shades of grey. The four scenarios are:

(1) 'decline and disaster', which may be interpreted as decline, chaos and the problem of the inner city;
(2) 'business as usual' – the status quo with slow or intermittent growth;
(3) 'hyper-expansion' – high tech, rapid growth;
(4) 'sane, humane, ecological' – sustainable development.

Decline, chaos and the problem of the inner city

The most pessimistic scenario, that of decline and chaos, is also the most difficult to analyse. The scenario was not included in Robertson's 1986 publication

Future Work. It may be regarded as melodramatic or as scaremongering. Is the society really likely to collapse? Is it even likely to experience a gradual decline into chaos?

The answer is that such a possibility must indeed be considered. This is the *Blade Runner* and social polarisation scenario. The future will be just like the present, only more so. It will be both glossy and shabby, wealthy and poor, only more so. Some cities and some residential areas will prosper, but others will decline into poverty, crime and pollution. Public policy involves a constant search for balance between the principles of wealth creation and social welfare with, in addition, an increasing concern with a third principle of environmental protection. The decline and chaos theory essentially assumes that this balancing act breaks down.

The scenario of chaos is additionally important because of its historical implications for urban planning. The concept of planning arose at the end of the nineteenth century as a reaction against the disorder of the laissez-faire industrial city. Later, Mannheim (1940) argued explicitly for planning, meaning the guidance of society from a central point, as a means of countering irrationality and social disintegration. The key question for Mannheim was not whether to plan, but how to plan.

Therein lies a problem. Arguing for planning as an antidote to chaos is liable to overreaction. Planning becomes the guardian of rationality and any deviation from the logic of the plan becomes an indication of decadence. Planning becomes over-ambitious, over-prescriptive and over-centralised. Mannheim's work suffers exactly from these tendencies. Irrespective of the possibility of decentralisation, a 'planned society' for Mannheim 'will always have to rely upon a very strong centralised bureaucracy' (p. 320). Personal freedom is possible in such a world, but has to be confined to 'the creation of free zones within the planned structure' (p. 379).

However, other more democratic formulations of planning are possible. It is possible to work out a justification for planning that is more directly related to the interests of individuals and communities and that is, as a result, more decentralised. For example, Lefèbvre (1968) has argued that planning should be based on the concept of the 'right to the city', meaning the right to participate in the life of the city and including the right to housing. In this formulation, planning and other forms of public intervention are justified where either chaos or the workings of capitalist development deny that right.

In Britain, the concept of the inner city provides a means of operationalising fears of decline and chaos. The inner city is, in part, a real place characterised by a loss of employment, a lack of private investment and a high level of poverty amongst its residents. (See, for example, the analysis of the 1991 Census, undertaken by Atkins *et al.*, 1966) In addition, the inner city is a place of the imagination – a negative utopia. Harrison (1986, p. 21) writes of the inner city as 'a universe apart, an alien world devoid of almost every feature of an ideal environment . . . a symbol and summation of the dark side of a whole society'. As Harrison also notes, the deprived local authority estate projects a similar negative image. This is 'the inner city's inner city', a place where problems are concentrated into an 'even smaller and more intimate space, where they can interact more destructively' (p. 225).

The opinion survey firm, MORI have undertaken a survey of residents' perception of inner city areas, defined as places of the most intense social deprivation. The results show that most local residents did not consider the inner city as a wholly undesirable place to live. Local residents were generally loyal to their area. They thought that conditions in their area were better than those in other, nearby places. Again, this suggests a need for sensitivity and local consultation in planning and renewal strategies. On the other hand, views of change were generally negative. A larger proportion of residents thought that things had got worse rather than got better or stayed the same (Robson *et al.*, 1994, pp. 335–366). The main exception was that attitudes were more optimistic where public resources had been concentrated (p. x). In the view of residents, the presence or absence of violent crime was the most significant influence on the quality of life, followed by the quality of health care and the cost of living.

Fear of violence is a common theme in accounts of life in the inner city, and it leads, in turn, to what Hillman (1994, pp. 40–41) calls the 'fortress city'. This is a city where affluent property owners either move out to the apparently safer suburbs or invest heavily in surveillance systems and security measures. The fortress city allows the better-off to avoid the dangers of inner city living, but only at considerable expense. To an extent the fortress city already exists. Security guards are present at the entrances to larger offices and record all visitors. Smart cards and push-button codes control access to different rooms within buildings. Entry phones protect lesser buildings, including blocks of flats. Security cameras monitor city centres. Private developers build new estates according to the principles of defensible space. Individual households incorporate increasingly sophisticated security devices to prevent unauthorised entry into their homes.

In the future, if the fear of crime increases, security measures will become even more widespread. Local residents will demand that security cameras monitor all residential streets and not, as at present, merely those in the city centre. Private security men will patrol middle class areas and not, as at present, merely a few blocks of flats. Existing streets may become closed by electronic gates, with entry phone systems controlling access much in the same way as they already control access to individual blocks of flats. In the United States gated communities are already common in Los Angeles (Ellin, 1996, pp. 69–74). The contemporary post-modern city may be more diverse than its predecessors. However, diversity may become expressed through the creation of new barriers.

The status quo with slow or intermittent growth

There is an uncertain line between decline and chaos and the status quo. Much depends on the climate of influential public opinion and the priorities of the government in power. As Sassen (1991, p. 329) asks:

'At what point is the fact of homelessness a cost also for the leading growth sectors: How many times do high-income executives have to step over the bodies of homeless persons till this becomes an unacceptable fact or discomfort? At what point does the increasing poverty of large numbers of workers begin to interfere with the performance of core industries?'

At what point, one might add, does the cost of pollution in all its various forms pose intolerable risks for the health and comfort of the whole urban population.

The continuation of the status quo means a continuation of business-oriented policies in urban renewal and planning. In this scenario, public policies are generally subservient to the demands of the economic system. They promote economic growth and the emergence of an 'enterprise culture' amongst residents. However, public policy is also sensitive to demands for social justice, to the possibility of social disorder and, in the case of planning control, to the demands of local groups for environmental protection.

The assumptions of the status quo are clearly expressed in a policy statement *Action for Cities* (HM Government, 1988). The document contains a section entitled *Better Homes and Attractive Cities*. This expresses two priorities, to secure a wider quality of good housing available for rent, and to buy and improve conditions and opportunities for people living in Council estates. In addition, this same section contains a commitment for the continuation of existing policies in favour of 'greening the cities'. Otherwise, the emphasis is on the needs of business. 'A city,' the document states, 'can only grow if its local businesses grow and are successful'.

The language of *Action for Cities* is selectively biased towards a free-market Conservative ideology. Words associated with the welfare state and with planning are avoided. There are no adjectives such as 'social', 'collective', 'equal' and 'unequal', and no nouns such as 'local authorities', 'communities', 'needs' or 'poverty'. Instead, the emphasis is on the words associated with self-help and individual initiative, words such as 'enterprise', 'choice', 'freedom' and 'prosperity'.

Yet the substance of *Action for Cities* is not completely out-of-line with the position of other political parties. For example, an earlier policy statement, *Policy for the Inner Cities*, published by a Labour government also placed much emphasis on the promotion of business opportunities and the attraction of private investment (DoE, 1977). Likewise, a broadly based Labour party pressure group City 2020 (Anon, 1995) has declared its support for a partnership with the private sector and has even stated that 'the private sector has been neglected by government for the past fifteen years and its regenerative involvement has been marginalised'. The main difference between the policies pursued by a Conservative government and those pursued by a Labour or Liberal coalition government is that the latter are more likely to accept the existence of market failure and more likely to allow local authorities to determine the priorities for action.

The status quo is characterised by a variety of problems which require different solutions and different types of policy intervention (see, for example, Ascher, 1995, pp. 234–242). These different types of intervention will surely continue. They may be listed as follows:

❑ piecemeal measures of control that anticipate and resolve potential problems in the relation between new development and their surroundings;
❑ strict measures of control that attempt to preserve areas of historic or architectural importance;
❑ public investment programmes that seek to provide infrastructure or services, including low cost housing that the private sector finds unprofitable;
❑ selective renewal programmes that attempt to make disadvantaged areas more attractive to private developers;
❑ area management of the type practised in town centres and social housing estates and that seek to co-ordinate existing services and to prevent the emergence of problems.

Intervention in response to specific problems means a loosely organised process in which different styles of decision-making co-exist with one another. It means a combination of closely co-ordinated exercises in urban design for prestige schemes; broad strategic planning policies that indicate priority areas for growth and constraint, and various renewal and housing policies that involve selective grant aid. Applied to the inner city, business as usual means managed decline. Despite public investment, big cities will continue to lose housing as a result of declining household size, an absence of suitable development sites and the preference of many employers for sites away from urban traffic congestion.

High tech, rapid growth

If private businesses and public authorities succeed in the promotion of economic growth, the result will be the third scenario, that of high tech, rapid growth. This is best regarded as a variant of the status quo. The policy priorities and the social problems will be much the same as before. Rapid economic growth may provide more funds for investment by public authorities. However, the experience of the 1980s and 1990s is that economic growth will not solve problems of poverty or poor environment and that it will not create large numbers of jobs. The optimistic interpretation is that rapid growth and affluence will lead to more leisure opportunities. The pessimistic view is of increased unemployment and increased economic inequalities.

The advantages and limitations of rapid growth, as applied to housing, can be understood through a distinction between material and positional goods (Hirsch, 1977). Material goods are those that are receptive to mechanisation or technological innovation, without deterioration in quality. Positional goods, in contrast, are those that are either scarce in some absolute or socially imposed sense or subject to deterioration through mass production and more extensive use.

Housing has a material aspect. Continued economic growth can lead to a higher rate of house building. The building of more houses may, in turn, reduce housing shortages and enable the formation of more households. A reduction in housing shortages, one might suppose, will lead to lower prices for people to rent and buy and so enable more young people to leave the family home, if they so wish. Moreover, material affluence and technological progress will enable people to live in larger dwellings, equipped with a full range of labour-saving appliances.

At the same time, housing also has a positional aspect that is insensitive to economic growth. Economic growth will not resolve the problem of unpopular and stigmatised estates. Social stigmatisation is a product of social processes and trends, including the level of violent crime, that are independent of the level of economic prosperity. Likewise, economic growth will not counter tendencies towards urban sprawl or reduce the consumption of greenfield sites.

A distinctive feature of rapid growth lies in an increased tendency for the existing building stock to become obsolete:

❑ either because existing buildings, including existing houses, fail to meet new comfort levels;
❑ or because they fail to meet the demands of new forms of communications technology, for example teleworking;
❑ or because existing patterns of urban development are overtaken by new trends.

The built environment will have to become more flexible; it will have to be upgraded more frequently or replaced.

In the most prosperous places, it is possible that, unlike current practice, private developers will undertake the modernisation of the older housing stock. Attractive older areas, especially areas of architectural and historic importance, will be rehabilitated to a high standard. Elsewhere in these prosperous places. private developers will replace older property by up-market flats and high density/low-rise courtyard housing. The results will be an increase in the density of the built form and possibly, depending on occupancy rates, an increase in the population of some urban neighbourhoods. However, even in conditions of rapid growth, private redevelopment will probably remain uncommon. Private developers will find the task of urban redevelopment too complex and too costly and will generally prefer greenfield sites.

Rapid growth will not be an even process with growth distributed equally in different regions and cities. Some places will be subject to intensive development pressures. Here the local authorities will probably demand higher contributions from developers to pay for physical and social infrastructure and to provide some form of compensation to existing residents. This is certainly the experience of growth areas in the United States, in California and Florida. Even in Britain some planning authorities, mostly in the counties in the South of England, have started to charge developers for the additional financial burdens that arise from economic growth. In the long term, land owners rather than consumers will pay the additional costs associated with development charges. However, the pressure of development in growth areas will encourage inflation in land prices and will probably lead to an overall increase in housing costs.

The concentration of growth in specific places will facilitate the development of new towns and so-called 'edge cities', based on peripheral transport networks, shopping and commercial centres. As part of this, existing out of town and suburban centres will acquire housing. In California, for example, shortages of housing land have led social housing developers to build flats and houses over shopping centre car parks. In the London Borough of Hammersmith, the Peabody Housing Trust has completed a similar type of scheme involving social housing over a Tesco supermarket (Housing Review, 1997).

Another possibility is the creation of massive new inner area 'supercities' involving a combination of flats, offices and recreational facilities. The prototypes already exist in the schemes undertaken for the Olympic Games in Barcelona, for La Défence in Paris and for Canary Wharf in the London Docklands (see *The Futurist*, May–June 1993). The scale of such schemes means that their development is a risky exercise, as the problems of Canary Wharf have demonstrated. However, as the experience of Canary Wharf also demonstrates, large-scale private development may prove profitable in the long term.

The concentration of growth in specific places is likely to promote decline elsewhere. Given the difficulties of private redevelopment, hyper-expansion implies the re-emergence of public policies for extensive clearance and rebuilding. Otherwise, hyper-expansion may, like the otherwise very different scenario of decline and chaos, lead to increasing vacancies in the urban building stock and increased dereliction in urban areas.

Sustainable development

The final scenario, that of sustainable development, has been the subject of extensive debate, in the official statements of government, within the professional literature in town planning and amongst the various environmental pressure groups. Sustainable development means development that minimises energy demand, that maximises the use of renewable resources, that will last and that creates a healthy environment.

A distinguishing feature of sustainable development is its longer-term time frame. For example, a business-like approach to urban planning might anticipate that rising energy costs will require the use of energy savings techniques and that this will influence the location and design of new housing. A business-like approach might also anticipate that residents will demand higher standards for air and water quality and that this demand will influence the locational decisions of international and national industry. In contrast, the sustainable development scenario assumes that the government takes a lead in such matters.

Compared with the other scenarios, sustainable development is an invented, rather than a projected, scenario. It is invented on the basis of a series of possible policy decisions and created through a clearly defined and detailed programme of action. Because sustainable development is an invented scenario, it is also more open to different interpretations. Sustainable development, like the environmental movements on which it is based, is characterised by a series of overlapping fault lines, for example:

❑ anti-growth versus controlled growth;
❑ social, concerned with changing life styles versus technical, making existing technology more sensitive to its effects;
❑ plan-led, relying on sanctions versus price dependent, relying on incentives;
❑ egalitarian versus inegalitarian.

To an extent, each of these opposites can be mixed with one another in a multitude of different ways. Egalitarian solutions may be combined with either social or technical approaches. Plan-led approaches may favour either no growth or controlled growth.

At the same time, the various distinctions may be understood as a confrontation between conservative and radical political attitudes, between perhaps a 'pale' or 'shallow' green philosophy and a more radical and utopian 'deep green' approach that is not open to compromise. From the viewpoint of political expediency, it is easier to argue in favour of controls on growth, rather than the complete cessation of economic growth. It is simpler to find technical solutions within the status quo than to change the way of life of the population. Finally, it is generally less controversial to accept rather than to introduce radical changes in the existing unequal distribution of income and wealth.

The divisions in environmental thought extend to the future of the big city. Anti-urbanism has a long history in utopian thought in town planning. It is, for example, a theme in the original proposals that Howard (1985) made to break up big industrial cities in favour of small garden cities. Anti-urbanism remains a common theme in green or environmental thinking. For example, Robertson (1986; 1990) argues in favour of a fresh movement of people out of cities on a variety of grounds, including that this will promote 'rural values'. Clark *et al.* (1993, p. 146) gave argued in favour of a 'self-support economy' that involves 'more land for outbuildings and outdoor activities ... and a general reduction in net residential densities'. Finally, Potts (1993) has argued, mainly on the basis of American experience, for the development of homes that are completely independent of urban services such as water, sewerage and power and that, as a result, promote a 'self-reliant, sustainable lifestyle'. In Britain, the movement for ecological build has similar implications for independent, self-sufficient living, free of urban services.

There are obvious problems with anti-urbanism. Abandonment of the city would not permit the recycling of the existing building stock or the reuse of vacant sites. It would also not offer a reliable method of promoting 'rural values', even assuming that these latter can be satisfactorily defined. The movement of urban residents to rural areas might simply enable more people to pursue high consumption, urban life styles in the countryside. Finally, of course, the desirability of dispersal is open to question on the grounds that it would lead to the loss of wildlife habitats and increase dependence on private motor traffic.

The same anti-urban bias expresses itself in a different way in a preference for natural rather than man-made products. Pearson (1989), writing as the 'Director of the eco and health consultancy Gaia Environments' has argued in favour of the 'natural house'. Likewise, Kanuka-Fuchs (1993, p. 3) writes of the principles of 'building biology' and 'bio-harmonic architecture' as including

> 'healthy building site ... natural building materials ... natural air filtration ... natural heating, healthy climate, solar energy, no toxic fumes ... natural magnetic fields'.

The problem is, of course, that the consumption of so-called 'natural' products can be dangerous and, compared to the processed products, more damaging on the environment. Asbestos is, for example, a natural material, but one that can cause cancer.

The divisions in environmental thought imply a degree of caution in anticipating the consequences for housing policy and urban planning. The detailed implications can only be worked out through democratic debate. The consequences are much clearer, if a radical version were to be implemented. In addition, the consequences are clearer if a distinct pro-urban stance is adopted and no mention is made of a preference for 'natural living' or 'natural products'.

Planning and urban policy would seek to improve both the functional or systems-like aspects of the city and those aspects that refer to the city as a home environment. Policies would aim to improve the energy efficiency of the city and to reduce pollution. Equally, they would aim to ensure that the city provides a varied and pleasant place to live, with a housing stock of which the residents can be proud. In such circumstances, many lines of policy would be clear. One might envisage the following:

❏ Renewal strategies are planned and co-ordinated at a local level in a way that brings empty property back into use, promotes the participation of the community and respects the character of a place.
❏ Where developers undertake new build, this is located within walking distance of public transport links, is sited on derelict or under-used land, uses recycled materials, is subject to stringent controls concerning its durability and build quality, and is designed in the form of well-insulated, compact accommodation that, wherever possible, uses a combination of active and passive solar energy systems. Established environmental guidelines are now available for designers and builders (see Prior and Bartlett, 1995).
❏ New housing and rehabilitation schemes conform to some notion of a lifetime standard and are designed to satisfy a diversity of housing needs, including those of disabled people.
❏ Finally, measures are taken to improve the broader environment of urban areas. As part of this, a determined effort is made to increase the use of public transport and to protect pedestrians and residents from traffic nuisances and pollution.

Nevertheless, uncertainties remain. First, in relation to new house building, debates continue about whether sustainable development should attempt to restrain demand. An analogy may be drawn between household formation and the demand for car use. It is now widely accepted that measures to satisfy the incessant demand for motor travel can and should be mitigated by an awareness of their environmental costs and their costs to the public purse. Should we likewise accept that it may not be possible to satisfy a demand for a separate home for every single person who wishes one?

One might argue that a failure to satisfy demand is irresponsible in its implication for people in need. However, housing needs do not have to be met by new house building. It is equally possible, within the framework of a restraint policy, for social housing agencies to acquire existing properties and to redistribute existing housing space.

At present, town planning policies often involve localised restraints, for instance in Green Belts, whilst attempting to satisfy housing need and demand at a district-wide or national level. National and regional restraint is more controversial. The report of an enquiry into housing needs, undertaken by the Town and Country Planning Association, notes that, at a national and regional level, 'the majority view seemed to be that demand and need should be met' (Breheny and Hall, 1996, p. 64). Nevertheless, as the report also shows, there is no consensus. Some environmentalists continue to argue in favour of restraint.

Second, doubts remain about the future scale of demolition. The usual view of a sustainable renewal policy, following Leather and Mackintosh (1994), is a policy that helps owners to look after and care for their property. Such a sustainable renewal policy is open to various interpretations about the relative importance and cost effectiveness of improvement grants, of compulsory measures (for instance through placing new insurance requirements on owners), and of help and advice services. However, the various interpretations all seek to stop further disrepair, to tackle existing repair problems and to protect the existing stock against the need for demolition.

In contrast, the *Energy Report* of the English House Condition Survey 1991 (DoE, 1996, p. 9) states that,

> 'over 1 in 5 dwellings are not physically capable of being made energy efficient at reasonable cost. It would appear that for the medium term, the most cost effective strategies would be those that aim to replace the very worst stock.'

Though the report is not completely clear, it is unlikely that demolition could be justified by conventional economic assessments. The crucial consideration is the balance of energy use. Piecemeal improvements to the older stock do not lead to reduced energy consumption. The occupiers merely take advantage of lower or more predictable heating costs to increase their comfort levels. Savings are only likely if the property can be improved to a high standard.

The debates about demand restraint and about energy use express a continuing dilemma about the scope of public intervention in private life styles. Should the promotion of sustainable development require individuals to share a home with others, if, given the chance, they would prefer to live alone? Likewise, should the promotion of sustainable development require people to move out of a home that they would otherwise have accepted as adequate?

CONCLUSIONS

The two types of future study, trend impact analysis and scenario analysis, lead to different types of conclusion. The former type of analysis is essentially an exercise in identifying specific trends and assessing their likely impact. It asks the question: 'how will people be housed in the future?' The latter, scenario analysis, is an inclusive method. It brings different factors together in a statement of the future that incorporates an assumption about community values. It asks the question: 'how will cities and societies be organised?'

Trend impact analysis implies a series of specific points. For example:

❏ The short-term, conservative character of the building industry implies the possibility of a mismatch between existing practice and the demands of a changing society. There is a need for government agency (and this has to be a government agency given the sums of money involved) to take the lead in preparing new models of innovative housing and to provide training programmes that will enable the workforce to use a wider range of construction methods. Rudlin and Falk (1995) state that innovative models of housing should reflect four considerations of cost, comfort, conservation and community. Clearly, such considerations should be taken into account. However, it is also possible to identify more focused priorities. The government should encourage private developers and housing associations to explore:
  ○ new types of housing for single adults;
  ○ new construction methods for high density flats, including those methods that use concrete panels and are commonly used in Germany and the Netherlands.
❏ Innovation is, however, unlikely to lead to rapid improvements in efficiency or value-for-money. The main justification for innovation is to provide a wider range of house types suitable for different planning situations and household types.
❏ Trends in the use of housing have mixed implications for the spatial pattern of housing demand. Trends in personal consumption are usually said to lead to a demand for larger dwellings in more spacious surroundings and therefore to a preference for greenfield sites either in the countryside or the suburbs. Patterns of demand amongst affluent retired households also suggest a preference for the quiet of the countryside or for a combination of quiet and convenience such as might be realised near the centre of a small country town. On the other hand, the likely growth of single adult households and of dual career households suggest a trend towards higher density living and possibly towards urban locations. Another possible trend, that of teleworking, is likely either to be small or neutral in its effect on urban patterns.

Scenario analysis is best regarded as a means of coping with uncertainty. It implies that the future urban environment will evolve from a shifting combination of different trends and alternatives. Scenario analysis implies, in part, an open-ended, technical attitude to change, where the analyst or researcher merely points out the implications of a specific innovation, policy or trend. It implies a degree of realism about the persistence of trends. For example, it is not realistic to expect a sudden shift in favour of urban house building. However, scenario analysis is not completely open-ended or free of policy prescriptions. Scenarios of chaos are clearly a negative utopia which public policy should avoid. Conversely, so long as an explicitly egalitarian and pro-urban approach is adopted, sustainable development must surely be regarded as a desirable state that is worth working towards.

Different scenarios have to be combined to provide an adequate definition of housing quality. Quality in housing means that people live in a safe area with a secure future. Quality means that people live in a home that can meet their demands as consumers for the foreseeable future. Finally, quality in housing means that people live in a way that minimises the impact on the environment.

References

ACE (Access Committee for England) (1992) *Building Homes for Successive Generations*, ACE, London.

ADC – see the Association of District Councils.

Ahrentzen, S. (1989) Space, time, and activity in the home: a gender analysis. *Journal of Environmental Psychology*, **9** 89–101.

Aldous, T. (1992) *Urban Villages: a Concept for Creating Mixed Use Urban Developments on a Sustainable Scale*, Urban Villages Group, London.

AMA – see the Association of Metropolitan Authorities.

Ambrose, I. (1994) A house of mirrors: reflections on housing policy and housing quality. *In* Tanninen, T., Ambrose, I. and Siksio, O. (eds). *Transitional Housing Systems*, CIB Publications, Rotterdam.

Almendola, G. (1989) The mirror house/ L'habitat miroir, in *EUROPAN 89, Lifestyles – Housing Architecture/Modes de vie – Architectures du Logement*, Editions Regirex-France, Paris.

Amphoux, P. (1989) The conditional habitat/L'habitat conditionnel, in *EUROPAN 89, Lifestyles – Housing Architecture/Modes de vie – Architectures du Logement*, Editions Regirex-France, Paris.

Andersen, H.S. (1995) Explanations of decay and renewal in the housing market: what can Europe learn from American research? *Netherlands Journal of Housing and the Built Environment*, **10** (1) 65–85.

Anderson, R., Bulos, M. A. and Walker, S. R. (1985) *Tower Blocks*, The Polytechnic of the South Bank and the Institute of Housing, London.

Anon. (1981) *Practice Notes 2, Unfitness*, Shelter National Housing Aid Trust, London.

Anon. (1988) *Better Homes for the Future*, Birmingham City Council Housing Department, Birmingham.

Anon. (1993) *Housing Design Handbook: Energy and Internal Layout*, The Building Research Establishment, Watford.

Anon. (c. 1995) *Cities for the Future, A New Urban Policy*, City 2020/The Labour Party, London.

Appleton, J. (1984) Prospects and refuges re-visited *Landscape Journal*, **3** (2) 91–103.

Armstrong, D. (ed) (undated, about 1985) *Miles Better, Miles to Go: The Story of Glasgow's Housing Associations*, The Housetalk Group, Glasgow.

Arnstein, S. (1969) A ladder of citizen participation. *American Institute of Planners Journal*, **35** (4) 216–224.

Ascher, F. (1995) *Métropolis ou l'avenir des villes*, Editions Odile Jacob, Paris.

Ash, J. (1982) Tenant participation: Part 1 A view of techniques. *Housing Review*, **31** (2) 55–57.

Ash, J. (1985) Weller Streets Housing Co-operative. *Housing Review*, **34** (4) 118–120.

Aspinall, P., Wilson, D. and Murie, A. (1995) *Factors Influencing Housing Satisfaction Among Older People*, The Centre for Urban and Regional Studies, Birmingham.

Association of Metropolitan Authorities (1981) *Ruin or Renewal: Choices for our Ageing Housing*, the AMA, London.

Association of Metropolitan Authorities (1986) *Achievements in Council Housing*, the AMA, London.

Atkins, D., Champion, T., Coombes, M., Dorling, D. and Woodward, R. (1996) *Urban Trends in England: Latest Evidence from the 1991 Census*, Department of the Environment, HMSO, London.

Audit Commission (1991) *Healthy Housing: The Role of Environmental Health Services*, HMSO, London.

Audit Commission (1996) *Within Site: Assessing Value for Money in Housing Associations' New Build Programmes*, The Housing Corporation and the Audit Commission, London.

Baldwin, J. and Bottoms, A. (1976) *The Urban Criminal: A Study in Sheffield*, Tavistock, London.

Barlow, J. and Gann, D. (1993a) Converting empty offices into flats. *Housing Research Findings*, 102 The Joseph Rowntree Foundation, York.

Barlow, J. and Gann, D. (1993b) *Offices into Flats*. The Joseph Rowntree Foundation, York.

Barritt, C. M. H. (1994) *The Building Act and Regulations Applied: Houses and Flats*. Longman Scientific, Harlow, Essex.

Béhar, D. and Rosenberg, S. (1990) La politique contractuelle de l'habitat à Mantes-la-Jolie. *Hommes et Migrations* (1133).

Bell, T., Bevington, P. and Crossley, R. (1990) Estate Management Boards – a way forward for Council tenants. *Housing Review*, July/August.

Bell, T. (1991) *Joining Forces: Estate Management Boards – A Practical Guide for Councils and Residents*. The Priority Estates Project, London.

Benwell Community Development Project (1978) *Slums on the Drawing Board*, The Project, Final Report No. 4, Newcastle.

Berk, S.F. (1988) Women's unpaid labour: home and community. *In* Stromberg, A. H. and Harkess, S. (eds) *Women Working: Theories and Facts in Perspective*, Mayfield Publishers, Mountain View, California.

Berry, F. (1974) *Housing: the Great British Failure*, Charles Knight, London.

Bibby, J. and Shepherd, J. (1997) Projecting rates of urbanisation in England, 1991–2016: method, policy application and results. *The Town Planning Review*, **68** (1) 93–124.

Birks, D. F. and Southan, J. M. (1992) An evaluation of the rationale of tenant satisfaction surveys. *Housing Studies*, **7** (4) 299–308.

Birmingham Community Forum (1983) *Are you being Enveloped? – a Residents' Guide to Enveloping*, the Community Forum, Birmingham.

Bishop, J., Davison, I., Rose, J., Kean, J., Hickling, D. and Silson, R. (1994) *Community Involvement in Planning and Development Processes*, Department of the Environment Planning Research Programme, HMSO, London.

Björklund, E. (ed.) (1994) *Good Nordic Housing*, Nordic Council of Ministers, Copenhagen.

Blackaby, R. (1986) Slum clearance – unwelcome option. *Housing*, 36.

Blackmon, T., Evason, E., Melaugh, M. and Woods, R. (1987) Housing and Health: a case study of two areas in West Belfast. In *Unhealthy Housing – prevention and remedies*. The Proceedings of a Conference held at the University of Warwick, pp. 13–15.

Bootsma, H. G. (1995) The influence of a work-oriented life-style on the residential choice of couples. *The Netherlands Journal of Housing and the Built Environment*, **10** (1) 45–64.

Bottoms, A. E. and Xanthos, P. (1981) Housing policy and crime in the British public sector. *In* Brantingham, P. and Brantingham, P. (eds) *Environmental Criminology*, Sage, Beverly Hills, California.

Bottoms, A. E., Mawby R. I. and Walker, M. (1987) A localised crime survey in contrasting areas of a city. *The British Journal of Criminology*, **27** (2).

Bowley, M. (1945) *Housing and the State*, George Allen and Unwin, London.

Bowron, A. J. M. (1992, unpublished) *A Question of Standards*. A paper prepared for the Joseph Rowntree Committee on Housing Standards.

Bozeat, N., Barrett, G. and Jones, G. (1992) The potential contribution for the planning to reducing travel demand. PTRC European Transport, Highways and Planning. *XXth Summer Annual Meeting, Environmental Issues*, Proceedings of Seminar B.

Bramley, G. (1993) Planning, the market and private housebuilding. *The Planner*, January.

Breheny, M., Gent, T. and Lock, D. (1993) *Alternative Development Patterns: New Settlements*, Department of the Environment, HMSO, London.

Bridge, G. (1990). *Gentrification, Class and Community: a study of Sands End, Fulham*, DPhil thesis, Nuffield College, Oxford University.

Breheny, M. and Hall, P. (1996) *The People – Where Will They Go?* National Report of the TCPA Regional Enquiry into Housing Need and Provision in England, The Town and Country Planning, Association, London.

Bright, J. (1986) Safety and security on council housing estates: the safe neighbourhoods unit. *Housing Review*, July/August.

Bright, J. (1987) Community safety on housing estates. *Housing Review*, September/October.

Broadbent, H. (1993) We can rebuild it. *Housing*, July.

Brookes, J. A. and Hughes, K. (1975) Housing redevelopment and rehabilitation. *The Town Planning Review*, **46** (2).

Brown, B. B. and Bentley, D. L. (1993) Residential burglars judge risk: the role of territoriality. *Journal of Environmental Psychology*, **13** 51–61.

Brown, F. E. and Steadman, J. P. (1987) The analysis and interpretation of small house plans: some contemporary examples. *Environment and Planning B: Planning and Design*, **14** 407–438.

Brown, F. E. and Steadmnan, J. P. (1991) The morphology of British housing: an empirical basis for policy and research. Part 1: Functional and dimensional characteristics. Part 2: Topological characteristics. *Environment and Planning B: Planning and Design*, **18** 227–299, 385–415.

Brunt, T. (1982) Housing case study, envelope treatments. *Architects Journal*, December, 75–76.

Building Cost Information Service (1995). *Surveys of Tender Prices*, The Royal Institution of Chartered Surveyors, London.

Burbidge, M. (1975) The standards tenants want. *Housing Review*, November–December.

Burnett, J. (1991) *A Social History of Housing* 2nd edn., Routledge, London.

Burridge, R. and Ormandy, D. (1993) The legal environment of housing conditions. *In* Burridge, R. and Ormandy, D. (eds) (1993) *Unhealthy Housing: Research Remedies and Reform*, E. & FN Spon, London.

Burridge, R., Ormandy, D. and Battersby, R. (1993) *Monitoring the New Housing Fitness Standard*, The Department of the Environment, HMSO, London.

Byrne, D., Harrison, S., Keithley, J. and McCarthy, P. (1986) *Housing and Health*, Gower, Aldershot.

Calthorpe, P. (1993) *The Next American Metropolis*, Princeton Architectural Press, New York.

Campinos-Dubernet, M. (1992) La diversité des bâtiments européens: l'incidence des modèles nationaux. *In* Campagnac, E. (ed.) *Les Grands Groupes de la Construction: De nouveaux acteurs urbains?* L'Harmattan, Paris, pp. 155–165.

Canter, D. and Brown, J. (1978) *Searching for and buying a home*, The Alliance Building Society Housing Research Unit, The Department of Psychology, University of Surrey, Guildford.

Canter, D. (1983) The purposive evaluation of places: a facet approach. *Environment and Behaviour* 15 (6) 659–698.

Canter, D. (1985) (ed.) *Facet Theory: Approaches to Social Research*, Springer Verlag, New York.

Carey, L. and Mapes, R. (1972) *The Sociology of Planning: a study of social activity on new housing estates*, Batsford, London.

Carlestam, G. (1989) My home and my house: two perspectives on human settlement. Prepared for *The Meaning and Use of Home and Neighbourhood*, National Swedish Institute for Building Research, Gävle, Sweden, August 21–23. Cited by Gurney, C. M. (1995) (with minor amendments, 1996), pp. 86–91.

Carley, M. (1990) *Housing and Neighbourhood Renewal, Britain's New Urban Challenge*, The Policy Studies Institute, London.

Cassel, E. (1993) *The Continuing Care Retirement Community: A Guidebook for Consumers*, American Association of Homes for the Ageing, Washington D.C.

Central Housing Advisory Committee (1966) *Our older homes – a call for action*. Report of the sub-committee on standards of housing fitness (The Denington Report), The Ministry of Housing and Local Government, HMSO, London.

CHAC – see Central Housing Advisory Committee.

Chadwick, W. (1988) Is demolition and new build better than renovation? *Municipal Journal*, 9 September.

Chamberlain, O. and Goodchild, B. (1994) *An Evaluation of the Social Housing Over Shops Initiative of the Housing Corporation*, The Housing Corporation, London.

Champion, T. and Dorling, D. (1994) Population change for Britain's functional regions, 1951–91. *Population Trends 77*, HMSO, London, 14–23.

Chapman, D. and Houghton, R. (1991) Design guidance – An art of relationship? *Planning*, 29 March.

Chermayeff, S. and Alexander, C. (1963) *Community and Privacy*, Penguin Books, Harmondsworth, Middlesex.

Cheshire County Council (1976) *Planning Standards – Open Space*, Cheshire County Council.

Cheshire, P. and Sheppard, S. (1989) British planning policy and access to housing: some empirical estimates. *Urban Studies*, 26 469–485.

Choay, F. (1965) *L'Urbanisme, Utopies et Réalités*, Editions du Seuil, Paris.

Christensen, D. L. and Carp, F. M. (1987) PEQI-based environmental predictors of the residential satisfaction of older women. *Journal of Environmental Psychology* 7 45–64.

Christophersen, J. (1995) *The Growth of Good Housing, Promotion and Regulation of Dwelling Quality in Norway*, The Norwegian State Housing Bank, Oslo.

Civic Trust (1988) *Urban Wasteland Now*. The Civic Trust, London.

Clark, M., Burall, P. and Roberts, P. (1993) A sustainable economy. *In* Blowers, A. (ed.) *Planning for a Sustainable Environment, A Report by the Town and Country Planning Association*, Earthscan, London.

Clarke, F. (1992) Sent up the stairs. *Roof*, November/December.

Clarke, L. and Wall, C. (1996): Skills and the construction process. *Joseph Rowntree Housing Research Findings*, No. 172, York.

Cohen, S. and Young, M. (eds) (1981) *The Manufacture of News*, Constable, London.

Cole, I. (1996) The impossible journey? From 'social exclusion' to 'social balance' in new housing association developments in England. A paper presented to *The Housing Studies Association Conference on Housing and Social Exclusion*, University of Birmingham, 16 and 17 September.

Cole, I. and Smith, Y. (1995) From estate action to estate agreement. *Housing Research Findings* 159, The Joseph Rowntree Foundation, York.

Coleman, A. (1985) *Utopia on Trial*, Hilary Shipman, London.

Colin Buchanan and Partners (1971) *The Prospect for Housing*, The Nationwide Building Society.

Collins, K. J. (1993) Cold-and heat-related illnesses in the indoor environment. *In* Burridge, R. and Ormandy, D. (eds) (1993) *Unhealthy Housing: Research, Remedies and Reform*, E & FN Spon, London.

Colquhoun, I. and Fauset, P. G. (1991) *Housing Design in Practice*. Longman Scientific and Technical, Harlow, Essex.

Commission of the European Communities (1990) *Green Paper on the Urban Environment*, Luxembourg, L-2920, the Commission of the European Communities, Directorate General for Environment, Nuclear Safety and Civil Protection, EUR 12902 EN.

Committee appointed by the President of the Local Government Board and the Secretary for Scotland to consider questions of building construction in connection with the provision of dwellings for the working classes (The Tudor Walters Committee) (1918). *Report*, HMSO, Cd 9191, London.

Conzen, M. R. G. (1968) The use of town plans in the study of urban history. *In* Dyos, H. J. (ed.) *The Study of Urban History*, Edward Arnold, London.

Cooney, E. W. (1974) High flats in local authority housing in England and Wales. *In* Sutcliffe, A. (ed.) *Multi-storey Living, The British Working Class experience*, Croom Helm, London.

Cooper Lybrand and Associates (1986) *The Impact of Grants on Urban Housing and Greenfields*, The Housing Research Foundation, London.

Cooper Marcus, C. and Sarkissian, W. (1986) *Housing as if People Mattered*, The University of California Press, Berkeley, California.

County Council of Essex (1973) *A Design Guide for Residential Areas*, The County Council.

Course Team – Technology Foundation Course (1988) *Living with Technology: Block 1: Home*, The Open University Press, Milton Keynes.

Crawford, D. (ed.) (1975) *A Decade of British Housing: 1963–1973*, The Architectural Press, London.

Crockett, D. (1990) Suburban redevelopment: an appraisal of recent pressures and policy responses in an outer London borough. *The Planner*, 10 August.

Crook, T. (1984) An enhanced role for the private sector. *The Planner*, April.

Cullen, G. (1961) *The Concise Townscape*. Butterworth Architecture, London.

Cullen, J. and Turner, M. (1982) The return of the native? Public response to 'build for sale' housing in Liverpool. *Housing Review*, September–October, 159–161.

Cullingworth, J. B. (1966) *Housing and Local Government*, George Allen and Unwin, London.

Damer, S. (1974) Wine alley: the sociology of a dreadful enclosure. *Sociological Review*, 221–248.

Daubner, W. (1994) Wege zur Kostenreduzierung im Wohnungsbau/Ways to reduce costs in Housing Construction. *Betonwerk + Fertigteil Technik/Concrete Precasting Plant and Technology* (9) 1994.

Davey, J. (1996) Equity release for older home-owners. *Housing Research Findings* 188, The Joseph Rowntree Foundation, York.

Davison, I. (1990) *Good Design in Housing*, The House Builders Federation, London.

Day, C. (1993) *Places of the Soul*, The Aquarian Press, London.

Delafons, J. (1991) Planning int he USA – paying for development. *The Planner*, June, 8–9.

Dennis, F. (1990) HATs: Who needs them? *Housing*, November.

Department of the Environment – see DoE.

Di Salvo, P., Ermisch, J. and Joshi, H. (1995) Household formation and tenure decision among the 1958 birth cohort. *Housing Research Findings*, 164, The Joseph Rowntree Foundation, York.

Dible, J. and Webster, J. (1981) *Residential Renewal in Scottish Cities*, The National Building Agency, Edinburgh.

DoE (1971) *Safety in the home*. Design Bulletin 13, HMSO, London.

DoE (1972) *The estate outside the dwelling*. Design Bulletin 25, HMSO, London.

DoE (1974) *Housing for people who are physically handicapped* Circular 74/74, HMSO, London.

DoE (1975) *Housing: needs and action*. Circular 24/75, HMSO, London.

DoE (1977) *Policy for the inner cities*, Cmnd. 6845, HMSO, London.

DoE (1978) *The economic assessment of housing renewal schemes*. The Department of the Environment, Improvement Research Note 4-78, London.

DoE (1979) *English House Condition Survey 1976 Part 2 Report of the Social Survey*, HMSO, London.

DoE (1980a) *Development control – policy and practice*. Circular 22/80, HMSO, London.

DoE (1980b) *Housing Requirements: a Guide to Information and Techniques*, HMSO, London.

DoE (1982) *English House Condition Survey 1981 Part 1 The Report of the Physical Condition Survey*, HMSO, London.

DoE (1983a) *English House Conditions Survey 1981 Part 2 Report of the Interview and Local Authority Survey*, HMSO, London.

DoE (1983b) *Tackling Priority Estates*, HMSO, London.

DoE (1985) *Home Improvement – A New Approach*, HMSO, London.

DoE (1989) Draft *Planning Policy Guidance Note 3: Housing*.

DoE (1990a) *Local Government and Housing Act 1989: area renewal, unfitness, slum clearance and enforcement action* Circular 6/90, HMSO, London.

DoE (1990b) *The Government's Expenditure Plans 1990–91 to 1992–93, Chapter 8 – Environment*, HMSO, London, Cmnd 1008.

DoE (1991) *Planning and Compensation Act 1991: planning obligations.* Circular 16/91, HMSO, London.

DoE (1992a) *Annual Report: The Government's Expenditure Plans 1991–92 to 1993–94*, HMSO, London, Cmnd. 1508.

DoE (1992b) *Planning Policy Guidance: General Policy and Principles*, the Department of the Environment, PPG1 (revised), London.

DoE (1992c) *Planning Policy Guidance: Housing*, the Department of the Environment, PPG3 (revised), London.

DoE (1992d) *Planning Policy Guidance: The Countryside and the Rural Economy*, the Department of the Environment, PPG7, London.

DoE (1992e) *Tenant Involvement and the Right to Manage: A Consultation Paper*, the Department of the Environment, the Welsh Office, London.

DoE (1993) *Englishouse Condition Survey 1991*, the Department of the Environment, HMSO, London.

DoE (1995) *Planning Policy Guidance: Green Belts*, the Department of the Environment, PPG2 (revised), London.

DoE (1996a) *Private sector renewal: a strategic approach* Circular 17/96, HMSO, London.

DoE (1996b) *The English House Condition Survey 1991, Energy Report*, HMSO, London.

DoE and DoT (1977) *Design Bulletin 32, Residential Roads and Footpaths: Layout Considerations*, HMSO, London.

Dominguez, K. (1990) Time adaptive housing. *In* Wilkes, J. A. (ed.) *Encyclopaedia of Architecture: Design, Engineering and Construction*, 5, John Wiley, New York.

Donnelly, D. (1980) Are we satisfied with housing satisfaction? *Built Environment*, 6 29–34.

Donnison, D. (1991) The scope and limits of the community-based approach. *In* Robertson, D. and Sims, D. (eds) *Glasgow: Some Lessons in Urban Renewal*, City of Glasgow District Council.

Driver, E. (writing as part of the Nottingham Law School and of Frere Cholmeley Bischoff) Securing low-cost housing in perpetuity. *Housing Research Findings*, 115 The Joseph Rowntree Foundation, York.

Drooglever Fortuyn, J. (1993) *A busy life: the use of time and space in dual earner families.* Doctoral Thesis, The University of Amsterdam (Title in Dutch: *Een Druk Bestaan: Tudsbesteding en rumtegebruik van tweeverdieners met kindered.*) Amsterdam.

Dudley Report – see the Ministry of Health.

Duncan, P. and Halsall, B. (1995) *Building Homes People Want*, The National Federation of Housing Associations, London.

Duncan, S. (1988) *Public Problems, Private Solutions*, Department of the Environment, HMSO, London.

Duncan, S. J. (1985) The house as symbol of social structure. *In* Altman, I. and Werner, C. (eds) *Home Environments*, Plenum Press, New York.

Duncan, T. L. C. (1976) *Housing Action Areas in Scotland*, The Planning Exchange Research Paper No. 3, Glasgow.

Dunmore, K. (1992) *Planning for Affordable Housing: a Practical Guide*, The Institute of Housing/The House Builders Federation, London.

Edwards, B. (1992) *London Docklands: Urban Design in an Age of Deregulation*, Butterworth Architecture, Oxford.

Ellin, N. (1996) *Postmodern Urbanism*, Blackwell, Oxford.

Energy Efficiency Office (1992) *Good Practice Case Study: Energy Efficiency in New Housing*, Department of the Environment, London.

Errazurez, I. (1946) Some types of housing in Liverpool. *The Town Planning Review* **XIX** (2) 57–68.

Estate Action and the Department of the Environment (1991) *Handbook of Estate Improvement, No. 2: External Areas*, HMSO London.

European Commission – see Commission of the European Communities.

Evans, A. (1973) *The Economics of Residential Location*, Macmillan, London.

Evans, A. (1987) Urban or rural development. *In An Environment for Growth*, The Adam Smith Institute, London.

Everett, R. (1980) *Passive Solar in Milton Keynes*, Energy Research Group, Research Report ERG 031, The Open University, Milton Keynes.

Farrell, G. (1992) Multiple victimisation: its extent and significance. *International Review of Victimology*, 7 85–102.

Farthing, S. and Lambert, C. (on behalf of the University of the West of England and Oldfield King Planning) (1996) *Land, Planning and Housing Associations*, The Housing Corporation, Source Report No. 10, London.

Fennell, G. (1986) *Anchor Tenants' Survey Report*, Anchor Housing Association, Oxford.

Flett, H. (1984) Dispersal policies in council housing: argument and evidence. *In* Ward, R. (ed.) *Race and Residence in Britain: Approaches to Differential Treatment in Housing*, The Economic and Social Research Council, London.

Foot, M. (1975) *Aneurin Bevan, 1945–1969*, Granada Publishing, St Albans.

Forty, A. and Moss, H. (1980) A housing style for troubled consumers: the success of the neo-vernacular. *Architectural Review* **167** (996) 73–78.

Foster, J. and Hope, T. (1994) *Housing, Community and Crime: the Impact of the Priority Estates Project*, A Home Office Research and Planning Unit Report, HMSO, London.

Friedan, B. (1981) *The Second Stage*, Summit Books, New York.

Furbey, R. and Goodchild, B. (1986a) Attitudes to environment. *Housing* **22** (3).

Furbey, R. and Goodchild, B. (1986b) *Housing in use: a study of design and standards in the public sector*, Pavic Publications, Sheffield.

Furbey, R. and Goodchild, B. (1986c) Method and methodology in housing user research. *Housing Studies* **1** (3) 166–182.

Geddes, P. (1968) *Cities in Evolution*, Ernest Benn, London. (Originally published in 1915.)

Gee, D. (1974) *Slum Clearance*, Shelter, London.

Gibb, K., Munro, M. and McGregor, A. (1995) *The Scottish Housebuilding Industry: Opportunity or Constraint?* Research Report 44, Scottish Homes, Edinburgh.

Gibson, M. S. and Langstaff, M. J. (1982) *An Introduction to Urban Renewal*, Hutchinson, London.

Glass, R. (1964) *London, Aspects of Change*, MacGibbon and Gee, London.

GLC – see the Greater London Council.

Glendinning, R., Allen, P. and Young, H. (1989) *The Sale of Local Authority Housing to the Private Sector*, Department of the Environment, HMSO, London.

Glennerster, H. and Turner, T. (1993) *Estate Based Housing Management: An Evaluation*, Department of the Environment, HMSO, London.

Goldsmith, S. (1975) Wheelchair housing. HDD Occasional Paper 2/75, Department of the Environment, Housing Development Directorate, London. Reprinted from *The Architects' Journal*, 26 June.

Goldsmith, S. (1984) *Designing for the disabled.*, 3rd edn., fully revised, RIBA publications, London.

Goodchild, B. (1984) Housing layout, housing quality and residential density. *Housing Review*, July/August.

Goodchild, B. (1987) Local authority flats: a study in area management and design. *The Town Planning Review*, 58, (3) 293–316.

Goodchild, B. (1989) French lessons. *Roof*, January/February.

Goodchild, B. (1990) Planning and the modern/postmodern debate. *The Town Planning Review*, 61 (2).

Goodchild, B. (1991) Postmodernism and housing: a guide to design theory. *Housing Studies*, 6 (2).

Goodchild, B. (1992) Land allocation for housing, a review of practice and possibilities in England. *Housing Studies*, 7 (1).

Goodchild, B., Booth, C. and Henneberry, J. (1996) Impact fees: a review of alternatives and their implications for planning practice in Britain. *The Town Planning Review*, 67 (2) 161–182.

Goodchild, B., Chamberlain, O. and Beatty, C. (1996) *Volume Procurement: Operation Breakthrough Evaluated*, The Housing Corporation, London.

Goodchild, B., Chamberlain, O., Dalgleish, K. and Lawrence, B. (1997) *Crime and The Home Front*, York Publishing Services, York.

Goodchild, B., Duckworth, H. and Simmonite, A. (1984) *New Housing in the City: a case study of the inner area of Sheffield*, Pavic Publications, Sheffield City Polytechnic.

Goodchild, B. and Furbey, R. (1986) Standards in housing design: a review of the main changes since the Parker Morris report (1961). *Land Development Studies*, 3 79–89.

Gordon, T. J. (1992) The methods of future research. *The Annals of the American Academy of Political and Social Science*, 522 25–35.

Grant, M. G. (1991) Betterment again? The planning balance in the 1990s. Papers from a conference held at Oxford, September 1991, organised by the Bar Council, the Law Council and the Royal Institution of Chartered Surveyors. *Journal of Planning and Environmental Law*, Occasional Paper No. 18, Sweet and Maxwell, London.

Greater London Council (1978) *Housing Layout*, The Architectural Press, London.

Greater London Council (1985) *Planning for Housing*, The County Hall, London.

Greater London Council (1986) *Housing Standards, A Survey of New Build Local Authority housing in London 1981–1984*, The County Hall, London.

Gregory, P. and Hainsworth, M. (1993) Chameleons or trojan horses? The strange case of housing action trusts. *Housing Studies*, 8 (2) 109–119.

Griffiths, M., Park, J., Smith, R., Stirling,T. and Trott, T. (1996) Community lettings in practice. *Housing Research Findings*, No. 171, The Joseph Rowntree Foundation, York.

Guiton, J. (1982) *Le Corbusier: Textes Choisis, Architecture et Urbanisme*, Editions du Moniteur, Paris.

Gurney, C. M. (1995) *Meanings home and home ownership: myths, histories and experiences.* A thesis submitted to the University of Bristol for the award of a Doctor of Philosophy (with minor amendments, 1996).

Habraken, N. J. (1971) *Supports: An Alternative to Mass Housing*, The Architectural Press, London.

Hall, P., Gracey, H., Drewett, R. and Thomas, R. (1973). *The Containment of Urban England* 1 and 2, George Allen and Unwin, London.

Hall, T. (1990) Design control: a call for a new approach. *The Planner*, 5 October, 14–18.

Hambleton, R. and Hoggett, P. (1987) Beyond bureaucratic paternalism. *In* Hambleton, R. and Hoggett, P. (eds) *Decentralisation ahnd Democracy: Localising Public Services*, Occasional Paper 28, The University of Bristol School of Advanced Urban Studies, Bristol.

Harrison, A. (1986) Can you measure housing quality, a summary of research undertaken by DEGW for the Housing Corporation and the Department of the Environment and presented at a Housing Corporation Conference. *Quality and Competitiveness in Social Housing*, 22 May.

Harrison, P. (1983) *Inside the Inner City*, Penguin Books, Harmondsworth, Middlesex.

HBF – see House Builders Federation

HDD – see Housing Development Directorate.

Hebbert, M. (1978) How many to the acre? *Estates Gazette*, **246** 725–727.

Hedges, B. and Clemens, S. (1994) *Housing Attitudes Survey*, Housing Research Report, Department of the Environment, HMSO, London.

Heijden van der, H. and Visscher, H. (1995) *Housing Quality in The Netherlands*, Delft (unpublished).

Hester, R. T. (1975) *Neighbourhood Space*, Dowden, Hutchinson and Ross, Stroudsburg, Pennsylvania.

Heywood, F. and Naz, M. R. (1990) *Clearance: The View from the Street*, The Community Forum, Birmingham.

Heywood, F. (1992) Aiming at housing satisfaction. *The Planner*, 7 February.

Hillier Parker (1991) *Nottingham Employment Land Study for Nottingham City Council, Final Report*, Hillier Parker (unpublished), London.

Hillier, W. and Hanson, J. (1984) *The social logic of space*, Cambridge University Press, Cambridge.

Hillier, W., Burdett, R., Peponis, J. and Penn, A. (1987) Creating life: or, does architecture create anything? *Architecture and Behaviour*, **3** (3).

Hillman, J. (1994) *Telelifestyles and the Flexicity*, The European Foundation for the Improvement of Living and Working Conditions, L-2985 Luxembourg. The Office for Official Publications of the European Communities, Luxembourg.

Hirsch, F. (1977) *Social Limits to Growth*. Routledge and Kegan Paul, London.

HM Government (1988) *Action for Cities*, HMSO, London.

HM Government (1995) *Our Future Homes: Opportunity, Choice, Responsibility*, Cm 2901, HMSO, London.

Hole, W. V. and Attenburrow, J. J. (1966) *Houses and People: a Review of User Studies at the Building Research Station*, HMSO, London.

Holmans, A. (1995) Housing demand and need in England, 1991–2011. *Housing Research Findings*, 157, The Joseph Rowntree Memorial Trust, York.

Holmans, A. (1996) Meeting housing needs in the private rented sector. *In* Wolcox, S. (ed.) *Housing Review 1996/97*, The Joseph Rowntree Foundation, York.

Homes for the Future – see Institute of Housing, Royal Institute of British Architects, 1984.

Hope, T. and Hough, M. (1988) Area, crime and incivilities: a profile from the British Crime Survey. *In* Hope, T. and Shaw, M.(eds) *Communities and Crime Reduction*, Home Office Research and Planning Unit, HMSO, London.

Hope, T. and Shaw, M. (1988) Community approaches. *In* Hope, T. and Shaw, M. (eds) *Community and Crime Reduction*, The Home Office Research and Planning Unit, HMSO, London.

Horelli, L. and Vepsä, K. (1994) In search of supportive structures for everyday life. *In* Altman, I. and Churchman, A. (eds) *Women and the Environment*, Plenum Press, New York.

Hough, J. M. (1980) Introduction. *In* Clarke, R. V. G. and Mayhew, P. (eds) *Designing Out Crime*, The Home Office Research Unit, HMSO, London.

House Builders Federation (1987) *Private Housebuilding in the Inner Cities*, The House Builders Federation, London.

House of Commons Environment Committee, Session 1982–83 (1983) *The Problems of Management of Urban Renewal (the role of the private sector)*, Minutes of Evidence, Tuesday 26 April, The Building Societies Association, HC 325–i, HMSO, London.

House of Commons Environment Committee, Session 1983–84 (1984) *First Report – Green Belt and Land for Housing*, HMSO, London, HC 275–1, 275i–xii.

Housing Centre Trust Seminar (1983) Report, *The Housing Review*, **32** (4) July–August.

Housing Corporation (1983) *Design and Contract Criteria for Fair Rent Projects*, Issue 2/3, HMSO, London.

Housing Corporation (1993) *Scheme Development Standards*, The Housing Corporation, London.

Housing Development Directorate (1980) *Starter Homes: a Report of a DoE Survey of New Small Houses and Flats for Sale*, Department of the Environment, HDD Occasional Paper 2/80, HMSO, London.

Housing Development Directorate (1981) *A Survey of Tenants' Attitudes to Recently Completed Estates*, Department of the Environment, HDD Occasional Paper 2/81, HMSO, London.

Howard, E. (1985) *Garden Cities of Tomorrow*, Attic, Eastbourne.

Hunt, D. R. G. and Gidman, M. I. (1982) A national field survey of house temperatures. *Building and Environment*, **17** (2) 107–124.

Hussell, D. (1994) A new settlement for Cambridgeshire. *Town and Country Planning*, **63** (12) 340–342.

Huyssen, A. (1984) Mapping the postmodern. *New German Critique*, Fall edition, No. 33.

Ineichen, B. (1993) *Homes and Health, How Housing and Health Interact*, E & FN Spon, London.

Institute of Advanced Architectural Studies, University of York (1993) *Housing Design Studies Overview*, ETSU (the Energy Technology Support Unit), HMSO, London.

Institute of Housing, Royal Institute of British Architects (1983) *Homes for the Future*, London.

Institute of Housing, Royal Institute of British Architects (1988) *Tenant Participation in Housing Design: A Guide for Action*, Royal Institution of Chartered Surveyors, London.

Institute of Housing (1992) *A Radical Consensus: New Ideas for Housing in the 1990s*, the Institute of Housing, Coventry.

IoH – see Institute of Housing.

Jacobs, J. (1965) *The Death and Life of Great American Cities*, Penguin Books, Harmondsworth.

Jenks, M. (1983) Residential roads researched. *Architects' Journal*, 29 June.

Joseph Rowntree Foundation (1994) *Inquiry into Planning for Housing*, The Joseph Rowntree Foundation, York.

Joseph Rowntree Foundation/Trotter, E. (1992) Accessibility in action. Supplement to *Innovations in Social Housing*, 3, The Joseph Rowntree Foundation, York.

JRF – see the Joseph Rowntree Foundation.

Junior RICS – The Junior Organisation of the Royal Institution of Chartered Surveyors (1993) *The Spare Space? Project*, The RICS (unpublished), London.

Kanuka-Fuchs, R. (1993) Green architecture: Designing an ecologically sound dwelling. *In* Inan, M. (ed.) *Housing America in the Twenty-First Century*, The Proceedings of the Conference, American Society of Civil Engineers, New York.

Karn, V. (1978) Housing policies which handicap inner cities. *New Society*, 11 May.

Karn, V. (1996) Trends in the regulation of new housing quality in Western Europe. *Journal of the European Network for Housing Research*, **4/96**.

Karn, V. and Lucas, J. (1995) *Home-Owners and Clearance: an Evaluation of Rebuilding Grants*, Department of the Environment, HMSO, London.

Karn, V. and Sheridan, L. (1994) *New Homes in the 1990s*, The Joseph Rowntree Foundation, York.

Karn, V. and Sheridan, L. (1994) *Housing Quality: a Practical Guide for Tenants and their Representatives*, The Joseph Rowntree Foundation, York.

Karn, V. and Whittle, B. (1978) Birmingham's urban cosmetics. *Roof*, November, 163.

King, A.D. (1984) *The Bungalow: The Production of a Low Global Culture*, Routledge and Kegan Paul, London.

Kirby, K., Finch, H. and Wood, D. (1988) *The Organisation of Housing Management in English Local Authorities*, The DoE, HMSO, London.

Kruythoff, H. (1993) Urban and suburban types of low earner households in the Randstad. *The Netherlands Journal of Housing and the Built Environment*, **8** (2) 211–236.

Kuper, L. (1953) Blueprint for living together. *In* Kuper, I. (ed.) *Living in Towns*, Cresset Press, London.

Lacaze, J.-P. (1989) Urbanisme et réhabilitation. *In* Duport, J.-P. (ed.) *Réhabilitation de l'habitat en France*, Economica, Paris, pp. 19–28.

Le Dantec, J.-P. (1991) For a Baroque approach to cities and architecture. *Architecture et Comportement/Architecture and Behaviour* 7 (4).

Leather, P. (1993) Putting our houses in order. *Inside Housing*, 2 July.

Leather, P. and Mackintosh, S. (1994) Ways of encouraging home maintenance, an overview. *In* Leather, P. and Mackintosh, S. (eds) *Encouraging Housing Maintenance in the Private Sector*, SAUS Publications, Bristol.

Leather, P. and Mackintosh, S. (1994a) *The Future of Housing Renewal Policy*, SAUS Publications in association with the Joseph Rowntree Foundation, Bristol.

Leather, P. and Mackintosh, S. (1997) Towards sustainable policies for housing renewal. *In* Williams, P. (ed.) *Directions in Housing Policy: Towards Sustainable Housing Policies for the UK*, Paul Chapman, London.

Leather, P. and Reid, M. (1989) *Investing in Older Housing: A Study of Housing Improvement in Bristol*, University of Bristol School for Advanced Urban Studies, Bristol.

Ledewitz, S. (1991) A review of 'the social logic of space' *The Journal of Architectural and Planning Research*, **8** (3).

Lefèbvre, H. (1968) *Le droit à la ville*, Paris Editions Anthropos. Reprinted in Ansay, P. and Schoonbrodt (eds) (1989) *Penser la ville choix de textes philosophiques*, Archives d'Architecture Moderne, Bruxelles, pp. 477–479.

Lefèbvre, H. Preface to Boudon, P. (1969) *Lived-in Architecture, Le Corbusier's Pessac*

Revisited, Lund Humphries, London. (French original, *Pessac de le Corbusier*, Paris, 1969, second edition, by Dunod and Bordas, Paris, 1985.)

Leicester City Council Housing Department (1995) *Policy and Practice Guide*, Leicester City Council.

Littlewood, J. and Mason, S. (1984) *Taking the Initiative: A Survey of Low Cost Home Owners*, Department of the Environment, HMSO, London.

Littlewood, J. and Tinker, A. (1981) *Families in Flats*, Department of the Environment, HMSO, London.

Llewelyn-Davies (1994a) *Providing More Homes in Urban Areas*, SAUS Publications, University of Bristol, Bristol.

Llewelyn-Davies (1994b) *The Quality of London's Residential Environment*, The London Planning Advisory Committee, London.

Llewelyn-Davies (1996) The re-use of 'brownfield' land for housing *Housing Research Findings*, 170, The Joseph Rowntree Foundation, York.

Llewelyn-Davies, Weeks, Forestier-Walker & Bor (1970) *The Plan for Milton Keynes*, The Milton Keynes Development Corporation, Milton Keynes.

Loewen, L. J., Steel, G. D. and Suedfeld, P. (1993) Perceived safety from crime in the urban environment. *Journal of Environmental Psychology* 13, 323–331.

London Planning Advisory Committee (1995) *Borough Density Standards* (unpublished).

London Research Centre (1994) *Houses in Multiple Occupation in London*, The London Planning Advisory Committee, London.

LPAC – see London Planning Advisory Committee.

LRC – see London Research Centre.

Lynch, K. (1960) *The Image of the City*, The MIT Press, Cambridge, Massachusetts.

Lynch, K. (1989) *Site Planning*, The MIT Press, Cambridge, Massachusetts.

MacEwen, M. (1991) *Housing, Race and Law: the British Experience*, Routledge and Kegan Paul, London.

McCafferty, P. (1989) *A Study of Co-operative Housing*, The DoE, HMSO, London.

McCarthy, J. and Buckley, M. (1982) *Birmingham Enveloping Schemes Survey*, a report prepared for the Department of the Environment, Research Bureau Limited, London.

McDonald, A. (1986) *The Weller Way*, Faber and Faber, London.

McGregor, A., Kintrea, K., Fitzpatrick, I. and Urquhart, A. (1995) *Interim Evaluation of the Wester Hailes Partnership*, The Scottish Office Central Research Unit, Environmental Research Programme Research Findings No. 14, Edinburgh.

McKie, R.(1971) *Housing and the Whitehall Bulldozer*, Hobart Paper No. 52, The Institute of Economic Affairs, London.

McKie, R. (1974) Cellular renewal. *The Town Planning Review*, 45 (3) 274–290.

Mackintosh, S. and Leather, P. (eds) (1992a) *Home Improvement under the New Regime*, University of Bristol School for Advanced Urban Studies, Occasional Paper 38, Bristol.

Mackintosh, S. and Leather, P. (1992b) The role of the private sector in housing renewal, lessons from the neighbourhood services experiment in England. *Housing Studies*, 7 (3).

Mackintosh, S. and Leather, P. (1992c) *Staying Put Revisited*, The Anchor Housing Trust, Oxford.

Mackintosh, S. and Leather, P. (1993) *Renovation File*, The Anchor Housing Trust, Oxford.

Mackintosh, S. Means, R. and Leather, P. (1990) *Housing in Later Life: the Housing*

Finance Implications of an Ageing Society, The School for Advanced Urban Studies, Bristol.

Maclennan, D. (1983) Housing rehabilitation in Glasgow. *Housing Review*, November/December.

Maclennan, D. (1987) Rehabilitation older housing. *In* Donnison, D. and Middleton, A. (eds) *Regenerating the Inner City*, Routledge and Kegan Paul, London.

Maclennan, D., Munro, M. and Lamont, D. (1987) New owner occupied housing. *In* Donnison, D. and Middleton, A. (eds) *Regenerating the Inner city*, Routledge and Kegan Paul, London.

Maheu, J. (1989) European cultural identity/L'identité culturelle européenne. In *EUROPAN 89, Lifestyles – Housing Architecture/Modes de vie – Architectures du Logement*, Editions Regirex-France, Paris.

Makkar, L. (1979) *A Concept of the Low Energy House as an Integrated System*, SLC Energy Group, London.

Malpass, P. and Murie, A. (1982) *Housing Policy and Practice*, Macmillan, London.

Mannheim, K. (1940) *Man and Society in an Age of Reconstruction*, Routledge and Kegan Paul, London.

Mant, D. C. and Muir Gray, J. A. (1986) *Building Regulation and Health*, The Building Research Establishment, Watford.

Markus, T. A., Brierley, E. and Gray, A. (1972) *Criteria of sunshine, daylight, visual privacy and view in housing*, University of Strathclyde Building Performance Research Unit, Glasgow.

Martin, L. and March, L. (1972) *Urban Space and Structures*, The University Press, Cambridge.

Mason, T. (1995) Short Note: Housing in the periphery – Scottish housing from a European perspective. *Scandinavian Housing and Planning Research*, **12** 31–37.

Mass Observation (1943) *An Enquiry into People's Homes*, John Murray, London.

Matrix (1984) *Making Space: Women and the Man-Made Environment*, Pluto, London.

Mawby, R. (1977) Defensible space: a theoretical and empirical appraisal. *Urban Studies*, **14** (2).

Mayhew, P., Aye Maung, N. and Mirrlees-Black, C. (1993). *The 1992 British Crime Survey*, A Home Office Research and Planning Unit Report, HMSO, London.

Mayhew, P., Elliott, D. and Dowds, L. (1989) *The 1988 British Crime Survey*, A Home Office Research and Planning Unit Report, HMSO, London.

MELT (Ministère de l'Equipement, du Logement et des Transports) Direction de l'habitat et de la construction (1992) *Reglement de Construction, Bâtiments d'Habitation*. Paris.

Merrett, S. (1979) *State Housing in Britain*, Routledge and Kegan Paul, London.

MHLG – see Ministry of Housing and Local Government.

Milton Keynes Development Corporation (1975) *Residential Design Feedback, Report of Studies* (unpublished).

Milton Keynes Development Corporation (1992) *The Milton Keynes Planning Manual*, Chesterton Consulting, London.

Ministry of Health (1994) The Design of Dwellings: Report of the Design of Dwellings Sub-Committee of the Central Housing Advisory Committee, HMSO, London.

Ministry of Housing and Local Government (1952) *The Density of Residential Areas*, HMSO, London.

Ministry of Housing and Local Government (1961) *Homes for Today and Tomorrow* (the Parker Morris report), HMSO, London.

Ministry of Housing and Local Government (1969) *Housing Act, 1969, Area Improvement*, Circular 65/69, HMSO, London.

Ministry of Housing and Local Government (1969) *People and Planning: Report of the Committee on Public Participation in Planning* (the Skeffington report), HMSO, London.

Ministry of Reconstruction Advisory Council, Women's Housing Sub-Committee (1919), *Final Report*, HMSO, London, Cd 9232.

Mitchell, H. T. (1982) A social contract – to halt housing decay. *Contact*, (1).

Moore, P. (1992) Renovation: is group repair the answer? *In* Mackintosh S. and Leather, P. (eds) (1992) *Home Improvement under the New Regime*, University of Bristol School for Advanced Urban Studies, Occasional Paper 38, Bristol.

Moore, R. (1980) *Reconditioning the Slums*, Polytechnic of Central London School of Environment, Planning Unit, Planning Studies No. 7, London.

Moore, R. (1987) The development and role of standards for the older housing stock. *In Unhealthy Housing – Prevention and Remedies*, the Proceedings of a Conference held at the University of Warwick.

Mormiche, P. (1993) Des logements toujours plus vastes. *In La Société Française, Données Sociales 1993*, INSEE, Paris.

Morris, J. (1992) New approaches to clearance and rebuilding. *In* Mackintosh, S. and Leather, P. (eds) (1992) *Home Improvement under the New Regime*, University of Bristol School for Advanced Urban Studies, Occasional Paper 38, Bristol.

Mulder, I., Meijden, van de, J. (1991) A multiplicity of answers to the way in which towns are designed. *In* Rebois, D. (ed.) *EUROPAN 2: Living in the city – re-interpretation of urban sites, European results*, Editions Regirex-France, Paris, pp. 31–35.

Mullins, D., Marsh, A. Niner, P. and Symon, P. (1993) An Evaluation of the Housing Corporation Rural Programme, The Rural Development Commission, Salisbury (Wiltshire).

Munro, M. and Madigan, R. (1989) Do you ever think about us? *The Architects' Journal*, 20 and 27 December.

Munro, W. and Lane, R. (1990) An environmental assessment of the residential areas of Harrow. *The Planner*, 12 January.

Muthesius, S. (1982) *The English Terraced House*, Yale University Press, New Haven and London.

Myers, D., Baer, E. C., Seong-Youn Choi (1996) The changing problem of overcrowded housing. *American Planning Association Journal*, Winter 66–83.

National Economic Development Office (1971) *New homes in the cities: the role of the private developer in urban renewal in England and Wales*, HMSO, London.

National Home Improvement Council (1985) *Improving our Homes*, the NHIC, London.

Needleman, L. (1965) *The Economics of Housing*, The Staples Press, London.

Needleman, L. (1969) The comparative economics of improvement and new building. *Urban Studies*, **6** (2) 196–209.

Newman, O. (1972) *Defensible Space: Crime Prevention through Urban Design*, Macmillan, New York.

NHIC – see the National Home Improvement Council.

Nicholls, D. C., Turner, D. M., Kirby-Smith, R. and Cullen, J. D. (University of Cambridge Department of Land Economy) (1981) *Private Housing Development Process*, Department of Environment Inner Cities Research Programme No. 4, HMSO, London.

Niner, P. and Forrest, R. (1982) *Housing Action Area Policy and Progress, the Residents Perspective*, The Centre for Urban and Regional Studies, University of Birmingham, Research Memorandum 91, Birmingham.

Noble, J. (1982) Activities and spaces *Architects' Journal Supplement*, 15 December.

Noble, J., Bennett, G. and Jenks, M. (1987) *Roads and Parking in Private Sector Housing Schemes*, The Housing Research Foundation, London.

OECD (Organisation for Economic Co-operation and Development) (1995) *Women in the City*, OECD, Paris.

Orlans, H. (1952) *Stevenage: a sociological study of a new town*, Greenwood Press, Westport, Connecticut.

Osborn, S. (1993) *Crime Prevention on Council Estates*, The Department of the Environment, HMSO, London.

Oseland, N. A. (1991) *An evaluation of space in new homes: physical factors*, Building Research Establishment, Note N73/91, Watford.

Oseland, N. A. and Donald, I. (1993) The evaluation of space in homes: a facet study. *Journal of Environmental Psychology*, 13 251–261.

Oseland, N. A. and Raw, G. J. (1991) Room size and adequacy of space in small homes. *Building and Environment*, 26 (4) 141–147.

Pacione, M. (1990) The site selection process of speculative residential developers in an urban area. *Housing Studies*, 5 (4) 219–228.

Page, D. (1993) *Building for communities: a study of new housing association estates*, The Joseph Rowntree Foundation, York.

Parker Morris Report – see Ministry of Housing and Local Government, 1961.

Pearson, D. (1989) *The Natural House Book*, Gaia Books Ltd, London.

Peatross, F. D. (1992) Changing lives/changing spaces: an investigation of the relationships between gender orientation and behaviours and spatial preferences in residential kitchens. *The Journal of Architectural and Planning Research*, 9 (3) 239–257.

Perkins, D. D., Wandersman, A., Rich, R. C. and Taylor, R. B. (1993) The physical environment of street crime: defensible space, territoriality and incivilities. *Journal of Environmental Psychology*, 13 29–39.

Perry, J. (1991) The case for clearance. *Housing*, June/July.

Petherick, A., Fraser, R. (1992) *Living over the Shop: A Handbook for Practitioners*, The LOTS project, University of York, York.

Pharoah, T. (1992) Traffic growth or limitation: filling the policy vacuum. *PTRC European Transport, Highways and Planning, XXth Summer Annual Meeting, Environmental Issues*, Proceedings of Seminar B.

Phippen, P. (1982) Housing design: an approach to design. *Architects' Journal*, 24 November, 75–88.

PIC–Peat Marwick Mclintock – see Property Investment Company Ltd–Peat Marwick Mclintock.

Potts, M. (1993) *The Independent Home*, Chelsea Green, Post Mills Vermont.

Power, A. (1984) *Local Housing Management: A Priority Estates Project Survey*, Department of the Environment, HMSO, London.

Power, A. (1987) *Property before People*, Allen and Unwin, London.

Power, A. (1991) *Running to Stand Still, Progress in Local Management on Twenty Unpopular Housing Estates*, PEP Ltd, London.

Power, A. (1995) Progress and polarisation on twenty council estates. *Housing Research Findings*, 151, The Joseph Rowntree Foundation, York.

Poyner, B. and Webb, B. (1991) *Crime Free Housing*, Butterworth Architecture, Oxford.

Prescott-Clarke, P., Atkins, J. and Clemens, S. (1993) *Tenant Feedback: A Step by Step Guide to Tenant Satisfaction Surveys*, Department of the Environment, HMSO, London.

Price Waterhouse (1993) *Evaluation of the Urban Development Grant, Urban Regeneration Grant and City Grant*, Department of the Environment, HMSO, London.

Priemus, H. and Metselaar, G. (1992) *Urban Renewal Policy in a European Perspective*, Delft University Press, Delft.

Prior, J. J. and Bartlee, P. B. (1995) *The Environmental Standard: Homes for a Greener World*, the Building Research Establishment, Watford.

PRO – Property Investment Company Ltd – Peat Marwick McLintock (1989) *Housing Action Trust Studies*, the Department of the Environment, London.

Purdue, M., Healey, P. and Ellis, F. (1992) Planning gain and the grant of planning permission in the United States' test of the 'rational nexus' the appropriate solution. *Journal of Planning and Environmental Law*, November, 1012–1024.

Ragone, G. (1989) Standard of living and individual space/Niveau de vie et espace individuel. In *EUROPAN 89, Lifestyles – Housing Architecture/Modes de vie – Architectures du Logement*, Editions Regirex-France, Paris.

Rapoport, A. (1968) The personal element in housing: an argument for open-ended design. *Royal Institute of British Architects' Journal*, **75** (7) 300–307.

Rapoport, A. (1977) *Human Aspects of Urban Form*, Pergamon Press, Oxford.

Rapoport, A. (1982) *The Meaning of the Built Environment*, Sage, Beverly Hills, California.

Ratcliffe, J. and Stubbs, M. (1996) *Urban Planning and Real Estate Development*, UCL Press, London.

Ravetz, A. (1980). *Remaking Cities*, Croom Helm, London.

Ravetz, A. with Turkington, R. (1995) *The Place of Home, English Domestic Environments, 1914–2000*, E & FN Spon, London.

Raw, G. J. and Prior, J. J. (1993) The environmental assessment of new houses. *In* Burridge, R. and Ormandy, D. (eds) (1993) *Unhealthy Housing: Research, Remedies and Reform*, E & FN Spon, London.

Reade, E. J. (1982) Residential decay, household movement and class structure. *Policy and Politics*, **10** (1).

Rebois, D. (1991) From one *EUROPAN* to another. *In* Rebois, D. (ed.) *EUROPAN 2: Living in the city – re-interpretation of urban sites, European results*, Editions Regirex-France, Paris, p. 7.

Reeves, D. (1986) Building for sale under licence. *In* Booth, P. and Crook, T. (eds) *Low Cost Home Ownership*, Gower, Aldershot, Hampshire.

Rennie, A. M. (1981) *Design of Dwellings for the Elderly: the Measurement of Optimum Height of Shelves and Spaces Required for Various Domestic Activities*, The Institute for Consumer Ergonomics, the University of Technology, Loughborough, Loughborough, Leicestershire.

Research Associates (1988) *Designing and selling three and four bedroom houses*, Research Associates Ltd, Stone (Staffordshire).

Reynolds, F. (1986) *The Problem Housing Estate*, Gower, Aldershot, Hampshire.

Richardson, R., Gillespie, A. and Cornford, J. (1995) Low marks for rural home work. *Town and Country Planning*, March, 82–84.

Robertson, D. and Bailey, N. (1996) *Review of the Impact of Housing Action Areas*, Research Report 47, Scottish Homes, Edinburgh.

Robertson, D. and Sim, D. (1991) Introduction. *In* Robertson, D. and Sim, D. (eds) *Glasgow: some lessons in urban renewal*, City of Glasgow District Council Glasgow.

Robertson, J. (1986) *Future Work, Jobs, Self Employment and Leisure after the Industrial Age*, Gower/Maurice Temple Smith, London.

Robertson, J. (1990) Alternative futures for cities, in Cadman, D. and Payne, G. (eds.) *The Living City: Towards a Sustainable Future*, Routledge and Kegan Paul, London.

Robson, B., Parkinson, M. and Robinson, F. (with others) (1994) *Assessing Impact of Urban Policy*, HMSO, London.

Roe, W. (1995) Lessons from Bell Farm Estate, York, *Housing Summary*, 11, The Joseph Rowntree Foundation, York.

Rogerson, J. (1979) The social effects of rehabilitation. *In* Brand, J. (ed.) Proceedings of a conference, *The Rehabilitation of Older Housing*, organised by the Strathclyde Area Survey, Strathclyde University, Glasgow.

Rolfe, S. and Leather, P. (1995) Improving the efficiency of the housing repair and maintenance industry. *Housing Research Findings*, 163, the Joseph Rowntree Foundation, York.

Rowe, C. and Koetter, F. (about 1978) *Collage City*, MIT Press, Cambridge, MA. and London.

Rowe, P. G. (1993) *Modernity and Housing*, the MIT Press, Cambridge, MA.

Royal Commission on Housing in Scotland (1917) *Report of the Royal Commission on the Housing of the Industrial Population of Scotland, Rural and Urban*, HMSO, Edinburgh, Cd. 8731.

Royal Town Planning Institute (1981) *Renewal of Older Housing Areas: in the 1980s*, a policy prepared by the Housing Working Party, The RTPI, London.

Rudlin, D. and Falk, N. (1995) *21st Century Homes, Building to Last*, Joseph Rowntree Foundation, URBED, London.

Sassen, S. (1991) *The Global City*, Princeton University Press, Princeton, New Jersey.

Savills (1992) *The Market for Residential Developments in the 1990s*, Savills Agricultural and Residential Ltd, London.

Saw, P. (1996) Housing associations and the private lender *Supplement to the Joseph Rowntree Foundation Housing Research Findings*, 192.

Schneider, U. (1989) Alternative living: freedom for women. In *EUROPAN 89, Lifestyles – Housing Architecture/Modes de vie Architectures du Logement*, Editions Regirex-France, Paris.

Schofield, J. A. (1995) Home automation takes off. *Design News*, 4 October, 84–87.

School of Land and Building Studies (1987) *Housing Land in Urban Areas, Leicester*, Leicester Polytechnic, Leicester.

Scottish Development Department (1967) Scottish Housing Advisory Committee, *Scotland's Older Houses*, Report of the Sub-Committee on unfit housing, HMSO, Edinburgh.

Scottish Homes (1993) *Scottish House Condition Survey 1991*, Scottish Homes, Edinburgh.

Scottish Homes (1996a) *The Physical Quality of Housing: A Framework for Action*, Scottish Homes, Edinburgh.

Scottish Homes (1996b) *The Physical Quality of Housing. Housing for Older People and Disabled People: A Consultation on Design Guidance*, Scottish Homes, Edinburgh.

Scottish Office Development Department (1996) *National Planning Policy Guidelines: Land for Housing*, HMSO, Edinburgh (NPPG3).

SDD – see Scottish Development Department.

Selby, R., Westover, T., Anderson, J. and Weidemann, S. (1987) *Resident Satisfaction: a means to better housing. Volume I: Research and Recommendations*, Urbana, Illinois.

Housing Research and Development Programme. University of Illinois at Urbana–Champaign.

Shankland, G., Willmott, P. and Jordan, D. (1977) *Inner London: Policies for Dispersal and Balance, Final Report of the Lambeth Inner Area Study*, DoE, HMSO, London.

Shapland, J., Wiles, P. and Wilcox, P. (1994) *Targeted Crime Prevention for Local Areas: Principles and Methods*, The Home Office Police Department, London.

Sherman, L.W., Gartin, P. R., Buerger, M. E. (1989) Hot spots of predatory crime: routine activities and the criminology of place. *Criminology*, **27** (1) 27–55.

Sim, D. (1993) *British Housing Design*, Longman and the Institute of Housing, London and Coventry.

Sitte, C. (1965) *City Planning According to Artistic Principles*. New York Random House. (Translated from the German by G. R. Collins and C. C. Collins.)

Sixsmith, J. (1986) The meaning of home: an exploratory study of environmental experience. *Journal of Environmental Psychology*, **6** 281–298.

Skogan, W. G. (1988) Disorder, crime and community decline, in Hope, T. and Shaw, M. (eds) *Communities and Crime Reduction*, Home Office Research and Planning Unit, HMSO, London.

SLABS – see School of Land and Building Studies.

Smith, M. (1989) *Guide to Housing*, 3rd edn., The Housing Centre Trust, London.

Smith, R. and Burbidge, M. (1973) *Density and Residents' Satisfaction*, Sociological Research Branch of the Department of the Environment (unpublished), London.

Smith, S. (1994) The essential qualities of the home, *Journal of Environmental Psychology* **14**, 31–46.

SNU – see Safe Neighbourhoods Unit.

Social Housing Unit. *More than just a Builder*, The House Builders' Federation, London.

SPAZIDEA (1992) *Construire le logement en France et en Italie*, Plan, Construction et Architecture, Paris.

Squire, R. (1988) *New Housing in Sheffield's Inner City*. BSc (hons) dissertation, Sheffield City Polytechnic.

Steele, A. Somerville, P. and Galvin, G. (1995) The effectiveness of estate agreements. *Housing Research Findings* 160, The Joseph Rowntree Foundation, York.

Stewart, K. (with Waterton, J.) (1994) *Health and Housing*, Scottish Homes Working Paper, Edinburgh.

Stoker, G. and Brindley, T. (1985) Asian politics and housing renewal. *Policy and Politics*, **13** (3) 281–303.

Stollard, P., Osborn, S., Shaftoe, H. and Croucher, K. (1991) *Safer Neighbourhoods*, The Safe Neighbourhoods Unit, London.

Stollard, P., Groucher, K., Osborn, S., Shaftoe, H. and Warren, F. (1991) *Crime Prevention through Housing Design*, London.

Thomas, A. D. (1986) *Housing and Urban Renewal*, George Allen and Unwin, London.

Tickell, S. and Hughes, N. (1979) Social effects of housing rehabilitation. *Housing Review*, May–June, 78–79.

Town and Country Planning Association (1996) Land use planning implications of housing projections. *Housing Research Findings*, 187, The Joseph Rowntree Foundation, York.

Tudor Walters – see the Committee appointed by the President of the Local Government Board and the Secretary for Scotland.

Turkington, R. (1994) Pondering on Poundbury. *Town and Country Planning* **63** (12) p. 342.

Turner, J. F. C. (1976) *Housing by People*, Marion Boyars, London.

URBED (Urban and Economic Development Group) (1944) *Vital and Viable Town Centres: Meeting the Challenge*, Department of the Environment, HMSO, London.

Vale, R. and Vale, B. (1995) Green house living – balancing need and greed. *Town and Country Planning*, January 16–18.

Venturi, R. (1976) A house is more than a home. *Progressive Architecture*, August.

Venturi, R., Scott Brown, D. and Izenour, S. (1972) *Learning from Las Vegas*, MIT Press, Cambridge, MA.

Voutsadakis, S. (1989) *Housing for People with Disabilities*, Islington Borough Council (2nd edn.), London.

Walentowicz, P. (1992) *Housing association development after the 1988 Housing Act Housing Research Findings*, 56, The Joseph Rowntree Memorial Trust, York.

Walmsley, D. J. (1988) *Urban living: the individual in the city*, Longman Scientific and Technical, Harlow, Essex.

Ward, C. (1976) *Housing: An Anarchist Approach*, Freedom Press, London.

Ward, S. V. (1992) The garden city campaign: an overview. *In* Ward, S. V. (ed.) *The Garden City: Past, Present and Future*, E & F N Spon, London.

Warnes, A. M. (1994) Cities and elderly people., *Urban Studies*, 31 (4/5) 799–816.

Wates, N. and Knevitt, C. (1987) *Community Architecture: How People are Creating their own Environment*, Penguin, Harmondsworth.

Welsh Office (1996) *Planning Guidance (Wales): Planning Policy*, HMSO, Cardiff.

Werner, K. (1991) Fragmentation and juncture. *Architecture and Behaviour/Architecture et Comportement*, 7 (4).

Wester Hailes Partnership, Community Safety Unit (1996) *Crime in Wester Hailes*.

Westminster City Council (1980) *Living at Higher Densities*. Westminser City Council Planning Department, London.

Wheatley, J. (MP) (1923) *Homes or Hutches, a speech delivered in Parliament on 24th April when moving the Labour Party motion for the rejection of the Tory Housing Bill]*, The Scottish Council of the Independent Labour Party, Glasgow.

Wheeler, R. (1985) *Don't Move: We've Got you Covered*. The Institute of Housing, London.

Which? (1984) Buying a new house, July.

Whitehand, J. W. R., Larkham, P. J. and Jones, A. N. (1992) The changing suburban landscape in postwar England. *In* Whitehand, J. W. R. and Larkham P. J. (eds) *Urban Landscapes: International Perspectives*, Routledge, London.

Wilcox, S. (ed.) (1996) *Housing Review 1996/97*, The Joseph Rowntree Foundation, York.

Williams, G. (1990) Development niches and specialist housebuilders – an overview of private sheltered housing in Britain. *Housing Studies*, 5 (1) 14–23.

Williams, G. and Bell, P. (1992) The 'exceptions' initiative in rural housing – the story so far. *Town and Country Planning*, May, 143–144.

Williams, R. (1993) *Housing Standards in Scotland*. Draft paper given to a seminar of the European Network of Housing Research, Housing Quality Working Party, held at Salford University, 23 April.

Willis, M. (1963) Designing for privacy: what is privacy? *Architects' Journal*, 29 May 1137–1141.

Wilmott, P. and Murie, A. (1988) *Polarisation and Social Housing*, Policy Studies Institute, London.

Wilson, J. K. and Kelling, G. (1982) Broken windows. *The Atlantic Monthly*, March.

Wilson, J. R. (1982) The measurement of domestic activity space. *Ergonomics*, **25** (5) 401–418.

Wilson, S. (1980) Vandalism and defensible space on London housing estates. *In* Clarke, R. V. G. and Mayhew, P. (eds) *Designing Out Crime*, The Home Office Research Unit, HMSO, London.

Winch, G. and Campagnac, E. (1995) The organisation of building projects: an Anglo/ French comparison. *Construction Management and Economics*, **13** 3–14.

Windle, R. and Mackie, A. M. (1992) *Survey on Public Acceptability of Traffic Calming Schemes*, Department of Transport, Transport and Road Research Laboratory, Contractor Report 298.

Winter, J., Coombes, T. and Farthing, S. (1993) Satisfaction with space around the home on large private estates. *The Town Planning Review*, **64** (1).

Woodford, G., Williams, K. and Hill, N. (1974) *The Value of Standards for the External Residential Environment*, the Department of the Environment, Research Report 6, London.

Woodin, S., Delves, C. and Wadhams, C. (1996) *Just what the Doctor Ordered*. Produced for the Comprehensive Estates Initiative of the London Borough of Hackney for National Housing Week.

World Health Organisation (WHO) (1972) *Health Hazard of the Human Environment*, WHO, Geneva.

Young, J. (1992) The rising demand for law and order and our Maginot Lines of defence against crime. *In* Abercrombie, N. and Warde, A. (eds) *Social Change in Contemporary Britain*, Polity Press, Oxford.

Young, K. and Kramer, J. (1978) *Strategy and Conflict in Metropolitan Housing*, Heinemann, London.

Zipfel, T. (1989) *Estate Management Boards: an Introduction*, the Priority Estates Project, London.

Index